EASTERN FORTRESS

EASTERN FORTRESS

A MILITARY HISTORY OF HONG KONG, 1840–1970

KWONG CHI MAN AND TSOI YIU LUN

HKU PRESS
香港大學出版社

Hong Kong University Press
The University of Hong Kong
Pok Fu Lam Road
Hong Kong
https://hkupress.hku.hk

ISBN 978-988-8208-70-8 (*Hardback*)
ISBN 978-988-8208-71-5 (*Paperback*)

British Library Cataloguing-in-Publication Data
A catalogue record for this book is available from the British Library.

Digitally printed

Cover image: View of Victoria Harbour, Hong Kong, from the Peak. The battleship at anchor is the HMS *Duke of York*. © Imperial War Museum IWM-SE 6470

Contents

List of Illustrations — ix

Foreword — xi

Preface — xv

Note on Transliteration and Measurements — xix

Abbreviations — xxi

1 Introduction — 1
Themes and Structure 1
Sources 2
Military Geography of Hong Kong 3

2 A British Foothold in China, 1839–1861 — 9
The First Opium War and the Taking of Hong Kong 9
Early Defence and Garrison, 1841–1861 10
Hong Kong during the Second Opium War, 1856–1861 14
Conclusion 16

3 Hong Kong in an Imperial Defence System, 1861–1883 — 17
Increasing Strategic Importance, Land Use and Military Contribution 17
Hong Kong and Imperial Defence 19
The First Steps: The Milne Committee of 1878 21
Hong Kong and Imperial Defence: The Carnarvon Report, 1879–1883 26
Conclusion 32

4 Hong Kong Defence during the Age of Empires, 1883–1919 — 33
Strategic Role of Hong Kong during the Age of Imperialism 33
Military Contribution, Venereal Disease and Plague 35
Modernization of the Batteries, 1883–1912 39
The Defence Schemes, 1889–1901 46
The Acquisition of the New Territories and the Six-Day War of 1899 49
Turning to Landward Defence, 1901–1914 52
Hong Kong during the First World War and the Kowloon Defence Line 65
Conclusion 68

5 Treaty, Air Force and Landward Defence, 1920–1939 — 71
British Imperial Defence, 1919–1939 71

Impacts of the Washington Treaty 74
The Interwar Garrison 79
Hong Kong as an Offensive Base: Defence Reviews of 1927–1930 82
The Decision to Build the Gin Drinker's Line, 1931–1935 89
The Hong Kong Defence Scheme of 1936 94
*Hong Kong as "Outpost": The Far Eastern Appreciation of 1937 and the Refortification
    Plan of 1938* 96
Defences in Hong Kong, 1935–1941 107
Conclusion 115

6   The International Situation and Hong Kong Defence, 1939–1941   117
The European War and Hong Kong Defence Policy 117
The Fall of France and Its Impact 120
Peace through Deterrence: The Strategy of Sir Robert Brooke-Popham 126
Collective Security: The Actions of Other Allied Powers 131
Canadian Reinforcement and the Rapid Deterioration of US-Japan Relations 134
Alerts before the War 140
Conclusion 141

7   Hong Kong before the War   143
Hong Kong Unprepared? 143
Overview of Internal Situation 144
British, Chinese and Japanese Intelligence Activities in Pre-war Hong Kong 146
Economic Contribution of Hong Kong during the Early Stages of the War 151
War Preparation by the Hong Kong Government 154
Conclusion 159

8   The Fall of Hong Kong, December 1941   161
The Larger Context of the Hong Kong Operation of 1941 161
The Arrival of Brigadier Lawson and the Second Canadian Reinforcement 162
British Redeployment in November 1941 164
Japanese Planning and Deployment 167
The Battle of Hong Kong 1941 171
The Battle of Hong Kong: A Military Assessment 222

9   Hong Kong under the Japanese Occupation, 1942–1945   225
Japanese Defence of Hong Kong and Allied Counterattacks 225
The British Army Aid Group and the East River Column 230
Conclusion 234

10   The Defence of Hong Kong during the Early Stages of the Cold War,   235
        1945–1960
The Cold War and British Strategic Contraction 235
Continuing the Policy of Deterrence, 1946–1950 237
Anglo-American Cooperation on Hong Kong Defence, 1950–1960 242
The Post-Korean War Garrison 250
The Final Tests: The 1956 and 1967 Riots and Aftermath 255
Conclusion 259

11 Conclusions 261

The Strategic Role of Hong Kong and Its Defence 261
Making Defence Policies 264
Military and Urban Development 265
The Garrison and Hong Kong 265
Summary 266

Appendices 269

Appendix I: Bibliographical Review 269
Appendix II: British Command Structure in Hong Kong 271
Appendix III: British Army Commanders at Hong Kong, 1843–1960 272
Appendix IV: Commanders of China Station, 1865–1941 274

Notes 277

References 325

Index 341

Illustrations

Figures

1. Hong Kong in Asia   *4*
2. Hong Kong in 1941   *5*
3. Early defence of Hong Kong, 1850   *11*
4. Long-term defence layout proposed by the Milne Committee   *23*
5. Defence layout proposed by Col. Crossman, 1881   *30*
6. RN submarines being repaired in the Royal Naval Dockyard, 1910s   *39*
7. French armoured cruiser *Montcalm*, an improved version of *Dupuy de Lôme*, built in 1898   *40*
8. Coastal guns in Hong Kong, 1886   *41*
9. Coastal batteries in Hong Kong, 1906   *44*
10. Guns proposed by the Owen Committee, 1906–1912   *45*
11. Line drawings of HMS *Swiftsure* and HMS *Triumph*, 1900   *58*
12. Anderson's proposed Kowloon defence line, 1911   *60*
13. HMS *Medway* and the submarines of the China Station, c. 1930s   *75*
14. HMS *Hermes* in dry dock in Hong Kong   *76*
15. The British Geisha House (Brothel) on Stonecutters Island, 1935   *81*
16. Layout of the Gin Drinker's Line   *108*
17. Shing Mun Redoubt, December 1941   *109*
18. Pillbox disguised as a house (PB 305)   *110*
19. Removing 9.2-inch guns from Devil's Peak   *112*
20. Coastal and AA guns in Hong Kong, 1941   *113*
21. Japanese plan against Hong Kong, 1941   *169*
22. Japanese invasion of Hong Kong, 8 December 1941   *173*
23. Situation near Shing Mun, 9 December 1941   *175*
24. Evacuation of the Mainland Brigade, 11–13 December 1941   *181*
25. British defence of Hong Kong Island East, 14–18 December 1941   *187*
26. Japanese landing on Hong Kong Island, 18 December 1941   *196*
27. Japanese penetration, early morning, 19 December 1941   *199*
28. Battle of Wong Nai Chung Gap, 08:30–12:00, 19 December 1941   *200*

29. British counterattack on Hong Kong Island, 15:00–04:00, 19–20 December 1941   *203*

30. Japanese advance renewed, morning, 21 December 1941   *207*

31. Wallis's counterattack, 21 December 1941   *210*

32. Final position, 15:00, 25 December 1941   *220*

33. Cartoon mocking the inability of the British to hold Hong Kong, 1967   *252*

Tables

1.   Distance between Hong Kong and major ports in Asia   *4*

2.   Probability of foggy days noted in the Defence Scheme of 1910   *7*

3.   Hong Kong garrison, May–June 1854   *14*

4.   Temporary armaments for the stations suggested by the Milne Committee   *26*

5.   Garrisons for the stations outlined by the Milne Committee   *26*

6.   Proposals to the Carnarvon Committee, 1879–1881   *28*

7.   Proposals to the Carnarvon Committee (garrison size), 1879–1881   *28*

8.   Proposals to the Carnarvon Committee (cost in £), 1879–1881   *29*

9.   Naval strength of the major powers, 1887–1891   *32*

10. British dry-docks East of Suez, 1914   *34*

11. British, French and Russian naval strength in Asia, 1902   *36*

12. Military contribution of Hong Kong, 1892–1917 (in HKD)   *36*

13. Comparison of RMLs, RBLs and BLs, 1880–1890s   *41*

14. Asian port defences, as estimated by Lambton, 1908   *54*

15. The Kowloon–New Territories Line designed by Gen. Anderson, 1911   *61*

16. The Island Line designed by Gen. Anderson, 1911   *62*

17. Hong Kong landward defence, as envisaged by Maj. Gen. Anderson, 1913   *64*

18. Major units of the China Station, December 1919   *75*

19. Major units of the China Station, June 1939   *76*

20. Budget for the improvement of Hong Kong defence (Army), 1936–1940   *93*

21. Sections of the Gin Drinker's Line, 1935   *107*

22. Coastal defences on Hong Kong Island, 1938   *113*

23. Hong Kong-built Empire ships   *152*

24. Minesweepers built in Hong Kong, 1941   *153*

25. New departments of the Hong Kong government, 1937–1941   *156*

26. Japanese plan against Hong Kong Island, 18 December 1941   *192*

27. Order of battle of the 2nd China Fleet, January 1942   *226*

28. Japanese army units near Hong Kong, August 1945   *230*

29. Guerrilla activities as recorded by the 2nd China Fleet, 1942–1945   *234*

30. Military expenditure of the Hong Kong government, 1949–1970   *251*

31. Hong Kong Defence Force, civil defence units, as well as auxiliary forces strength and nationality, 1959   *254*

Foreword

The closure to Britain's involvement in the affairs of Hong Kong, signalled by the handover of sovereignty to the People's Republic of China in 1997 and marking the definite end to any British pretensions to a continued military role in East Asia, prompts the question of how we should look back on Hong Kong's military role. The authors of *Eastern Fortress* take up this challenge with aplomb. In analyzing Hong Kong's history as a British military outpost, they look at the issue from both the British and the local Hong Kong perspectives. They base their analysis on a wide reading in British, American and Japanese archives as well as a thorough familiarity with military history more generally. The result is a study which not only is hugely well informed and superbly documented, but also places the history of Hong Kong in a wide context, making it relevant to students of military affairs, British imperial history, and the history of Hong Kong. It is a real achievement and will become the starting point for any further research on Hong Kong's military role.

As *Eastern Fortress* makes clear, Hong Kong was for Britain an asset but also a liability. Hong Kong became a British colony as a result of the 1838–1842 Opium War when the British fought their way into Guangzhou and blocked the Grand Canal to stop taxes arriving in Beijing, thus compelling the Qing dynasty to sign the Treaty of Nanjing, the first of the Unequal Treaties as they became known later. If perceived insults to British dignity were one cause of the Opium War, it was also the case that for its economic health Britain needed to build up a trade network in "the East" to make up for the loss of its colonies in "the West" as a result of the late 18th century revolutions in the Americas. Until the Napoleonic Wars were over, little could be done. But once they were and the industrial revolution had begun to deliver economic and financial success, as well as better weapons, including the *Nemesis*, the first steam-driven naval vessel put to devastating effect during the Opium War, Britain set about the task with energy and determination. So Hong Kong became the easternmost major bastion of British power, a position that would give Britain a role in South China and East Asian affairs for a century and a half.

But Hong Kong also made the British military position vulnerable to overextension. Hong Kong was far away from Britain, which meant that until the arrival of the telegraph, London could do little if local commanders took action off their own bat, as they did during the 1856–1860 Arrow War. During much of the 19th century many soldiers died from tropical diseases to which they were not immune. The acquisition of Kowloon and the New Territories toward the end of the 19th century in some ways weakened the British position, as it now had a land border with China that was difficult to defend. And Hong Kong Island was always vulnerable to market strikes, as became clear, for instance, during the rise of the Nationalists in the 1920s. To make Hong Kong militarily secure, Britain would have had to occupy a significant swathe of land and invest heavily in building up its military presence in it. The occupation of Guangzhou during the Arrow War was difficult, demonstrating that it was one thing to defeat Qing forces in a pitched battle but quite another to occupy and govern a large city. This, and the 1857 Indian Uprising, ensured that little enthusiasm remained for building large colonies in China. During the Opium War, Hong Kong was acquired in a bout of British aggression, but after the Arrow War it became a bit of a bluff, depending more on the threat than the actuality of force. That threat was worth maintaining because of the influence it gave Britain in East Asian affairs, and as such it proved an investment that paid handsome dividends. But Britain never really wanted to put in the effort, or spend the treasure, to turn Hong Kong into a true fortress: too difficult, too far away, too risky, and too costly.

The great strength of *Eastern Fortress* is its broad approach to examining how these realities worked themselves out over time. This is not a narrow military history, focusing on the number of troops stationed in Hong Kong at any given time, the type of arms these forces possessed, the ships the British navy maintained in port, or the aircraft the RAF deployed at the Kai Tak aerodrome. Nor is it an account of a single war such as the Opium War, the Arrow War, or the Japanese conquest of Hong Kong in December 1941. Rather, *Eastern Fortress* looks at the *longue durée* of the British military involvement in Hong Kong, which is analyzed consistently, and convincingly, from its position in British imperial strategy. It tells us about the thinking of military strategists and political leaders in London, showing how their views were shaped by, of course, imperial strategy, as well as available resources, personalities, and British diplomatic relations. Importantly, it demonstrates that while the Hong Kong government was usually consulted, military strategy trumped local political imperatives. This broad perspective allows the authors to bring out an important tension in British imperial strategy, namely the rivalry between Singapore and Hong Kong for preferment in British strategy. Singapore became increasingly favoured as India, a colony, outpaced China, a semi-colony, not only economically but also in the British public imagination and in the British official mind.

Eastern Fortress is path-breaking in another way as well. Military history is a field that has focused on big topics and big events such as, in the case of Western historians, the 19th century arms race, the causes of the First World War, the impact of industrialization on the conduct of war, the Battle of Stalingrad, and the emergence of total war. In Chinese history, while the Opium War has been studied at great length, for more recent periods it has been the War of Resistance, the Boxer Rebellion, and the 1894–1895 Sino-Japanese War that have received far more attention. Neither Western nor Chinese historians have paid much attention to Hong Kong, in the case of the first probably because they considered it largely irrelevant and in the case of the latter perhaps because they did not consider it a legitimate topic in Chinese history, or perhaps because Hong Kong's military history was regarded as somewhat embarrassing. Both will find food for thought in *Eastern Fortress.* The book forms an important illustration of the fact that military history can be enriched, and enlivened, by delving into its backwaters.

Hong Kong has many identities, some of them contradictory, including as a free port, a haven for capitalist enterprise, a centre for smuggling, and an example of British law-based governance. The significance of its development as being a British military outpost, however, is one of the many thought-provoking suggestions of *Eastern Fortress.* The ways that British military needs shaped the pattern of its urban development as well as sanitary and hygiene regulation, that military life was frequently and visibly interwoven with public life in Hong Kong, and that the Hong Kong garrison was important in maintaining stability and order in the city, including during the Cold War, form important insights.

For the foreseeable future, Hong Kong will not have a serious military role. The garrison of the People's Liberation Army now stationed in Hong Kong is small and, largely confined to barracks, it remains inconspicuous. Whether many decades from now, when the arrangements struck for the 1997 transfer of sovereignty become obsolescent, *Eastern Fortress* will be followed by a study with the word "Chinese" in the title is an open, and intriguing, question for the future. But that its military inconspicuousness today is not the natural order of things is one important lesson of this study.

Hans van de Ven
October 2013

Preface

It is truly gratifying to see the defenders of Hong Kong from all nationalities properly commemorated every November at the Cenotaph in Central.

This book is inspired by *Between Two Oceans: A Military History of Singapore* (1999), a comprehensive study of the military history of an island nation with a similar experience to that of Hong Kong.

We hope our work can shed new light on the various aspects of the military history of British Hong Kong and, more importantly, elucidate the strategic-military importance of Hong Kong during a significant part of its modern history. During the process of writing this book, we were delighted to find that the source materials for this topic in the relevant languages were far richer than we had ever expected. As many parts of the military history of Hong Kong have yet to be studied systematically, most of the content of this book relies on primary historical sources.

We would like to thank our teachers, colleagues and friends. Without their assistance and support, this book could not have been finished. Prof. Yip Hon Ming of the Chinese University of Hong Kong (CUHK), Prof. Hans van de Ven of Cambridge University, Prof. Rana Mitter of Oxford University, Prof. Frederick Cheung Hok Ming of CUHK, Prof. Chow Kai Wing, Prof. Lee Kam Keung, Prof. Mak King Sang and Dr. Wong Man Kong of Hong Kong Baptist University (HKBU) and Dr. James Stewart, Jr. all guided and supported this project, providing invaluable advice and encouragement throughout the sometimes arduous writing process. Naval historian Prof. Gerald Jordan (1932–2012) urged one of the authors of this volume to pursue an academic career; his words thereby changed the life of that author.

The completion of this book would have been impossible without the generous support provided by the Advanced Institute for Contemporary China Studies at HKBU. Dr. Karen Xu Zhihua, Dr. Mark Chow Man Kwong, Ms. Cavis Choi, Ms. Teresa Tsang and Ms. Jane Lee rendered crucial assistance to the authors. Ms. Ada Au-Yeung Pui Man's map work elevated the readability and lucidity of this work to a whole new level. Unless otherwise stated, the maps were all drawn by the expert hands of Ada.

We owe a lot to a number of friends who provided vital criticisms and suggestions. Among them, Mr. Dennis Cheung Tsun Lam followed the entire writing process and shared his thoughts both as an expert in the field and a thoughtful reader. Mr. Tim Ko and Mr. Bill Lake very generously provided us with rare photographs on the military history of Hong Kong, and offered invaluable advice. We are also extremely fortunate to have been aided by a number of distinguished individuals who served in the British military forces, including the late Mr. Fung Ying Kei MBE, Mr. Peter Choi, Dan Waters, Capt. Ronald Taylor, and Capt. James Chan. The late Mr. Chan On Kwok, son of the legendary Admiral Chan Chak, provided us with Admiral Chan's diary, which was key to our understanding of the Battle of Hong Kong in 1941. Ms. Gillian Wallis and Ms. Myf Payne, relatives of Brigadier General Cedric Wallis, kindly shared with us extremely rare photos of Wallis. The Hong Kong Ex-Servicemen's Assocation and the Hong Kong World War II Veterans Association also rendered vital support in our work. We would especially like to thank Capt. Lam Ping Wai, Capt. Derek Leung Hing Chuen, Capt. Kenny Yau Wai Kee, Mr. Jimmy Kong Kim Hung, Mr. Sin Ting-kwong, Mr. Famby Kwan, Mr. Bernard Yuen, Mr. Lo Dip Koon, Mr. Danny Chung and Mr. Danny Wong.

Mr. Christopher Young and Mr. Michael Broom of the Royal Asiatic Society (Hong Kong Branch), Mr. Chan Sui-jeung (author of *East River Column*), Mr. Philip Snow (author of *The Fall of Hong Kong*), Mr. Tony Banham (author of *Not the Slightest Chance*), Mr. Tim Luard (author of *Escape from Hong Kong*), Mr. Geoffrey Emerson (author of *Hong Kong Internment*), Mr. Bill Lake (producer of *Battle for a Barren Rock*), Mr. Richard Hide (chair of HongKong Escape Re-enactment Organization HERO), Prof. Lawrence Lai Wai-chung and Prof. Ho Chi Wing (authors of various works on the Gin Drinker's Line, the Shing Mun Redoubt, and the battle for Wong Nai Chung Gap), Mr. Choi Chohong, Mr. Jerry Lee (grandson of Mrs. C. R. Lee), Mr. James O'Neill (grandson of John Laird), Mr. Jeff Lee and Mr. Yim Chi Tak all generously shared their thoughts with us about this work. During the process of writing, we were also fortunate to be able to learn from Ms. Susanna Siu of the Hong Kong Museum of History, Ms. Rosa Yau and Ms. April Yip of the Hong Kong Museum of Coastal Defence, Ms. Kitty But of the Hong Kong Maritime Museum, Dr. Lam Kam Yuen of the Hong Kong Heritage Museum, Ms. Ada Yau, Mr. Ray Ma and Mr. Jeffer Mak of the Antiques and Monuments Office.

On countless occasions, the authors received vital assistance from archivists and librarians in Hong Kong, the United Kingdom, Japan and Australia. In particular, the authors would like to thank the National Archives in Kew, Ms. Diana Manipud and Ms. Lianne Smith of the Liddell-Hart Center for Military Archives at King's College, University of London, Ms. Jessica Lau and Mr. Bernard Hui of the

Public Records Office Hong Kong, the staff of the Japan Center for Asian Historical Records, Ms. Kiya Mika of the National Diet Library, and Mr. Lai Kai Yan of the Hong Kong Public Library. Special thanks should also be extended to Mr. Anthony Wong and Ms. Furihata Chiaki, who helped the authors collect part of the Japanese archival sources.

Everyone mentioned above deserves all the credit of this work, while the authors alone are responsible for all its faults and defects.

This book is dedicated to the Chinese, British, Indian, Canadian and other nationalities who served, fought and died to protect Hong Kong.

Kwong Chi Man
Tsoi Yiu Lun
April 2013

Note on Transliteration and Measurements

Throughout this work we have used the pinyin system for Chinese and the Hepburn system for Japanese names and terms. There are exceptions to this rule as some names are better known in other romanization systems: Chiang Kai-shek (instead of Jiang Jieshi in pinyin), Kuomintang, KMT (instead of Guomindang, GMD), and Sun Yat-sen (Sun Zhongshan).

As for measurements, since the British usually used inches, yards and miles during the period concerned, conversion to decimal measurements such as millimetre, metre and kilometre is provided in parentheses. Many military measurements appear in short form (e.g. pounder as pdr.). A full list of abbreviations is provided.

Abbreviations

2CF	2nd China Expeditionary Fleet
2RS	2nd Battalion, The Royal Scots Regiment
AA	anti-air
ACMB	anti-coastal motorboat
Adm.	Admiral
ADMO	Assistant Director of Military Operations
ARP	Air Raid Precaution Department
BAAG	British Army Aid Group
BL	Breech Loader
Bn.	Battalion
BPF	British Pacific Fleet
Brig.	Brigadier
Capt.	Captain
CATF	China Air Task Force
CCP	Chinese Communist Party
CDC	Colonial Defence Committee
Cdre.	Commodore
CID	Committee of Imperial Defence
C-in-C	Commander-in-Chief
Cmdr.	Commander
CO	Colonial Office, Commanding Officer
Col.	Colonel
COS	Chiefs of Staff Committee
Coy	Company (military unit)
CSHQ	Combined Service Headquarters
DCLI	Duke of Cornwall's Light Infantry
DELS	Defence Electric Lights
DFW	Directorate of Fortifications and Works
Div	Division
DMO	Deputy Director of Military Operation

FECB	Far Eastern Combined Bureau
FO	Foreign Office
GCHQ	Government Communication Headquarters
Gen.	General
GOC	General Officer Commanding
HCE	Higher Colonial Establishment
HKD	Hong Kong dollar
HKMSC	Hong Kong Military Service Corps
HKR	Hong Kong Regiment
HKSRA	Hong Kong Singapore Royal Artillery
HKVDC	Hong Kong Volunteer Defence Corps
HMG	heavy machine-gun
HMS	Her/His Majesty's Ship
HQ	headquarters
IJA	Imperial Japanese Army
IJN	Imperial Japanese Navy
Inf	Infantry
JACAR	Japan Center for Asian Historical Records
JCS	Joint Chiefs of Staff (US)
JPC	Joint Planning Sub-committee
KMT	Kuomintang, the Chinese Nationalist Party
KSLI	King's Shropshire Light Infantry
LCE	Lower Colonial Establishment
Lt.	Lieutenant
Lt. Col.	Lieutenant Colonel
Lt. Gen.	Lieutenant General
Maj.	Major
Maj. Gen.	Major General
Med. Bty.	Medium Battery
MG	machine-gun
MOD	Ministry of Defence
MTB	motor torpedo boat
Mtn. Bty.	Mountain Battery
NSC	National Security Council (US)
ODC	Overseas Defence Committee
OP	observation post
PB	pillbox
PLA	People's Liberation Army
PRC	People's Republic of China
PWD	Public Works Department

QF	quick-firing gun
RA	Royal Artillery
RAF	Royal Air Force
RBL	Rifled Breech Loader
RE	Royal Engineers
Rear Adm.	Rear Admiral
Rgt.	Regiment
RHKR	Royal Hong Kong Regiment
RML	Rifled Muzzle Loader
RN	Royal Navy
RNVR	Royal Naval Volunteer Reserve
RR	Royal Rifles of Canada
RSM	Regimental Sergeant Major
SEATO	Southeast Asia Treaty Organization
SIS	Secret Intelligence Service
SOE	Special Operations Executive
TF38	Task Force 38
USAAF	U.S. Army Air Force
USIS	U.S. Information Service
VD	venereal disease
Vice Adm.	Vice Admiral
WO	War Office

INTRODUCTION

The islands of the south [China Sea] were of utmost importance ... If under our control, our southern border would be secure ... They [the British] travelled far away and put so much effort into taking this island [Hong Kong]; as a result, they are now able to hold the key to the south and control our country's front gate.

—Wu Guangpei (吳廣霈), a secretary of Li Hongzhang, 1881

This remote but important station should be fortified and garrisoned as the chief British stronghold in the East.

—John Pope Hennessy, Governor of Hong Kong, 1878

Themes and Structure

This book is an introduction to the military history of Hong Kong. More than narrating important events such as the Battle of the New Territories in 1899, the Japanese invasion of Hong Kong in 1941 and the riots in 1956 and 1967, it tries to examine a number of interrelated themes and to explore their historical significance. First, it critically examines, through British, American, Japanese and Chinese historical sources, the changing strategic role of Hong Kong and the British defence policy for the colony from 1841 to 1970. It attempts to highlight the roles of cosmopolitan politics in Britain, international relations, financial considerations and technological change in the making of Hong Kong defence policies. In addition, this work examines the social and policy implications of the British military presence in Hong Kong, and the relationship between colonial government and metropole in aspects such as garrison finances, land use and hygiene.

Through the use of previously unseen archival sources, this work also tries to shed new light on ongoing debates within Hong Kong military history, such as on the British perception of the relative importance of Hong Kong and Singapore during the 19th and 20th centuries; changing defence plans and facilities; the controversial "Gin Drinker's Line," built during the 1930s; British preparations and planning for the Japanese threat throughout the interwar period (1919–1939); the performance of the British and Japanese forces and the role of the Chinese during the invasion of December 1941; and the British, Chinese and American policies for Hong Kong during the early phase of the Cold War.

This book is divided into eleven chapters. The Introduction describes the aim, structure and features of the book, and provides an overview of the primary sources used. An outline of the geographical features of Hong Kong is included. Chapter 2 discusses the defence and strategic roles of Hong Kong during the early decades of the British takeover. Chapter 3 illustrates the place of Hong Kong in British discussions of imperial defence and the impact of the emergence of iron- and steamships on the defence of Hong Kong.

Chapter 4 examines the problem of Hong Kong defence during the late 19th century, when Britain faced the challenge of rising powers such as the United States and Japan. It also elucidates the emergence of the defence line in Kowloon before and during the First World War. Chapters 5, 6 and 7 all focus on the inter-war period, which receives special attention as it sets the stage for the fall of Hong Kong in December 1941. Chapter 5 outlines the prolonged discussion from 1919 to 1938 over the defence of Hong Kong and the actual structures built, such as the Gin Drinker's Line. Chapter 6 examines the changing international situation from 1938 to 1941 and British responses concerning the defence policy for Hong Kong. It contributes to the ongoing discussion over the preparedness of the Hong Kong garrison and the Canadian reinforcement by highlighting the role of Air Chief Marshal Sir Robert Brooke-Popham, the British Commander-in-Chief of the Far East. Chapter 7 focuses on the situation in Hong Kong before the Japanese invasion, the economic contribution of the colony to Britain and China during the early stages of the Second World War, and the consequences of the colonial government's war preparations.

Chapter 8 revisits the Battle of Hong Kong through British, Japanese and Chinese sources, while Chapter 9 focuses on the period of Japanese occupation. Chapter 10 deals with the post-1945 military history of Hong Kong, highlighting the British, Chinese and American strategic considerations and major events such as the gradual disarmament of Hong Kong and the large-scale riots in 1956 and 1967. Chapter 11 summarizes the book and briefly discusses several major historical questions. Chapters 1 to 7, 9 to 11 of this manuscript were written by Kwong Chi Man; Chapter 8 was written by both Tsoi Yiu Lun and Kwong Chi Man.

Sources

The major sources consulted for this book are declassified archival sources from Britain, Japan, China, Hong Kong and the United States. Many of these sources are unpublished. Most of the British sources consulted lie in the National Archives of the United Kingdom and the Liddell Hart Centre for Military Archives, King's College London. They provide important details, including the defence schemes for Hong Kong from 1889 to the 1930s, the defence reports written by various organizations and the Armed Services, and the minutes of cabinet committees such as the Committee of Imperial Defence. For example, the report of Major General Frederick Barron, the Inspector of Fixed Defences, provides details as to the design, planning and construction of the notorious Gin Drinker's Line, built during the 1930s to resist a possible Japanese invasion. British archival sources also offer much insight into British planning before the Japanese invasion, the battle of December 1941 and post-World War II defence.

This book also utilizes, for the first time, a large number of Japanese documents from the Japan Center for Asian Historical Records and the National Institute for Defense Studies. These documents not only provide a fresh perspective for the study of the Battle of Hong Kong, but also offer more important and previously unseen information such as the actual design and detail of each and every pillbox of the Gin Drinker's Line, the Japanese defence arrangements in Hong Kong during the Second World War, and Japanese intelligence activities before the invasion. Chinese sources, such as the Qing and Republican archival materials, are also used. In particular, the documents of the Nationalist government (國民政府) of China and the diary of Admiral Chan Chak are most useful.

Military Geography of Hong Kong

Hong Kong lies at the centre of the Western Pacific region, midway between Singapore and Japan. It controls the estuary of the Pearl River Delta and is one of the best seaports along the South China coast. In the 19th and early 20th centuries, ocean traffic between East Asia, Europe and the Americas usually followed the route of Hong Kong–Singapore–India–Cape of Good Hope (later, the Suez Canal). This made Hong Kong one of the most important seaports in Asia during a substantial part of the period covered by this book.

In 1881, Wu Guangpei (吳廣霈), a secretary of Li Hongzhang, noted the strategic importance of Hong Kong in the age of steam:

> The islands of the south [China Sea] were of utmost importance . . . If under our control, our southern border would be secure . . . They [the British] travelled far away and put so much effort into taking this island [Hong Kong]; as a result, they are now able to hold the key to the south and control our country's front gate.[1]

As Hong Kong was an important strategic node in the Western Pacific (Table 1, Figure 1), the British used it as a major naval base soon after acquiring it from the Qing in 1842. In 1865, the China Station, a permanent station of the Royal Navy, was established, with its headquarters placed in Hong Kong until 1940 (Appendix II). After the Second World War, Hong Kong remained a major naval base, until the British withdrawal from East of Suez in the 1960s.

Table 1   Distance between Hong Kong and major ports in Asia[2]

Ports	Distance (km)	Ports	Distance (km)
Weihaiwei	1,891	Incheon	1,915
Singapore	2,334	Shanghai	1,303
Labuan	1,706	Guangzhou (Canton)	129
Yokohama	2,151	Macao	56
Taipei	563	Halong Bay	740
Port Arthur (Lüshun)	2,012	Hanoi	869
Vladivostok	2,655	Saigon	1,497
Jiaozhou (Kiaochow)	1,818	Manila	1,104

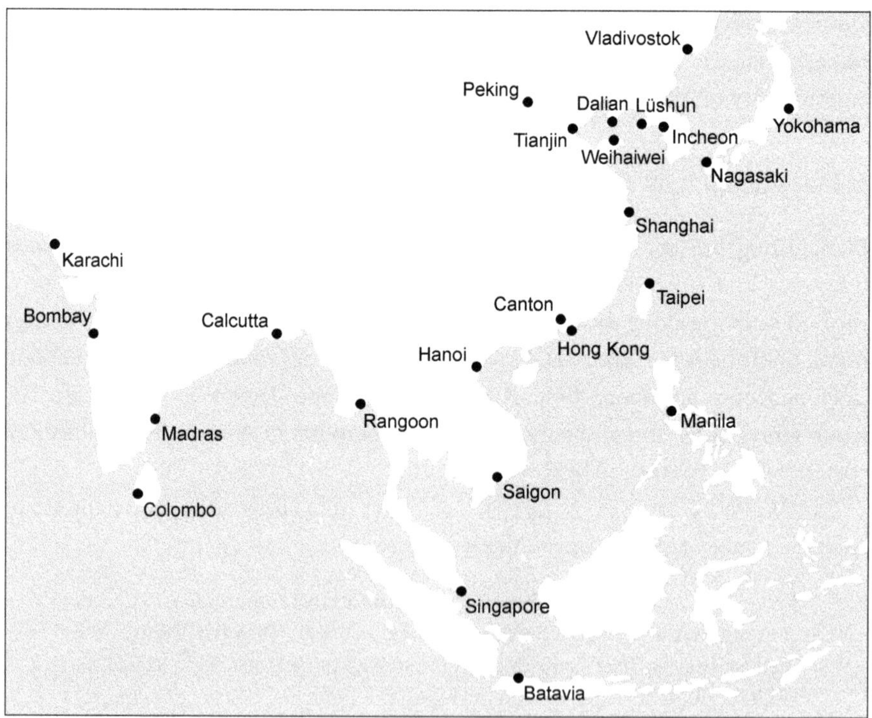

Figure 1   Hong Kong in Asia

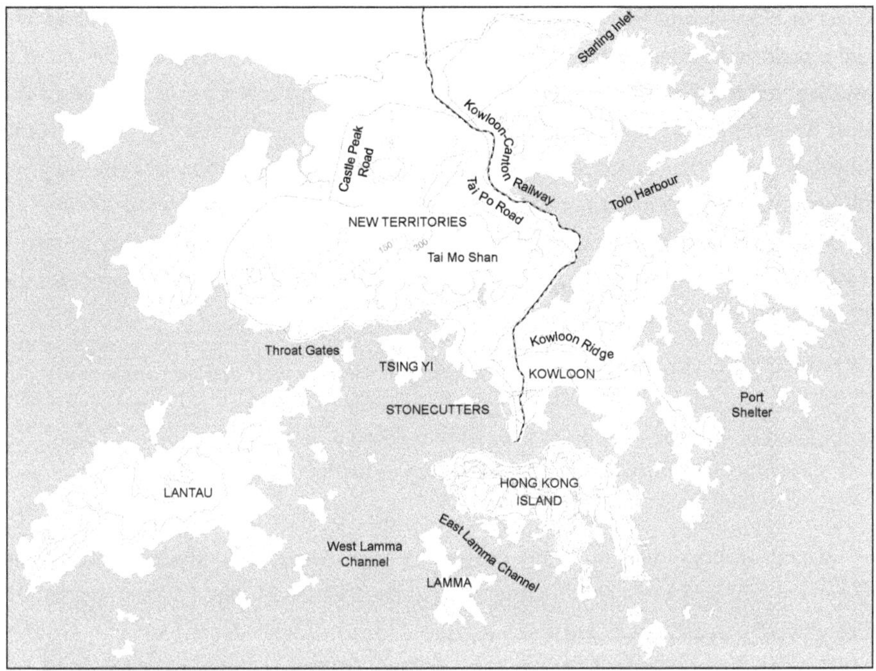

Figure 2   Hong Kong in 1941

Geographically, Hong Kong may be divided into three parts: Hong Kong Island; Kowloon and the New Territories adjacent to mainland China; and the more than 260 islands within Hong Kong waters (Figure 2). The total area of Hong Kong Island is currently 80 km² (2013). The island is divided into two parts by the two mountain ranges cutting across the island from east to west. They are in turn divided by Wong Nai Chung Gap in the middle of the island. From west to east, the western range includes Mount Davis (269 m), High West (494 m), the Peak (552 m), Mount Kellett (501 m), Mount Gough (479 m), Mount Cameron (439 m) and Mount Nicholson (430 m). The eastern range includes Jardine's Lookout (433 m), Violet Hill (433 m), Mount Butler (436 m), The Twins (386 m), Mount Stanley (364 m), Mount Parker (528 m), Mount Collinson (348 m) and Mount Pottinger (312 m). After years of reclamation and urbanization, the northern coast of the island has been built up since the 1980s. The island also has two peninsulas, both (Stanley and D'Aguilar) are found on the southeast shore.

The Kowloon Peninsula was incorporated into the colony of Hong Kong in 1860. Its area expanded from about 7 km² to more than 11 km² in the period of British rule. Before the 1920s, the peninsula consisted largely of farmland, with several hills such as Ho Man Tin Hill. The peninsula points like a dagger towards the northern coast of Hong Kong Island. Protected by the mountains on Hong Kong Island and the Kowloon Peninsula, Victoria Harbour between the peninsula and the island is an ideal natural harbour. From 1841, the harbour has been regarded as one of the best deepwater harbours in Asia. In 1863, Guo Songtao, the first Qing minister to London, noted that Lyemun, the eastern entrance of the harbour, was the "key" to Hong Kong defence as it may be easily enclosed by the surrounding mountains.[3]

Major General William Gascoigne, commander of the Hong Kong garrison from 1898 to 1903, used the analogy of India to describe the terrain of Kowloon and the New Territories:

> This chain of hills runs for two-thirds of the way due west and east, and then sharply recurves for the remaining distance to the south. The western and eastern flanks rest on the sea, and it thus forms a barrier wall affording many facilities for defence, and represents to Kowloon in miniature degree much what the Himalayan range does to India.[4]

A continuous mountain range covers the area from the northwest of Kowloon (near Lai Chi Kok) to the Sai Kung Peninsula east of Junk Bay (Tseung Kwan O). From west to east, there are Piper's Hill (223 m), Eagle's Nest (305 m), Golden Hill (369 m), Beacon Hill (458 m), Lion Rock (495 m), Unicorn Ridge (437 m), Temple Hill (488 m), Tate's Cairn (577 m) and Kowloon Peak (603 m). Along the so-called "Kowloon Ridge" mentioned above, there are numerous passes; most of these existed before the construction of the tunnel of the Kowloon-Canton Railway. From west to east, there are Smuggler's Pass, Beacon Hill Pass, Grasscutters Pass, Customs Pass, Shatin Pass, Kowloon Pass and Lead Mine Pass. From the 1880s, the British garrison had already talked of occupying this area in order to protect Kowloon more effectively. Soon after the British takeover of the New Territories in 1899, plans were laid to fortify the area against an enemy invasion.

To the north of the Kowloon Ridge, are more mountains, such as Needle Hill (532 m), Tai Mo Shan (957 m) and Grassy Hill (647 m). Together they form the Shing Mun Valley, which became the Shing Mun Reservoir in 1937. Another mountain range stretches from Tai Mo Shan to present-day Tuen Mun, including the mountains Shek Lung Kung (473 m), Lin Fa Shan[5] (578 m), the Tai Lam area and Castle Peak (583 m). To the north of this string of mountains, are the plains of Yuen Long, Kam Tin and Shek Kong. The northeastern part of the plain is surrounded by the mountains of Lam Tsuen, which also separate the Kam Tin plain with Tai Po. Northwest of Yuen Long and modern-day Tin Sui Wai is Deep Bay. The relief of the Hong Kong–China border that existed from 1899 to 1997, north of Lam Tsuen and stretching from Deep Bay to Shataukok from west to east, is relatively gentle. It should be noted that before 1945, most of these mountains had yet to be covered by forest and vegetation as they are nowadays. Thus, in the 1910s, the commander of the Hong Kong garrison actually proposed to plant cactus as obstacles on these mountains.[6]

The eastern part of the New Territories consists of a very broken coastline and numerous peninsulas. The largest of these include the Sai Kung Peninsula, located east of Kowloon. This rugged coastline has many coastal enclaves, such as Starling Inlet, Plover Cove, Tolo Harbour, Port Shelter and Junk Bay. Fortunately, as the British found out, many of them are too small and isolated to create a serious problem for defenders. Because of currents and tidal surges, the western part of the New Territories is not suitable for large-scale amphibious operations.

Before the emergence of large steel vessels in the last decade of the 19th century, ships entering Hong Kong were of shallow draught and able to use most of the entrances to Victoria Harbour. Later, as the ships became larger and harbour traffic control more elaborate, most ships entering the harbour used Tathong Channel (east of Lyemun), Kap Shui Mun (Throat Gates) and East Lamma Channel (between Hong Kong and Lamma islands). Although the West Lamma Channel (between Lamma and Lantau islands) was wider, the depth of the former could reach as deep as thirty metres, allowing larger vessels to enter.

In general, Hong Kong has rugged relief. Except for reclaimed land and the Yuen Long–Kam Tin area, Hong Kong lacks flat land. Broken terrain dominates the island and the mainland; the major islands are also hilly. The lack of flat land prevented the British from constructing a large military air base throughout the colonial period. While this feature allowed the defenders to use the broken terrain to their advantage, it also proved to be a major problem for the garrison after the First World War.

The climate of Hong Kong is generally hot and humid in summer (June to September) and cold in winter (November to March). The likelihood of fog is high due to the high humidity. Using the statistics of 1883 to 1903, the Defence Scheme of 1910 suggested an average of 147 foggy days each year, of which "March, April, May and June were the most foggy months, and September, October and November the least" (see Table 2).[7]

Table 2 Probability of foggy days noted in the Defence Scheme of 1910

Fog appearing between 609.6 m and 304.8 m	Probability	Fog appearing between 304.8 m and 243.84 m	Probability
Jan, Feb, July, Aug	42.0%	Jan, May, June	14.0%
Mar, April, May, June	64.0%	Feb, Mar, Apr	33.0%
Sep, Oct, Nov, Dec	15.0%	July to Dec	5.5%

Precipitation in Hong Kong is concentrated between May and September. The temperature during this part of the year is also the highest. Typhoons from the Western Pacific usually attack Hong Kong during these months. Thus, the China Station usually left Hong Kong for North China or Japan in summer, and stayed in Hong Kong for training between October and March.

2

A BRITISH FOOTHOLD IN CHINA, 1839–1861

To retain Hong Kong will require the loss of a whole regiment every three years, and that to have 700 effective men, it is necessary to maintain 1,400.

—Major General D'Aguilar, 1845

The First Opium War and the Taking of Hong Kong

As the story of the Opium War has been told many times, this chapter gives only a brief description of events and focuses instead on the importance of Hong Kong as a staging area for British military activities on the China coast in the mid-19th century.[1] As early as 1806, the East India Company had noted the advantages of the anchorage between Hong Kong Island and the Kowloon Peninsula.[2] During the Napoleonic War and the War of 1812, the British Royal Navy was already active in the South China Sea.[3] When Imperial Commissioner Lin Zexu (林則徐) pressured the British merchants in Guangzhou to hand in their opium stocks by threatening to cut off food and water supplies in March 1839, Charles Elliot, the British Plenipotentiary to China, led the British merchants and their ships to Hong Kong. The first shot of the First Opium War (1839–1842) was fired at Hong Kong, when Elliot ordered on 4 September 1839 the bombardment of the Qing war junks and batteries near Kowloon.

When London decided to dispatch more troops to China in November 1839, the anchorage off Kowloon and Hong Kong Island was already a shelter for British warships and merchantmen operating in South China. The objective of the British expedition of forty-four ships that arrived off Hong Kong from India in June 1840 was not Hong Kong but Chusan Islands, some 1,000 kilometres northeast of Hong Kong. Within two months after its arrival, the expedition had captured Dinghai of Chusan and sent a warship near Tianjin. While Charles Elliot and Chinese High Commissioner Qishan (琦善) were still negotiating, the British captured the batteries at Bogue to keep up the pressure. On 25 January 1841, before Qishan and Elliot had concluded a treaty (the Convention of Chuenpee), Commander Edward Belcher was ordered to land a party of sailors and marines at what would become

Possession Point on Hong Kong Island.[4] The British expedition, which had 448 men die of disease between 13 July and 31 December 1840, abandoned Chusan and bivouacked at Hong Kong.[5]

As London was not satisfied with the Convention of Chuenpee, Elliot was replaced by Henry Pottinger, who brought additional troops. Soon after Pottinger arrived, in August, British forces recaptured Dinghai and took Xiamen and Ningbo. Reinforcements and replacement troops continued to reach China from India, using Hong Kong as a staging and resting area. By July 1842, the British forces about to attack Zhenjiang (Chinkiangfu) amounted to "9,000 bayonets," excluding the Royal Marines and the navy.[6] When British forces reached Nanjing, the Qing sent Qiying (耆英) to negotiate with Pottinger, ceding Hong Kong Island to the British through the Treaty of Nanking in August 1842. After more than a year of British occupation, Hong Kong became the first formal British possession along the China coast.

Early Defence and Garrison, 1841–1861

As John Carroll has pointed out, Hong Kong during the early colonial period was hardly a successful commercial port.[7] It was more of a military station and logistic hub for British activities on the China coast. Thus, even before the conclusion of the Treaty of Nanking, the British had already erected a temporary battery on Kellett Island and a naval store at West Point.[8] Before 1842, however, no permanent structures were built because the island was seen only as a bargaining chip in exchange for Chusan.[9]

As the Hong Kong garrison suffered heavily from disease, the British tried to build permanent structures to house the garrison and to protect the town of Victoria and the harbour. The first permanent British defensive structures in Hong Kong were the Wellington, Murray and Royal batteries (all located near modern-day Admiralty). Two barracks, named Victoria and Murray, were also built on nearby hillocks. These structures were designed by a Royal Engineers officer, Major Edward Aldrich, who was sent to Hong Kong by the War Office in 1843. These structures, all finished by 1847, formed the early defence of the colony (Figure 3). Temporary barracks were also erected in different parts of the island. Barracks for the Indian garrison were located at Sai Ying Pun; others were erected at Stanley, Tai Tam and Tin Wan in the south. One hundred and fifty thousand silver dollars was spent on these works, with another one hundred thousand dollars as land premium.[10]

The gravest threat facing the garrison during this period was not foreign invasions but disease. From November 1842 to late 1843, of the 526 officers and men of the 55th Regiment of Foot, 242 died of disease. Major General D'Aguilar, the garrison commander, noted in 1845 that "to retain Hong Kong will require the loss of a whole regiment every three years, and that to have 700 effective men, it is necessary to maintain 1,400." *The Illustrated London News* also noted that "the graveyard was soon filled and another was required from the Surveyor-General, who found it difficult to point out a proper spot."[11] Disease was so lethal that the navy was unwilling to install any permanent shore facilities. Until the late 1840s, the naval headquarters was on the decommissioned ship-of-the-line HMS *Minden*, which also served as the harbour ship. Even so, Captain Le Fleming Senhouse, the first Senior Naval Officer (SNO), died of disease.[12]

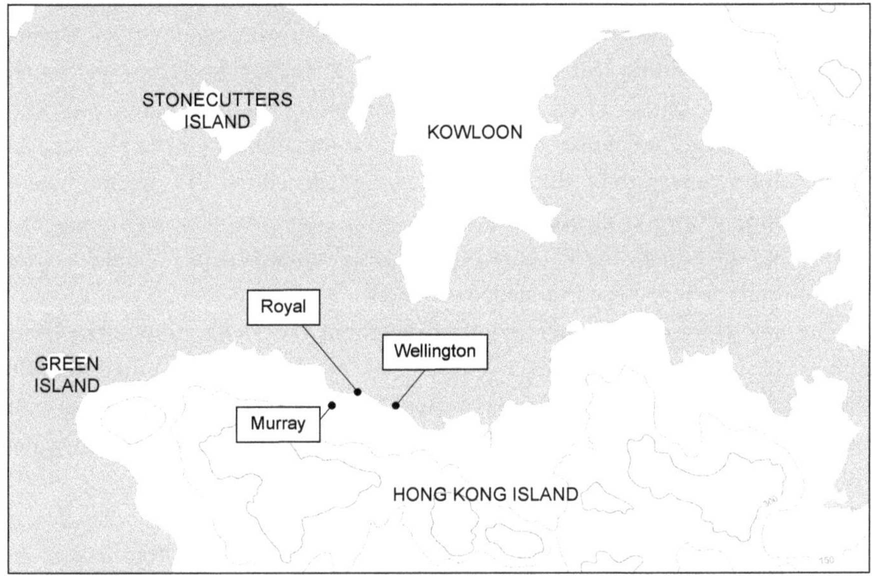

Figure 3   Early defence of Hong Kong, 1850[13]

The most lethal disease of all was malaria. It was argued that the absence of permanent barracks was the cause of the high fatalities suffered by the garrison. On the other hand, as Lieutenant John Ouchterlony, the first garrison engineer, pointed out, the lack of crown land in the town of Victoria had prevented the construction of such barracks. Many Royal Engineers troopers and officers responsible for the construction work also succumbed to disease.[14] Garrison duties outside the barracks were very dangerous for European soldiers. When twenty soldiers were sent to Lyemun during the 1840s, five were dead in five weeks and six had to be hospitalized.[15] As Christopher Munn has noted, the high mortality rate of the garrison led to widespread desertion, self-inflicted wounds, heavy drinking and occasional suicide.[16]

Other acute problems facing the early garrison were venereal disease (VD), drunkenness and desertion. The problem with VD was an obvious result of the gender imbalance in the colony and would haunt the garrison for some time to come.[17] For example, one-third of the crew of the only ship-of-the-line at Hong Kong (HMS *Winchester*, 60 guns) was infected by VD.[18] When Colonial Surgeon J. Murray arrived in 1859, he found that "both among naval and military invalids the syphilitic amount to nearly twenty-five percent of the whole."[19] To curb the spread of VD, Governor John Bowring introduced in 1857 "An Ordinance for Checking the Spread of Venereal Diseases," which put all brothels and prostitutes serving the Europeans under a registration and examination system. A decade later, it became the Contagious Disease Ordinance, introduced in other parts of the British Empire. The infected prostitutes would be sent to the Lock Hospital until they were cured or dead. The measure caused much resistance among the prostitutes, who were forced to undergo unfamiliar and humiliating examinations by male physicians.[20] According to Murray, the ordinance significantly reduced the VD infection rate of the garrison.[21] However, as later pointed out by the commission set up by Governor Hennessy to investigate the VD control measures, the infection rate of the European garrison and the Royal Navy remained serious.[22]

The new colony was rather chaotic throughout the 1840s despite the heavy military presence. Colonial Treasurer Robert Montgomery Martin noted that "the European inhabitants are obliged to sleep with loaded pistols; frequently to turn out of their beds at midnight to protect their lives and property from gangs of armed robbers, who are ready to sacrifice their number if they can obtain a large plunder."[23] The garrison was equally unruly. As early as 1841, there were already Indian deserters.[24] *The Friend of China* received a letter in 1842 claiming that "the disgraceful scenes of which our streets are the arena, call loudly for magisterial interferences, each day they become worse and worse . . . I can only allude to the drunker delinquencies of our soldiers and sailors . . ."[25] Until the 1850s, deserters tried to leave on the American whalers calling at the colony.[26]

During this period, the main defence of Hong Kong was the East Indies and China Station of the Royal Navy, formed in 1844 after a separation of the East Indies and China squadrons.[27] The British naval presence on one hand was used to coerce the Qing, and on the other was employed to deter potential enemies that could threaten the British diplomatic and economic interests.[28] During the early days of the colonial rule, the Governor of Hong Kong, who concurrently served as the Plenipotentiary in China and Superintendent of British Trade, always tried to control the movement of the ships of the Royal Navy despite the protest of the Commander-in-Chief of the China Squadron, who was also based in Hong Kong.[29]

The issue was not sorted out until the later period, when improved communication (by telegraph) allowed London to enforce central control over British political and military operations in East Asia.

When Lieutenant Colonel Chesney, commander of the Royal Artillery at Hong Kong, arrived in July 1843, he noted that there were three ships-of-the-line stationed in Victoria Harbour.[30] According to *The Navy List* of 1848, the East Indies and China Station and the Pacific Station had two third-rate battleships (64 to 80 guns), seven fifth-rate frigates (32 to 44 guns), three sixth-rates (20 to 28 guns) and fifteen sloops (16 to 18 guns).[31] In 1861, the East Indies and China Station had eighty warships and 8,000 officers and men.[32] Although it was smaller than either the Channel or the Mediterranean fleets, it was enough to secure British naval supremacy in Asia.

The Royal Navy fought a number of battles against large fleets of Chinese pirates. In September and October 1849, HMS *Columbine*, HMS *Fury* and HMS *Medea* attacked the pirate lair of Chui A-poo at Bias Bay. During the ensuing battle, twenty-six pirate junks were destroyed and more than 400 pirates killed. Chui was captured later by Chinese authorities but was handed back to the British; he killed himself in gaol.[33] Later, HMS *Columbine* and a Sino-British fleet together destroyed the pirate fleet of Sap Ng Tsai near Cochinchina, killing as many as 1,700 pirates and sinking more than sixty ships.[34] Another major action was the Anglo-American expedition against Chinese pirates at Ty-ho Bay, near modern-day Lantau Island, in 1854. Again, hundreds of pirates were killed or captured. Although small-scale pirate attacks persisted until the late 1930s, large pirate fleets no longer existed near Hong Kong after these actions. The change was also the result of the introduction, from the 1860s, of the Water Police and of ship registration.[35]

Under the aegis of the Royal Navy, only a few coastal batteries and usually two regiments (one British and one Indian) were kept in Hong Kong. In order to cut costs, London even hired Indian gun lascars to replace European gunners. In 1847, the Hong Kong Singapore Artillery (later renamed the Hong Kong Singapore Royal Artillery, or HKSRA), consisting of one subedar and eighty-eight gun lascars, was formed.[36] The military expenditure of Hong Kong decreased from £80,778 in 1848 to £50,346 in 1853.[37]

In March 1854, because of a dispute over Palestine and the Ottoman Empire, a war broke out, pitching Britain and France against Russia. Although the war was later known as the Crimean War, fighting was not confined to the Crimean Peninsula. In the Pacific theatre, other than the ill-fated expedition against Petropavlovsk led by Rear Admiral David Price, the situation was largely quiet. Soon after the news of the war arrived, both Governor Bowring and Vice Admiral James Stirling, the Commander-in-Chief of the East Indies and China Station, left Hong Kong for Japan with the main body of the fleet, including the ship-of-the-line HMS *Winchester*, frigate HMS *Spartan* and steam frigate *Barracuda*.[38] They went to Japan to prevent Russian warships from using the Japanese ports. In effect, however, they forced the opening of the country by a show of force.[39] At that time, the garrison consisted of merely 565 men of all ranks, with only 357 fit for combat (Table 3).

Table 3   Hong Kong garrison, May–June 1854[40]

	Officers	Ranks	Fit for duty
59th Foot	11	412	263
Artillery	4	53	28
Gun Lascars	1	84	66
Total	16	549	357

To prepare for a Russian attack, the garrison installed spare guns on the guard ship HMS *Hercules* and converted the vessel into a floating battery that could cover both sides of the harbour.[41] By June 1854, a temporary battery was built at West Point to support HMS *Hercules* and the existing batteries. Together, these batteries had thirty-two 32-pounders, six 24-pounders, three 10-inch and two 8-inch mortars.[42]

Pirates and local armed groups in South China probably posed a larger threat to Hong Kong during the Crimean War. In May 1854, William Caine, the acting governor, reported that there was a pirate fleet of nineteen ships near Hong Kong. Meanwhile, adherents of the Heaven and Earth Society (天地會) wreaked havoc in Guangdong Province, capturing the Kowloon Walled City in August. Kowloon was thoroughly looted.[43] As the colony was seemingly threatened from different sides, the first volunteer militia, known as The Hong Kong Volunteers, was formed in that year. It was led by Caine and had ninety-nine men at its peak. Most of the volunteers were staff of the British trading and shipping companies. At that time, there were only three hundred British males in the colony. The Volunteers existed only for a few months, as the situation improved. It was revived briefly between 1863 and 1865, and was not reformed until 1878.[44] During the war, both Governor Bowring and Admiral Stirling asked for and received help from the Chinese authority in Guangzhou to suppress the pirates near Hong Kong.[45]

Hong Kong during the Second Opium War, 1856–1861

Soon after the Crimean War, Britain and the Qing started another war over treaty revision and the Arrow Incident of October 1856. As Sino-British tensions were heightened, Governor Bowring introduced a curfew. In January 1857, about four hundred European inhabitants were poisoned by the bread produced in a Chinese bakery. The owner of the bakery, himself poisoned, was found not guilty and expelled from the colony.[46] Although the event was most likely an accident, the heightened tension persuaded Bowring to revive the Hong Kong Volunteers. However, the proposal was not carried out.[47]

During the Second Opium War, Hong Kong was again the base of the British land and naval forces operating in China. Although the Indian Mutiny of 1857 delayed the British operation, the Royal Navy had launched from Hong Kong a series of actions against the Qing fleet and batteries at Lantau and the Pearl River estuary. By December 1857, 7,000 troops were concentrated in Hong Kong or its vicinity. The British also hired hundreds of Hakka coolies to form the Canton Coolie Corps, providing them with uniforms and an insignia. It was possibly the first Anglo-Chinese military unit to be formed.[48] By May 1858, the British had captured Guangzhou, Nantou and Taku Fort, near Tianjin. The Qing offered peace and negotiated the Treaty of Tianjin with Britain, France, Russia and the United States.

It was during the Second Opium War that the British decided to extend the colony of Hong Kong to include Kowloon Peninsula. In June 1858, the British government instructed Lord Elgin, the High Commissioner to China, to acquire Kowloon and Stonecutters while ratifying the Treaty of Tianjin with the Qing. However, the fleet carrying him to Beijing exchanged fire with Taku Fort as it forced its way into Baihe in June 1859. This action led to renewed fighting; the British occupied Kowloon on 18 March 1860.[49] Harry Parkes, the British consul at Guangzhou, demanded that the Commissioner of Guangdong and Guangxi, Lao Chongguang (勞崇光), lease Kowloon and Stonecutters to the British. It was stipulated in the "contract" that, as long as the British were able to pay the rent on time, the Qing was forbidden to retake the territories. In addition, the lease would be in force before the British had concluded any permanent treaties with the Qing over the ownership of Kowloon. After Lao signed the leasehold, the inhabitants of Kowloon were notified that the territory was British. In the same month, two British regiments were sent from Hong Kong to recapture Chusan. By June 1860, British forces in China consisted of 14,000 men, with most having passed through or been garrisoned at Hong Kong.[50] These forces were to be sent north to attack Beijing and Tianjin with French forces from Ningbo. After the British and French had captured Beijing and burnt the Summer Palace, the Qing ratified the Treaty of Tianjin and signed the Treaty of Peking that ceded the Kowloon Peninsula and Stonecutters to Britain in October 1860. When the peninsula was formally transferred in January 1861, the British had already been garrisoned on it for almost a year.

Conclusion

Between 1841 and 1861, the Royal Navy enjoyed unchallenged supremacy in East Asia, with the exception perhaps of the littoral area, where piracy was still rife. The British Army also enjoyed a considerable advantage over the Qing and other powers in Asia. The British ability to project power in Asia was unprecedented. Possessing the strategic points of Singapore and Hong Kong, the British were able to send credible military forces to North China during the two Opium Wars. During these campaigns, Hong Kong acted as the anchorage of the expeditionary fleets, providing not only provisions but also accommodation and medical care. Although disease claimed many lives during the early days of occupation, the death rate of the garrison steadily declined as medical services improved and as permanent structures on Hong Kong Island were built. The whole process of turning Hong Kong into a valuable strategic possession did not, however, come without a price: between 1841 and 1866, 5,375 British and Indian officers and men died in the colony. All were buried in Happy Valley; most had died of disease.[51]

While the British enjoyed unchallenged military superiority in East Asia, the problem of Hong Kong defence was relatively simple. However, as military technologies developed rapidly during subsequent decades, and as France, Russia and the United States gradually industrialized and turned their focus to Asia, the defence of Hong Kong became an increasingly difficult and complex issue from the 1860s.

3

HONG KONG IN AN IMPERIAL DEFENCE SYSTEM, 1861–1883

> Were Singapore or Hong Kong taken, each part of the empire would suffer in proportion to its India and China trade; and so on. If our squadrons are tied to these places because they are not defended nor have adequate garrisons in war, the water districts of which they are the centres would be left without efficient protection, and similar results follow.
>
> —John Colomb, *The Defence of Great and Greater Britain* (1879)

Increasing Strategic Importance, Land Use and Military Contribution

By 1861, Hong Kong had become a busy military depot. After the barracks and hospitals had been built, Hong Kong's role as the British logistic base in Asia became more important. For example, it was the staging area for British forces during the Anglo-Satsuma War of 1863. The war was a punitive expedition against the Satsuma Clan of Kyushu, as it refused to apologize and pay an indemnity after a samurai had killed or wounded three British subjects. In April 1866, F. Davies, a musician of the 20th Regiment of Foot, returned to Hong Kong on a steam transport ship after serving as a garrison troop at Kyushu. He noted "upwards of a thousand ships of all countries at anchor in security," including the vessels of the China Station, formed in 1865. He also noted that "the barracks are justly considered as the finest in the world . . . there is also a splendid hospital capable of accommodating eight hundred soldiers," and the colony had "everything you would find in a large European City."[1] Even the Americans utilized the strategic potential of Hong Kong. In 1853, the U.S. Pacific Squadron under Commodore Matthew Perry went to Japan via Hong Kong, waiting a year in the colony for the reply of the Tokugawa Shogunate.[2] A decade later, Rear Admiral Henry Bell of the U.S. East Indian Squadron rented a godown on Hong Kong Island for a rent of US$200 per month. It was argued that Hong Kong was a better base than Macao because of its steady supply of food and fuel. In addition, it received mail from China and around the world one day before Macao.[3]

The occupation of Kowloon allowed the British to control the two sides of Victoria Harbour and to secure a substantial part of the anchorage. Even before the conclusion of the Treaty of Peking, a heated debate had begun between the colonial and military authorities over the issue of land use in Kowloon. In April 1860, Rear Admiral John Hope of the China Station suggested reserving the majority of the land in Kowloon for military use. Governor Hercules Robinson rejected the proposal, arguing that it would hinder commercial development. A joint civilian-military committee was formed to discuss the issue, but no consensus was reached. The General Officer Commanding Hong Kong, Lieutenant General James Hope Grant, then proposed to relocate the military facilities of Hong Kong to Kowloon.[4] It seems that the British were less worried at that time about the possibility of Kowloon being attacked from the landward side. After two years of bargaining, a compromise was finally reached, with part of the land at Tsim Sha Tsui, Hung Hom and Stonecutters being given to the military, while the rest would be sold by the colonial authority. The Royal Navy established a coal store in the southwestern part of Kowloon, while the army reserved land for battery and barracks near modern-day Tsim Sha Tsui.[5]

The regular payment to Britain of a military contribution was established during this period. In 1863, London asked Hong Kong to contribute £20,000, or 20 percent of the total military expenditure of the colony. William Mercer, the acting governor, resisted the measure by arguing that the empire rather than the colony should be responsible for its defence, as Hong Kong was a regional military station. When the Legislative Council debated the issue in 1864, the colonial treasurer joined the unofficial members opposed to the measure.[6] Despite the opposition, Hong Kong was required to pay £20,000 per annum (or $92,000 in 1865) or 16.5 percent of its total gross revenue (the larger amount applied) to Britain from 1865.[7] The amount was, according to Edward Cardwell, the Secretary of State for the Colonies, "very reasonable."[8] This practice was not changed until the early 1890s, when London asked for an increase in the contribution.

The discipline of the garrison during the 1860s remained unsatisfactory. In 1858, a police inspector suggested: "Hong Kong at the time was very much crowded with sailors and soldiers, they used to send a large portion, and I believe half a ship's company, from different ships on shore on the same day, and it gave rise to drunkenness, riots, and occasional contests with the numerically small police we had."[9] In September 1864, a riot broke out in the City of Victoria, the result of fighting among European sailors, soldiers from the 99th Regiment and the local police. Several men were killed; the newly formed Hong Kong Volunteers were called out to maintain order.[10] In 1865, the 2nd Battalion, 9th Regiment of Foot had court-martialled 103 men, issuing 200 lashes and 4,882 days of imprisonment. Of the soldiers tried, fifty-nine were charged for "habitual drunkenness" and other charges, including "violence to superiors and insubordination," "desertion" and "drunk on duty under arms."[11] In 1867, an extraordinary case highlighted the unequal legal system of the colony, the inefficient police system and the problem of military discipline. Thomas Banbury, a deserter of the 20th Regiment, was caught near Aberdeen after two months of searching. He had committed numerous robberies and rapes during his escape, but was released as no witnesses for the prosecution appeared. He raped more women before finally being caught by an Indian constable. This time, even with a number of Chinese women appearing as witnesses, he was sentenced to only two years of hard labour.[12]

Hong Kong had yet to become a safe city. Speaking to a parliamentary committee dealing with the high mortality of the British troops in Hong Kong, Lieutenant General James Hope Grant noted that "you are liable to be robbed at any time in the town (City of Victoria)" and that "it is not safe to ride two miles out of the town." Not even the European troops were safe; on one occasion, seven European soldiers were sent on a boat to transport some money. Six were murdered during an ambush and the seventh escaped death by jumping overboard.[13]

Hong Kong and Imperial Defence

"Pax Britannica" was seemingly secure after the Crimean War, the Indian Rebellion and the Second Opium War. The British Empire and its global trade network were protected by the Royal Navy, which remained unchallenged until the 1890s. Thus, as Donald Schurman has suggested, the "attention paid (by the British government) to defence problems during the years 1868–1887 was hardly commensurate with the growth and population of the empire."[14] When Edward Cardwell became the Secretary of State for War, he pulled British troops out of Canada, Australia and New Zealand. On the other hand, in response to the invasion scares of the 1860s, expensive fortifications were built across the United Kingdom.

Although the British government might not be interested in imperial defence, rapid technological change took place; a new appreciation of the geopolitical value and the defence requirement of the empire re-emerged from the mid-19th century.[15] In the late 1850s, Sir William Armstrong designed the rifled breech-loading gun (RBL), heralding a new generation of guns with longer range and higher accuracy. These guns used explosive shells that quickly rendered wooden warships obsolete. In 1860, HMS *Warrior*, built entirely of iron and powered by steam, entered service. Two years before that, the French had already launched the ironclad *La Gloire*. The emergence of HMS *Warrior* and *La Gloire* not only changed naval tactics but also logistics. Although ironclads were faster and stronger, their effective range of operation was shorter than wooden warships, and they relied on a steady stream of coal supply that might not be found in overseas ports. Their iron hulls also needed larger dockyards for repair. It was thus necessary to store coal reserves and to establish modern repair facilities at far-flung bases such as Hong Kong.

The question of how to protect these bases soon attracted attention from the government and the public. John Colomb, a former Royal Navy captain whose brother was a vice admiral, was an important advocate of imperial defence. He published influential pamphlets such as *The Protection of Our Commerce and Distribution of Our Naval Forces Considered* (1867) and *The Defence of Great and Greater Britain* (1879). He was active in societies such as the Royal Colonial Institute. Colomb believed that the two services had equal responsibility in imperial defence. As the fleet had to concentrate on Europe to protect the British Isles, the communication of the British Empire had to be maintained by a system of ports protected by coastal guns and garrisons and connected with telegraph lines. With such a system, the Royal Navy could be deployed freely to meet overseas threats.

Colomb suggested that Gibraltar, Malta, Halifax, Bermuda, the Bahamas, Jamaica, Antigua, Aden, Bombay, Cape Comerin, Trincomalee, King George Sound, Singapore and Hong Kong were suitable bases for the imperial defence network. In *The Defence of Great and Greater Britain*, he used the example of Hong Kong and Singapore to illustrate the importance of maintaining an adequate defence for the ports:

> Were Singapore or Hong Kong taken, each part of the empire would suffer in proportion to its India and China trade; and so on. If our squadrons are tied to these places because they are not defended nor have adequate garrisons in war, the water districts of which they are the centres would be left without efficient protection, and similar results follow.[16]

Matthew Marsh, a member of parliament (MP) with extensive experience in Australia, suggested that the navy alone could not guarantee the security of the empire:

> Ships only were of no use for these purposes; in these days of steam it was necessary that we should have depots of coal and places where ships could refit, with garrisons to protect them; and what [I] maintained was that if we had not colonies, we should be forced to have arsenals and garrisons all over the world. In the absence of colonies, we already maintained such military stations as Gibraltar, Malta, Bermuda, and Hong Kong…[17]

Similar voices could be heard from the bureaucracy. From 1856, Colonel William Jervois, the Assistant Inspector General of Fortifications and secretary of the Defence Committee of the War Office, had also advocated arming the overseas ports. From 1863 to 1874, he studied the defence of the colonies. He suggested that it was necessary to fortify Hong Kong, as it was the only refuge for the British in China and the only British possession protecting the Sino-British trade, which brought about an annual income of £5,000,000.[18] He proposed to seal off the entrances of Victoria Harbour by placing new batteries at Stonecutters Island, West Point, Possession Point, Kellett Island, the western side of the Kowloon Peninsula and the northern shore of Lyemun. However, the proposal was shelved by the government.[19]

In 1875, Jervois was entrusted by Admiral Alexander Milne, another proponent of imperial defence, to study the issue again. He criticized the government for having neglected the issue for decades, noting the undefended state of ports such as Hong Kong. He devised a plan costing £950,000 to fortify eleven coaling stations, and reinforced his argument by suggesting that the cost was equal to only two ironclads. Again, no action was taken by the cabinet. However, events soon forced the British to strengthen the defence of their coaling stations.

The First Steps: The Milne Committee of 1878

In 1877, an Anglo-Russian war became a real possibility, as the Russians attempted to reassert their influence in the Balkans and the Black Sea area at the expense of the Ottoman Empire, which was backed by Britain. The discussion over imperial defence was thus revived. The secretary of the Defence Committee, Colonel Nugent, outlined in April 1877 the principles in prioritizing the defence of overseas bases. The principles included "proximity to passing commerce," "position vis-à-vis the nearest naval squadron" and "position vis-à-vis likely enemy attack." According to these principles, the order of priority was Cape of Good Hope, Hong Kong, Singapore, Saint Lucia, King George Sound, Trincomalee, Mauritius, Vancouver, the Falklands and Ascension Island.[20] Nugent highlighted the importance of Hong Kong:

> It is absolutely necessary to support and develop this [Sino-British] trade, and to hold a firm position from which we may interpose as our interests demand, in the event of hostile combinations between the Russians, the Chinese and the Americans.[21]

He also noted the potential danger of "losing face" in China and India if Hong Kong was lost. From then on, the perceived importance of maintaining "face" by holding Hong Kong became an important rationale for generations of policymakers.

To alert the cabinet, Major General John Simmons, the Inspector of Fortifications, inserted in a report to the cabinet a paragraph about the danger facing the overseas possessions. The Defence Committee was authorized to draft a plan for £2,297,412 to fortify the coaling stations. Although the plan was again shelved in 1877, mounting Anglo-Russian tension in early 1878 led to the formation of the first interdepartmental committee on imperial defence. In March 1878, the ad hoc Colonial Defence Committee held the first meeting. Chaired by Admiral Milne, who had asked Colonel Jervois to study imperial defence, members of the committee included representatives from the army, the navy and the Colonial Office. The committee was known as the Milne Committee after its chairman.

The committee was to "consider how to provide some early and temporary defence in case of any sudden outbreak of hostilities." Only the Cape of Good Hope, Mauritius, Ceylon, Singapore and Hong Kong were studied.[22] Based on naval intelligence, the committee assumed that the Russians had only four ironclads in the Pacific, armed with 7-inch and 9-inch guns.[23] This assumption became the basis for defence arrangements. The first recommendation made by the committee was to distribute the thirty-four spare 7-inch Rifled Muzzle Loaders (RMLs) stored in the United Kingdom to the coaling stations. This meagre number of guns suggests the negligent attitude of the British government towards imperial defence throughout the 1860s and 1870s.

The committee reiterated the strategic importance of Hong Kong as a commercial and military station:

> [Hong Kong] is the extreme station possessed by Great Britain in the Chinese Seas, and is the centre of a very large trade . . . It also possesses naval and military establishments, and is well provided with docks, well supplied with shears, engineers' and carpenters' shops, foundries, and every requirement for making extensive repairs to ships of war and merchant vessels . . . its importance, both as a coaling and refitting station for the ships of Her Majesty's fleet employed in protecting the extensive British interest in these seas, and as a safe port of refuge for commercial ships, cannot be exaggerated.[24]

Despite its importance, Hong Kong's defences had been deteriorating since the Crimean War. Only the Murray and Wellington batteries still existed, and their line of fire was blocked by the rapidly expanding town. The former was not even armed. Six naval 7-inch RBLs were in the stores.[25]

The committee adopted Jervois's idea of sealing off the entrances of the harbour with guns and mines, also noting the need to defend Kowloon, where the coal store was located. It abandoned the idea of placing batteries on the Kowloon side of Lyemun, as it was too isolated and difficult to reinforce.

A temporary scheme was outlined. In all, twenty-one guns were to be mounted on temporary batteries. After the batteries were finished, the 32-pounders were to be replaced by the heavier 64- or 80-pounders to deter enemy warships. The unreliable 7-inch RBLs were to be replaced by the older but more reliable 7-inch RMLs, so that all the large-calibre guns in Hong Kong would be uniformed.[26]

The committee also recommended doubling the garrison into a force of 1,800 infantry and 200 artillerymen. Local police and the Portuguese were seen as

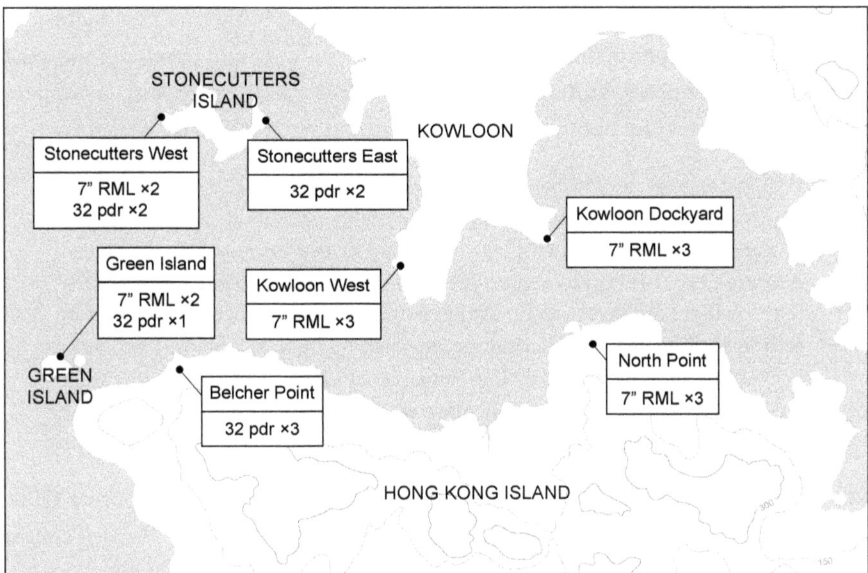

Figure 4 Long-term defence layout proposed by the Milne Committee[27]

potential sources of manpower. At that time, the Portuguese community, most of whose members had come from Macao, was the second largest foreign community in Hong Kong after the British.[28] To prevent the enemy attacking Victoria City from the rear, defensive works at the mountain gaps from Mount Davis to Quarry Bay were planned. Two gunboats armed with 10-inch RMLs and submarine mines were to be sent. The committee approached the defence issue not only from the coastal perspective, but saw both land and sea defences as forming one coherent and mutually supporting system.

The implementation of these recommendations was less than smooth, as tension existed among the Hong Kong government, the garrison commanders and the services. In March 1878, Governor John Pope Hennessy was instructed by the Colonial Office to study the defence issue. Hennessy conferred with Admiral Alfred Ryder, Commander-in-Chief of the China Station; both agreed that proper defences should be erected near the entrances of the harbour rather than in the town. When Hennessy asked Colonel Alfred Bassano, acting garrison commander, and Lieutenant Colonel William Stuart of the Royal Engineers for their opinion, the two officers proposed simply updating the existing batteries in Victoria. Hennessy informed Bassano of the navy's wish to close the harbour entrances with guns, but was ignored.[29]

When the Colonial Office instructed Hennessy to reorganize defences according to the recommendations of the Milne Committee, Bassano and Stuart again refused to cooperate. They argued that it was possible to place only one new battery on Stonecutters Island, to be manned only by The Volunteers, and to rebuild the existing batteries. Hennessy wrote to the Colonial Office that the garrison's uncooperative attitude forced him to buy expensive private land in the Victoria City:

> Whilst it was my duty to express my views frankly to Colonel Bassano on these points, I had not the slightest hesitation in giving him all the assistance in my power to carry out his own plans and those of the Commanding Engineer. Bassano's experience and ability, apart from his official position, entitle him to my fullest confidence and most hearty cooperation. I therefore assisted in getting for him, from private owners, the new sites he wanted in the town, and, in every other way, the Local Government is cordially working with the military authorities, who have already made rapid progress with the batteries they are raising . . .[30]

When Hennessy's complaint reached London in June 1878, the Colonial Office passed the report to the War Office and mocked the latter's apparent lack of control over its commanders:

> it is not quite clear from this despatch whether the military authorities were fully acted on the telegraphic instructions sent at the request of the Secretary of State for War, or whether they felt at liberty to depart from the decisions taken at head-quarters without further reference home?[31]

Despite the garrison commanders' reluctance to conduct large-scale works, Hennessy reported in May that new batteries were being built on Bonham Road, Stonecutters, the southern tip of Kowloon, the Kowloon Docks, North Point and West Point.[32] The Wellington Battery was relegated for training purposes. Hennessy might possibly have exaggerated the reluctance of the officers to carry out the recommendations of the Milne Committee, but the reorganized defences differed from what had been envisaged. A month later, Hennessy reported that most of the temporary works were finished, thanks to the work of more than 2,000 Chinese workers. The cost of the works was £5,000, paid by the local government.[33]

As for naval defences, both the Milne Committee and Hennessy asked for torpedoes, but the Admiralty was unwilling to provide any, as it believed that sending torpedo experts to far-flung colonies was too extravagant and the men would "become thoroughly inefficient from having little or nothing to do." The Royal Navy sent only HMS *Esk* and HMS *Tweed*, two 363-ton gunboats armed with three 64-pounders to support HMS *Wvyern*, the 2,750-ton guard ship armed with four 229-mm RBLs.[34]

Another issue was the establishment of a Chinese regiment. The idea was first proposed in 1866 by Lieutenant General James Hope Grant, who had led the expedition to China in 1860, to replace British troops, who were prone to disease and premature death. He noted that the Chinese were potentially "fine soldiers."[35] The Milne Committee suggested organizing local civilians such as the Portuguese into a volunteer unit, and also raised the possibility of using the Chinese as auxiliary troops. Hennessy, who was interested in elevating the status of the Chinese, went a step further and proposed recruiting the Chinese as soldiers.[36]

In February 1878, Hennessy first proposed re-establishing the Hong Kong Defence Force, the local volunteer unit of British nationals. He then urged the Colonial Office to consider forming a Chinese unit. He used the example of the West Indian regiments to illustrate the importance of having colonial troops to defend overseas ports and serve as auxiliaries abroad. "With a proper recruiting system," he argued, "it might be possible to raise at least 20,000 Chinamen of good physique for service in India, or indeed, in any part of the world." If the troops were led by European officers, he added, they "would be found as amenable to strict discipline and as courageous in the face of the enemy as any Colonial soldiers."[37] Hennessy's idea was supported by Lieutenant General Edward Donovan, the General Officer Commanding China, Hong Kong and the Straits Settlements, and by Colonel Bassano. Hennessy also suggested that hiring Chinese troops could prevent "fine regiments" such as the 74th Highlanders, depleted after stationing in Hong Kong, from "being weakened and rendered sickly by this climate and by the temptations to drink and vice which around here [Hong Kong]."[38]

Hennessy claimed that the officers who "took an interest in studying Chinese character, and gain in that way an intelligent sympathy with the natives" would agree with him. However, when the Marquis of Salisbury, who was Foreign Secretary, asked Thomas Wade, the British Minister to China who had helped establish the Chinese Maritime Customs Service and contributed to the invention of the Wade-Giles transcription system, about the issue, Wade replied that "he was sorry to see a large force of Chinese employed in Hong Kong," as they "could certainly not be relied upon if there were any misunderstanding between the Chinese government and our own." He suggested that if the government insisted on hiring Chinese troops, then it should do it at Singapore, and that the troops should be sent far away from China. Only a small number of Chinese auxiliaries should be hired in Hong Kong.[39] Although the issue dragged on until 1880, the War Office had abandoned the idea of establishing independent Chinese units when the Duke of Cambridge expressed his reservations on the matter.[40]

As the threat of an Anglo-Russian war subsided after the conclusion of the Treaty of San Stefano, London asked Hennessy in July 1878 to stop all ongoing works.[41] In his reply, Hennessy reiterated the need to turn the colony into the "stronghold in the East."[42] In all, Hong Kong received much attention from the Milne Committee: it received the largest amount of funding, and was recommended to keep a large regular garrison compared to other colonies (Tables 4 and 5).

Table 4 Temporary armaments for the stations suggested by the Milne Committee[43]

Stations	Armaments		Cost (£)				Total
	7-inch	6.3-in*	Works	Guns	Mines	Gunboats	
Hong Kong	8	7	30,000	12,200	7,000	26,000	75,200
Singapore	13	6	21,800	16,600	5,000	26,000	69,400
Cape Town	10	6	17,600	13,600	3,000	13,000	47,200
Galle	6	6	9,900	9,600	—	—	19,500
Port Elizabeth	6	4	10,400	8,400	—	—	18,800
Trincomalee	7	4	6,600	9,400	2,000	—	18,000
Colombo	6	3	5,100	7,800	—	—	12,900
St. Louis	2	—	400	2,000	2,000	—	4,400
Total	58	36	101,800	79,600	19,000	65,000	265,400

* RML 64-pdrs

Table 5 Garrisons for the stations outlined by the Milne Committee[44]

Stations	Current Strength			Planned Strength				
	Regular			Regular		Local		
	Art	Eng	Inf	Art	Inf	Art	Inf	Cav
Hong Kong	194	17	928	200	1,800	100	1,000	—
Cape of Good Hope#	241	72	3,537	200	1,000	400	2,000	100
Mauritius	115	5	318	100	1,000	150	—	—
Ceylon^	295	4	900	300	800	100	400	—
Cape Colony*	95	—	950	100	1,000	150	—	—
Total	940	98	6,618	900	5,600	900	3,400	100

\# including Cape Town, Port Elizabeth and St. Louis
^ including Trincomalee, Galle and Colombo
* including Singapore, Malacca and Penang

Hong Kong and Imperial Defence: The Carnarvon Report, 1879–1883

After the Milne Committee had submitted its report, General John Simmons proposed to the War Office that a standing committee for imperial defence be set up. However, as the war scare subsided and as Lord Carnarvon, the Colonial Secretary who supported the idea, left office in January 1878, the progress in forming the committee was slow. It was not until the summer of 1879 that Whitehall decided to form another ad hoc committee to deal with the long-term defence policy for overseas possessions.

The new committee, formed in July 1879, was known as the Royal Commission Appointed to Inquire into the Defence of British Possessions and Commerce Abroad (hereafter the Carnarvon Committee). It was chaired by Lord Carnarvon, and its members included Simmons, Lord Milne, two members of parliament and a representative from the Treasury. Colomb, who wanted to join the committee, was not appointed. This surprised his contemporaries who believed he was one of the more influential figures behind the idea of imperial defence.[45]

It took three years for the Carnarvon Committee to finish its study. The delay was caused not only by the breadth and depth of the topic but also by the return to government of the Liberals, who opposed overseas military commitments and the existence of the committee. The Liberal MP John Bright ridiculed the committee's "insane scheme" of "[defending] half of the world."[46] Still, with little help from the government, the committee finished three reports in three years. Most important, it pointed out the need for "an organised system of defences of the important colonial ports and naval stations" so that the navy could be deployed freely to meet various threats.[47]

The committee asked three different parties to work on the long-term defence requirements and structures of Hong Kong: the War Office, the Local Committee and Colonel William Crossman of the Royal Engineers, sent by the War Office to inspect the situation on the spot (Table 6).

The War Office scheme was drafted by Colonel Nugent, who believed that as Britain might face as many as three powers simultaneously in Asia, it was necessary to arm Hong Kong adequately so that it could serve as a "port of refuge" and a "depot to be denied to an enemy."[48] Nugent calculated that Russia alone could field twenty steamships in Asia, of which three would be armed with eight to ten inches of armour. To counter these ships, he proposed to install 10-inch RMLs or 10.4-inch BLs (10.4-inch BL Mark I) in Hong Kong. By reinforcing existing batteries and building new ones, the number of batteries in Hong Kong would be increased to eight (Kowloon Docks, North Point, Quarry Bay, Kowloon West, Belcher Point, as well as East, West and Central of Stonecutters Island). Nugent also suggested new infantry positions and barracks on Mount Gough. To prevent the enemy from shelling the island after taking Kowloon, infantry positions and batteries were also proposed for Kowloon and Stonecutters Island. The total garrison envisaged was 2,400 men (Table 7).

Table 6   Proposals to the Carnarvon Committee, 1879–1881

Locations	War Office	Local Committee	Col. Crossman
Kowloon Docks	10-in RML# x 1 9-in RML x 3	10-in RML x 4	10-in RML x 4
North Point	10-in RML x 1 9-in RML x 3	9-in RML x 3 64-pdr SB x 1	9-in RML x 3 64-pdr SB x 1
Quarry Bay	10-in RML x 3 64-pdr SB x 2	10-in RML x 4 64-pdr SB x 2	10-in RML x 4 64-pdr SB x 2
Kowloon East*	—	9-in RML x 2	9-in RML x 2 64-pdr SB x 1
Kowloon West^	9-in RML x 3 64-pdr SB x 1	10-in RML x 3 64-pdr SB x 1	10-in RML x 3 64-pdr SB x 1
Stonecutters East	7-in RML x 2	7-in RML x 2	7-in RML x 2
Stonecutters West	10-in RML x 2	10-in RML x 3	10-in RML x 3 64-pdr SB x 1
Stonecutters Central	10-in RML x 2	9-in RML x 2	9-in RML x 2
Stonecutters North	—	64-pdr SB x 1	—
Belcher Point	10-in RML x 3	10-in RML x 3 64-pdr SB x 1	10-in RML x 3
Total	10-in RML x 12 9-in RML x 9 7-in RML x 2 64-pdr SB x 3	10-in RML x 17 9-in RML x 7 7-in RML x 2 64-pdr SB x 6	10-in RML x 17 9-in RML x 7 7-in RML x 2 64-pdr SB x 5

\# or 10.4-inch BL

* modern-day Tsim Sha Tsui East

^ modern-day Tsim Sha Tsui West

Table 7   Proposals to the Carnarvon Committee (garrison size), 1879–1881

Proposals	War Office	Local Committee	Col. Crossman
Infantry	1,800	1,860	2,000
Cavalry	200	200	50
Artillery	360	386	562
Engineers	60	60	60
Total	2,420	2,506	2,672

Table 8   Proposals to the Carnarvon Committee (cost in £), 1879–1881

Proposals	War Office	Local Committee	Col. Crossman
Batteries	73,920	98,574	93,908
Guns	65,178	77,545	77,545
Mines	19,000	19,000	4,000
Barracks	100,000	143,600	114,240*
Inf. positions	4,000	1,400	25,000
Cav. and Mtn. guns	—	11,112	500
Coastal defence	26,000	79,300	80,000
Total	288,098	430,531	395,193

* £25,000 would be used to build a hospital.

The second proposal was put forward by the Local Committee, which consisted of the infantry, cavalry and artillery commanders in Hong Kong, Acting Colonial Secretary Walter Deane and Commander John Jones of the Royal Navy. It largely concurred with the War Office on the selection of battery sites, but proposed two more batteries on Stonecutters and in Kowloon East. It also proposed to increase the naval defence by an addition of conventional mines and of four torpedo boats armed with spar torpedoes. As for land defence, the committee suggested introducing Indian cavalrymen, who could ride on Chinese ponies instead of European breeds, to be responsible for transport and reconnaissance duties. The committee rejected the idea of building barracks on high points, as it was argued that the lookouts and signal stations on the Peak, Mount Kellett, Stanley Gap and Beacon Hill, as well as the infantry positions in Victoria Gap, Mount Gough, Wan Chai Gap and Stanley Gap would suffice. It was proposed that the garrison be concentrated in the western part of the island, holding only the heights and gaps towards the town.[49]

The third proposal was drafted by Colonel Crossman of the Royal Engineers, who had visited Hong Kong with the Local Committee in September 1881. Unsurprisingly, Crossman's proposal was similar to that of the Local Committee, although he paid more attention to the problem of land defence. He treated the land defence of the colony as a mutually supporting system, abandoning the idea of splitting the garrison to defend the batteries. For the same reason, he also gave up the defence of the Stanley Gap and Little Hong Kong. Crossman noted the need to incorporate the newly built Tai Tam Reservoir in future defence planning. He believed it was necessary to maintain communications between the batteries on the two sides of the Kowloon Peninsula and to protect their rear by placing two 64-pounder guns on the landward position. This was arguably the first British attempt to establish a defensive position *across* the Kowloon Peninsula to defend against a landward attack (Figure 5).[50]

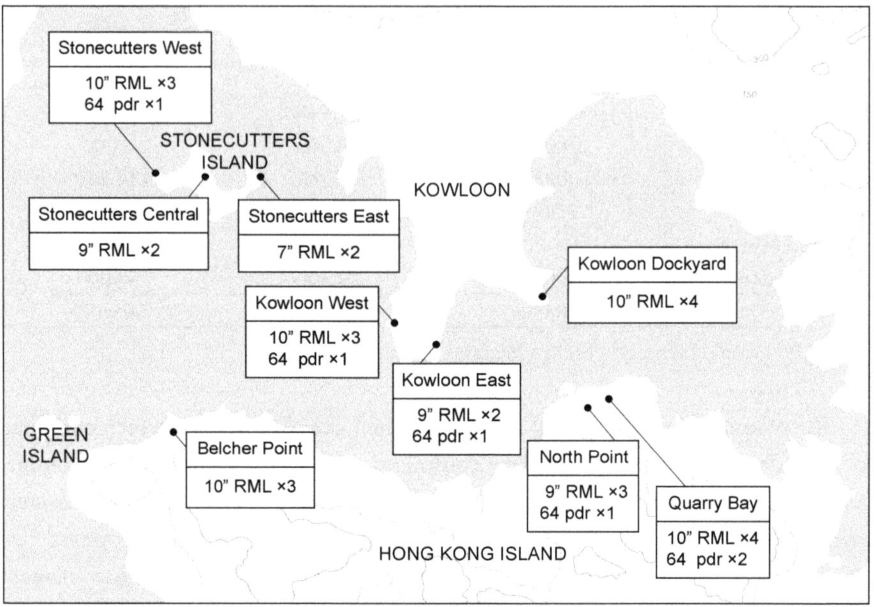

Figure 5   Defence layout proposed by Col. Crossman, 1881[51]

The Carnarvon Committee concluded that, due to the commercial and military importance of Hong Kong, it had "no hesitation in saying that [it] must be adequately defended and garrisoned, and no time should be lost in making it strong enough to withstand for some time, alone and unaided, the attack of an enemy."[52] The committee adopted Crossman's proposal, including his idea of concentrating all military facilities in Causeway Bay.[53] However, the Royal Navy objected, and operated in the Central District until 1993.[54]

The Carnarvon Committee also dealt with the issue of Chinese troops. After the inconclusive discussion in 1878, Hennessy raised the issue again.[55] However, General Donovan, who previously had supported the idea, changed his mind as he believed that the insanitary habits of the Chinese might contaminate his European troops.[56] In response, Hennessy quoted Admiral Robert Coote, the Commander-in-Chief of the China Station, who pointed out that the Hakka population might provide good soldiers.[57] In July 1880, Hennessy tried to solicit the support of Colonel Charles "Chinese" Gordon, the famous imperial adventurer, in his campaign for Chinese regiments. When Gordon passed through Hong Kong, Hennessy invited him to become the commander of the "Chinese Regiment." Gordon wrote a lengthy letter to London, in which he advocated an Anglo-Chinese alliance to counter Russia at the cost of abandoning opium trade. He then outlined his scheme to revive his Ever Victorious Army (*Changshengjun*) in Hong Kong, which he had helped create during the Taiping Rebellion:

> With respect to the force required for the defence of Hong Kong a nucleus of Chinese troops ought to be now formed. They would be perfectly trustworthy, if under officers who have some tact; they ought to be under a stricter discipline than Europeans in some matters, and a laxer discipline in others; they, each man, ought to be obliged to supply two guarantees for their behaviour; they ought to be allowed their women, whether they are married or not.
>
> My opinion would be dead against their being put under Generals commanding the troops, who only indirectly should oversee them. I have never found a regular General who was capable of commanding foreign levies. Probyn and Fane's Horse succeeded because they were in a great measure free of General's interference . . .
>
> I would begin with 250 Chinese. I would have but few European instructors, and those men who would not bully the poor devils because they do not understand English. The non-commissioned officers should be Chinese. I would so organise the force that it could be increased to 1,000. I would also put 100 or 200 in artillery.
>
> All rubbish of "goose step, right face, left face," etc., which our regular drills delights in, ought to be left untaught.
>
> I consider, if the nucleus was thus formed, you would be able to have, in a short time, any amount of good troops, who would take the place of those poor chocolate sepoys of India, with their castes, etc.[58]

Gordon's plan remained on paper, as the Commander-in-Chief of the Forces, the Duke of Cambridge, ruled it out. He also decided that the Hong Kong Defence Force would consist solely of Europeans. The Chinese would be recruited only as auxiliaries, and then only when Indians and Malays were unavailable.[59] The idea of a Hong Kong Regiment within the British Army was not realized until 1941.

The defence of Hong Kong remained weak until the mid-1880s, as many of the recommendations of the Milne and Carnarvon committees were not carried out. The inaction was not entirely the result of bureaucracy or financial considerations. There was little incentive to improve defences. Although Russia remained a potential threat, its navy was negligible. After the disastrous Franco-Prussian War of 1870, France too was no longer a serious naval threat (Table 9). At that time, the heavy units of the China Station, such as HMS *Audacious*[60] and HMS *Shannon*,[61] possessed more guns than all the batteries in Hong Kong combined. In addition, the Royal Navy was more inclined towards offensive actions and use of close blockades against enemy ports (as in the action against Sevastopol in 1854–1855) than defending bases. Thus, it was natural for London to invest in offensive arms such as ironclads rather than coastal batteries, which were seen as a second line of defence. For example, HMS *Inflexible*, an ironclad battleship, cost £812,200, more than the cost of the works in Singapore and Hong Kong proposed by the Carnarvon

Committee.[62] In addition, as will be discussed, the rapid change in weapon technology during subsequent decades explained the hesitation of planners to invest in fixed defences.

Table 9   Naval strength of the major powers, 1887–1891[63]

Class	Britain			France			Russia		
	No.	Tonnage	Guns*	No.	Tonnage	Guns	No.	Tonnage	Guns
First**	24	234,440	106	10	105,245	38	7	65,879	26
Second^	24	143,140	102	18	126,270	72	4	26,862	14
Third#	11	92,110	135	5	23,508	32	11	27,088	69
Total	59	469,690	343	33	255,023	142	22	119,829	109

* more than 9-tons

** ironclad or First Rate, steel made, with no less than 9-inch armour and displacement of 8,500 tons

^ Second Rate, steel-made or protected, with no less than 8-inch armour but displacement of less than 8,500 tons

\# First Rate, steel-made or protected, with no less than 4- to 6-inch armour

Conclusion

As the Royal Navy remained unchallenged during this period, London had little incentive to invest in the defence of Hong Kong. Lack of real change, however, did not mean that the committees were irrelevant. They highlighted the need to conceptualize the defence policy of the British Empire as a whole. They also established Hong Kong's status as the most important British base in Asia until after the First World War, when the British were no longer willing and able to deploy large fleets in Asia.

As the new iron-steamer warships had to rely on established bases for supplies and repairs, Hong Kong became—like Malta, Gibraltar and Singapore—one of the British overseas possessions that formed a closely knit network for Royal Navy operations. It was also established that the mission of defending Hong Kong lay on the shoulders of the army, as the navy was expected to operate away from base, fighting offensive actions. However, because of the peculiar geographical features of Hong Kong, the navy's role in littoral defence remained important. Through the repeated discussions of the committees, basic requirements, force structure and perceived threats came to be clearly outlined. The defensive structures (batteries and mines), the garrison and the port-defence vessels were now seen as parts of a mutually supporting system rather than as separate entities. This period also witnessed the realization of the need to defend Kowloon, an idea that contributed to the subsequent acquisition of the New Territories and other attempts to defend the Hong Kong–China border.

4

HONG KONG DEFENCE DURING THE AGE OF EMPIRES, 1883–1919

No powerful attack could even be made so long as England retains the command of the China Seas, but if this command is lost, even if only for a short time, an attack in force will certainly be made upon this very valuable possession.

—Colonial Defence Committee, 1889

The possession by Great Britain of the country between the Kowloon Hills and the Sham Chun River is, in one respect, a source of weakness, because it makes it possible for one of the Great Powers to land an army within striking distance of Hong Kong, without violating the neutrality of Chinese territory.

—Major General Charles Anderson,
General Officer Commanding Hong Kong, 1910

Fixed [coastal] defences, however formidable, will not render a fortress secure against attack by an expeditionary force.

—Colonial Defence Committee on Hong Kong defence, 1911

Strategic Role of Hong Kong during the Age of Imperialism

The international situation in Asia changed drastically between 1880 and 1914. Germany became an economic and military powerhouse after its unification in 1871. After the ascendancy of Kaiser Wilhelm II to the throne in 1890, it also became an ambitious naval power and the most threatening potential enemy of Britain. France and Russia also made much progress in Asia. The former consolidated its control over Indochina after its victory over the Qing in 1884–1885 and leased a foothold at Guangzhouwan in 1892. When the weakness of the Qing was fully exposed during the Sino-Japanese War of 1894–1895, these powers established bases along the China coast. In 1897, the German East Asia Squadron (Ostasiengeschwader) arrived in Qingdao (Tsingtao) and leased the port for ninety-nine years. In the following year, the Russians leased Port Arthur (Lüshun); the British leased the New Territories and Weihaiwei, also for ninety-nine years. In the same year, the United States became a new Pacific power after wresting control of the Philippines from the Spaniards. During the early 1900s, the Russians built a sizeable fleet and a naval base at Port Arthur that led to much British concern. However, it was soon destroyed by Japan, a British ally since 1902, during the Russo-Japanese War of 1904–1905. The British quickly realized that the replacement of Russia by Japan as the predominant naval power in the Northeast Pacific was a latent threat to Hong Kong and the empire.

Between 1883 and 1919, Hong Kong became one of the major shipping and financial centres of Asia. While the opium trade remained an important source of income, other commercial activities also brought much wealth to the colony and the metropole. In 1908, the Commander-in-Chief of the China Station estimated that the trade related to Hong Kong amounted to £45,000,000 per annum.[1] According to Japanese intelligence, over 1,260,000 tons of coal was imported to the colony in 1909 alone.[2] The importance of the colony as a naval base was also enhanced, with the completion of dockyards such as the Cosmopolitan (1880), Taikoo (1902) and the Royal Naval Dockyard (1903). They were the few British dock facilities that could accommodate battleships in Asia before the Sembawang Base in Singapore was operational in the late 1930s (Table 10).

Hong Kong still served as the major staging area for British forces in Asia. During the Boxer War of 1899–1901, numerous British and Indian formations passed through Hong Kong, which also sent the Hong Kong Regiment (consisting of Indian troops) to relieve the Foreign Legation in Beijing. After the conclusion of the Boxer Protocol in 1901, British troops were allowed to garrison at Beijing, Tianjin and Shanghai. Before that, the British had already garrisoned at Weihaiwei. Hong Kong was the rear area for these garrisons.

Table 10   British dry-docks East of Suez, 1914[3]

Name	No.	Dry-docks' size (in feet)
Mauritius	1	384 ft. x 60 ft., one smaller
Bombay	1	500 ft. x 65 ft.
Colombo	1	708 ft. x 85 ft.
Penang	1	343 ft. x 46 ft.
Singapore	5	467 ft. x 65 ft.; 478 ft. x 60 ft.; 400 ft. x 47 ft.; 450 ft. x 52 ft.; 846 ft. x 100 ft.
Hong Kong	8	555 ft. x 95 ft.; 750 ft. x 88 ft.; 700 ft. x 86 ft.; 432 ft. x 84 ft.; 466 ft. x 85 ft., three smaller
Adelaide	1	500 ft. x 60 ft.
Brisbane	1	431 ft. x 55 ft.
Sydney	7	638 ft. x 84 ft.; 477 ft. x 59 ft.; 675 ft. x 83 ft., four smaller
Melbourne	4	470 ft. x 80 ft., three smaller
Auckland	2	521 ft. x 80 ft., one smaller

Hong Kong was also used by other powers, and even revolutionaries, as a strategic springboard. During the Sino-French War of 1884, the French fleet attacking Taiwan and Fujian called at Hong Kong. This caused much resentment among the Chinese residents, leading to a strike and a riot that had to be quelled by the garrison.[4] When the United States was at war with Spain in 1898, the U.S. Asiatic Squadron was anchored and refuelled in Mirs Bay of what would become the New Territories. To avoid the embarrassment of evicting or interning the US warships, the British delayed the occupation of the New Territories until 1899.[5] From the 1890s, Chinese revolutionary organizations such as Xingzhonghui (興中會), Huaxinghui (華興會) and, later, Tongmenghui (同盟會) were all active in Hong Kong.[6] As early as 1872, anti-Spanish Filipino revolutionaries also used the colony as their base. The colony was the intelligence centre and rear base for José Rizal in the 1890s. During the Spanish-American War, the Filipino revolutionaries made a deal with Rear Admiral George Dewey of the U.S. Asiatic Squadron, who promised to ship them back to the Philippines.[7]

The mechanism of British defence policymaking also witnessed much change. Most important, two permanent committees emerged and were responsible for drafting, reviewing and coordinating the defence policies of the empire as a whole. In 1885, the Colonial Defence Committee (CDC) became a permanent body that consisted of representatives of the army, the navy and the bureaucracy (it was renamed the Overseas Defence Committee in 1911). In 1902, the Committee of Imperial Defence (CID) was established. It was chaired by the Prime Minister and its members included the Foreign Secretary, the First Lord of the Admiralty, the First Sea Lord, the Chief of Imperial General Staff (CIGS), and intelligence and planning heads such as the Director of Naval Intelligence.[8] Together with departments within the services such as the Directorate of Military Operations of the War Office, the two standing committees reviewed the defence of Hong Kong amid rapid changes in military technology, in domestic and international situations, and in the economic outlook of Britain.

Military Contribution, Venereal Disease and Plague

Under the protection of a strong China Station (Table 11), the size of the Hong Kong garrison remained at two to three battalions of infantry, the garrison artillery and smaller Royal Artillery and Royal Engineers units. In 1898, the infantry garrison had only 1,167 men. As David French has suggested, the main role of the army in the colonies was to "project an image of strength" through parades and other imperial ceremonies, such as the arrival and departure of governors.[9] When

Japan became a British ally in 1902, the British naval presence in Hong Kong was reduced, although a number of capital ships still remained. In 1906, in response to the German naval threat in North Sea, the heavy units of the China Station were redeployed to European waters. There was not a single battleship in Hong Kong until 1912.

Table 11   British, French and Russian naval strength in Asia, 1902[10]

Class	Britain			France			Russia		
	No.	Tonnage	Guns*	No.	Tonnage	Guns	No.	Tonnage	Guns
Battleship	5	60,000	20	1	9,430	4	5	51,206	20
Arm. Cru^	2	11,200	8	0	—	—	6	55,623	0
Pro. Cru#	13	68,845	0	5	28,391	0	2	2,500	0
Destroyers	6	—	—	0	—	—	0	—	—
Gunboats	16	—	—	6	—	—	2	—	—

* 12-inch to 9.2-inch guns only
^ Armoured Cruisers
# Protected Cruisers

During this period, the practice of sending military contributions underwent some changes that had a profound impact on the public finances of Hong Kong. Between 1865 and 1890, the military contribution remained at £20,000. The actual amount paid in terms of the Hong Kong dollar fluctuated following changes in the price of silver, generally increasing from around $90,000 to $120,000 in 1890. That year, London demanded that the military contribution be doubled. This demand enraged the unofficial members of the Legislative Council. The Hong Kong government was also reluctant to allow a substantial increase. On the other hand, Viscount Knutsford, the Secretary of State for the Colonies, pointed out that the Hong Kong government was paying only a portion of the £180,000 being spent on the defence of the colony.[11] Thus, Hong Kong doubled its military contribution until 1900, when the amount was fixed again at 20 percent of total government revenue.[12] However, just what constituted "government revenue" was constantly debated. To minimize the chargeable revenue, the government maximized land premiums and minimized rent, as the former was not chargeable. The government was also unwilling to raise taxes or to add new services, as 20 percent of the new income would go to military contribution.[13] Although there were continuous petitions to decrease the contribution, the issue was settled until the 1930s (Table 12).

Table 12   Military contribution of Hong Kong, 1892–1917 (in HKD)[14]

Year	1892	1897	1902	1907	1912	1917
Contribution	269,005	476,869	949,804	1,239,594	1,421,352	2,813,700

During this largely peaceful period, the garrison had to fight against VD, annual plague epidemics and a devastating storm. In 1867, the Contagious Disease Ordinance was amended as the Contagious Disease Act (CD Act), according to the same law introduced in Britain. However, the act faced increasing public censure as it was seen as oppressive and unjust. Governor Hennessy also opposed the act, appointing a committee to show that the control measures were largely ineffective.[15] When the CD Act was finally repealed in Britain in 1883, Hong Kong kept a partial system that allowed prostitutes to receive examination on a voluntary basis. The examination and registration system was completely abolished under much pressure from London in 1894.[16]

The abolition of the CD Act and the control measures, however, did not solve the problem. In April 1896, Vice Admiral Alexander Buller, Commander-in-Chief of the China Station, wrote to Governor William Robinson to ask for "any steps which could be taken to mitigate this dreadful complaint." He forwarded a letter written by the surgeon of the fleet, who had discovered the prevalence of all types of VD in his flagship.[17] A year later, a staggering 499 out of 1,000 men of the garrison had to be admitted to hospital for VD treatment. As formal registration and examination systems were loathed by the British public and rejected by Whitehall, the Hong Kong government adopted a workaround by closing down brothels that had not been examined and "overlooking" those that allowed their prostitutes to be examined. From then on, a new examination system existed quasi-legally in Hong Kong, and was in place well into the first half of the 20th century.[18] Meanwhile, prostitution remained a major business. As the Japanese naval intelligence pointed out, in 1910, 143 out of 376 Japanese women in the colony were prostitutes.[19]

The discipline of the British forces in Hong Kong was at times poor during the zenith of imperialism and racial discrimination. This was partly shown by the high rate of VD infection among the troops. In 1880, as a result of the Army Discipline and Regulation Act of 1879, the War Office recommended that the Colonial Office instruct the Hong Kong government to select one "authorised Prison" to house military convicts.[20] As a result, the Victoria Gaol became the military prison of Hong Kong. When Hong Kong became a staging point for large deployments, the problem of military discipline was amplified accordingly. In 1901 alone, 127 military prisoners were admitted to the Victoria Gaol.[21] The intake of military convicts fluctuated, from over a hundred to fewer than ten during the first decade of the 20th century.[22] As noted by a visitor to Hong Kong in 1877, the British officers treated Chinese "as if they were a very inferior kind of animal to themselves."[23] These abuses might not be found in the record. The misbehaviour of the troops towards the Chinese, whose national consciousness was starting to emerge, often led to unexpected results. For example, Yang Quyun, an early revolutionary and a close associate of Sun Yat-sen, had a fistfight with British sailors in Hong Kong who maltreated coolies. This event partly prompted him to engage in the revolutionary movement.[24]

The garrison saw extensive action during the outbreak of bubonic plague in 1894. The plague, which started in early May, soon overwhelmed the local authorities. Upon the governor's request, the King's Shropshire Light Infantry (KSLI) sent 380 officers and men to assist. The Royal Navy also provided medical assistance; a hospital ship was used to house all infected residents. As the origin and treatment of the plague had yet to be discovered, the colonial authority could only forcefully remove, through the use of armed soldiers, dead and infected residents, predominantly Chinese, from their homes. The troops then cleared the crowded residential area in Taipingshan. These measures were resented by the Chinese and the Qing authority at Guangzhou. The governor asked the Royal Navy to deploy HMS *Tweed* at the harbour as a deterrent. The Chinese houses in Taipingshan were later demolished by the Royal Engineers, and their inhabitants moved to present-day Sheung Wan. In all, more than 2,500 men and women died, including the officer commanding the cleaning and removal parties and six KSLI troopers.[25] As for social disturbances, the garrison was called out to suppress the anti-French and -government riot during the Sino-French War of 1884. The riot was the result of the government's decision to allow French warships to be resupplied at Hong Kong. During the dockers' strike of 1895, the garrison sent 400 soldiers to work at the pier for twelve hours every day.[26] The garrison was again called out after a devastating typhoon struck Hong Kong and killed over 10,000 people in September 1906.[27]

From 1886, a small number of Hong Kong Chinese were recruited as assistants to the divers in the Hong Kong Submarine Mining Company. Their number increased to seventy in 1893.[28] They were among the first Hong Kong Chinese soldiers to serve in the British Army during the colonial period. Their Chinese name—*shui leipao-bing* (literally "submarine miner," 水雷砲兵)—became for the subsequent century a synonym for Hong Kong Chinese soldiers serving in the British Army. The unit participated in the Six-Day War and the Boxer Uprising, but was disbanded in 1906, when the Royal Engineers handed the submarine mining service to the Royal Navy.[29] The Chinese sappers were transferred to the 40th (Fortress) Company, a local engineers unit.

This period also witnessed extensive improvement of the military facilities in Hong Kong, such as the expansion of the Royal Naval Dockyard and the construction of the Whitfield Barracks at Tsim Sha Tsui. The attempts of the colonial government to induce the Royal Navy to move away from Victoria City had consistently

Figure 6   RN submarines being repaired in the Royal Naval Dockyard, 1910s (Tim Ko)

failed. In the early 1900s, the navy had substantially expanded its base and built a naval dockyard by reclamation.[30] Three submarines could simultaneously be repaired at the new naval dockyard, making it one of the largest repair facilities of the Royal Navy in Asia (Figure 6).[31] In the 1860s, only matsheds were built in Kowloon to house part of the garrison. When the Hong Kong Regiment was formed in 1892, the Whitfield Barracks was built at the cost of £65,700.[32] The complex gradually expanded by the 1910s into one that had eighty-five blocks. As discussed below, the armaments and planning of the garrison also underwent extensive changes.

Modernization of the Batteries, 1883–1912

From the 1880s, the development of military technology had accelerated. The most important change was in land and naval artillery. As mentioned, the British had briefly adopted Rifled Breech Loaders (RBLs, hereafter simply BLs) in the 1860s, but they were replaced by RMLs because of their high cost and unreliability. After the emergence of interrupted screws, smokeless powders and new types of shell casings, the reliability and capability of the BLs had far exceeded that of the RMLs. In 1879, the Admiralty authorized the development of a new type of heavy BL. Three years later, the 9.2-inch (233.7 mm) BL was in production. As Table 13 shows, the power and range of the new BL guns could easily outmatch any RML. In the late 1880s, the British introduced the 4.7-inch quick-firing guns (QF) on warships. As the cartridge for the QF guns included both shell and propellant, their loading time was much shorter than ordinary artillery pieces. This allowed guns of

Figure 7 French armoured cruiser *Montcalm*, an improved version of *Dupuy de Lôme*, built in 1898[33]

medium to small size (6-inch or below) to fire much faster than their predecessors and the larger pieces.

Rapid changes in warship design also occurred during this period. By the 1880s, steam-powered warships made of steel had become the norm. Although some warships still kept their rigging and masts, they were more the products of a transitional period. In 1888, the French armoured cruiser *Dupuy de Lôme* (6,300 tons), the first of its kind, was put into service. It had a heavy armour belt of 100 mm at its thickest, a pair of 7.6-inch (193 mm) guns, over twenty smaller guns and torpedo-launching tubes (Figure 7). It was much stronger than the British "protected-cruisers" (cruisers without an armour belt) serving in the foreign stations. The armoured cruiser was the brainchild of the Jeune École of the French Navy, which advocated the construction of many smaller but faster vessels to disrupt British overseas trade. Although the French could never build enough warships, large or small, to actually threaten Britain, the emergence of new guns and ships forced British planners to rethink the defence of its overseas possessions, including Hong Kong.

In this context, the defence of Hong Kong experienced fundamental changes. After the Carnarvon Committee had recommended Colonel Crossman's scheme in 1883, the scheme was revised by Major General Andrew Clarke, the Inspector General of Fortifications. In the context of rapid technological change, Clarke decided not to fully implement Crossman's scheme. He also proposed deploying the most powerful guns at the batteries that would actually be built. The plan called for the installation of 9.2-inch BLs at Stonecutters West, Belcher Point and Quarry Bay,

Table 13   Comparison of RMLs, RBLs and BLs, 1880–1890s[34]

Type	Muzzle Velocity (m/s)	Penetration (mm)*	Range (m)
10-in RML	420.3	297	4,572
9-in RML	438.9	102	4,572
7-in RML	464.8	102	4,572
7-in RBL#	335.3	123	4,572
10-in BL	640.1	538	11,500
9.2-in BL	629.4	478	14,000–16,000
6-in BL	585.2	262	12,000

*   Fire from 914 m (1,000 yards)

\#   RBL: Rifled Breech Loader

while the guns in the West Kowloon Battery would be changed to 10-inch RMLs. Clarke's proposal was further revised by the Inspector General of Artillery, Major General W. Reilly, who suggested that only British gunners should be allowed to handle the 9.2-inch BLs as he doubted whether the Indian gunners were up to the job. He also urged replacing all 7-inch RMLs, installed in Hong Kong from 1878, with the larger 9-inch RMLs.[35] Clarke and Reilly's proposals heralded a new phase of battery construction in Hong Kong.

Figure 8 shows the layout of Hong Kong defence in 1886. Only the eastern entrance of Victoria Harbour had a relatively complete defence. The western

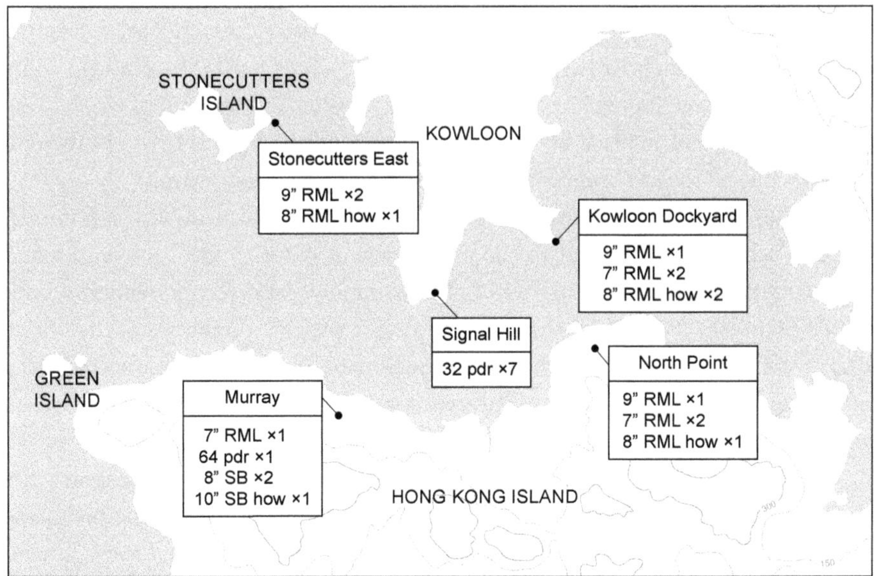

Figure 8   Coastal guns in Hong Kong, 1886[36] (how = howitzer)

approach was weakly covered by the guns at Stonecutters and the Murray Battery, which was already buried in the town. If the Murray Battery actually exchanged fire with intruding warships, the damage on the city would be immense.

In 1886, the Foreign Intelligence Committee of the Admiralty also recommended installing new BLs and QFs in Hong Kong. A Royal Engineers–Royal Artillery Committee was formed by the War Office to review the schemes drafted by Clarke and Reilly. It agreed that BLs and QFs should be installed, and that the defence perimeter of the island should be extended to Lyemun to cover the newly developed North Point and Taikoo. To cover the flank of this area and to prevent the enemy from dominating Lyemun and the Devil's Peak, an infantry position should also be prepared at Sai Wan Hill. QFs should be installed at Lyemun, Stonecutters and Belcher Point to prevent surprise attacks by enemy torpedo boats. This recommendation shows the British understanding of the threat posed by the Jeune École.[37] The War Office sent Lieutenant Colonel Fairfax Ellis and Lieutenant Colonel G. Baker to Hong Kong; they produced another report illustrating the defects of the existing batteries in July 1886. The North Point Battery, they argued, was too exposed, while the bamboo screen erected around it only made it more conspicuous. They proposed installing modern rangefinders for the batteries and more medium-sized QFs to deter modern warships.[38]

The Colonial Office instructed the Hong Kong government in July 1886 to prepare £116,000 for the construction of the new batteries.[39] The total expenditure was around HK$700,000, all paid by Hong Kong.[40] Between 1886 and 1889, the colony received (or was receiving) five 10-inch BLs, three 10-inch RMLs, two 9.2-inch BLs, eight 9-inch RMLs and six 6-inch BLs.[41] Thus, by 1889, although some of the batteries were not yet operational, the discussion and revision of Hong Kong defence that had taken place since 1877 was largely finished. Until 1894, the focus of planners turned to the Hong Kong Defence Scheme (see next section).

In 1894, the Local Committee requested more QFs to deal with a potential torpedo boat attack. This led to the installation of 4.7-inch QFs at Lyemun and Stonecutters South Battery in 1895.[42] The committee also recommended installing 12-pounders at the Belcher Battery and replacing the mountings of the 6-inch BLs at the Lyemun Redoubt with hydro-pneumatic disappearing mountings. The mountings of the 6-inch guns at Stonecutters West and the Belcher Battery were also changed accordingly.

Between 1894 and 1906, Hong Kong was equipped with a secret weapon—the Brennan torpedo. It was invented by the Irish-born Louis Brennan, who had made its prototype as early as 1874. It was claimed to be a type of guided torpedo controlled by a wire linking the torpedo with a control station. The War Office formed a special committee to study Brennan's design and in 1883 granted him £5,000 to improve it.[43] The Royal Navy, however, rejected the device, due to the impossibility of installing it on a warship. After the problems of depth, control and speed were purportedly solved, the War Office granted another £110,000 to Brennan to produce the torpedoes in 1887. The contract was so expensive that it led to some dissension in parliament, but the War Office refused to explain, as the torpedo was deemed a "secret."[44]

The Brennan torpedo was indeed treated as a national secret. Only a few Royal Engineers officers were told about how it worked, and although *Brassey's Naval Annual* had mentioned its "tremendous speed" in its table of contents, the paragraphs about the torpedo were deleted.[45] The staff of Brennan's factory were divided into sections, so as to be unaware of the work of others. The devices that controlled the depth and direction of the torpedoes were sealed in black boxes and sent separately. They were locked in safes during peacetime, and could only be opened with keys carried by two officers. The process of unlocking the black boxes and arming the torpedoes was so complicated that the torpedoes were useless in emergencies.[46] This problem did not seem to trouble the War Office, which installed Brennan torpedo stations at Plymouth and at overseas ports such as Cork and Malta. Between 1892 and 1894, a launching station was built near the Lyemun Redoubt; it was first mentioned in the Defence Scheme of 1897. It belonged to the Submarine Mining section of the Royal Engineers; the position of Station Torpedo Officer was held by the Officer Commanding, Submarine Mining. Under his command were ten European (British) officers and men.[47]

After the Qing agreed to lease the New Territories in 1898, the Committee on Armaments of Certain Stations at Home and Abroad proposed reorganizing the defences of Victoria Harbour. The committee recommended replacing the disappearing mountings of the 6-inch guns at Lyemun Redoubt with open barbettes, to increase their rate of fire. Additional 6-inch BLs at Pakshawan and 6- and 9.2-inch BLs on the newly acquired Devil's Peak were proposed, to cover the Lyemun Channel. Inner-port batteries such as the Kowloon Docks Battery would be decommissioned, and the North Point Battery would be redesigned to carry 6-inch BLs. As for the defence of the western approach, the committee recommended installing 6-inch BLs at the West Kowloon Battery and erecting a new battery near modern-day Lung Fu Shan on Hong Kong Island.[48]

The above recommendations were studied by the Armament Committee of the War Office (the successor of the Royal Artillery–Royal Engineers Committee). It added that the mountings of all 10- and 6-inch BLs should be changed, and the 6-inch BLs at Devil's Peak, Pakshawan, West Kowloon and North Point should

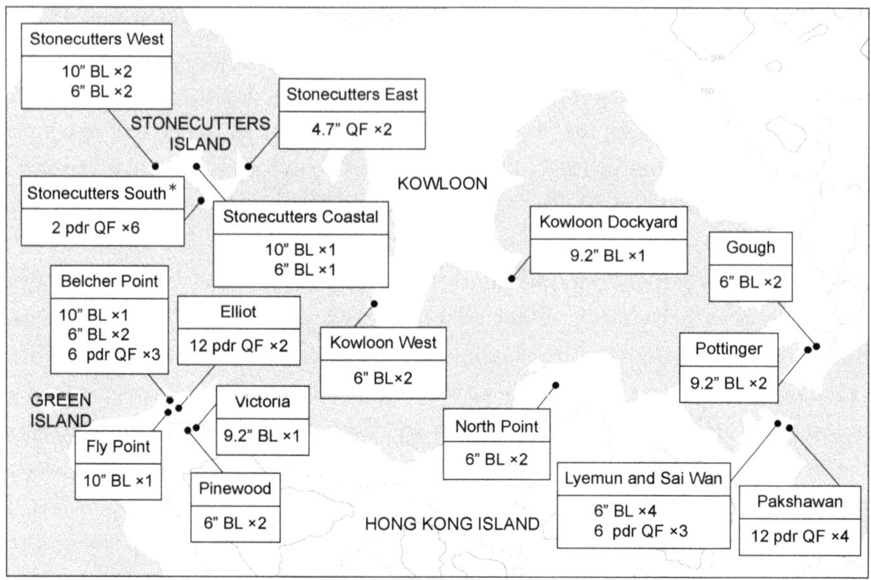

Figure 9   Coastal batteries in Hong Kong, 1906[49]

use the latest centre pivot mountings. A plan of £244,485 to build and renovate the batteries was finally approved; the Hong Kong government was responsible for £90,000. From 1900 to 1905, a new group of batteries were built and most of the existing ones were renovated (Figure 9).

Lyemun
- Pottinger Battery (operational in 1902);[50] Gough Battery (completed in 1903); Pakshawan (operational in 1903)

Stonecutters
- Albion Battery (operational in 1904); Centurion Battery (operational in 1905); Stonecutters (operational in 1906–1907); Stonecutters East (operational in 1900)

Hong Kong Island
- Belcher Point Battery (operational in 1905–1906); Elliot Battery (operational in 1900); Pinewood Battery (operational in 1905)

After the Russo-Japanese War of 1904–1905, the defence layout was again revised.[51] In 1906, the War Office appointed a committee chaired by Colonel John F. Owen to study Hong Kong defence with Royal Artillery, Royal Engineers and Royal Navy representatives. The Owen Committee reported that Hong Kong would face the "Class A Attack," as it was the most important British port in Asia and a base of Royal Navy capital ships. This meant that it might be attacked by capital ships of a foreign power.[52] The committee found that the existing defence aimed at guarding Victoria Harbour against intruding warships rather than long-range bombardment by enemy capital ships. Indeed, during the Russo-Japanese War, the Japanese had tried to subdue Port Arthur by long-range naval and land bombardment. The likely targets included the City of Victoria and the dockyards.

The Owen Committee recommended dismantling most of the existing batteries, some of them only recently built, and replacing them with a system of fortifications that guarded the entrances of the harbour. In all, only the Pakshawan, Lyemun, Pottinger, Gough, Stonecutters West, Albion and Belcher batteries remained (Figure 10).[53] A new fortress would be built at Mount Davis on Hong Kong Island, housing five 9.2-inch BLs to guard the western approach.[54] The 6- and 9.2-inch BLs recommended by the committee were of the latest design. The 6-inch BL Mark VII had a range of 14,000 metres, while the new 9.2-inch BL Mark X had a range of 18,000 metres. Although the guns of the capital ships theoretically had longer range, enemy warships had to close well within the range of the guns in Hong Kong in order to engage effectively, because of their limited fire control system. The committee explained that these guns could deter enemy warships, as they might not want to risk being damaged by coastal guns before engaging the British fleet.

As the new batteries were more expensive than the existing ones and as the number of gunners increased after the revision, it is unlikely that the above-mentioned scheme was merely a product of retrenchment.[55] Thus, cost considerations

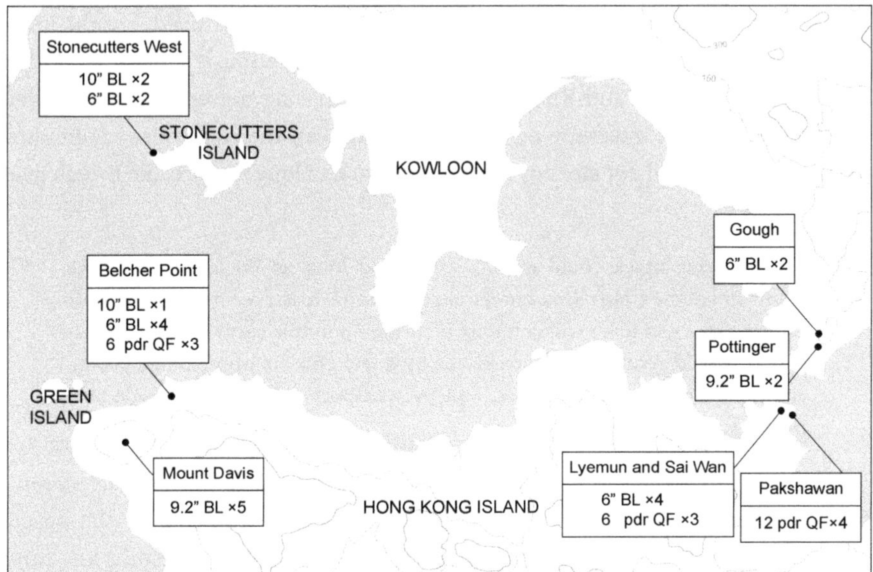

Figure 10   Guns proposed by the Owen Committee, 1906–1912[56]

might not be the sole factor for such an arrangement. From 1906, a new round of battery construction started according to Owen's scheme; it continued until the completion of the Mount Davis Fortress in 1912.

The Defence Schemes, 1889–1901

The problem of Hong Kong defence had both coastal and land dimensions. The two issues were tackled by the defence schemes drafted by the Local Committee, which consisted of military and naval representatives. From 1886 to 1970, numerous defence schemes were drafted. The schemes were to provide the garrison clear courses of action in times of war. They involved not only strategic background and operational arrangements, but also deployment, logistics and communication detail. This section uses the defence schemes from between 1889 and 1910s to fill in a missing part of British discussions about Hong Kong defence.

Soon after the Colonial Defence Committee (CDC) had been formed in 1885, it requested the overseas garrisons to draft detailed defence schemes. However, the committee found the first defence scheme submitted by Hong Kong in 1887 too vague and asked the Local Committee to rewrite it, based on the one submitted by Natal.[57] Thus, it was not until July 1889 that Hong Kong was able to submit a completed scheme to Britain. The Local Committee, chaired by the General Officer Commanding Hong Kong, Lieutenant General William Cameron, suggested that with the loss of Hong Kong, "all British power in the Chinese Seas and the Western Pacific is at an end, and that not only would our trade be destroyed, but the independence of our rising Colonies in Australasia would be seriously threatened."[58] The committee saw France and Russia as the most menacing powers, and considered that the Qing might intervene on their side. However, the committee maintained that the colony would not face any large-scale attack so long as a sizeable British fleet was present:

> No powerful attack could even be made so long as England retains the command of the China Seas, but if this command is lost, even if only for a short time, an attack in force will certainly be made upon this very valuable possession. It would probably be carried out by a few cruisers of moderate power, accompanied by smaller vessels, and by transports carrying a considerable body of troops.[59]

Still, a land invasion was possible if the Royal Navy was temporarily absent. Cameron and the Local Committee rejected the idea of resisting on the beach, instead dividing the 1,707 men garrison into three "sections" to defend a line from the Peak to Mount Cameron through Mount Gough, another line from Lyemun to North Point, and Kowloon Peninsula and Stonecutters. In short, the defenders would form a ring encircling the City of Victoria, with separate elements stationing at Stonecutters. Cameron believed that, as the line between the Peak and Mount Cameron was the most crucial, "under no circumstances do the Committee consider it advisable to withdraw the troops available for the southern defence." The south shore of the island would be protected only by armed police, who would be "in telegraphic communication with headquarters."[60]

To augment the small garrison, the scheme planned to erect "redoubts (stone and earth fieldworks with all-around fire)" at "hill above North Point Battery, hill above Belcher Point Battery, Victoria Peak, High West, Mount Kellett, Mount Gough, Sanitarium, Mount Cameron, and the hill adjoining Kowloon East Battery." Houses that might block the firing arc would be demolished; some would be requisitioned.[61] Given the small size of the garrison and the lack of communication on the island during the 1880s, it was sensible not to defend the south shore. Had the garrison tried to resist a landing on the south shore, it might be decimated by naval bombardment, or enemy forces could bypass and isolate it by landing elsewhere. Cameron chose to conserve his force for a prolonged struggle in the mountains of the island. The idea was based on the assumption that Hong Kong would be relieved by the navy, which would retain/retake control of the South China Sea. Thus, the scheme was rational in the context of British naval superiority. In fact, in 1886–1888, the Russian Navy dropped a plan of attacking Hong Kong with several cruisers carrying 2,000 to 3,000 soldiers, because it realized that it could not challenge the British navy.[62]

The CDC was satisfied with Cameron's scheme, judging that the need to reinforce Hong Kong was remote so long as the Royal Navy remained strong. It suggested that "taking the China and Australian Stations together, Great Britain will possess a great naval preponderance which it will be extremely difficult to disturb."[63] Still, given the colony's commercial and military importance, the CDC thought it necessary to prepare for the defence of Hong Kong against attack in force from Indochina or Vladivostok. A landing from the south shore of the island raised particular concern. The garrison was urged to study all possible landing places and their communications, and to prepare details of the fieldworks that would be constructed in war. Machine-guns and light field guns were sent upon Cameron's request.[64]

In 1894, the General Officer Commanding Hong Kong, Major General George Barker, was asked by the War Office to revise the existing scheme, to take into account the new Hong Kong Regiment and the new batteries. The new scheme abandoned the idea of building large redoubts on mountaintops, as they might tie down many troops and their line of sight might be blocked by heavy fog. A system of blockhouses on the island and a small flying column that could harass the landing enemy were envisaged. After fighting against the flying column, the enemy ashore would meet a second line of defence consisting of trenches and blockhouses located near mountain spurs that could not be shelled from the sea.[65] In all, temporary infantry positions on the beaches and thirteen locations for blockhouses and trenches were planned. The scheme of 1894 was an improvement as it highlighted the importance of cover and terrain in absorbing enemy firepower. Like Cameron's plan, Barker's goal was to wait for Royal Navy reinforcement, thus he also refused to delegate most of his resources to defending the beaches.

While Hong Kong was seemingly secure because of a strong naval presence, its residents felt less assured. Between 20 September and 8 October, the *China Mail* serialized *The Back Door*, a novel about the hypothetical fall of Hong Kong to a Franco-Russian expedition over three-and-a-half days in 1897.[66] In *The Back Door*, three Russian transport ships, escorted by destroyers and torpedo boats, landed troops in Aberdeen. As the telecommunication line between the south shore and the headquarters was cut, the invading force of 4,000 men had already marched into Wong Nai Chung Gap before the garrison was assembled. The 2,000-strong garrison made a gallant stand in the gap, but rioting engulfed the City of Victoria. The small Royal Navy detachment tried to attack the invading fleet but was annihilated. Although the first invasion was beaten back in a daring night attack, the garrison had already lost half of its strength. When the French and Russian forces landed another 14,000 men on the island and Kowloon, the defenders were eventually eliminated after a last stand on Stonecutters.[67]

The Colonial Office received the novel from Hong Kong, but it was noted by an official as being "irrelevant."[68] The work also had no impact on the new Defence Scheme of 1897 or the discussions about reorganizing the coastal guns. It has been suggested that London was reluctant to fortify the south shore largely because of cost considerations.[69] However, long before the novel was published, the planners had already discussed in detail the military threats facing Hong Kong and possible enemy courses of action. From 1889, the planners envisaged a landing on the south shore of the island or a cruiser raid before the declaration of war. The Defence Scheme of 1897 estimated that the French and the Russians could deploy only 2,000 men at most for a raid against Hong Kong. When the General Officer Commanding Hong Kong, Major General Wilsone Black, revised the scheme, he noted that a member of the Local Committee had raised much concern about the defence of the south shore, and that the committee had also noted the absence of lateral roads between Victoria Gap, Wan Chai Gap and Wong Nai Chung Gap.[70] These problems were all mentioned in *The Back Door*. Thus, the novel was possibly written by this disgruntled member of the committee in an attempt to raise the authorities' aware-ness about these problems. Black, however, assured Governor Robinson that the current garrison, by holding the mountain gaps leading towards the city, would be adequate for dealing with a raid of 2,000 men.[71]

Black's estimation about the size of a possible invading force was largely accurate. As discussed, the Russians contemplated deploying only 2,000 to 3,000 men against Hong Kong during the 1880s. When Britain, France and Russia were on the brink of war during the Fashoda Incident in 1898, the French found that their navy was no match against the British everywhere. When the French approached the Russians for assistance, the latter found that their fleets in the Baltic and Black seas were iso-lated and that their fleet in Asia could not even handle an Anglo-Japanese invasion against their Asian coast. On the other hand, the Royal Navy was confident that its cruisers at Weihaiwei were enough to handle the Russian fleet in Vladivostok, while its heavy units in Hong Kong could quickly eliminate the French fleet in Indochina.[72] With the immense threat of the China Station, it was unlikely that the French and the Russians would be able to protect their Asian possessions, let alone launch an expedition of 18,000 men against Hong Kong. Thus, it was natural for the more informed officers in Hong Kong and London to ignore *The Back Door*.

The Acquisition of the New Territories and the Six-Day War of 1899

When the defence perimeter of Hong Kong was extended to Lyemun in the 1880s, there were already proposals to incorporate part of the Chinese mainland in order to establish complete control over Lyemun Channel. In 1884, the General Officer Commanding Hong Kong, Lieutenant General John Sargent, first formally proposed to extend the boundary. His successor, Major General William Cameron, revived the idea in 1886, but was turned down by the Imperial Defence Committee.[73] The Anglo-Chinese business communities were also interested in the land of the New Territories, and lobbied the government to expand the colony.

In 1895, the CDC again recommended that the government facilitate a perpet-ual lease of part of Xin'an County (新安縣).[74] The extension was to prevent the occupation by other powers of the heights on the other side of Lyemun Channel that overlooked the Lyemun Redoubt and Pakshawan Battery.[75] However, it was not until the French had leased the Leizhou Peninsula and claimed Yunnan, Guizhou and Guangxi as her sphere of influence that London instructed the British Minister to China, Claude MacDonald, to demand that the Qing lease what would become the New Territories. The discussion between MacDonald and the Qing led in June 1898 to the conclusion of the Convention for the Extension of Hong Kong Territory.

Although the British could have occupied the New Territories in July, they delayed moving in until April 1899 because of the Spanish-American War and the problem of demarcation. The Hong Kong government had intended to occupy the village of Shum Chun as well, but the plan was dropped due to Chinese protest. When the British tried to occupy the territory, however, they had an engagement with the inhabitants of the New Territories whose repercussions could still be felt after 1997.

Governor Henry Blake asked the Colonial Office to allow him to occupy the New Territories in early April 1899 before the rainy season began. However, as the Qing government urged MacDonald to delay the occupation, Blake was asked to take formal action only on 15 April. On 27 and 28 March, Francis Henry May (Governor of Hong Kong, 1912–1919), the commissioner of police, went to Tai Po to build a matshed for the official ceremony of the occupation but met resistance from the inhabitants.[76]

In the following days, the elders of some villages of the New Territories held meetings to discuss their next move. The elders believed that a solid resistance could reverse the decision of the Hong Kong government, which was (according to the elders) misled by colony businessmen who were already buying land in the area.[77] Thus, it was decided that neighbouring villages should be invited (in some cases, coerced) to join the resistance movement. Leaflets about the anti-British campaign were posted across the New Territories.[78] The villagers also gathered able-bodied men and arms.[79] By 7 April, over 1,332 pounds (604.2 kg) of gunpowder and twenty small cannons, six larger cannons and twenty-eight jingals were collected.[80]

On 1 April, Blake was still reporting to the Colonial Office that the anti-British movement "shall be nipped in the bud." He urged the Chinese authority of Guangzhou to help suppress the movement, but Tan Zhonglin, the Governor General of Guangdong and Guangxi, was not interested in stopping Chinese villagers from joining the anti-British movement.[81]

When Henry May returned to Tai Po on 3 April to inspect the matshed, he was greeted by villagers throwing stones, bricks and furniture. May tried to hold the matshed with Sikh police that night, but they were driven back to the island when a large group of villagers appeared. General Gascoigne rushed to the scene on the destroyer HMS *Fame* with troops from the 2nd Battalion of the Royal Welsh Fusiliers.[82] Stewart Lockhart, the Colonial Secretary, also arrived on HMS *Whiting*, which was damaged in the process when she hit a rock.[83] When Gascoigne arrived the next morning, he gathered the villagers at Tai Po to listen to the proclamation of Lockhart, who claimed that any resistance would be suppressed and the territory would become formally British on 17 April.[84]

The movement continued to gain force even after Lockhart promised to respect the land rights of the villagers. Workers sent to the New Territories to post the British proclamation were killed. The villagers formed the "Tai Ping Gong Kuk" (太平公局) on 10 April to coordinate their efforts. Villagers from the mainland also entered the New Territories to participate in the movement.[85]

The situation escalated before the ceremony. After the matshed at Tai Po was burnt down again on 14 April, the Hong Kong government sent Captain Edmund Berger and three Jemadars to lead 122 men from the Hong Kong Regiment (HKR) to the scene on the following day.[86] Although Berger was ordered not to use force unless attacked, he found himself outnumbered and surrounded by villagers upon arrival. He estimated that as many as 1,200 armed villagers had occupied the surrounding heights. When the HKR was bombarded by the villagers' cannons, Berger ordered his men to return fire with long-range rifle volleys and to occupy a small top near the matshed. As the villagers were equipped only with primitive firearms, only one HKR trooper was wounded.

The two sides exchanged fire until late afternoon, when HMS *Fame* returned to Tolo Harbour to resupply Berger's men. Captain Long from the HKR also took overall command. Lieutenant Roger Keyes, the young captain of the destroyer, led a landing party to join the HKR.[87] With the support of the 12- and 6-pounder QFs of HMS *Fame*, the villagers were dispersed before sunset.[88]

The villagers had originally planned to ambush the British during the ceremony on 17 April, but the engagement on the 15th disrupted the plans of both sides.[89] The Hong Kong government decided to hold the ceremony one day earlier, dispatching three hundred HKR soldiers to Tai Po, led by Lieutenant Colonel John Retallick and Lieutenant Colonel N. P. O'Gorman. They were supported by a company of Hong Kong and Singapore Artillery, led by Captain C. S. Simmonds.[90]

The ceremony on 16 April ended without incident, as both sides were preparing for the coming clash. The villagers gathered their "braves" and started to prepare artillery and jingal positions on Shelter Trench Hill at the entrance of Lam Tsuen Gap and on the hill near Pun Chung Village. The British encamped on a small hill called Flagstaff Hill and patrolled the surrounding area. Gascoigne himself led a large patrol on the morning of the 17th and penetrated into the Lam Tsuen Gap, but was unable to locate any insurgents. At noon on the 17th, the villagers approached the British camp in force.[91] Gascoigne, who had just returned from patrol, organized a force under Captain Berger's command to attack the insurgents. At around 13:00, troops under Berger moved towards Shelter Trench Hill and captured it before turning to Fong Ma Pu (放馬埔), near Lam Tsuen, in the afternoon. Simmonds and his artillery followed, but he lost contact with Berger and withdrew towards Fanling.

The HKR penetrated into Lam Tsuen Gap and pursued the villagers until 17:00. By then, the British had advanced to Sheung Tsuen and captured three cannons.

On 18 April, Berger's contingent was joined by the bulk of the forces from Flagstaff Hill led by Lieutenant Colonel O'Gorman. By 14:00, they were already approaching Pat Heung and Kam Tin. At 14:30, the British encountered over 1,200 villagers near Shek Tau Wai (石頭圍). O'Gorman estimated that around one-third of them had come from the mainland.[92] The villagers attacked in three skirmish lines under the cover of small cannons and jingals. As Lockhart noted, the British would have had "a warmer time" had the insurgents possessed modern weapons.[93] Berger and his troops, some 350 men from the HKR and RN landing party, took position along a dry riverbank and unleashed a hailstorm of bullets on the incoming insurgents when they were two hundred yards away. Patrick Hase has estimated that at least 450 to 500 villagers were killed in the battle.[94] After this engagement, Gascoigne landed his men near Deep Bay and eventually joined O'Gorman and Berger at Kam Tin, ending the insurgency.

As Hase has pointed out, the British handled the campaign clumsily despite suffering minimal losses (a few injured men). They were unable to gather much knowledge about the strength and direction of the insurgents; their logistics were appalling; communication between infantry and artillery was ineffective; and their command system flawed. As Gascoigne, Lockhart and O'Gorman wanted to shift the blame of heavy casualties on the villagers, all tried to fudge in their reports.[95] Indeed, if the British had shown adequate force at the beginning of the event and established good communication with the villagers, the engagements on 17 and 18 April could have been avoided.

After the battle, the New Territories became an integral part of the colony. Although the British were able to control both sides of Victoria Harbour and the islands surrounding Hong Kong, the defence perimeter was significantly enlarged and new defence problems appeared.

Turning to Landward Defence, 1901–1914

Before the British occupied the New Territories, planners had already examined the defensibility of the additional territories. In January 1899, the Committee of Imperial Defence (CID) suggested that, while the beaches of Mirs Bay were large enough for a sizeable invasion, invaders would not attack from the landward direction, as much time would be wasted traversing the mountains between Kowloon and the New Territories.[96] However, Gascoigne, who had fought in the New Territories, noted in the Defence Scheme of 1901 that the Kowloon Ridge was disadvantageous to defenders:

> These hills command the whole of Kowloon at a range from 5,000 to 6,000 yards, and would afford a very strong position to an enemy effecting a landing on the mainland unless denied to him. A footing on those hills would, moreover, enable him, in all probability, to mount guns of heavy calibre on them, which would endanger the safety of Hong Kong itself.[97]

When assessing possible attackers, Gascoigne suggested that "it is hardly probable that a Chinese army would, in view of recent events, have the enterprise to make an advance on Hong Kong from Canton . . . (the task) would prove insuperable to it in its present state of inefficiency."[98] The "recent event" referred to the Boxer War of 1900. The most probable attackers were identified as Japan and France, the latter probably with Russian assistance.[99]

The 1901 scheme suggested that the enemy might try to destroy the harbour facilities or to take Hong Kong through a surprise landing before the declaration of war. Such an attack could be carried out by one or a few cruisers carrying thousands of troops. In response, the scheme set out three objectives for the garrison:

1. Block the entrance of enemy ships into Victoria Harbour
2. Hold the central ridge of Hong Kong Island
3. Hold the passes over the hills running across Kowloon Peninsula[100]

The garrison of 4,700 infantry and artillery was divided into four parts and distributed to Stonecutters, the City of Victoria, Wong Nai Chung Gap and Lyemun, with reserves at Kowloon and Hong Kong Island. Around 1,200 men would be deployed in Kowloon and along the Kowloon Ridge.[101] The 1901 scheme was the first plan to suggest holding Kowloon Ridge against an attack from the north. Its focus was the mountain passes, which would be fortified when war seemed likely.[102]

In 1903, the CID estimated the scale of potential attacks against Hong Kong to be 4,000 men, based on the fact that the Russians and the French had secured Port Arthur and Indochina. It maintained that, as long as the Royal Navy controlled the South China Sea, Hong Kong would be safe from larger scale attacks.[103] This decision had little impact on the Defence Scheme of 1903, which was more or less the same as that of 1901.[104] As the safety of Hong Kong was further guaranteed by the Anglo-Japanese Alliance of 1902, subsequent defence schemes were largely unchanged until 1908. After the Russian fleet in Vladivostok was eliminated during the Russo-Japanese War, the British even withdrew the underwater mines in Hong Kong.[105]

                                                         Eastern Fortress

The issue of Hong Kong defence was left untouched until 1908, when Admiral Hedworth Lambton started a controversy about the state of defence. In October 1908, Governor Frederick Lugard wrote to Lambton, the Commander-in-Chief of China Station, to inquire about the construction of a breakwater at Junk Bay to protect anchoring warships from possible torpedo attacks. Instead, Lambton criticized the CID and the CDC's decision (based on the recommendations of the Owen Committee) to dismantle a large number of coastal guns. He suggested that the defences were "entirely futile, and insufficient, and that their conception shows a complete inappreciation of what modern war will really mean."[106] As the Royal Navy had withdrawn its battleships back to Europe, Lambton argued that he and the residents of Hong Kong were "absolutely at the mercy of America."[107] His cruisers, armed with 9.2- and 6-inch guns, were no match against modern battleships.

Lambton estimated that the enemy might deploy as many as three standard battleships (12,000–16,000 tons, armed with four 10.5- to 12-inch BLs and numerous 6- and 8-inch BLs) to attack Victoria Harbour. As the Owen Committee suggested that only three 9.2-inch BLs would suffice for Lyemun, it would mean one gun for each battleship if the enemy attacked from the east, or one facing fourteen guns larger than 6-inch. Lambton concluded that the arrangement was "preposterous" and that the fortress of Mount Davis would "end up like Vesuvius" in facing a modern battleship. After the destruction of the batteries, enemy warships could easily dominate the harbour, as the inner batteries and the submarine mines (including the Brennan torpedo station) were decommissioned. He also argued that the 9.2-inch BLs could do only minimal damage to modern battleships at the range of 5,000 to 7,000 metres. To Lambton, at least eight to twelve 12- or 14-inch BLs were needed, equivalent to the number of guns of a latest dreadnought.[108]

Lambton's idea contradicted the basic strategy of the Victorian and Edwardian navy. The navy was understood by contemporaries as an offensive tool; naval supremacy was maintained not by coastal guns but by the number of capital ships. To divert

Table 14 Asian port defences, as estimated by Lambton, 1908

| | USA | Russia | Germany | Britain |
	Manila and Subic	Vladivostok	Qingdao	Hong Kong
Heavy and medium-sized guns	12" x 8 (18^)*	11" x 12	11" x 11 (4)	9.2" x 8
	10" x 3 (4)	10" x 24	9.4" x (2)#	6" x 11
	6" x 20 (7)	9" x 18	8.27" x (4)#	
		6" x 68	6" x 11 (7)	
Trade value (£)	6,400,000	304,500	5,100,000	45,000,000

* actual number in parentheses
^ Most of them were howitzers with a range of 14,000 metres.
# originally installed by the Qing

resources from dreadnoughts to coastal guns would be a waste of resources, which, although abundant, were not unlimited. Lambton produced a list comparing the Asian ports controlled by other powers to show the unpreparedness of Britain (Table 14). However, the other powers had expensive coastal defences installed precisely because of the Anglo-Japanese naval preponderance in Asia. The small number of guns in Hong Kong revealed the initiative enjoyed by the British. Lambton also over-estimated the advantage of capital ships over coastal guns. The Anglo-French failure to force through the Bosphorus Channel in 1916 revealed that modern coastal guns and submarine mines, if competently handled and supported by undersea mines, still had some edge over battleships. As will be shown in subsequent chapters, the 9.2-inch guns in Hong Kong were indeed valid deterrence until 1941.

Before Lugard submitted Lambton's criticism to London, he asked the General Officer Commanding South China, Major General Robert Broadwood,[109] to give his views. Broadwood, junior to Lambton in rank, submitted a measured rebuttal. He thought it was "inconceivable that such irreplaceable weapons as battleships would be risked in attempts to silence the forts," especially as the enemy warship might have to engage British naval reinforcements afterwards.[110] As for the problem of inner harbour defence, Broadwood also suggested reactivating the underwater mines or deploying submarines. He particularly noted that "a landing on the mainland would be the most tempting line for an attack" and that it was necessary to deploy at least ten battalions to prevent such an attack.[111] Lambton ridiculed Broadwood's ideas, claiming that the guns in Hong Kong "have no more chance of stopping a battle fleet than Dame Partington had of mopping up the Atlantic." He even wrote that Broadwood lacked the "obvious common sense of the business."[112]

The CDC and CID discussed the views of Lambton and Broadwood, with the latter laying down two principles for further discussion in June 1909:

- So long as the Anglo-Japanese Alliance remained in force, the British possessions in the Far East would be secure.
- Care should be taken sufficiently to reinforce the fleet in the Far East before the termination of the alliance in order to neutralize the danger from a preponderant Japanese fleet in China seas.[113]

The army and the navy were asked to prepare for a fresh study of Hong Kong defence under these two principles. The CDC also asked the Inspector General of the Forces, General John French, to inspect the colony. French reported in January 1910 that he largely agreed with Lambton's view. He suggested preserving the submarine mines, the Brennan torpedoes and the 6-inch BLs at the Kowloon East and Stonecutters East batteries. He also proposed installing two 9.2-inch BLs at Cape D'Aguilar to defend the south shore of Hong Kong Island (realized in 1941).[114]

The CDC then drafted a detailed memorandum after receiving the views of General French and the services in early 1911. The memorandum listed all possible ways of attack and countermeasures conceived before 1910:

Forms of Attack	**Countermeasures**
Long-range bombardment by a squadron of battleships with a view to the destruction of the naval dockyard or of warships in the harbour;	Eight 9.2-inch guns
Raids by night by unarmoured cruisers on merchant shipping lying in the harbour;	Eleven 6-inch guns; searchlights
Attacks by torpedo craft with a view to the destruction of the docks or warships in the harbour;	6-inch and smaller guns
Raiding attacks by two or three armed transports conveying in all a maximum landing force of 4,000 men, supported by a squadron of armoured vessels.[115]	Garrison of one British battalion, two Indian battalions and other auxiliary troops, 4,212 in total

The CDC suggested that, although the Royal Navy had no capital ships in Asia, it had more battleships than any other two navies combined. Thus, it was reasonable to assume that the navy could reinforce Hong Kong in weeks. After discussing the military potential of China, the United States, France, Russia, Germany and Japan, the memorandum concluded that only Japan could launch an attack in force against Hong Kong that could not be handled by the colony's defence. Quoting the Admiralty's report, the CDC believed that the colony would have to defend itself for three weeks before relief. Within those three weeks, Hong Kong would have to withstand the forms of attack mentioned above, and "attack by a squadron of armoured ships attempting to enter the inner waters to land men from the ships to capture the place by *coup-de-main*" and "attack by a formidable expeditionary force landed on or in the vicinity of Hong Kong."[116]

The CDC agreed that Japanese armoured ships could approach Hong Kong Island from the southeast of Cape Collinson with the cover of the coastline. When they had reached Cape Collinson, some could run for Junk Bay and exchange fire with the Lyemun batteries, while the rest rushed into the harbour. If the enemy attacked from the west, they could take cover behind Lamma Island until reaching Wu-lo-tsui Point (葫蘆咀), which was only 6,400 metres from the Mount Davis Battery. They could then dash into the harbour through Sulphur Channel (3,600 metres from Mount Davis). To counter these attacks, the CDC recommended installing 9.2-inch howitzers on Mount Parker and the Peak to rain plunging fire down on the intruding warships. It also recommended reactivating the underwater mines and the Brennan torpedoes.[117] The committee rejected the proposal of installing 9.2-inch BLs at Cape D'Aguilar, as they would be outside the defence perimeter and unable to assist other batteries.[118]

The CDC agreed with Broadwood and the War Office that Hong Kong might be attacked by a "formidable" landing force. It also suggested that "fixed [coastal] defences, however formidable, will not render a fortress secure against attack by an expeditionary force."[119] This memorandum and the War Office report were among the first serious studies of land attacks against Hong Kong. The CDC believed that, although the current garrison could handle a raid of 4,000 men, it could not resist a large-scale attack. The War Office estimated that the Japanese could field as many as 48,000 men in Hong Kong. As Hong Kong Island was protected by submarines and coastal defence vessels, the Japanese would not try to attack directly. Instead, they would first land in the New Territories and then march to Kowloon. To resist this attack, at least 15,000 men would be needed to defend the rugged terrain along Kowloon Ridge. This estimation was even more generous than the one proposed by Broadwood (ten battalions, or around 12,000 men).[120]

The idea of expanding the garrison to 20,000 men was deemed financially and diplomatically unfeasible. It also conflicted with Secretary of State for War Richard Haldane's attempt to build an expeditionary army of six divisions for continental commitments.[121] Thus, the CDC refused to make such a recommendation. It was also deemed impossible to reinforce Hong Kong if tensions mounted between Britain and Japan, as such a move would be provocative. If the government decided to end the Anglo-Japanese Alliance, recommended the CDC, then it should "reassert the British naval supremacy in the China Seas."[122]

The CID reviewed the CDC memorandum in January 1911. The participants of the meeting included Prime Minister Herbert Asquith, First Sea Lord Admiral Arthur Wilson, General French, Foreign Secretary Sir Edward Grey, Secretary of State for India Lord Crewe and others. French suggested that the colony could be defended by around 14,000 men as the terrain in the New Territories would pose much trouble for the attackers. The navy suggested that the China Station should be made strong enough to threaten the Japanese sea lane towards Hong Kong, and that submarines could force the Japanese to land further away from the colony. The solution found, however, was simply the continuation of the Anglo-Japanese Alliance. While the Secretary of State for India pointed out that Australia, New Zealand and Canada all opposed the alliance, Sir Edward Grey suggested that it was necessary to enlighten the colonies about the difficulties brought by its termination.[123]

Consensus was finally reached in March 1911, when it was agreed that the alliance would be continued, and that the British government should "sufficiently reinforce the fleet in the Far East to deter the Japanese from bringing transports to the neighbourhood of Hong Kong with a view to effecting a landing in force." The CID agreed to increase the number of guns and to expand the garrison by one more battalion (though this was not carried out). The Royal Navy would also send three submarines and two destroyers for coastal defence.[124] The navy had much faith in its submarines. Vice Admiral Alfred Winsloe, the successor of Admiral Lambton, suggested that the "moral effect of a submarine is very great, more than is warranted by her offensive powers, as it is human nature to fear most what is unseen."[125]

From then on, high-level discussions about Hong Kong defence were discontinued until the end of the Anglo-Japanese Alliance was in sight in the late 1910s. The CID also dropped a proposal to install the 12-inch BLs after the alliance was renewed in 1912.[126] In the same year, the Mount Davis Fortress became operational. In 1913, the Royal Navy dispatched two pre-dreadnoughts to Asia. The battleships, HMS *Swiftsure* and HMS *Triumph*, were originally built by Armstrong for Chile (Figure 11). The two ships were each armed with four 10-inch BLs, fourteen 7.5-inch BLs and twenty smaller guns. The firepower of each of them was stronger than all the batteries in Hong Kong combined.[127] This also explains why the four 9.2-inch howitzers proposed by the CDC were never sent.

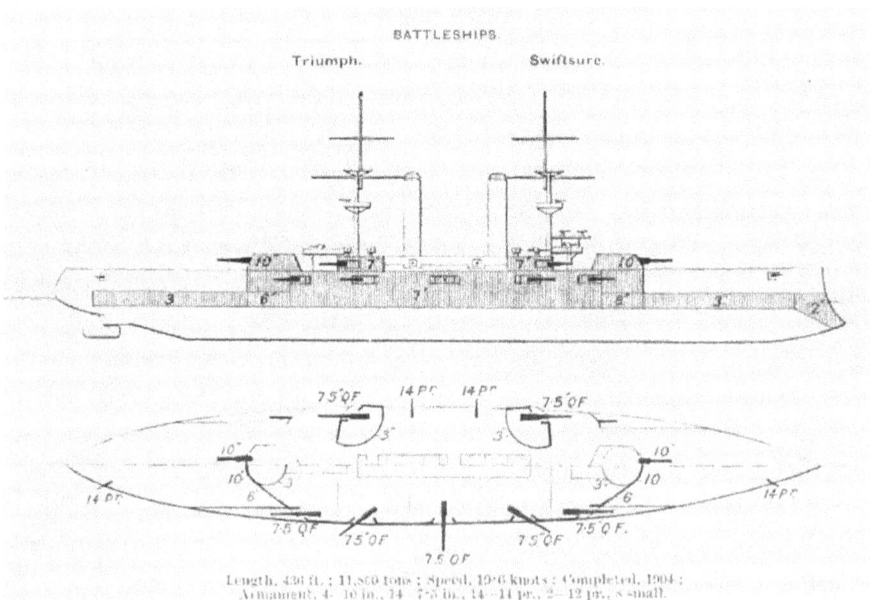

Figure 11   Line drawings of HMS *Swiftsure* and HMS *Triumph*, 1900[128]

From the 1910s, the focus of planners gradually shifted to "landward defence." The first proponent of constructing a permanent defensive line along Kowloon Ridge was Broadwood's successor, Major General Charles Anderson. Anderson started his career as a junior officer of the Royal Horse Artillery. He had participated in the Second Anglo-Afghan War and the Anglo-Burma War, before serving in the North West Frontier from 1897 to 1907. To defend the mountainous area against nomadic tribesmen, the British had built a large number of blockhouses and forti-fied posts. Soon after Anderson arrived, the Battle of Saragarhi (1897) took place, during which a small Indian garrison of twenty-one men held a fortified post against more than a thousand tribesmen with firearms. Although the garrison was overrun, it absorbed the momentum of the attack and inflicted hundreds of casualties on the tribesmen. During the South African War of 1899–1902, the British built numer-ous blockhouses to protect vital points and their lines of communication.[129] These examples possibly inspired Anderson to contemplate a "Kowloon Line."

Anderson formulated the idea when revising the Defence Scheme in 1910. Although his objective was to hold Hong Kong Island, he noted the importance of preventing the enemy from occupying Kowloon Ridge, which could dominate the island:

> The possession by Great Britain of the country between the Kowloon Hills and the Sham Chun River is, in one respect, a source of weakness, because it makes it possible for one of the Great Powers to land an army within striking distance of Hong Kong, without violating the neutrality of Chinese territory.
>
> It would, of course, be desirable to watch and guard the various possible landing places on the mainland, and to establish strong advanced posts in the difficult country north of the Kowloon Hills, but with the garrison avail-able neither can be done without dangerously weakening the main lines of defence.[130]

The garrison had to prevent the situation described above. As only one battalion could be spared for the defence of the mainland, he believed that it was necessary to provide it with fortifications and artillery support. In all, he planned a line of nine miles (15 km) that stretched from Devil's Peak to Lai Chi Kok. Artillery position would be built at Chiu Lan Chu (Tsiu Lan Shue 蕉欄樹, modern-day Anderson Quarry), Tate's Cairn, Crown Point (modern-day Sap Yi Fat) and Eagle's Nest. Trenches and temporary blockhouses would be built at Devil's Peak, Hai Wan Hill (Chiu Keng Wan Hill 照鏡環山), Yau Tong Village, Chiu Lan Chu, Chin Lan Chu Bridge (Tseng Lan Shue 井欄樹橋), Customs Hill, Customs Pass, Hill 1804, 1886 and 1770 (near Temple Hill), Grasscutters Pass, Kowloon Pass, Railway Pass, Beacon Hill Pass, Kowloon Reservoir (built in 1910), Piper's Hill and, finally, Lai Chi Kok (Figure 12).

Anderson then submitted a more elaborate proposal of the defensive line to the War Office in May 1911. He estimated that enemy forces would land in Mirs Bay, and that the small detachment resisting the landing would be gradually pushed southwards. Kowloon Ridge, according to Anderson, lacked depth to contain an enemy attack: "[after brief resistance in the New Territories] the garrison stands at bay within its line of <u>defence</u> [emphasis original], not within its line of <u>defences</u>, for there is none."[131] Thus, it was necessary to reinforce the line with permanent structures to delay the Japanese advance and to protect the batteries at Devil's Peak.[132]

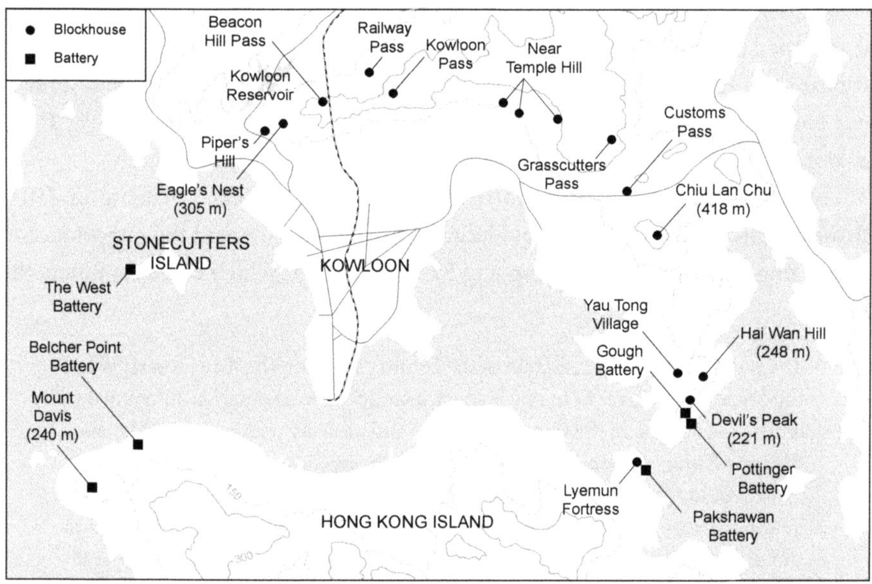

Figure 12   Anderson's proposed Kowloon defence line, 1911[133]

He planned a defensive line consisted of redoubts, blockhouses and artillery positions stretching from Lyemun to Lai Chi Kok. It would be divided into six sections, held by half of the garrison (2,000 men) (Table 15). The sections could support each other through the lateral roads along Kowloon Ridge. Some would actually be built, such as the Anderson Road behind Section II.

Anderson suggested that, even though other parts of the Kowloon line might be lost, the garrison could protect the batteries in Devil's Peak with Sections I and II, together with a fallback position across the Kowloon Peninsula near Ho Man Tin. Thus, the two sections had most of the heavy equipment.[134] Section VI, which stretched from Beacon Hill to the coastline near Lai Chi Kok, also received attention. Anderson suggested building two large redoubts on the eastern and western

Table 15   The Kowloon–New Territories Line designed by Gen. Anderson, 1911

Section	Location	Equipment	Garrison
I	Devil's Peak to Yau Tong Village (or Lau Tong Village)	5 small redoubts that could withstand bombardment, with barbette 6 MGs 2 mobile searchlights	48 in forward position 130 in redoubts 222 reserves Total: 400
II	Yau Tong Village to Customs Pass (near modern-day Kowloon Peak)	3 redoubts with guns 6 guns 3 MGs 1 mobile searchlight	69 in forward position 80 in redoubts 251 reserves Total: 400
III	Customs Pass to Temple Hill	1 redoubt with guns 2 guns A number of blockhouses	60 in forward position 30 in redoubts 50 in blockhouses 160 reserves Total: 300
IV	Temple Hill to Kowloon Pass	1 redoubt with guns 2 small redoubts 2 guns 1 MG	67 in forward position 70 in redoubts 113 reserves Total: 250
V	Kowloon Pass to Beacon Hill	2 small redoubts 2 MGs 1 mobile searchlight	54 in forward position 40 in redoubts 156 reserves Total: 250
VI	Beacon Hill to Lai Chi Kok	2 redoubts with guns 3 blockhouses 4 guns 6 MGs 1 mobile searchlight	79 in forward position 120 in redoubts 201 reserves Total: 400

ridges of Eagle's Nest, and a number of smaller machine-gun blockhouses. The guns at Stonecutters were to support this section.[135] As for Sections III, IV and V, as it was believed that large forces and heavy artillery could not penetrate these passes, only smaller detachments would be deployed there.[136]

As most of the movable guns (guns other than those installed in the batteries) were very large and could only be hauled to prepared positions by men or pack animals, it would be impossible to redeploy them during the battle. Thus, Anderson suggested having most of these guns installed in the large redoubts and forming a mobile mountain gun battery. He also proposed to plant cactus on the bare mountains on the mainland to serve as additional defence.[137]

Table 16 The Island Line designed by Gen. Anderson, 1911[138]

Section	Location	Equipment	Garrison
VII	Stonecutters and Mount Davis	4 small redoubts 10 MGs	125 in forward position 180 in redoubts 95 reserves Total: 400
VIII	High West to Middle Gap (modern-day Wong Nai Chung Gap)	3 redoubts with guns 10 guns 6 MGs 1 mobile searchlight	185 in forward position 70 in redoubts 145 reserves Total: 400
IX	Middle Gap to Tytam Harbour via Tytam (Tai Tam)	1 redoubt with guns 2 guns 4 MGs Several blockhouses	200 in forward position 20 in redoubts 80 reserves Total: 300
X	Quarry Bay Gap to Mount Parker, including Sai Wan Bay	2 redoubts with guns 6 guns 6 MGs 1 mobile searchlight	180 in forward position 50 in redoubts 70 reserves Total: 300
XI	Lyemun Peninsula and Pakshawan	Existing Lyemun fortress and redoubt at Pakshawan	60 in forward position 40 reserves Total: 100

As for Hong Kong Island, Anderson shared the idea of his predecessors that the garrison was too small to hold all the beaches. Thus, it was necessary to establish strong positions on the mountains and the passes towards the urban area and Taikoo Dockyard. The five sections on Hong Kong Island formed a continuous line cutting the island into two parts along the mountain ridges. In all, 1,500 infantry and eighteen guns would be deployed, with five companies of infantry as reserves (Table 16).

In his conclusion, Anderson proposed expanding the Hong Kong Volunteer Defence Force (HKVDF) to man the redoubts and blockhouses so that the regulars could be used for mobile operations. He was confident that as many as 600 to 700 men from the British population would serve in the HKVDF. Should all his recommendations be implemented, he believed, the colony would be "reasonably secure" against an attack of 4,000 men for a period of time (the one-month period before relief suggested by the CDC). However, he also argued that the garrison had to be expanded to around 20,000 if Hong Kong had to face a larger invasion.[139] As noted in the Defence Scheme of 1911, some of the temporary structures had already been built on Kowloon Ridge, but they were only weak blockhouses, "proof against rifle fire but not against the fire of mountain guns."[140]

In January 1912, the War Office authorized Anderson to build the defences in the eastern part of Kowloon Ridge and a road from Devil's Peak to Customs Pass.[141] Two months later, Anderson tested the defence of Hong Kong when he invited two Indian battalions passing through the colony to act as invaders. After the exercise, Anderson suggested that the current force level was unable to withstand even an attack of 4,000 men, as the enemy might concentrate its forces and penetrate Kowloon Ridge in one stroke. He also mentioned that China, which had just become a republic, might attack Hong Kong in a few years' time: "It can only be a matter of a few years before the danger that China may wish to recover her Territory... her present lack of sea power would confine her action to the Mainland..."[142] In response to Anderson's letter, the Assistant Director of Military Operations (ADMO) proposed reconsidering the force level of Hong Kong and estimating when "the Chinese [would] be sufficiently organised to be taken into account as possible attackers."[143]

Anderson discussed the Kowloon defence line with the DMO and the Directorate of Fortifications and Works (DFW) in London. It was agreed that the garrison was to protect the batteries and naval establishments and to prevent the enemy from "establishing observing parties on the Kowloon hills in order to bring indirect fire to bear in the valleys to the north or east of the hills." Anderson was asked to provide infantry defences for the batteries, and to construct a "main line of infantry defences on the mainland across the neck of the Kowloon Peninsula" as well as "self-contained redoubts armed with the heavy guns of the movable armaments on the Kowloon hills between Devil's Peak and Lai-chi-kok" that could withstand prolonged attack. Anderson was also instructed to build "redoubts" to cover the valves and machinery of the reservoirs (Table 17).[144]

During the discussion, the idea surfaced that China might be a potential enemy and that Hong Kong must be retained as a means of projecting British prestige in Asia. In December 1912, the Overseas Defence Committee (the successor of CDC, hereafter ODC) discussed Anderson's proposals. The request for immediate reinforcement was rejected, as the ODC believed that none of the powers could attack Hong Kong with more than 2,000 men, except Japan, the United States and China. The ODC then turned to the question of whether it was necessary to provide the garrison with "permanent or semi-permanent defence works on the land side of the fortress."[145] It was noted that the Chinese New Army from Guangzhou was a force to be reckoned with, and that its efficiency might be improved further. Moreover, it was estimated that a railway linking Guangzhou and Beijing would be finished by 1915, making Hong Kong vulnerable to a larger-scale attack from China. Thus, the ODC approved Anderson's plan in principle.[146]

The CID then reconfirmed the assumption that Hong Kong would not be attacked by other powers, except China, with more than 2,000 men. This decision precluded Hong Kong from expanding its garrison. As for China, the CID's only recommendation was to "carefully observe" its military development.[147] Anderson reiterated the Chinese threat, and again asked the War Office to provide more troops and permanent defence.[148] Lieutenant General Ian Hamilton, the Inspector General of Overseas Forces who was sent to investigate by the War Office, concluded that Hong Kong should be abandoned. Not all agreed. Brigadier Henry Wilson, the Director of Military Operations (DMO), suggested that such a move would be "a deplorable sign of weakness and would shake our position in the East to its very foundation."[149] Wilson proposed that the Foreign Office should be asked whether the government considered China a future enemy. The Foreign Office replied that the government had decided to hold Hong Kong against a Chinese attack.[150] From then on, the "prestige" factor remained important in British defence policy for Hong Kong.

As the government had made clear its intention to hold Hong Kong, Wilson suggested building the planned works. However, the works could be constructed "at leisure" as China was not an immediate threat. The works were scheduled to be finished in 1918.[151] Accordingly, Anderson submitted a revised plan in July 1913. In all, nineteen caponiers and one redoubt would be built to protect the Belcher, Gough, Pakshawan, Sai Wan and Mount Davis batteries. Redoubts equipped with machine-guns and artillery would be built at Sai Wan, Railway Pass, Crown Point, Garter Ridge, Shatin Pass and Temple Hill. A line consisting of firing trenches for nine to twelve companies would be dug across Kowloon Peninsula, from Ma Tau Kok to the Cosmopolitan Dock via the Yau Ma Tei Railway Station. In all, these defences were equipped with seventy machine-guns, a considerable number for a pre-World War I defence.[152]

Anderson's plan, however, was not supported by his successor, Major General Francis Kelly, a military engineer. Soon after he arrived, he proposed abandoning Anderson's plan. He believed that, as China remained weak and Japan was a British ally for the near future, the plan, with a total cost of £100,000, was unnecessary. He

Table 17   Hong Kong landward defence, as envisaged by Maj. Gen. Anderson, 1913[153]

	Locations	Equipment	MGs
Battery Defences	Belcher Battery	Caponier x 4	5
	Gough Battery	Caponier x 3	4
	Pakshawan Battery	Caponier x 4, light gun x 2	6
	Sai Wan Battery	Redoubt x 1	1
	Mount Davis Battery	Caponier x 8, Trench, 5-inch Howitzer x 2	16

Table 17 (*cont.*)

	Locations	Equipment	MGs
Kowloon Defences	Devil's Peak Line	Redoubt x 1, 5-inch Howitzer x 2, light gun x 2	5
	Railway Tunnel	Redoubt x 1, 10-pounder x 2	2
	Garter Gap	Redoubt x 1, 15-pounder x 1	2
	Crown Point	Redoubt x 1, 5-inch Howitzer x 2, 4.7-inch gun x 2	2
	Shatin Pass	15-pounder x 1	—
	Temple Hill	Redoubt x 1	2
	Kowloon Line (Ma Tau Kok to Tai Kok Tsui)	5-inch Howitzer x 2, 15-pounder, light gun x 2	9
Island Defences	Island Line (1): from Belcher Battery to the crossroad of Craigmin Road and Gough Hill Road, via High West and Mount Austin	Redoubt x 2, 10-pounder x 4^	7
	Island Line (2): Magazine Gap to Morrison Hill via Wan Chai Gap, Black's Link, and Happy Valley		4
	Mount Parker		—
Stonecutters		4.7-inch gun x 2	5

^ Armament for the two sections of the Island Line

also believed that the redoubts could only tie down the garrison without causing much trouble to the enemy. He proposed forming three flying columns, each consisting of one battalion (the garrison had one British and two Indian battalions). The only features of Anderson's plan retained were the line across the Kowloon Peninsula as a fallback position for mobile columns and the infantry defences of the batteries.[154] Kelly's counterproposal caught the attention of the DMO, who found that "there seems to be a lack of clearness as to the purpose for which the barrier forts are required."[155] The matter was not resolved until the outbreak of the First World War in August 1914.

Hong Kong during the First World War and the Kowloon Defence Line

On 4 August 1914, Britain declared war on Germany when the latter invaded Belgium. Although Hong Kong was far away from the main battlefields, she was also affected by the war. A day after the declaration of war, all gunners were in position, and the garrison battalions, including the 2nd Battalion, Duke of Cornwall's Light Infantry (DCLI), the 8th Regiment Rajput and the 126th Infantry, Indian Army, were concentrated in their barracks. The French armoured cruiser *Dupleix* entered Victoria Harbour to join the China Fleet. The battleship of the China Station, HMS *Triumph*, was put at sea with an Anglo-French fleet.[156] To make up for the deficiency of its marine contingent, the DCLI lent 108 of its men to HMS *Triumph*.[157]

The only credible military threat to Hong Kong at the beginning of the war was the German East Asiatic Squadron, which consisted of the armoured cruisers *Scharnhorst* and *Gneisenau*. Governor Francis Henry May established an early warning system to protect Hong Kong from these ships. If hostile ships were sighted, HMS *Tamar* would fire three blank shots and hoist a red flag. A red flag would also be hoisted at the Peak.[158] Three auxiliary cruisers, previously steamers of the Canadian Pacific Line and P&O, were converted in Hong Kong.[159] The garrison was understandably nervous. On the rainy afternoon of 12 August, a Japanese merchantman *Shikoku Maru* tried to enter the harbour without stopping off Cape Collinson in accordance with the wartime regulation. She had not known of the outbreak of war when leaving Ishigaki Island. After several failed attempts to stop the ship by the examination officer, she was judged to be a German blockship. A red flag was hoisted and the Pakshawan Battery fired five plugged shots into the ship, killing one of its sailors. A board of inquiry justified the action and concluded that the captain of the *Shikoku Maru* should be held responsible.[160] No reparation was made; the event is not found in narratives about Hong Kong during the First World War. With the destruction of *Scharnhorst* and *Gneisenau* in December 1914 off the Falklands, tensions gradually subsided.[161] Still, at least 60,000 Chinese residents fled to mainland China, fearing Hong Kong might be attacked.[162]

During the war, the Hong Kong government acquired the power to appropriate properties, to demand that residents serve and to control prices. Inhabitants could also be tried by a court martial.[163] In October 1914, it took over German-owned companies and interned Germans at Hung Hom. Only one escape attempt was recorded, in which three German men dug a tunnel and left the camp in 1916. They were, however, apprehended at Fanling by Indian constables.[164] The government continued to increase its power over information, publications, harbour activities, transport and production. It was also given power to arrest without warrant.[165] As Norman Miners has suggested, however, the government seldom used these emergency powers throughout the war, except to appropriate German properties and control prices.[166] In December 1914, the General Officer Commanding Hong Kong, General Kelly, noted the "very strong anti-British feeling among the Indian Police, the Indian Watchmen and the Indian residents" and urged the colonial government to pay more attention.[167] Although an Indian mutiny actually took place in Singapore in February 1915 as a result of the Ghadar Party's agitation, no similar incidents occurred in Hong Kong.

Hong Kong contributed a considerable amount of money and manpower. In all, at least $12,000,000 was given to Britain.[168] By the end of 1914, residents had donated £17,000 to the National Relief Fund. In early 1915, the Chinese and English residents donated two fighters to the Royal Flying Corps.[169] However, only a few actually joined the war. By early 1915, only nine residents received commissions in the armed services, and only forty-seven volunteered.[170] More residents were drafted when London introduced the Military Service Ordinance of 1917, which required all males between the ages of eighteen and fifty-five to serve. Some served in Hong Kong Volunteer Defence Force, reformed into Hong Kong Volunteer Defence Corps (HKVDC) in 1920; others were sent overseas. Of the 463 men from Hong Kong who participated in the Great War, 75 died.[171] In addition, thousands of Hong Kong Chinese worked on the Allied merchant marine as stokers or trimmers, of which 535 died on seventy-five vessels sunk by mines, German submarines or merchant raiders.[172] While there were more than 100,000 Chinese labourers from different parts of the country serving on the Western Front, the Hong Kong Chinese labourers were sent mainly to the Middle East, where they worked as members of the Indian Military Works Services and of the Inland Water Transport, Royal Engineers. Three hundred and eighty-four of them died of disease, exposure or in accidents.[173] In 1915, the 1st Company of the HKSRA was sent to the Middle East upon the request of its regimental commander. When revolution broke out in Russia, the Hong Kong garrison (the 25th [Garrison] Middlesex Battalion) was sent to Vladivostok to support the pro-entente provisional government in the summer of 1918.[174]

A mainland defence line, as Anderson had advocated, was built as a result of the war. On 8 August 1914, the War Office ordered Kelly to build a temporary line across the Kowloon Peninsula. Kelly reported that he had finished the extra defences on Devil's Peak, Mount Davis, Hong Kong Island and Kowloon Peninsula. Fences, breastworks and trenches were also built around the premises of the batteries and the naval dockyard in January 1915. Most of the works were made of plywood and corrugated metal, and protected by barbed wire lines of 3.6 to 5.4 metres in width. They included firing trenches and ad hoc blockhouses. As Kelly suggested, they were temporary structures that could last only three to four years.[175] A formidable enemy encountered by the garrison was urban sprawl. When describing the state of the Kowloon defence line in 1915, the Royal Engineers commander noted that it was being eaten up by urban development:

> There is a large scheme of road construction and development in progress
> which will include the whole of the selected position . . . If however, as is more
> probable, the conditions change for the worse, then the line of the Kowloon
> Hills must be reoccupied.[176]

His worries soon became reality after the war.

The half-hearted nature of these works, built by a commanding officer opposed to the plan, was soon revealed. When Kelly's successor, Major General Francis Ventris, inspected the works in 1917, he found that many of them were already worn out, and the choice of position was poor. Many parts of the line actually faced paddy fields that blocked their fire, but no accurate maps were available for the garrison to reorganize the line.[177] There was little or no attempt made to utilize the advantage of crossfire by placing the positions in the spurs. The redoubts, built at exposed positions, could be easily overrun.[178] It seems that the line was also an unwelcome obstacle to the rapid development of Kowloon, and that Kelly only finished the work to satisfy the War Office. As Asia was secure, the War Office only told Ventris to maintain the existing works in April 1918. It also suggested that a comprehensive review would be undertaken after the war, when many surplus machine-guns could be sent to the colony.[179] Many of these guns proved their worth during the battle in 1941.

Conclusion

This period witnessed the emergence of a defensive system in Hong Kong that focused mainly on Victoria Harbour. The issues of defence arrangement and defence policy were constantly debated, even during the First World War. From the 1880s to 1900s, in the context of rapid technological change, especially the transformation from muzzle-loading to breech-loading artillery, the British defended Hong Kong mainly by maintaining their naval supremacy in Asia rather than investing in coastal defence. Thus, the man on the spot always noted the insufficiency of Hong Kong defence. This awareness was reflected in publications such as *The Back Door*. Still, many batteries, such as the fortresses of Lyemun and Mount Davis, which played an important role during subsequent periods, were constructed. New weapons such as machine-guns, Brennan torpedoes, torpedo boats and even submarines were introduced. After 1906, however, as a result of the German naval threat, the Royal Navy was no longer able to deploy large battle fleets in Asian waters. This fact motivated the British to reconsider Hong Kong defence.

The incorporation of the New Territories was another important change for the planners. On the one hand, it allowed the British to completely control Victoria Harbour, but on the other it forced the British to defend Kowloon Ridge, which could command the harbour. The garrison commanders tried to solve this problem by deploying mobile columns on the mainland. When Anderson arrived, however, a radical approach of building permanent defensive lines was proposed. This proposal marked a shift of focus from coastal to landward defence. Although Hong Kong was far from the main battlefields of the First World War, it was one of the crucial turning points for the history of Hong Kong defence, as a landward defence line was constructed across Kowloon Peninsula during the war. As the line built during the Great War was soon engulfed by urban sprawl, the need to construct a new line along the Kowloon Ridge was constantly debated during the subsequent period, as the international situation changed.

5

TREATY, AIR FORCE AND LANDWARD DEFENCE, 1920–1939

> We should now face more frankly the question of the defensibility of Hong Kong. In the campaign envisaged, the position of Hong Kong cannot be regarded as other than parlous in the extreme. By holding it we are giving a hostage to fortune. In attempting to retrieve that hostage we may well jeopardize the very limited resources wherewith otherwise we can hardly fail to achieve eventual victory, resources which, in any case, might subsequently be essential to our security elsewhere.
>
> —Wing Commander Arthur Harris, RAF; member of the
> Joint Planning Sub-committee, 1937

British Imperial Defence, 1919–1939

After the First World War, the German threat to British naval supremacy ended with the destruction of the High Seas Fleet (Hochseeflotte). Russian naval power was also significantly reduced because of the war and the revolution. France and the United States posed no immediate threat. The only threat facing Britain during the interwar period in Asia was Japan, her ally since 1902. Soon after the war, British military planners questioned Japan's designs on Asia. In 1925, Admiral Roger Keyes, the Deputy Chief of the Naval Staff who had participated in the Six-Day War as a lieutenant, wrote to Winston Churchill, then Chancellor of the Exchequer, that unless the British sufficiently strengthened their Asian possessions, the Japanese would turn the Europeans out of China, just as they had expelled the Chinese from Korea, the Russians from Manchuria, and the Germans from Qingdao.[1]

Meanwhile, Hong Kong remained one of the British political, economic and intelligence centres in Asia, although the British investment in Shanghai was larger. The colony also remained one of the places on which British "prestige" in Asia rested. To defend this important but vulnerable possession became a major problem for British planners and the government.

Although Britain had won the Great War, she had paid a high price: around 1,200,000 British and imperial and dominion subjects were dead because of the war. The war drained financial resources and contributed to the post-war recession that ultimately led to the General Strike of 1926. The price for victory also convinced a generation of politicians and planners to avoid the next Great War. On the other hand, Britain emerged from the war as the only superpower of the world, with global commitments and possessions. Studies of the interwar period tend to see Britain as a declining power, but it was hardly the case, at least in the eyes of contemporaries. Britain controlled all the major strategic straits of the world except the Taiwan Strait and the Panama Canal. The British also took over ex-Ottoman territories such as Iraq and German colonies in Africa and Oceania. As David Edgerton points out, the British spent only slightly less on arms (at the constant prices of 1913) during the interwar period than in the early 1910s, when the country had been in a naval arms race with imperial Germany.[2]

The impression that British military forces were in decline was the result of increased commitments, demobilization and the emergence of the Royal Air Force (RAF) (which had divided the share of the army and the navy in defence budgets). During the "Naval Holiday" between 1922 and 1936, Britain built more cruisers and aircraft carriers than Japan and the United States. She was able to modernize most of her battleships. The cost of modernizing a battleship was, as Edgerton suggests, sometimes higher than that of building one from scratch. The Royal Navy also made some headway in developing its naval air power, only lagging behind during the latter half of the 1930s as the result of a struggle with the RAF.[3] The size of the British Army shrank quickly after the war, but it operated globally and developed its armoured warfare theories. By 1939, it was able to equip and send to France a highly mechanized force.[4] Due to the political support it had gathered, the RAF remained a considerable force throughout the period, unmatched before the emergence of the German Luftwaffe.

Despite these achievements, the British military faced a tremendous limiting force, at least in the eyes of planners. To ensure that Britain could sustain the next Great War, seen as a long war of attrition that would require the total mobilization of national resources, politicians and the Treasury chose to rebuild the financial health of the nation by curtailing military spending. In 1919, the government introduced for the first time the "Ten Years Rule," which stipulated that Britain would not have to fight another war against a great power in the coming decade. In 1928, the rule was set to renew daily by the Chancellor of the Exchequer, Winston Churchill. The increase in real military spending was thus frozen until 1932.[5] Although the British military was able to maintain its efficiency and continue to develop new arms and doctrines, little could be done to augment the defence of overseas possessions. The services also competed constantly for scarce resources.

In this context, Hong Kong was used by the Royal Navy as a bargaining chip for more resources. In 1919, Lord Jellicoe, commander of the British Grand Fleet between 1914 and 1916, was sent by the British government to study the required naval forces in Asia. His suggestion, to form a combined fleet funded by Britain, Australia and New Zealand, received a cold reception. The Royal Navy then put forward the War Memorandum (Eastern), a plan for a possible Anglo-Japanese war, in 1920. The early versions of the war memorandum were more or less plans to redeploy the British fleet from Europe to Asia. They assumed that the navy would have to impose a blockade to defeat Japan. To do this effectively, a decisive victory over the Japanese battle fleet had to be achieved. The plan provided the rationale for a Singapore naval base, as the navy needed a first-class base in Asia to support a fleet. In retrospect, however, whether Britain had the resources to undertake a long war in Asia against Japan was in question. Moreover, Winston Churchill repeatedly pointed out that such a long and costly war against Japan was hardly worthwhile, as Britain had no vital interest in the area that would justify it. Thus, as Christopher Bell and Andrew Field suggest, the War Memorandum (Eastern) was more a rationale to ask for more resources from the government.[6]

In the Royal Navy's scheme, Hong Kong was deemed too vulnerable to landward attack to be the main base, but it was still seen as a viable offensive base by some naval officers until the late 1930s.[7] Without Hong Kong, it was argued, the navy would be unable to impose a close blockade against Japan, thus compromising the viability of its plan. This understanding affected the British defence policies for Hong Kong during this period. In fact, during this period, all the services tried to use Hong Kong as a bargaining chip for more resources. However, all gave up eventually because of the proximity of Hong Kong to the Japanese stronghold of Taiwan, the peculiar geography of the colony and, above all, the inability of the British to maintain a strong naval presence in Asia.

The mechanism of British defence policymaking had witnessed some changes after the First World War. The most important of them was the formation of the Chiefs of Staff Committee (COS) in 1923 and the Joint Planning Sub-committee in 1927 (JPC). The COS consisted of the chiefs of staff of the three armed services, and was the mechanism by which the services could exchange their views over defence policies and advise the civilian government on military matters. The JPC consisted of the heads of the planning departments of the services. Together they drafted plans and proposals such as the defence reports of Hong Kong, and were also responsible for making and modifying war plans according to the changing international situation. The lack of communication between the army and the navy over defence planning during previous periods was thus partly rectified.

Impacts of the Washington Treaty

A major factor affecting Hong Kong defence was the Washington Treaty, concluded by Britain, France, Japan, Italy and the United States in 1922. The powers agreed to maintain the status quo in Asia and to limit warship construction (the beginning of the "Naval Holiday") and construction of coastal defences in their Asian possessions. Article XIX of the treaty read:

> No new fortifications or naval bases shall be established in the territories and possessions specified; that no measures shall be taken to increase the existing naval facilities for the repair and maintenance of naval forces, and that no increase shall be made in the coast defences of the territories and possessions above specified. This restriction, however, does not preclude such repair and replacement of worn-out weapons and equipment as is customary in naval and military establishments in time of peace. [8]

Thus, Hong Kong was forbidden to build or upgrade its "coastal" defences between 1922 and 1936. This posed a new challenge for planners who had to improve the defences of the colony.

As suggested above, the early versions of the War Memorandum (Eastern) saw Hong Kong as an indispensable base for the Royal Navy's offensive against Japan. As early as October 1919, the navy had suggested to the Committee of Imperial Defence (CID) that it was necessary to review the "nature and scale" of Hong Kong defence.[9] In February 1920, General Henry Wilson, Chief of Imperial General Staff (CIGS) who had been involved in the previous discussion of landward defence, pointed out the difficulties of providing an adequate garrison in the face of financial stringency and demobilization:

> Whilst the scale of attack and defence of our naval bases and defended ports has temporarily been greatly reduced in the majority of cases as a result of the war, our bases in the Far East, and particularly Hong Kong, are a salient exception. So long as we can depend on our alliance with Japan we may rest content with a scale of defence sufficient to protect the base against a small raiding attack by land or sea. With Japan neutral we may have to face a considerably stronger attack from the Chinese mainland whilst, with Japan hostile, it is quite clear that it would be beyond our power to provide a garrison which could hold the place against a determined effort on the part of Japan for the period of three months stipulated by the Navy.[10]

Wilson also suggested that the current garrison and defences could not even deal with the incursion of a modernized Chinese army. Thus, he argued that, if the Japanese could not help defending Hong Kong, then the colony should be demilitarized and turned into a commercial port like Shanghai, with only a token garrison for maintaining internal order.[11] As the bulk of the British Army was demobilized and the rest of it committed in Russia, Crimea, the Middle East and the Caucasus, Wilson was naturally unwilling to spare troops for the defence of a far-flung colony that could be protected by an ally.

However, the Washington Treaty ended the Anglo-Japanese Alliance. The navy was largely able to follow the CID's previous recommendation of "sufficiently [reinforcing] the fleet in the Far East to deter the Japanese from bringing transports to the neighbourhood of Hong Kong with a view to effecting a landing in force." The Royal Navy had a squadron of three to five heavy cruisers, a flotilla of submarines (the 4th Submarine Flotilla) and an aircraft carrier (HMS *Hermes* or HMS *Eagle*) (Tables 18, 19; Figures 13, 14) in China. Although they could not match the full weight of the Japanese navy, their presence could not be discounted until the early 1940s, when the Japanese had developed a significant advantage in naval aviation. Before the outbreak of the European War in 1939, there were as many as thirteen long-range submarines stationed in Hong Kong or Singapore, capable of threatening mainland Japan.

Table 18 Major units of the China Station, December 1919[12]

Formation	Name	Type	Notes
5th Cruiser Squadron	*Hawkins*	Heavy Cruiser	7.5" x 7, commissioned in 1919
	Cairo	Light Cruiser	6" x 5, 1919
	Carlisle	Light Cruiser	6" x 5, 1919
	Columbus	Light Cruiser	6" x 5, 1919
Aircraft Carrier	*Ark Royal*	Carrier	Converted, 8 planes
4th Submarine Flotilla	*Ambrose*	Sub Tender	Commissioned in 1915
	H Class x 1	Minesweeper	
	L Class x 6	Submarine	Built in the First World War
Harbour Defence	W Class x 2	Destroyer	At Hong Kong

Figure 13 HMS *Medway* and the submarines of the China Station, c. 1930s (Tim Ko)

Figure 14   HMS *Hermes* in dry dock in Hong Kong (Tim Ko)

Table 19   Major units of the China Station, June 1939[13]

Formation	Name	Type	Notes
5th Cruiser Squadron	*Cornwall*	Heavy Cruiser	8" x 8, 1928
	Kent	Heavy Cruiser	8" x 8, 1928
	Dorsetshire	Heavy Cruiser	8" x 8, 1930
	Birmingham	Light Cruiser	6" x 12, 1937
Aircraft Carrier	*Eagle*	Carrier	25–30 planes, 1918
4th Submarine Flotilla	D Class x 9	Destroyer	Commissioned from the 1930s
4th Submarine Flotilla	*Medway*	Sub Tender	Comm. 1928
	W Class x 1	Destroyer	Comm. 1918
	O Class x 4	Submarine	Long-range Sub for the Far East
	P Class x 4	Ditto.	Ditto.
	R Class x 4	Ditto.	Ditto.
	G Class x 1	Ditto.	Comm. 1936
Torpedo boats	6		At Hong Kong
Mine Layer	1		At Hong Kong
Harbour Defence	S Class x 4		At Hong Kong

In March 1926, Alex Flint, the Permanent Under-Secretary at the Admiralty, passed on to the CID the view of the naval chiefs expressed during the Flag Officers Conference in February 1925. The admirals believed that:

> The importance of Hong Kong requires no emphasis, but it may be stated, with confidence, that from the point of view of naval strategy its loss in the event of an Eastern War would be a disaster of the first magnitude, and that its capture would be an essential preliminary to active offensive operations in the Pacific . . .[14]

Given the importance attached to Hong Kong in the War Memorandum (Eastern), the admirals asked for "measures of a naval and military character . . . which would materially assist to prolong the power of the garrison to withstand attack" without "overstepping the limitations imposed by that (Washington) Agreement."[15] Thus, the wish to augment the defence of Hong Kong never died down with the conclusion of the Washington Treaty.

In response to the navy's recommendation, the Joint Overseas and Home Defence Sub-committee prioritized the rearmament of defended ports in May 1927. The committee recognized the importance of Hong Kong "not only for the protection of our immense interests in China, but also for all except the preliminary stages of a war in the Far East." They suggested that, "with circumspection," the defence of Hong Kong "can be reorganised and brought up to date on the basis of replacing obsolete material, without infringing either the spirit or the letter of the Treaty."[16] Hong Kong was ranked second, behind Singapore, among the ports that required improvement.

One of the steps taken was the conversion of Kai Tak Bund into a military air base. In May 1926, Governor Sir Cecil Clementi submitted to the CID a memorandum about converting the strip of reclaimed land on the eastern side of Kowloon Peninsula (Kai Tak Bund) into an air base, which had been used by the RAF as an airstrip for two years already. The CID had just accepted the Air Ministry's request for an air base. The COS, which was responsible for the actual selection of the site, recommended buying the Kai Tak Bund in the face of instability in China and of rising property prices.[17] The COS added that such a move did not violate the Washington Treaty:

> A levelled area of ground cannot be interpreted as an increase in coast defences. It is only when buildings are erected and aircraft actually located on the aerodrome that the question of legality appears to arise . . .[18]

The Hong Kong government bought Kai Tak Bund for HK$1,001,250 in December 1927.[19] Six months later, the British discovered that the Japanese had also constructed aerodromes in Taiwan and deployed fighter squadrons there. The CID decided to turn the "levelled area of ground" into an operational air base. The cabinet suggested that, if Japan protested, Britain would take the case to the League of Nations. It even put forward a strange argument that the air base was "for purposes of defence against landward attack [only]." [20] Nevertheless, Japan raised no protest and the air base (RAF Kai Tak) became operational in 1930.[21]

Although the Kai Tak air base was established only in 1930, the RAF had operated in Hong Kong from 1924, when HMS *Pegasus* arrived with four Fairley III seaplanes. They conducted the first aerial survey of the colony, and participated in the suppression of pirates at Mirs Bay and Bias Bay.[22] In 1927, the navy formed a "Far East Flight" of four seaplanes, dispatching it to fly from Plymouth to Hong Kong through the Middle East, India and Singapore.[23] The goal was to gauge the speed with which the planes could reach Hong Kong from Britain. When RAF Kai Tak was established, planes from HMS *Hermes* and HMS *Eagle* often operated from there. The base was assigned to the RAF Far East Command, formed also in 1930, with its headquarters in Singapore. From 1933 to 1935, the buildings of the base (upgraded to RAF Station in 1935) were reconstructed with concrete. However, its first permanent flight, deployed in 1936, consisted only of obsolete Horsley and Tiger Moth light bombers. In 1937, the Horsleys were replaced by three Vildebeest torpedo bombers, but they arrived without torpedo rack.[24]

Another step taken was to improve the guns of Hong Kong. In July 1925, the British informed the Japanese of their intention to replace the field guns in Hong Kong for the defence against "landward attack." The Japanese demurred, claiming that such a move violated the Washington Treaty and would "provide a very bad precedent."[25] Later in 1928, when British were considering changing the mountings of the coastal guns to increase their range, the Foreign Office argued that the idea was a violation of the treaty. The COS countered that the Japanese and Americans had installed the same mountings on their battleships. A corresponding increase in the range of the coastal guns was necessary to maintain the status quo. On the other hand, the Foreign Office argued that unless the army could prove that the guns could only attack land and air targets, any change was a violation. Maurice Hankey, secretary of the CID and a British delegate to the Washington Conference, supported the COS by suggesting that if Article XIX allowed only improvements of naval gunnery but not coastal guns, then the article violated the spirit of the treaty, which was to maintain the status quo in the Pacific, as it rendered coastal defences in Asia useless against modern warships.[26]

In response, the Foreign Office claimed that it would not oppose the scheme "provided that the Chiefs of Staff, as the expert advisers of His Majesty's Government in such matters, are prepared to defend, should the necessity arise, the thesis that these alterations do not involve an increase in the coast defence of that Colony within the meaning of article XIX of the Treaty." The Foreign Office also wryly pointed out that the arguments of the COS were exactly the same as those employed by the Germans when they were trying to rearm their coastal forts.[27] Still, the CID agreed in principle to install new mountings to the coastal guns in Hong Kong in 1928, although the actual work was not started until 1935. Other than the changes mentioned above, the defence planning of Hong Kong was constantly reviewed by planners throughout the period.

The Interwar Garrison

The interwar garrison continued to perform its duties and face old problems and adversaries. As the political situation in China steadily deteriorated, piracy returned to the South China coast. Piracy in the 1920s, however, was different from that of previous decades. The large pirate fleets of Chui A-poo or Sap Ng Tsai no longer existed; instead, the pirates of the 1920s acted like modern-day hijackers. Disguised as passengers, they seized ships when they had just left Hong Kong near Bias Bay. The capture of SS *Anking* in 1928 was a typical example. The China Navigation Company vessel was carrying over 1,000 passengers from Singapore to Amoy when it was hijacked by pirates who had boarded the ship in Singapore. They then redirected it to Bias Bay and looted the passengers. As the result of these attacks, the vital areas of the ships such as the bridge and boiler rooms were protected with fences, and detachments of Water Police were deployed on board.[28] Army detachments from the British garrison were also lent to the ships.[29]

The China Station had much trouble dealing with this kind of piracy, as it often occurred outside Hong Kong, and it was difficult to locate the pirates and their lairs. In October 1927, when the submarines L4 and L5 tried to stop pirates from controlling SS *Irene*, they were forced to sink the ship, which belonged to the Chinese government-owned China Merchants Steam Navigation Company. Although the pirates were apprehended and later hanged, twenty-eight passengers died and a diplomatic furor erupted. The Chinese government sued the commander of L4 in 1930, but he was acquitted.[30] The aircraft carriers of the China Station also participated in anti-piracy operations by sending planes over Bias Bay.[31] The China Station attacked villages at Bias Bay twice in 1925 and 1927, but pirate attacks occurred until 1941, when the movement of goods and travellers was interrupted by the war.

Despite these duties, the small garrison in Hong Kong enjoyed a leisurely life. The quality of life of the officers and men had improved substantially because of the devaluation of silver after the First World War. As Lieutenant (later Captain) Robert Ryder noted, "everything out here is ridiculously cheap." For example, a pair of "good brown brogues" cost only seven shillings and sixpence in Hong Kong, compared to thirty shillings in Britain. For a month's pay, Ryder bought himself a yacht. He was also able to enjoy different sports.[32] Ryder even went with four junior colleagues on a trip across the Pacific and Atlantic, covering a total of 26,099.5 kilometres on a small Chinese ketch, the *Tai Mo Shan*, in 1933–1934. To ensure his superior would allow them to go, Ryder and his band "added a comprehensive letter in which we explained that we were eager to collect meteorological data, information re currents and winds experienced, and any other details of a similar nature which might prove useful."[33] Less adventurous officers such as Lieutenant Commander J. S. Dalison of HMS *Moth* could travel on modern steamers that were "suitably primed with food and iced drinks" to Nanning if he wanted to get away from his ship.[34] However, this is not to suggest that the interwar garrison was entirely free from danger; in 1931, HMS *Poseidon*, one of the new long-range submarines for the China Station, was sunk after colliding with a Chinese freighter during training. Twenty-two of the crew, including one Chinese steward, were killed in the accident.[35]

The discipline of the servicemen remained a problem: a group brawl occurred between British and American sailors on the island in 1921, after the Royal Navy sailors threw a U.S. Navy sailor into the sea.[36] The problem of VD, which had defeated garrison commanders and governors in previous decades, remained serious, because of the prolonged peace and an increase in disposable income among the men. Sailors from the U.S. Asiatic Fleet enjoyed the same benefits—and shared the same problem. *Life* magazine noted in 1940 that

> the Wan Chai district, the prostitution section, is incredible. American sailors whose dollar is worth four Hong Kong dollars are very rich in Hong Kong terms . . . with the result that they need not patronise houses of prostitution . . . a sailor can afford to set up a little establishment in Wan Chai for the duration of his tour of duty . . .[37]

However, during the Battle of Hong Kong in December 1941, the "Angels of Wan Chai" assisted their beleaguered former customers.[38] Another group of women serving the British forces in Hong Kong was the famous Jenny's Side Party, which cleaned the hull of the Royal Navy warships from the interwar period until long after the Second World War.

Norman Miners has suggested that the VD control measures introduced in the 1890s had reduced the infection rate of the garrison to 7 percent in 1922. However, the statistics covering a longer period show that the actual infection rate of Hong Kong was higher than that of other stations.[39] In 1924, the Admiralty complained to the Colonial Office about the prevalence of VD among sailors in Hong Kong. In 1922 alone, 410 contracted VD in Hong Kong, compared to merely 10 in Singapore. Thus, the Admiralty urged the colonial government to revive the examination and registration systems.[40]

Figure 15   The British Geisha House (Brothel) on Stonecutters Island, 1935 (Bill Lake)

Meanwhile, the colonial government was under constant pressure to abolish even the existing control measures. A delegation of the National Council for Combatting Venereal Disease, led by Dr. Hallam and Mrs. Neville-Rolfe, visited Hong Kong in 1922. Although it received no help from the colonial government, the delegation gathered much information about the state of prostitution and venereal disease and published its findings. Like the Hennessy Commission that had studied the issue half a century previously, the delegation suggested that the controlling measures were ineffective in stopping the spread of VD among servicemen.[41] After the visit of the delegates of the council and the League of Nations, Governor Peel finally jettisoned the system of selective closures in 1931. The brothels serving European soldiers and sailors were the first to be closed. From then on and before the Japanese invasion in 1941, the Hong Kong government did not legislate on prostitutes and brothels. The VD infection rate among the troops, however, remained high; in 1938, more than one-fourth of the sailors were infected.[42]

While the war against VD continued, the fight between London and Hong Kong over the issue of military contribution was brought to a close. During the First World War, because of the unusual increase in the value of silver, the burden of the military contribution of Hong Kong was relatively light. However, soon after the war, the actual military contribution steadily increased, due to the fall in silver prices. The garrison added financial pressure to the colony—in addition to the military contribution. As Governor Reginald Stubbs noted, the military occupied some valuable land that could be sold. He wrote to the Colonial Office that "acres of some of the best building land in the heart of the city are merely dotted here and there with insignificant buildings and a large area in the best part of Kowloon is sparsely inhabited by mules."[43] To increase income without adding the burden of military contribution, the Hong Kong government started to sell land in the New Territories, especially those adjacent to Kowloon. This led to a backlash from the landed interest of the inhabitants of the New Territories, who formed the Committee for the Protection of Private Property in the Leased Territory in Kowloon (九龍租界維護民產委員會), which was later renamed by Governor Cecil Clementi as the Heung Yee Kuk.[44] Clementi proposed in vain to fix the military contribution at 25 percent of all rateable values in 1926. The argument was put to a rest (until the 1950s) when the Financial Secretary of Hong Kong, Sydney Caine, proposed fixing the annual military contribution at $6,000,000 for five years from 1938. Although the sum of money offered was larger than previous contributions, the proposal benefitted the colony because its income increased substantially in following years, due to the influx of refugees and the development of further industrialization.[45]

Hong Kong as an Offensive Base: Defence Reviews of 1927–1930

At the request of the CID, Governor Stubbs studied the defence of the colony with local army and navy commanders, submitting a very gloomy memorandum in February 1926. It was drafted by Vice Admiral Edwyn Alexander-Sinclair,[46] Commander-in-Chief of the China Station; Major General Charles Luard,[47] General Officer Commanding Hong Kong; the Local Committee and the major officers of HMS *Hermes*.[48]

The memorandum argued that, as the invaders could land on several spots simultaneously, it was futile for defenders to resist any landing attempt. The defenders should focus only on Hong Kong Island and conduct a delaying action on the mainland, until reinforcements arrived from Singapore. The minimum size of garrison required was four infantry battalions, 1,200 artillerymen and eighteen aircraft. It was concluded that the only way to protect Hong Kong as a naval base was to send a large fleet to protect it from any landing attempt.[49]

In short, the colonial government and the officers on the spot believed that the navy remained indispensable against invasions. However, they had hardly studied the issue seriously. For example, they even failed to refer to previous studies that had already pointed out many of the beaches in Hong Kong were unsuitable for landing larger bodies of troops. No attempt was made by them to consider the defence of the colony without naval supremacy, or the difficulties facing the invading force, let alone the ways to exploit them. The memorandum assumed that it was "not difficult" for the Japanese to ship a large army to Hong Kong. However, the memorandum was extremely optimistic about holding Hong Kong Island with four battalions. It should be noted that officers such as Alexander-Sinclair and Luard had had limited experience during the previous war. Alexander-Sinclair served on capital ships in the North Sea, while Luard had been a brigadier serving in the Middle East. It was hardly surprising that the former did not explore the issue of littoral defence and the latter the terrain of the New Territories. Still, the memorandum was the first systematic study of Hong Kong defence after the First World War; it laid down the basic objective of the garrison, which was to hold Hong Kong Island for as long as possible.

After Stubbs submitted his report, the COS instructed the newly formed Joint Planning Sub-committee (JPC) to study the defence requirements of Hong Kong. After months of study, the JPC submitted its memorandum in December 1927. The JPC consisted of Captain Wilfred Egerton,[50] the Director of Naval Plans, Colonel William Dobbie[51] from the General Staff and Wing Commander Richard Peck,[52] the Director of Operations and Intelligence, Air Ministry. Egerton, Dobbie and Peck were experienced staff officers responsible for the operational planning of the British military. Their report set the tone for subsequent studies. Some of their estimations, such as the general direction of enemy attack and British reactions, were surprisingly accurate, especially given the fact that the actual invasion took place more than a decade later.

The JPC introduced several "controlling factors" in their estimation: 1) Japan would fight against Britain alone; 2) a long period of tension would exist before the actual outbreak of war; 3) the Washington Treaty did not prohibit an aircraft garrison in Hong Kong; and 4) China would not be able to prevent any violation of her territorial integrity by either Japan or Britain.[53] These factors largely met the situation during the late 1920s. First, Britain faced no potential enemies except Japan and the Soviet Union, but the two countries were unlikely to form an alliance. Second, although the Anglo-Japanese Alliance had been terminated, there was no issue or conflict of interest over which Japan and Britain might immediately start fighting. Third, the issue of the air base was not seriously raised throughout the 1920s. Last, China was indeed at that time unable to defend its own territories.

The JPC adopted the navy's view that Hong Kong should be held "at all costs," due to its strategic importance:

> The capture of Hong Kong... would not only deprive the British Fleet of the best anchorage in the north China Sea, and valuable storage and repair facilities, but would also result in a large accretion of strength to Japan, since, thereby, the range of action of her naval forces would be increased and consequently her powers of resistance to any operations...[54]

The report also noted that the fall of Hong Kong would be a "serious blow" to British prestige and its recapture would "require a very great expenditure and effort."[55]

As the purpose of holding Hong Kong was to provide an offensive base for the British fleet, the JPC approached the problem from two levels:

> Can Hong Kong be so fortified and garrisoned as to preclude all reasonable possibility of the Japanese being able to interfere with the use of the harbour by the British Fleet on arrival?
>
> If this should prove to be impossible, what is the minimum provision which must be made to ensure i) that Hong Kong shall not pass into Japanese hands, and ii) that any menace which may have developed to the unrestricted use of the harbour, can be effectively dispelled after the arrival of the British Fleet?[56]

The JPC acknowledged the fact that Hong Kong had numerous beaches and coastal enclaves, but also pointed out that most of them were too small for any sizeable body of troops to land on. The most likely landing spots would be Hong Kong Island, Bias Bay and Starling Inlet. As the JPC believed that the Japanese would try to prevent the British from using Hong Kong as an offensive base, they would not risk serious losses by landing directly on the island. Instead, they might land at Starling Inlet or Bias Bay, and then proceed along the Kowloon-Canton Railway to bring Hong Kong Island into artillery range. To achieve this, the Japanese had to overcome Kowloon Ridge.[57]

The Japanese might deploy at least two divisions (twenty-four battalions) to attack Hong Kong. However, the Japanese could bring only a few heavy guns because of the rugged terrain of the New Territories. To ship two divisions to Hong Kong from Japan or Taiwan, more than a hundred transports of 3,000 tons or more would be needed. This amounted to 40 percent of all Japanese merchant ships travelling between China and Japan. Thus, it would be possible to discover the Japanese move early on by detecting changes in shipping schedules and related financial and insurance activities. On the other hand, the War Memorandum (Eastern) estimated that the British main fleet could reach Hong Kong from home waters in 45 to 55 days. If the tankers could be arranged beforehand, then only 44 days would be enough. Thus, the Japanese had only 44 to 54 days to travel to Hong Kong and to complete their mission.[58]

To hold Hong Kong for 44 to 54 days, the China Station had to disrupt the sea communications of the invading forces. The JPC prepared two plans for the garrison:

Complete Protection
Objective: To completely protect Hong Kong and its facilities

Missions:

- Imposing delay by all possible means on Japanese operations
- Ensuring the fortress against a *coup-de-main*
- Manning the fixed armament
- Defending Hong Kong Island
- Arranging for internal security and the protection of vulnerable points
- Opposing the enemy landing at Starling Inlet or where it is attempted on the Leased Territory
- Arranging for the defence of the shores of Tolo Harbour, Port Shelter and Junk Bay. Should the landing be successful, to fight delaying action along the Shataukok–Fanling–Tai Po defile and, if necessary, take up a defensive position on the Tai Mo Shan Line

Garrison Size:

- Ten Regular Infantry Battalions, plus the Hong Kong Volunteer Defence Corps; ten to twelve squadrons of aircraft

The JPC believed that if the garrison could be expanded to this level, then it could protect the naval facilities and even deter Japan.[59] Like all military plans, the above-mentioned proposal only reflected an ideal situation. The JPC also put forward a "minimum provision" that only defend Hong Kong Island and part of the naval facilities:

Minimum Provision

Objective: To hold Hong Kong and protect part of its facilities until the arrival of the main fleet

Missions:

- Providing sufficient force to ensure an adequate bridgehead being maintained on the mainland. This would entail the retention of the line Tide Cove–Gin Drinker's Bay.
- Preventing any actual Japanese landing as long as possible, and imposing on any forces which succeed in gaining a footing the maximum of delay before they can attack the bridgehead
- Providing a mobile reserve available to resist attempts to land elsewhere at points which would turn the main bridgehead position and cut off the forces delaying the landing about Starling Inlet
- Securing Hong Kong Island against a direct attack

Garrison Size:

- Eight Regular Infantry Battalions, plus the Hong Kong Volunteer Defence Corps; five to seven squadrons of aircraft

With a smaller size, the garrison could not resist the shelling of naval facilities on Kowloon and Hong Kong Island by the Japanese. As it was necessary to expel the Japanese forces from Kowloon and the New Territories after the arrival of the main fleet, the garrison had to keep a bridgehead behind the "Tide Cove–Gin Drinker's Bay Line." The JPC also estimated that the Japanese could field as many as 250 aircraft to bomb Hong Kong, dropping 25 to 35 tons of bombs every day. However, it would take some time for them to establish an air base in Chinese territory, as no aircraft could fly from Taiwan to Hong Kong directly in 1927. To counter this threat, at least twelve squadrons would be required. The RAF argued that anything less could only delay the Japanese from establishing their air base. In the "minimum" plan, the RAF would be relegated to reconnaissance and ground support roles only.[60]

Unlike the Hong Kong government in its memorandum, the JPC highlighted the possible problems the Japanese would face if they were to attack Hong Kong, such as limited time, logistics, loss of the initiative (after the arrival of the British fleet) and high risk (the attacking force had no route of retreat). Thus, the JPC argued that it was possible to defend Hong Kong, and reiterated the need to augment its defence without breaching the Washington Treaty, such as by upgrading the mountings of the coastal guns, surveying the islands and areas that could be used by the Japanese in South China, and improving "the communications in the Leased Territory, especially those south of the line Tide Cove–Gin Drinker's Bay."[61]

Although the JPC report of 1927 overestimated the scale of the Japanese attack and the British ability to hold Kowloon, it laid down a foundation for subsequent discussions by accurately predicting the Japanese route of advance and shifting the central issue of Hong Kong defence from coastal to landward defence. This shift paved the way for the construction of the Gin Drinker's Line.

Not all were satisfied with the JPC Report. In late 1927, Vice Admiral Reginald Tyrwhitt,[62] the new Commander-in-Chief of the China Station, instructed the services in Hong Kong to provide concrete suggestions for the revision of the JPC report. Tyrwhitt noted that the resistance of Hong Kong could delay Japanese actions against Singapore, thus supporting the British war effort even though it might not be used as a naval base.[63] Unlike his predecessor, Tyrwhitt had extensive experience in coastal and littoral warfare, as he had been the commander of the Harwich Force during the First World War. He disagreed with his predecessor's view that little could be done to harass the Japanese invasion if the China Station possessed no capital ships. He outlined five objectives for the navy, including destroying and disrupting enemy transports, forcing the enemy to land at more remote beaches, preventing the enemy from entering Guangzhou or from using the islands near Hong Kong as artillery positions, and stopping enemy warships or submarines from entering Victoria Harbour. He demanded more submarines, torpedo boats and mines, and urged the redeployment of Royal Navy gunboats in China to support ground operations and disrupt Japanese sea lanes.[64] Many of his suggestions were gradually realized throughout the interwar period.

As did the JPC report, the army estimated that the Japanese would attack from the north and might take Guangzhou as a preliminary step. It also mentioned the danger of a Japanese attack against Hong Kong Island while the garrison was engaged on the mainland. The defenceless state of the south shore of the island was also noted, and the garrison commander urged to upgrade the coastal gun mountings as soon as possible.[65]

The RAF commander was pessimistic about the prospect of holding Hong Kong, as Kai Tak was too small for any sizeable air force and the Japanese could establish air bases on the flat land in Guangdong. With its limited number of planes, the RAF could not achieve air superiority, and had to rely on the less effective seaplanes. As the territorial size of Hong Kong was too small, it also lacked the depth to detect and give early warning of air attacks in the daytime or at night. Worse, the Japanese air force could eventually reach Hong Kong directly from Taiwan as its aircraft improved.[66]

These revisions marked the gradual shift of the Royal Navy's role, from preventing landing to assisting ground operations. The army highlighted the need to strengthen the ability of the garrison to resist on the mainland and the difficulty of holding the island. The RAF raised the problem of fielding an adequate air force at Hong Kong to protect it from aerial attack. These different views continued to shape the defence arrangements for Hong Kong throughout the 1930s.

The JPC revisited the issue from political, strategic and operational levels, submitting a new report in 1930. The committee now consisted of Captain Roger Bellairs,[67] Colonel Clive Liddell,[68] and Wing Commander Richard Peck. The 1930 report adopted the same controlling factors and estimations of its predecessor. It also maintained that the main objective of the garrison was to protect the harbour facilities. However, it emphasized holding the island, as it argued that many of the damaged facilities could be repaired. It suggested that defenders should not rely on terrain alone to delay the Japanese, as they had been able to march quickly with little provision and luggage during previous wars. The need to hold Kowloon Ridge so that the Japanese could not shell Victoria Harbour effectively was also highlighted.[69]

The 1930 report agreed with its predecessor that only part of Kowloon and Hong Kong Island could be held until the arrival of the British fleet. The forces required, however, were different from those mentioned in the 1927 report:

Army

- Six infantry battalions (one Indian)
- Twelve 18-pounder howitzers; twenty 4.5-inch howitzers; four 6-inch guns, four 60-pounder guns; eighteen light guns (fifty-eight in total)
- One engineer company

Royal Navy

- Six submarines; five China gunboats (with 3- to 6-inch guns); minelayers and other auxiliaries; 1,500 mines; submarine boom

Royal Air Force

- Five squadrons

Three defensive lines were proposed for the defence of the mainland: 1) Shenzhen-Shataukok; 2) the line across Tai Mo Shan, with its flanks being Tolo Harbour and Kam Tin River; and 3) Tide Cove–Gin Drinker's Bay line.[70] The roads between these lines would be destroyed when the defenders shifted from one line to another. As the first two lines were too long to be defended effectively, the best position from which to hold Kowloon until the arrival of the fleet would be the final one:

> The Tide Cove–Gin Drinker's Bay line is a strong defensive position. The only approaches by road both on the east and west run on the edge of the sea and the main approaches, those on the east, are exposed for some thousands of yards to fire of machine guns and light artillery south of Tide Cove. Any frontal attacks on the position must be made over country impassable except to the most mobile infantry and down slopes exposed to the fire of all arms from the main position. A considerable portion of the front is protected by the precipitous gorge of the Shing Mun River, which, if swept with machine gun fire, is capable of stopping any attack southwards from Needle Hill . . .
>
> If, therefore, this line were strongly wired and good machine gun emplacements were prepared it should be possible for the line to be held by three battalions, with an increased establishment of machine guns . . .[71]

It was estimated that the Gin Drinker's Line could be held by three battalions with a stronger machine-gun complement until reinforcements arrived. As the Japanese could not send bombers directly from Taiwan, the garrison had a "reasonable chance of holding out" if it was provided with a fortified line and a new air base, as well as additional aircraft, coastal defence vessels and mines.[72] The JPC listed thirteen recommendations, such as updating the coastal guns, increasing the wartime garrison to six battalions together with adequate guns and vehicles, sending additional aircraft from India and finding "the most rapid method of constructing concrete machine gun emplacements."[73]

As the JPC recognized that it was impossible to reinforce Hong Kong substantially in peacetime or during the period of tension, it tried to make the most of the resources available on the spot. Thus, the report went into much detail about how to impose the maximum delay on the incoming Japanese forces on the mainland, by adopting World War I tactical experiences such as elastic defence and land-sea cooperation. It also highlighted the importance of static defences made of concrete, another crucial lesson from the last war (though not necessarily applicable in the next).

The 1930 report was the second concrete proposal for a permanent defensive position along the Kowloon Ridge after the one put forward by General Anderson in 1911–1913. When the JPC suggested building a defensive line along Kowloon Ridge, it was not proposing a Great Wall-like structure that could indefinitely stop a Japanese attack. Rather, the goal was to delay the enemy from dominating Kowloon Ridge (thus Victoria Harbour) for 44 to 54 days. Deducting the time needed by the Japanese to ship and unload troops and to reach the defensive line from the beach-head, the JPC expected the line would be held for three weeks at most. Even if the line was eventually breached, it might impose sufficient delay to protect Hong Kong Island before reinforcements arrived.

The Decision to Build the Gin Drinker's Line, 1931–1935

The British planners faced more problems in considering imperial defence, as the internal and external situations deteriorated in the early 1930s. In September 1931, part of the British Atlantic Fleet staged a bloodless mutiny in Invergordon because of an imminent salary cut. The event contributed to a sharp fall of the British pound, brought down the cabinet and forced Britain to abandon the gold standard. In the same month, the Japanese Kwantung Army invaded Manchuria; the event escalated into a short but intense Sino-Japanese conflagration at Shanghai in 1932. In Europe, Mussolini's Fascist Italy became increasingly aggressive; the rise of the Nazis in Germany in 1933 made the future even less predictable.

Ramsay MacDonald, the Labour Prime Minister, proposed reconsidering the Ten Years Rule as early as November 1930:

> As things stood, it could be assumed that we should have ten years to recover our position. Supposing, however, something happened next year which made it appear the ten-year period was too long, we could reduce the time to a shorter number of years. The situation was that no Government could adopt a policy of peace coupled with disarmament on absolutely hard and fast lines. Every morning it was necessary to look round and see what changes had occurred during the night . . . as one who saw all telegrams that came to his Government

from foreign parts, that he sometimes felt rather anxious . . . In short, what was wanted in considering Defence was flexibility and not dogmas.[74]

The COS stated that the Ten Years Rule must go because "all forms of political prophecy and assumptions of the continuance of peace are perhaps the most unreliable."[75] The state of defence in Asia was "about as bad as it could be":

> Our naval forces in the Far East include nothing larger than 10,000-ton cruisers armed with 8-inch guns . . . The Hong Kong gun defences are out of date, and such essential elements as mines, anti-submarine defences, boom defences and aircraft are lacking. There are insufficient anti-aircraft guns. One of the three battalions of the peace time garrison of Hong Kong and part of the movable armament are at Shanghai . . .
>
> The whole of our territory in the Far East, as well as the coastline of India and the Dominions and our vast trade and shipping, lies open to attack.[76]

The COS urged the government to revise the defence planning for Singapore, Hong Kong and Trincomalee. Although the cabinet had already approved in principle the conversion of the coastal gun mountings in Hong Kong, actual work had yet to be started because the CID had not finished its study on the relative merits of coastal guns and aircraft.[77] Several years would be needed to update the mountings, as Britain could furnish only twelve mountings a year even at full capacity. The mountings could not be changed all at the same time as this would render Hong Kong defenceless. Moreover, as Singapore was still unarmed, Hong Kong would have to wait.[78]

At least something was done in 1932 to augment Hong Kong defence. Six 3-inch anti-aircraft (AA) guns were shipped to Hong Kong, and the ammunition storage of the coastal guns was increased. The battalion at Shanghai was also transferred to Hong Kong, increasing the permanent garrison to three battalions. The COS also reconfirmed that the order of rearmament would be Singapore, Hong Kong, Trincomalee, Malta and Gibraltar.[79] The idea of abandoning Hong Kong was again rejected, as holding it as long as possible could "contain some enemy forces and thus possibly to gain time at Singapore, and in the hope that our seagoing submarines might have an opportunity to inflict losses on the attacking forces."[80] It was also expected that the Americans at Manila could deter the Japanese, and while the Americans were unlikely to offer much help, the British could approach the Chinese and the French.[81] The idea that Hong Kong could be held with Chinese, French and even American help persisted until 1941, as Britain was no longer able actually to deploy a strong fleet in Asia.

Still, although some attention was paid by the COS (and to a lesser extent the CID) to Hong Kong, little more could be done because the Singapore project had not been finished. The CID ruled in April 1933 that comprehensive improvements in Hong Kong could be implemented only after Singapore was secure.[82] Meanwhile, the Air Ministry became increasingly pessimistic about the defensibility of Hong Kong as it could not find flat land on which to build a larger air base.[83] The navy insisted on treating Hong Kong as an offensive base, even if it was only a means to keep the War Memorandum (Eastern) as a seemingly workable plan. From 1933, the Royal Navy contemplated building an alternative naval base on the south side of Hong Kong Island, for light cruisers, destroyers and submarines; it tried to persuade the Hong Kong government to support the project. The plan was only partially realized due to lack of money.[84] The army had considered deploying 9.2- and 12-inch howitzers in Hong Kong, but the idea was also shelved for the same reason.[85]

The JPC approached the issue of Hong Kong defence anew, submitting another report in July 1934. This time, the JPC was composed of Rear Admiral Edward King, Colonel Robert Haining,[86] and Wing Commander Arthur Harris.[87] It was instructed by the CID to consider "on the assumption that the Singapore base is secure, what measure can be taken for the relief or recapture of Hong Kong."[88] However, probably influenced by the senior officer of the committee (a rear admiral), the JPC first turned to the defence of Hong Kong:

> The strategic importance of Hong Kong is so great and its situation so precarious that it appeared important to consider whether "emergency" measures could not be taken to improve the situation during the period that must elapse before the full programme can be taken in hand.[89]

The JPC rejected the idea that Hong Kong should not be defended or was indefensible, but conceded that the previous proposals had been too ambitious to be fully implemented. Thus, the report was to approach the question "realistically." It suggested that the Shanghai Incident of 1932 had shown that the Japanese were able to construct air bases quickly on paddy fields. At least eleven squadrons (around 200 planes) could be brought to bear against Hong Kong. Thus, the only viable objective for the garrison was to hold Hong Kong Island, as it was impossible to protect the harbour facilities effectively against air attack.[90]

The focus of the study was still the landward attack. Again, the report believed that the best position from which the defenders could delay the Japanese attack (after actions in the New Territories) was the Tide Cove–Gin Drinker's line. With an invading force of two divisions, the Japanese could probably breach the line before the arrival of the British fleet. Thus, the JPC recommended providing material aids with which the defenders could offset their numerical disadvantage:

> If the main position is wired throughout its length and provided with concrete pillboxes, its capacity for defence can be greatly increased and it is by no means

> improbable that, with a small expenditure of money, the main line of defence with both flanks resting on the sea could be adequately defended by a comparatively small garrison. . . .
>
> Large concrete reservoirs and conduits are being constructed in the neighbourhood of Hong Kong in connection with the Shing Mun Valley water supply scheme, and lend themselves for incorporation in the defensive line.[91]

The purpose of the defensive line was clear: to replace precious manpower with concrete defences so that a limited goal could be achieved. By then, it was tacitly agreed that it was impossible to protect the harbour facilities. The 1934 report also recommended increasing the garrison to at least five battalions, updating the coastal gun mountings, sending more anti-aircraft guns and building another new air base in Pat Heung.[92] In October 1934, the COS endorsed the JPC's report and urged the CID and the cabinet to take action.[93] Some of the recommendations, such as building the Gin Drinker's Line, were finally being implemented.

The international situation continuously deteriorated afterwards. In October 1935, Italy invaded Abyssinia, straining Anglo-Italian relations almost to a breaking point. British control over the Suez Canal was directly threatened. This persuaded Admiral Roger Backhouse, Commander-in-Chief of the Home Fleet, to urge for a shift of attention of the Royal Navy from the Far East to the Mediterranean.[94] From then on, the army replaced the navy as the driving force behind improvements in Hong Kong defence. Between March and April 1935, Major General Frederick Barron, the Inspector of Fixed Defences, visited Hong Kong. Barron submitted a detailed report, endorsing the construction of the Gin Drinker's Line and the reorganization of the coastal batteries (discussed below).

In September 1935, General Archibald Montgomery-Massingberd, the CIGS, urged the CID and the Defence Requirement Committee to devote more resources to Hong Kong. He believed that, although the colony was "far from possessing the strategic importance of Singapore," it was an important naval base, the focus of vast British interests in China and a great entrepôt of trade and shipping. He also noted that the Japanese army was modernizing, and that the situation in Europe might not permit the British to dispatch large bodies of reinforcement to Asia. As the British should not rely on China (too weak) or America (too unreliable), Montgomery-Massingberd argued, they should immediately strengthen the defence of Hong Kong.[95]

Montgomery-Massingberd suggested that only the Royal Navy was currently taking measures to shore up Hong Kong defence. The RAF could send more planes only after 1938, and the air bases planned by the Air Ministry were all located outside the Gin Drinker's Line. Thus, Montgomery-Massingberd argued that the army had to do more. He adopted a typical bureaucratic approach, first outlining

Table 20   Budget for the improvement of Hong Kong defence (Army), 1936–1940

Within the terms of the Washington Treaty		
Capital Defences		**(£)**
	3 x 9.2-inch batteries (8 guns in total)*	558,000
	3 x 6-inch batteries (6 guns in total)	228,000
	2 x 4.7-inch batteries (4 guns in total)	29,000
	Rangefinders	60,000
	Communications	80,000
	Defence Electric Lights (DELS)	32,000
	Landward Defences	168,000
	Beach Defences	15,000
	AA Defences	220,000
	Magazines	100,000
	Misc. Stores	3,000
	Accommodations for Engineers and Artillerymen	476,000
	Equipment and Animals	28,000
	Infantry Barracks (4 battalions)	1,450,000
	Hospital	100,000
Recurrent annual expenditure on personnel		
	Lower Colonial Establishment, LCE	156,000
	Higher Colonial Establishment, HCE	80,000
	1 x Indian Battalion	78,000
Total		**3,863,000**
Possible additions if Washington Treaty was abrogated		
	1 x 15-inch battery*	698,000
	1 x 9.2-inch battery*	44,000
	Close Defences	10,000
	ACMB equipment^ and DELS	51,000
	Additional AA guns	66,000
	Additional accommodations for RA and RE	142,000
Personnel	RE and RA	60,000
Total		**1,071,000**

*   With ammunition

^   Anti-coastal motorboat

a lavish plan that involved ten infantry battalions. The objective of this plan was to protect the airfields outside the main defence line. He then proposed a "practical" plan that involved only six battalions. The objective was to hold Hong Kong Island only.[96] The budget for this plan for five years (from 1936 to 1940) was £3,863,000, more or less the cost of a King George V Class battleship (Table 20).[97] The cost of the Gin Drinker's Line, under the heading of "landward defence," was £168,000.

Thus, the line was built because it was a cheap way to make up for the numerical deficiency of the defenders.[98]

As the restrictions of the Washington Treaty on the coastal defence of Asian ports were lifted, the Defence Requirement Committee earmarked £300,000 per annum for East of Suez ports, except Singapore, in early 1936. The total amount allotted was £2,893,000, which would be paid in ten years until 1946. Another £150,000 each year was allotted to ports West of Suez. In December 1936, the War Office asked for an increase of the budget for the eastern ports to £750,000, so that the rearmament would be finished by 1940 to 1941.[99] At that time, the garrison units in Hong Kong were all switched to Higher Colonial Establishment, which means they were fully manned. Although the actual provision was not yet settled, the British had at last decided to invest in Hong Kong defence.

The Hong Kong Defence Scheme of 1936

As London gradually settled its Hong Kong policy and authorized the Gin Drinker's Line programme, Major General Arthur Bartholomew, the General Officer Commanding Hong Kong, drafted a new defence scheme to accommodate the new situation. In the section "Reasons for Undertaking Defence," it was suggested that Hong Kong was a "naval base," a "base for further operations" and an "important commercial port," the loss of which would be "a serious blow to our prestige."[100] The goal of the defenders would be to hold Hong Kong and to protect its naval facilities throughout the 54-day "period before relief" against a Japanese invasion.[101]

The scheme was based on the current garrison, which consisted of four infantry battalions plus the Hong Kong Volunteer Defence Corps. It was estimated that Hong Kong would be attacked by battleships and air force. The scheme scaled down the size of the first wave of the invading force to one division, as it argued that anything larger than that would be easily detected and attacked by British cruisers and submarines from Hong Kong. The scheme also predicted that the Japanese would attack southward from the New Territories, after landing at Starling Inlet or Mirs Bay. A Japanese landing directly on Hong Kong Island, under extensive naval and air cover, was also seen as possible.[102]

To protect Victoria Harbour and Hong Kong, the two entrances of the harbour and the coastline of Hong Kong Island were designated as defended areas. On the mainland, the Kowloon Ridge was a focal point of defenders and would be protected by "permanent concrete works." However, "protracted resistance on it (the Ridge) will be difficult," as it was too long. Thus, the defenders on the mainland should try to impose maximum delay when the enemy had landed. A small number of troops would be delegated to ambush the Japanese forces, while a large mobile reserve would be kept.[103]

The scheme outlined the communication and logistics arrangements in minute detail, together with the deployment and operational plans for each formation. With only four battalions at his disposal, Bartholomew decided to make full use of the Gin Drinker's Line. He divided the garrison into two parts, with the Mainland Brigade (three battalions) being deployed along the line and the Island Command (one battalion) defending Hong Kong Island. The HKVDC would be dispersed to man the pillboxes. The mobile artillery would be allotted to the Mainland Brigade. The Japanese were expected to advance along the Kowloon-Canton Railway and the Frontier Road (modern-day Castle Peak Road) and attack the line from two directions. The Mainland Brigade was ordered to resist at the landing site and impose delay on the enemy, exploiting the terrain along the way. He particularly noted the need to conserve manpower through "remarkable qualities of command and control."[104] The battle for the line was seen by the scheme as the "final battle" of the Mainland Brigade, where it would "fight the issue out to a finish in the Inner Line, which is organised in considerable depth for that purpose."[105] If the line was breached, the mainland garrison was expected to "dispute to the last man and the last round [in] the Line of Passes, such as Customs Pass, Tate's Pass, Grasscutters Pass, and Shatin Pass."[106]

The 1936 defence scheme was a rather extreme plan. It contained no provisions for the withdrawal of the mainland garrison to Hong Kong Island, envisioning a "last stand" style of battle. However, the adoption of this approach by Bartholomew by no means suggests that he was complacent about the Gin Drinker's Line. On the contrary, Bartholomew was aware of the inadequacy of using a small garrison to hold it. In 1936, he even supported the idea of holding informal talks with Li Zongren, the Governor of Guangxi, who had approached the British with the plan of sending Chinese troops to relieve Hong Kong should the Japanese attack.[107] However, John Dill, the Director of Military Operations (DMO), suggested that the idea of "a secret entente" with the southwestern Chinese was "not only impracticable but highly dangerous" as it might entice the Japanese to take overt action.[108] When he left Hong Kong in April 1938, Bartholomew urged the War Office to increase the garrison to eight battalions and five squadrons of aircraft.[109] Bartholomew's extreme approach was probably the only viable plan for a reduced garrison: a last stand inflicting serious enemy losses would cause the least damage to British prestige, even if capitulation was inevitable.

Hong Kong as "Outpost": The Far Eastern Appreciation of 1937 and the Refortification Plan of 1938

In a memo submitted to the Defence Requirement Committee in October 1935, the COS admitted that Hong Kong had already fallen into the "effective range" of the Japanese forces.[110] To defend Hong Kong became increasingly difficult. In January 1936, Japan signed the Anti-Communist Accord with Germany; although Britain was not identified openly as an enemy, a Japanese-German alliance looked menacing enough. A year later, the JPC finished a comprehensive study (the Far Eastern Appreciation of 1937) on possible British strategy in a war against Japan and/or Germany. One of the authors of the report was Captain Thomas Phillips,[111] the Director of Naval Plans and a strong supporter of the War Memorandum (Eastern). The disagreement between Captain Phillips and Wing Commander Arthur Harris of the RAF over the defensibility of Hong Kong would shape the defence of the colony in the years before 1941.

The Far Eastern Appreciation stated that the best way of defeating Japan was through blockade. Such a process might take as long as two or more years. Another way was to eliminate the Japanese fleet, which might avoid battle and turn the conflict into a war of attrition. The report highlighted the strength of the Japanese air force, and questioned the feasibility of using Hong Kong as an offensive base because of its vulnerability against air attack. The plan of establishing bases north of Hong Kong was seen as impracticable for the same reason. As the Royal Navy had to deal with threats from Germany and Italy in European waters, the report substantially lengthened the "period before relief" for Hong Kong, from 44 to 90 days.[112]

Although the potential value of Hong Kong as a naval base was still acknowledged, the memorandum admitted that the situation was declining:

> Reserves of war material and food in Hong Kong are at present held for 60 days. If the arrival of the fleet was delayed appreciably beyond 60 days and the Japanese had completely cut sea communication to Hong Kong, the position of the garrison would become precarious apart from direct Japanese attacks . . .
>
> The present weakness of our fixed and AA defences and lack of defending aircraft render the base facilities open to attack by naval bombardment as well as sea-borne and shore-based air attack. Even if other naval requirements do not permit the Japanese to employ a heavy scale of naval bombardment, the damage which could be inflicted by carrier-borne and shore-based air attack during the period of six weeks, which will probably elapse before the arrival of the British Fleet, will probably be sufficient to make it virtually useless as a repair base, and might deprive us of the great proportion of reserves of material held at Hong Kong.[113]

Thus, whether the British fleet would be sent to Hong Kong depended entirely on the prevailing situation and the experience against Japanese air attack. If the reinforcement fleet was deemed too weak to challenge the Japanese battle fleet, then it would be used only to extract the garrison, and Hong Kong would be abandoned. If Hong Kong was captured before that, the report warned against any hasty attempt to recapture it.

As British intelligence revealed that Japanese bombers were able to reach Hong Kong directly from Taiwan, the JPC abandoned the plan of attacking the Japanese landing convoy with the China Station. If Japan intervened during an Anglo-German war, the China fleet, including the submarines, would withdraw to Singapore. The report also recommended moving the China garrison (the battalion in North China) to Hong Kong and storing war materials in the colony. Hong Kong would not be reinforced until the main fleet arrived, and would be treated as an "outpost" that should be held as long as possible.[114]

The Far Eastern Appreciation had little faith in the Gin Drinker's Line, which was still being built:

> From Starling Inlet the Japanese are likely to advance along the road, via Fanling, towards Kowloon, some 19 miles distant. The valley connecting Starling Inlet and Fanling is one of the few open areas in the Leased Territory. The country between Fanling and Kowloon has few communications and facilitates guerrilla and delaying tactics by small bodies, though it also makes protracted resistance on an extended front difficult because, given time, attacking troops could use the broken ground to facilitate penetration or outflanking operation. The Japanese may, therefore, feel confident with their superior strength that they will at least have established contact with our final defensive position (the Gin Drinker's Line) within 2 or 3 weeks of landing.
>
> The Japanese may well have as much as a division with which to attack the Gin Drinker's Line and are not likely to anticipate much delay in capturing it, whether they use their superior numbers in a frontal attack or to turn the flanks by landings in rear of the position ... (However) the capture of the Island from the mainland may prove a difficult operation if the bulk of our troops succeed in withdrawing and reorganising; but as the Japanese were in procession of the Kowloon area, the naval base could be commanded by their medium howitzers and the whole of Hong Kong Island would be within range of their medium guns.[115]

To deal with a landward attack, two to three battalions should be used to conduct mobile defence in the area between Starling Inlet and the Gin Drinker's Line. At least six battalions would be needed to resist in the line for "some considerable time." Without six battalions, the line could be used only for a delaying action and the garrison should retreat to Hong Kong Island. The JPC also noted the need to extend the right flank of the line, in order to prevent a flanking attack from Tide Cove.[116]

The report discussed in detail the problem of reinforcing Hong Kong during an Anglo-German war. It first outlined the benefits of such a move:

- The powers of resistance of our garrison will be materially increased by such reinforcements and by the elimination of the possibility of any complete surprise.
- During the period before the Japanese declaration of war, we may have time to ship appreciable additional supplies to Hong Kong to increase the time for which the fortress can hold out against investment [siege].
- Though we may assume that Japan will not declare war on us unless she believes that the USSR and the USA will remain neutral, the action of these Powers must remain uncertain and the intervention of either might enable us to hold Hong Kong successfully.
- Any increase in the powers of resistance of Hong Kong would mean an increase in the scope of the Japanese expedition, which implies a greater liability in the event of Soviet or American intervention.
- Only while we remain in possession of Hong Kong can we hope in time of war to exercise material influence in China and to encourage Chinese resistance to Japan.

The move, however, had a number of drawbacks:

- Apart from the chance of the intervention of the USSR or the USA, it appears very uncertain whether the reinforced garrison could hold out against Japanese attacks until the fleet reaches Singapore. It is also uncertain whether the fleet will be strong enough even to cover the evacuation of Hong Kong.
- It is most unlikely that the fleet will be strong enough to make any use of the base at Hong Kong even if we succeeded in holding it and preserving its facilities under air attack.
- There is therefore a grave risk that whatever reinforcements are added to the garrison at Hong Kong will be sacrificed possibly to no useful purpose.
- Shifting the China battalions [two at the time the JPC was writing the memorandum] to Hong Kong and keeping only four battalions at the colony could divert fresh troops to more important fronts.
- The dispatch of any air forces to reinforce Hong Kong, and, if so, in what strength, must depend upon whether the full requirements of Singapore and other theatres have been previously satisfied. This possibility is remote.[117]

While the JPC acknowledged the need to hold Hong Kong to draw the attention of the United States and the USSR and to encourage Chinese resistance against Japan, the danger of losing the reinforcement together with the colony and the impossibility of protecting Hong Kong from air attack are also noted. Still, the JPC, possibly under the influence of the Royal Navy's representative, insisted on maintaining Hong Kong, due to the following "political and psychological" factors:

- If Japan was uncertain whether our war with Germany would give her the chance she is awaiting in the Far East, the withdrawal of four battalions from China [including Hong Kong] might convince her that her opportunity had come and might thus precipitate hostilities.
- The withdrawal might be interpreted in China as a confession of weakness and thus destroy our political influence in that country.
- The approved garrison at Hong Kong is six battalions. An essential feature of the plans for its defence has always been delaying action in the Leased Territory, which presupposes a garrison of at least four battalions. If at a time when war with Japan seems possible the garrison is not only not reinforced, but is even reduced, the troops may well feel that they are not being given a fighting chance, with the consequent effect on their morale.
- The moral effect on the British nationals and the Asiatic population in Hong Kong of a reduction of the garrison, which will inevitably be regarded as desertion in the circumstances envisaged, must also be taken into account.[118]

Thus, instead of reducing the garrison, the battalions in China should be sent to Hong Kong if an Anglo-German war broke out. Given its "political and psychological" importance, Hong Kong was not merely an "outpost," but a symbol that could attract Chinese, American and even Soviet cooperation. This argument was to be repeated numerous times between 1937 and 1941 and was the most forceful one for holding and reinforcing the colony.

The report was signed only by Captain Phillips and the army representative. A minority report was attached, written and signed by Arthur Harris, who rejected the above arguments. He suggested that, as Hong Kong could not be used as a base against Japan, it should be demilitarized:

> We should now face more frankly the question of the defensibility of Hong Kong. In the campaign envisaged, the position of Hong Kong cannot be regarded as other than parlous in the extreme. By holding it we are giving a hostage to fortune. In attempting to retrieve that hostage we may well jeopardize the very limited resources wherewith otherwise we can hardly fail to achieve eventual victory, resources which, in any case, might subsequently be essential to our security elsewhere.
>
> It is admitted that Hong Kong cannot hold out by itself indefinitely against operations on a serious scale. Even if it does hold out it is highly debatable whether it would be usable for the major purpose for which we might require it as an advanced naval operational base.
>
> We have, therefore, to face three alternatives:

- We must be prepared either to lose Hong Kong with its garrison after a comparatively short period, or
- We shall be forced to undertake operations for its relief.
- The final alternative is to declare Hong Kong an open port and to evacuate the garrison either before or at the inception of the war.

This course would certainly involve loss of prestige in the Far East generally, and in China in particular, possibly even to an extent which His Majesty's Government may consider unacceptable. It is, however, at least arguable whether, in an attempt to avert this lesser loss of prestige, we should accept the risk of the much greater loss of prestige which would ensue upon military defeat in an unsuccessful effort to defend Hong Kong.

To put Hong Kong in a reasonable state of defence, it would, in my opinion, require an effort and expenditure greatly in excess of that required for Singapore. Even then its geographical situation is such that, if indeed it were possible to secure it against capture or investment, it is impossible, in my opinion, to defend it against air attack by the Japanese air force to an extent which would prevent its profitable use as an operational naval base.

With regard to the related question of our trade with China, which has a bearing on alternative 3, our Chinese trade is but two percent of our total world trade. Whether Hong Kong is held, or not, the major proportion of that trade with China must suffer seriously, if not be held in abeyance, for the duration of any such a campaign.

To sum up, I am of the opinion that neither on the score of military necessity, practicability, prestige or trade necessity, are we justified in an attempt to hold (still lesser to use) Hong Kong in the face of determined attack by Japan.[119]

The planners chose to risk the loss of the Hong Kong garrison rather than give up the colony. In retrospect, the decision led in part to the loss of over 13,500 servicemen (roughly an entire division) in December 1941. However, it was in 1938 by no means an unreasonable course of action, as abandoning the colony might have led to a chain of events more disastrous than losing Hong Kong and its garrison. Abandoning Hong Kong before the war might have weakened the Chinese resistance against Japan and even convinced Chiang Kai-shek that the Anglo-American powers could do nothing to help him. Such a conviction might have led to the collapse of Chinese resistance, allowing the Japanese a free hand in tackling the Soviet Union in the north or the Anglo-American-Dutch-French possessions in the south. Thus, although Harris's idea was militarily more practical, it was politically short-sighted.

To prevent the gloomy view of Harris from affecting the dominions, this report was omitted in copies sent to Australia and New Zealand.[120] Harris was the first British officer since 1919 openly to reject the entire War Memorandum (Eastern) and the need to defend Hong Kong. As the efficiency of the Japanese air force remained uncertain, it seems that abandoning Hong Kong was too radical an idea and overlooked the potential political and psychological consequences. On the other hand, without any control of the air, the survivability of the garrison was in question. The Appreciation of 1937 revealed that, while the planners were aware of the problems of Hong Kong defence, little could be done because of limited resources and the impossibility of providing an adequate air cover.

The Appreciation of 1937 overthrew the Defence Scheme of 1936. The former proposed that the Gin Drinker's Line should not be the "final position" but only a temporary defence line; the defenders should focus on Hong Kong Island. This policy lasted until November 1941, when the Canadian reinforcement arrived.

In July 1937, the CID authorized the COS to discuss "in principle" whether Hong Kong should be rearmed or demilitarized.[121] None of the services, however, was willing to state openly that Hong Kong should be "abandoned." Sir Cyril Deverell, the CIGS, argued that he had "always felt that it was impossible to consider giving up Hong Kong," but "the problem of defence against shore-based air attack had never been properly faced," and "it was extremely difficult to make the place impregnable in view of the danger of attack by land and air from the landward side."[122] Lord Chatfield, the First Sea Lord and Chief of Naval Staff, argued that, while the Royal Navy might not be able to use its facilities, it was necessary to deny them to the Japanese. Moreover, once the decision of demilitarization was made, it would be "impossible later on to reverse it." He also noted the possibility that Japan might be weakened during a Sino-Japanese conflict, and China might be able to offer help.[123] Sir Cyril Newall, the Chief of Air Staff, suggested that, while the Joint Overseas and Home Defence Sub-committee was examining what was required to fortify Hong Kong for 90 days, other departments should be invited to investigate the implications of demilitarizing Hong Kong. Then the JPC could set forth to examine the issue.[124]

Before the Joint Overseas and Home Defence Sub-committee had completed its study, however, the situation changed drastically again. From July to December 1937, the Sino-Japanese conflict had escalated into a general war. In November, the KMT forces suffered a devastating defeat in the Shanghai-Nanjing area and were forced to withdraw inland. On 12 December, Japanese aircraft sank USS *Panay* near Nanjing. Six days later, the Foreign Office asked the COS to comment on the situation of Hong Kong. The Foreign Office believed that, if the Japanese captured Guangzhou, Hong Kong would be rendered "useless" and "untenable." Any attempt to demilitarize the colony, however, would damage the British position in Asia and the world. It was also impossible to ask the Americans for help.[125]

The COS held an emergency meeting to discuss the issue. The services believed that, while Japan could easily take Guangzhou and stop China from importing munitions from Hong Kong, the situation would be largely the same, as it was well known that the Japanese would attack from the land border. The COS also pointed out that Hong Kong had been a serious problem ever since the end of the Anglo-Japanese Alliance. This was a subtle criticism against the Foreign Office, which had supported ending the alliance. Although the decision to hold Hong Kong would not have changed, the garrison would lose a number of advantages if Guangzhou fell:

- The defenders could not attack the invading convoy;
- The RAF could not harass the landing;
- The invaders could reach (and overcome) the Gin Drinker's Line much earlier than the estimated twenty days;
- The Japanese could launch an aerial attack against Hong Kong as soon as hostilities began.[126]

Britain could do little to ease the Japanese pressure on Hong Kong, besides shortening the time of arrival of the British main fleet (only if Europe remained quiet). The idea of immediately reinforcing the garrison to six battalions was rejected, as this might "merely result in a greater sacrifice of life."[127] The COS judged that it was unlikely for Japan to start a war against Britain solely for Hong Kong, as she was fighting an expensive war against China and had to guard against the Soviet Union in Manchuria. On the other hand, it was impossible to prevent the Japanese from strangling the Hong Kong economy through a blockade.[128] The year of 1937 ended in peace, but the problem of Hong Kong defence was greater than ever.

The Joint Overseas and Home Defence Sub-committee finally submitted the Hong Kong Refortification memorandum to the CID in March 1938. To hold Hong Kong for 90 days, the sub-committee put forward three levels of defences:

> Standard A: that required to protect the harbour, with its facilities, so that it might be used by the main fleet as a base on its arrival (£23,326,000);
>
> Standard B: that required to give sufficient protection to the harbour, with the necessary facilities to enable it to be used as a base for submarines and small craft (£18,236,000);
>
> Standard C: that required to deny the use of the anchorage to an enemy (£4,940,000).[129]

At that time, over £5,181,000 had already been earmarked for rearmament projects in Hong Kong (of which £2,620,000 was actually disbursed from 1935). This amount already exceeded the amount required for Standard C.[130]

As the Japanese could send bombers directly from Taiwan and attack from the land frontier, it was necessary to have a larger garrison operating in the New Territories and additional air bases for more fighters if the port facilities had to be protected. The Standard A plan proposed building two airfields in the New

Territories and to protect them with part of the garrison. The coastal guns would also be enlarged substantially to deter naval attacks. The total forces and equipment needed for Standard A would be as follows:

Army
- Eight infantry battalions; three artillery brigades; one engineers company
- Four 15-inch guns; nine 9.2-inch guns (new mountings); thirty-six 6-inch guns
- Sixty-four 3.7- and 4.5-inch AA guns; seventy-two light AA

Navy
- Submarine boom; mines, shell-proof stores; underground oil tanks; underground magazine; concrete submarine pen

Air Force
- Airfields at Pat Heung, Ha Tsuen, Kwanti and Kam Tin
- Heavy machinery for repairing the landing strips; concrete for RAF Kai Tak[131]

Distribution
  Army: £13,100,000; Navy: £1,634,000; RAF: £6,092,000

Standard B was similar to Standard A, only without the 15-inch guns and some of the anti-aircraft guns. Both plans were massive in scale. As they were obviously too large to be implemented, the intention of the committee was clear: to recommend the more "realistic" Standard C. The aim of the Standard C plan was to prevent the Japanese from using the anchorage by holding Hong Kong Island. The Gin Drinker's Line would be used only for delaying purposes. The garrison would be expanded to six battalions and the anti-aircraft armament would be substantially increased. The RAF, however, had no role in this plan:

Army
- Six infantry battalions; two artillery brigades; one engineers company
- Five 9.2-inch guns (new mountings); three 9.2-inch guns; twenty 6-inch guns
- Thirty-two 3.7- and 4.5-inch AA guns; twenty-four light AA

Navy
- Minefields and submarine booms

Distribution
  Army: £4,700,000; Navy: £235,000; RAF: £5,000[132]

Although the memorandum did not recommend Standard C, it mentioned the likelihood of a Japanese invasion of Guangzhou, a move that would render the coastal defences irrelevant.[133]

Standard C was supported by the army. General John Gort, the new CIGS, said during a COS meeting in March 1938:

> Our plans for the defence of Hong Kong had always been based on the hypothesis of a landing attack by the Japanese on the mainland in the neighbourhood probably of Starling Inlet, but this hypothesis was really somewhat academic. The most serious problem at Hong Kong was that of intensive air attack on the closely packed urban areas in Kowloon and the Island, and this contingency had never been squarely faced. For the complete defence of the colony, a very large garrison and very heavy expenditure would be required, and these were, under present conditions, outside the range of practical politics. Therefore the best solution of the problem would be to base our defensive plans on a retirement to the Island. The Gin-Drinker's Line should only be held lightly, and the garrison would retire back, destroying the base facilities on the mainland. It is not only impossible, but also valueless, to try to hold the Gin-Drinker's Line to the end, since in any case the naval base would be subjected to shelling from the land and heavy aerial bombing. In these circumstances we should spend no more money on the installations of batteries and defences on the mainland at least until we knew what the outcome of the present Sino-Japanese war would be.[134]

Chief of Air Staff Newall sided with the army, suggesting that additional aircraft to Hong Kong would be a waste of resources as the Japanese could attack directly from Taiwan. Maurice Hankey, the secretary of the CID and COS, also pointed out that while Hong Kong might be useful, Britain did not have the resources for maintaining two "first-class" bases in Asia.[135] Lord Chatfield, the Chief of Naval Staff, insisted to invest in Hong Kong, at least preserving the plan of defending the Gin Drinker's Line:

> [I] recalled that the COS had very carefully considered the question of Hong Kong when their Far East Appreciation had been drawn up. They had decided that ... Hong Kong might possibly be able to hold out against attack on the Gin-Drinker's Line and that in these circumstances, on the arrival of the Fleet, the base could be used for further operations in the China Seas. Alternatively, the garrison might be driven back on to the Island, in which case they thought it would be possible for the Fleet to relieve it. All their plans had been drawn up accordingly with the idea of sending the Fleet out as quickly as possible to cut the Japanese line of communication with their home bases. [I] doubted very much whether air attack would in fact destroy the naval base facilities, particularly if proper anti-aircraft defences were installed. If it were now proposed to

destroy the base facilities ourselves and retire to the Island without seriously attempting to defend them, there would be no point in sending out the Fleet to Hong Kong at all.[136]

He also argued that, if the strength of the Royal Navy were to be cut down, outlying bases like Hong Kong should be strengthened to offset the weakness. However, he too recommended only that the existing projects be continued, such as the Gin Drinker's Line and relocation of batteries, and left the responsibility of abandoning Hong Kong to the two services by asking them to study the issue again.[137]

In May, the army submitted another report, opposing again any additional investment. The report reiterated that, as the Japanese could subdue Hong Kong from the air, the colony could no longer ease the military pressure faced by Singapore. In addition, the Gin Drinker's Line was too close to Kowloon to prevent the Japanese from shelling Victoria Harbour. As for the line itself, the army found a number of defects:

> A considerable amount of work has been done to provide machine gun emplacements, defended localities, and barbed wire entanglements. But the line is very long for any probable garrison; it has no depth; it can be outflanked by landings in its rear from the sea; it permits the enemy to be within artillery range of all the vulnerable area; and it has a large and excitable mass of Chinese immediately in its rear at Kowloon.
>
> Once battle is seriously joined, the longer this line is held the greater the chances of a breakthrough and the greater the chaos and suffering of the civilian population in the rear . . .
>
> It is not necessary that we should be in territorial occupation of the base and its facilities in order to deny them to the enemy. Concentration of the defences on the Island itself, using the Inner Line [i.e., the Gin Drinker's Line] for delaying purposes only, would suffice.[138]

If the garrison held only Hong Kong Island, then much money and resources could be saved for building more defences and shell-proof facilities on the island. The enemy would also be forced to launch frontal attacks against the island, and the responsibility of taking care of civilians in Kowloon would be shifted to the Japanese. Only four battalions and some additional field guns would be needed to hold the island.[139]

In the same month, the RAF released a similar report. However, to avoid being accused of "abandoning Hong Kong," the RAF maintained its "plan" of sending a squadron of seaplanes or close-support planes, promising that surplus planes could be sent in a few years' time.[140]

The Royal Navy finally backed down in July 1938, allowing the COS to change the defence policy. The new COS report suggested that "the present programme for the development of the Defences of Hong Kong will not fulfil the requirement of [the new] policy."[141] It highlighted again the problem of the Gin Drinker's Line and the lack of flat land for air bases within the defence perimeter. The line would be used for delaying purposes only; the garrison would concentrate on the island:

> We do not suggest that there should be no attempt at all to delay an enemy advance over the land frontier. Any resistance on the mainland must inevitably increase the difficulties of the enemy and compel him to employ larger force than he would otherwise have to use. We consider that the general defence scheme for the colony in such a contingency should be to delay the enemy from the frontier to the Gin Drinker's Line, mainly by demolitions, and subsequently to make a temporary stand on the Line itself. Resistance on this Line would not have to be continued long enough to endanger the chances of the infantry garrison retiring to the Island or to cause heavy casualties to the civilian population of Kowloon by the enemy's land bombardment.[142]

The COS proposed moving all the coastal guns to the island. Additional mobile artillery, shell-proof facilities, anti-aircraft guns and ammunition would be sent to defend it. Ongoing work on the Gin Drinker's Line should be finished, but new works would be cancelled. The COS indirectly admitted that little could be done to ease the air pressure as it suggested that strengthening Malaya might ease the air pressure faced by Hong Kong. The report warned that "it will be essential to keep secret the intention not to hold to the last the Gin Drinker's Line."[143] When Major General Arthur Grasett was appointed the General Officer Commanding Hong Kong in 1938, he was warned not to disclose this new policy.[144]

As a result of the COS report of July 1938, the defence scheme of Hong Kong changed from holding both Kowloon and Hong Kong Island to holding the island only. The Gin Drinker's Line, previously seen as the "Inner Line" and a final defensive position, was designated as a delaying position. The Foreign Office and the Colonial Office also shared the military's view that the mainland could not be defended. When the KMT government of China offered the sale of the sovereignty of the New Territories, the two ministries were cool to the idea.[145]

On 12 October 1938, as expected by the British military planners, two divisions of the Japanese 21st Army landed in Bias Bay. However, their target was not Hong Kong but Guangzhou. The KMT garrison was overrun in days. The fall of Guangzhou marked further deterioration of the strategic situation of Hong Kong.

Defences in Hong Kong, 1935–1941

The Washington Treaty limited the expansion of the coastal defence of Hong Kong between 1922 and 1936. Still, the British paid some attention to the colony and constructed a number of defence facilities. Among them, the Gin Drinker's Line, sometimes known as the "Maginot Line of the East," was the best known.[146] This section revisits the Gin Drinker's Line and other facilities built during the interwar period.

Gin Drinker's Line

As mentioned, the idea of a "Kowloon defensive line" appeared before the First World War. When the JPC recommended providing concrete defences for the garrison in the early 1930s, Major General Bartholomew started to design the line. In 1935, the Inspector of Fixed Defences, Major General Frederick Barron,[147] submitted a report about the feasibility of the line after visiting Hong Kong.[148] Barron described the state of Hong Kong defence as "deplorable," and identified the most probable form of attack not as seaward invasion, but attempts to capture Kowloon and Hong Kong Island from the landward frontier. Thus, he recommended providing a mobile garrison and a landward defence line in the New Territories.[149]

As a long siege was expected, he stressed the importance of imposing delay on the enemy. He divided the operation in the New Territories into three phases, namely "anti-landing action," "delay action from landing point/border to the main defence position," and the "final position." The so-called "final position" of about 19,200 metres (21,000 yards) was what would become the Gin Drinker's Line. Barron divided the line into four "localities" from left to right. A "locality" was a defended area with positions for all-round fire and mutual support. The lowest level of a locality was one for a platoon; a number of platoon-sized localities formed a company-sized locality; and so on. Thus, the so-called Gin Drinker's Line was not a "line" per se but four battalion-sized localities. This explains the numbering of the pillboxes along the line with initials from "1" to "4" (Table 21; Figure 16).

Table 21 Sections of the Gin Drinker's Line, 1935

Sections	Numbers	Areas
Left	4	Frontier Road near Castle Peak to Golden Hill
Left-Centre	3	Tai Po Road to Shing Mun Valley
Right-Centre	2	One Rise More to Tide Cove
Right	1	Junk Bay to One Rise More

Barron noted that enemy forces might take advantage of broken terrain, fog or darkness to penetrate the line. Thus, in addition to the pillboxes protected by barbed wire, he proposed the establishment of mutually supporting localities around the pillboxes so that, even if the enemy was able to penetrate one location, the entire line could still be held.[150] At least one locality was linked with underground tunnels and communication trenches—the Shing Mun Redoubt south of the Shing Mun Reservoir (Figure 16).

Barron believed that at least four battalions were required to man the line; among them, three would be constantly at the front with one as the reserve. The battalions responsible for the delaying action in the New Territories would also join the garrison of the line, making a total of six battalions available. In February 1937, the garrison began referring to the line officially as the "Inner Line," to distinguish it from the Hong Kong–China border (the "Outer Line") and the "Intermediate Position" between the two.[151]

Surviving archival sources only outline the construction process and the scale of the line. An undated note titled "Work Completed on Gin Drinker's Line" suggests that the first pillbox, No. 55, was completed on 20 December 1935. The second pillbox, No. 57, was finished on 4 March 1936. It is possible that the two pillboxes were experimental structures, as five more pillboxes (Nos. 56, 58, 60, 64 and 66) were completed in June 1936 alone—all were on the left sector.[152] More pillboxes

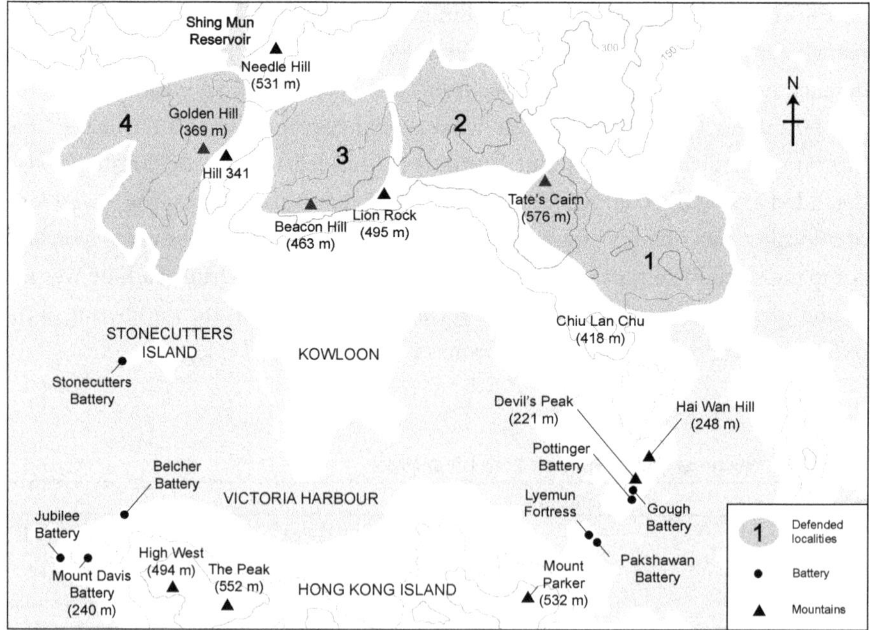

Figure 16   Layout of the Gin Drinker's Line[153]

were built in the next two years. According to another report submitted to the War Office in April 1938, twenty pillboxes were finished by the end of 1937. The annual report of public works for 1937 suggested that the Public Works Department had built three pillboxes (Nos. 53, 54 and 65) and "tunnels."[154] By April 1938, there were thirty-eight pillboxes completed, nineteen half-finished, and another thirty-three in a state of 85 percent completion. Nine splinter-proof headquarters were finished or almost finished, with two more half-finished. Three observation posts (OP), located at Shing Mun Redoubt, Smugglers' Ridge and Crown Point, were all finished. By then, barbed wire and apron fences were already erected at the Shing Mun Redoubt and some of the sectors.[155]

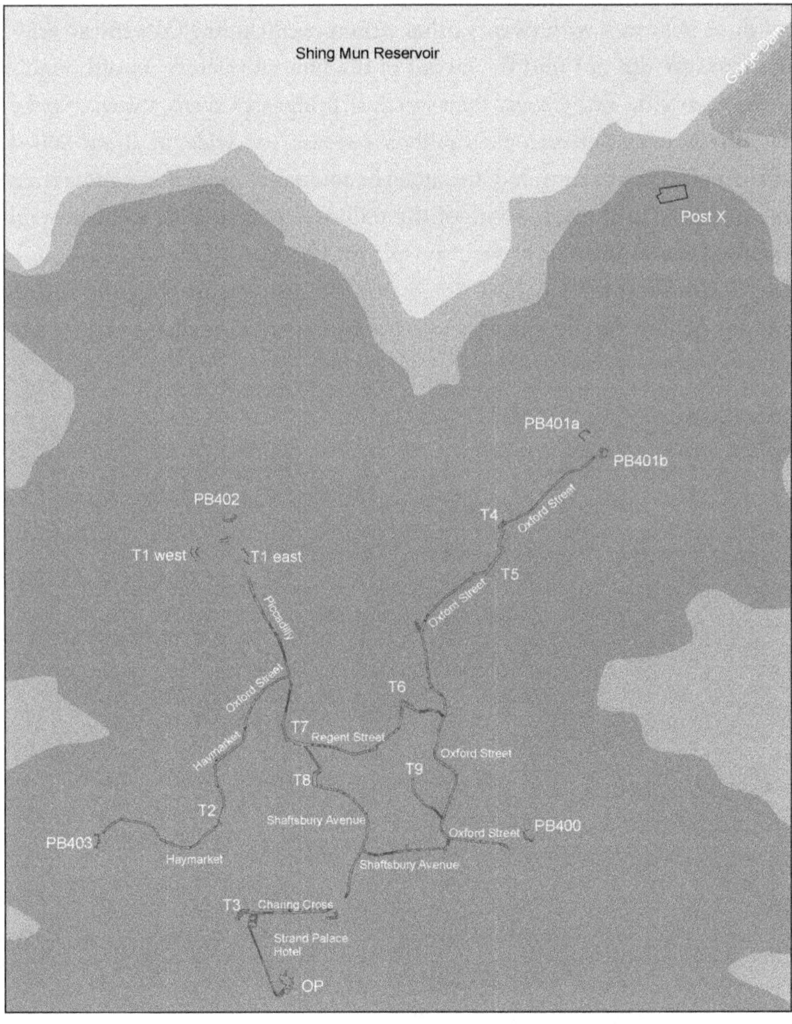

Figure 17   Shing Mun Redoubt, December 1941 (layout courtesy of Prof. Lawrence Lai)[156]

Since General Bartholomew's proposal has yet to be found, the total number of pillboxes planned remains unknown. However, Japanese sources and recent research allow us to discover the actual layout of the line and the number of pillboxes built. Japanese military engineers counted ninety-four *tochika* (pillboxes) after they captured the line. Headquarters, observation posts and bunkers are treated separately in the Japanese report, as only those with a British-assigned number (i.e., "PB 419") were treated as *tochika*. However, the progress report of the War Office in 1938 mentioned only ninety pillboxes, eleven headquarters and three observation posts. Of the pillboxes found by the Japanese, twenty-seven were found in the right sector, twenty-three in the centre-right, sixteen in the centre-left and twenty-eight in the left. Using aerial photographs and site inspections, Lawrence Lai and his team found ninety-three pillboxes, with twenty other structures including OPs and so on.[157]

The Japanese did not find the layout of the line satisfactory as, although many pillboxes had wide firing arcs, their vertical firing arcs were always blocked by terrain. The spacing between each pillbox was also too wide, at about 500–1,000 metres. If a pillbox was captured, the attacker could find more blind spots from pillboxes nearby.[158] In addition, some of the pillboxes were unable to blend with the surrounding environment and were conspicuous because of their half-hearted camouflage.[159] However, the Japanese noted that the concrete used by the British was of superior quality. As the line was half-finished, it is impossible to know whether

Figure 18   Pillbox disguised as a house (PB 305)[160]

these defects would have been rectified if the British had not suspended the project in 1938.

Island Defence

A large number of defences were built between 1935 and 1941 on the island, including a number of new batteries. The idea of reorganizing the batteries in Hong Kong was first put forward by Barron, whose plan was as follows:[161]

High Junk: 2 x 9.2-inch Mk X, 35°

Stanley: 3 x 9.2-inch Mk X, 35°

Mount Davis: 3 x 9.2-inch Mk X, 15°

Lyemun: 2 x 4.7-inch BL

Centurion: 2 x 4.7-inch Mk IX

Pakshawan: 2 x 6-inch Mk VII, 15°

Stonecutters Island: 3 x 6-inch Mk VII, 15°

Jubilee: 3 x 6-inch Mk VII, 15°

Cape Collinson: 3 x 6-inch Mk VII, 15°

In 1935, the War Office modified Barron's plan by moving two 6-inch BLs from the Cape Collinson and Jubilee batteries to Hallowes Hill of Sai Kung, and relocating the 4.7-inch guns to Chung Hom Kok and Port Shelter.[162] The works for the new Stanley Battery had already begun around the same time.[163] As the COS decided to concentrate on the island, the works on the batteries in the New Territories and Kowloon ceased in July 1938 (Figure 19). The 9.2-inch BLs for the proposed High Junk Battery were relocated to the Bokhara Battery at Cape D'Aguilar, which was finished in 1941. The guns in Stanley Battery were mounted on the new 35-degree mountings, which could be turned towards the mainland and cover as far as Tai Mo Shan. By 1941, the coastal guns were reorganized as follows (Figure 20):

Bokhara: 2 x 9.2-inch Mk X, 15°

Stanley: 3 x 9.2-inch Mk X, 35°

Mount Davis: 3 x 9.2-inch Mk X, 15°

Chung Hom Kok: 2 x 4.7-inch BL

Pakshawan: 2 x 6-inch Mk VII, 15°

Stonecutters Island: 2 x 6-inch Mk VII, 15°

Jubilee: 3 x 6-inch Mk VII, 15°

Chung Hom Kok: 2 x 6-inch Mk VII, 15°

Bluff Head: 2 x 6-inch Mk VII, 15°

Upper Belcher: 1 x 6-inch Mk VII, 15°

Cape Collinson: 2 x 6-inch Mk VII, 15°

Figure 19   Removing 9.2-inch guns from Devil's Peak (Tim Ko)

In addition to the coastal guns, a large number of defensive structures were built on the island, such as the headquarters in Wong Nai Chung Gap, the magazine in Shouson Hill and the pillboxes along the coast. By 1938, over fifty pillboxes and "splinter-proofs" (pillboxes with thinner walls) were built on the island, with a total number of 120 machine-guns, including the PB01, which inflicted serious losses on the Japanese Army in 1941 (Table 22). New anti-aircraft batteries were also built in Mount Davis, Kellett Bay, Brick Hill, Wong Nai Chung, Stanley, Sai Wan and Chung Hom Kok. Although there were plans to send more anti-aircraft guns to Hong Kong, they were not realized before the Japanese invasion. By 1941, the fixed anti-aircraft defences in Hong Kong were as follows:

Mount Davis: 3.7-inch x 2   Kellett Bay: 4.5-inch x 2
Brick Hill: 3-inch x 2   Wong Nai Chung: 3.7-inch x 2
Stanley: 3-inch x 2   Sai Wan: 3-inch x 4
Chung Hom Kok: 3-inch x 2

The Hong Kong Battle-Box

As British planners had predicted that Hong Kong would face intensive air attack, they decided to build an underground command post, called "Battle-box," below the Combined Service Headquarters (CSHQ) at modern-day Admiralty for the

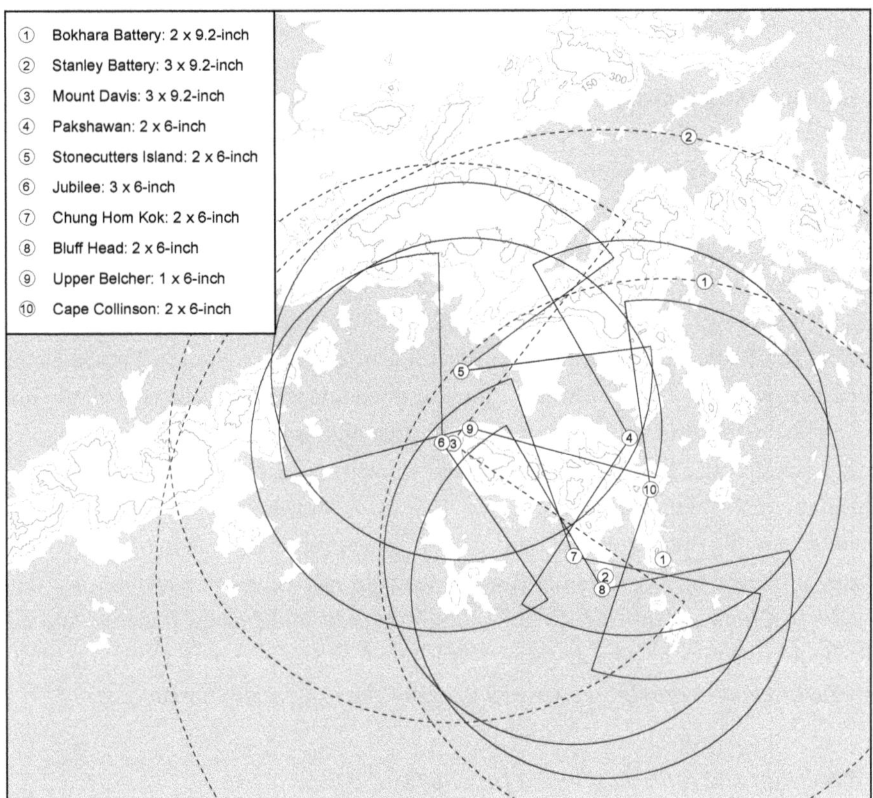

Figure 20   Coastal and AA guns in Hong Kong, 1941[164]

Table 22   Coastal defences on Hong Kong Island, 1938[165]

Area	Pillboxes	Splinter-proofs	Machine-guns
Right	4	15	42
Centre	3	13	34
Left	9	11	46
Total	16	39	122

garrison in 1935. When the CSHQ became operational two years later, the Battle-box was still in the process of being wired and ventilated; it was not ready until 1940. Its construction cost was supposedly divided among the three services equally, but the RAF refused to pay as much as the others from 1937 as it realized that its role was limited in Hong Kong.[166]

The Battle-box was between 8.5 and 15.5 metres underground, with a total floor area of 16,145 square feet (or 1,500 square metres). It was slightly larger than the Fort Canning Battle-box of Singapore. It had two entrances, one at the front and another at the rear. The concrete roof had a thickness of 2.28 metres. The structure was protected by a concrete layer of 1.35 metres thick and another layer of soil 1.2 metres thick between the roof and the concrete cover. The outer layers were for absorbing the explosions of shells or aerial bombs. As the Hong Kong Engineering Development Department discovered in 1983, the concrete used was of superior quality; after almost fifty years, no visible cracks were found.[167] The Battle-box had thirty-six rooms, completed with ventilation, generators, batteries, telephone exchange, lavatories, kitchen and other necessary facilities.

As no pre-war floor plan may be found, we are unable to understand the specific use of the Battle-box except as a command post of the garrison during the Battle of Hong Kong in 1941. However, the year it was decided to build the Battle-box coincided with the establishment of the British military signal intelligence (sigint) organization (the Far Eastern Combined Bureau), which had Hong Kong as its headquarters. When the Sino-Japanese War broke out in 1937, the navy had considered moving the Combined Bureau to Singapore for safety reasons. However, the army preferred to stay in Hong Kong as it could intercept radio communications between China and Taiwan. Even if Hong Kong was under siege, the army argued, it should continue to operate there.[168] It is possible that part of the function of the Battle-box was to provide a secure location for the Combined Bureau.

Minefields and Anti-Submarine Defences

As mentioned, from the 1920s it was suggested by naval planners that Hong Kong be equipped with a large number of mines and underwater defences to supplement the coastal guns. While the army was building the Gin Drinker's Line, the navy was also planning a "seaward defence" line. From 1935, the navy started to store submarine mines in Hong Kong. After the European War started, the navy sent a large number of mines, an anti-submarine boom and "indicator loop" to Hong Kong. The third item, invented by the Royal Navy in 1915, was used to detect submarines intruding into harbours or water channels. The loop could send warning signals to defenders and detonate nearby mines to destroy the intruders. The indicator loop at Scapa Flow destroyed an intruding U-boat in 1918. By July 1939, more than 1,250 conventional mines and 480 remote-controlled mines were sent to Hong Kong. In November, most of them were in position, including the indicator loop. The indicator loops resembled a continuous "sea wall" stretching from Lantau Island to Port Shelter through the south side of Lamma Island and Po Toi Islands. In addition, the eastern entrance of Victoria Harbour was protected by an anti-submarine boom; all ships entering and leaving the harbour had to be inspected by boom-control vessels.[169] Although these defences have received limited attention in Hong Kong historiography, together with the coastal guns they proved to be effective defences against the Japanese during the Battle of Hong Kong.

Conclusion

Facing multiple threats across the continents with strained resources, British planners found it increasingly difficult to secure Hong Kong. Instead of the "eastern fortress" envisioned by Governor Hennessy in the 1880s, Hong Kong became an "exposed outpost" by the late 1930s. This reveals the decline in confidence among British planners about the empire's ability to fulfil its global commitments, especially during the difficult financial circumstances of the 1930s. Worse still, the three services had very different ideas about how to defend this far-flung colony. The debate was part of a larger discussion during the interwar period about the potential of air power. As the colony lacked operational depth for containing a land invasion and air space for building an effective air defence with the technology of the time, Hong Kong was seen as especially vulnerable during this period. However, to sustain British rule in many parts of Asia, London had little choice but to retain Hong Kong as a symbol. After 1937, Hong Kong also became the symbol of the British determination to restrain Japan, as well as a more subtle symbol for the British support of Chinese resistance. Because of Hong Kong's political value, British planners devised numerous plans and projects for augmenting the defence of the colony, including construction of the Kai Tak air base, the Gin Drinker's Line and even a seaward defence line. Many of the actions taken during the Battle of Hong Kong in 1941 had already been envisioned by planners during the interwar period. In short, instead of abandoning the colony, the British never stopped planning for the defence of Hong Kong between 1919 and 1939.

6

THE INTERNATIONAL SITUATION AND HONG KONG DEFENCE, 1939–1941

Hong Kong is not a vital interest and the garrison could not long withstand Japanese attack. Even if we had a strong fleet in the Far East, it is doubtful whether Hong Kong could be held now that the Japanese are firmly established on the mainland of China; and it could not be used as an advanced naval base . . . In describing the position in this way, we do not mean to imply that we advocate immediate demilitarisation of Hong Kong, which, if it were undertaken by itself, would involve an incalculable loss of prestige.

—Far East Appreciation, 1940

Repercussions from early fall of Hong Kong would be very serious throughout the Far East. Demonstration at present juncture of our determination to defend Hong Kong would encourage Chinese in their resistance to Japan and would be important feature in our policy of firmness towards Japan which is calculated to reduce likelihood of aggression by her.

—Air Marshal Sir Robert Brooke-Popham, January 1941

The European War and Hong Kong Defence Policy

After the decision to concentrate on the island had been made in July 1938, the problem of Hong Kong defence was shelved. Because of its proximity to the area under Japanese control, Hong Kong became a strategic liability to Britain. The Japanese media openly claimed that Hong Kong had no longer any strategic value to China and Britain after the Japanese forces had captured Hainan Island in February 1939.[1] By then, the colony was surrounded on three sides (Taiwan, Guangzhou and Hainan). The Japanese sent "commercial" parties to the Paracel and Spratly islands and later occupied them openly. A Royal Navy survey ship was sent to observe the islands, but nothing was done after it was found that the islands were too small for aircraft to operate from. The Japanese even showed their ability to attack Hong Kong by bombing the Lo Wu Railway Station on 21 February 1939.[2] To counter the Japanese threat, Britain supported the Chinese Nationalist resistance. In late 1938, the Chiefs of Staff Committee (COS) proposed to offer loans to Chiang Kai-shek to shore up his confidence against the Japanese. It was pointed out that if Chiang surrendered, Britain could do little to protect its interests in Asia.[3]

The British also invited the French to help. Discussions had taken place in 1939 to study the possibility of reinforcing Hong Kong from French Indochina. However, as John Driefort has pointed out, "the British naturally tended to emphasize the role of naval defence in stopping Japan, but Admiral Sir Percy Noble had no fleet. The French stressed military operations to check, but they had no army."[4] Thus, when Anglo-Japanese relations almost reached the breaking point during the Tianjin Incident of June 1939, the COS replied that little could be done against Japan except to send two capital ships to Asia. Hong Kong "would have to be left with its own resources" as the China Station would join the defenders of Singapore.[5] The COS admitted that, unless the United States intervened, Britain could not defend its interests in Asia.[6]

After the Tianjin Incident, Britain was fully occupied by the European War that broke out in September 1939. However, as Japan was severely defeated during the Nomonhon Incident and the Soviets signed a non-aggression pact with Germany, the British gained a respite in Asia.[7] Major General Arthur Grasett, the General Officer Commanding Hong Kong, was still concerned about the state of defence. Grasett was born in Canada and joined the army when he was eighteen. He had served as a staff officer during the First World War in northern France, before being transferred to the General Staff in 1917. After the war, he went to the Staff College before serving in the Indian Army. He then worked in the War Office until 1931, when he was admitted to the Imperial Defence College. The commandant of the college by then was Air Chief Marshal Sir Robert Brooke-Popham, who later became Commander-in-Chief of the Far East from late 1940 to December 1941. Grasett became a brigadier in 1937, and was teaching at the Staff College before being appointed GOC Hong Kong.

Grasett urged the War Office for additional troops as early as May 1939. He believed that, with the two battalions from Shanghai and Tianjin, he could defend the Gin Drinker's Line.[8] In August 1939, he even proposed to Whitehall that, if reinforcements could not be sent, Britain should first ask Japan to sign an agreement renouncing any intention to attack in a given period, then minimize the size of the garrison. By so doing, Grasett argued, Britain could rid itself of a strategic burden. The Foreign Office, as Kent Fedorowich has pointed out, asked Grasett to abandon his "fantasies" and not to intervene in "high politics."[9]

Soon after the outbreak of the war, the Committee for Imperial Defence (CID) extended the "period before relief" for Singapore to 180 days, and asked the colony to store sufficient materials accordingly. The Port Defence Committee (successor of the Joint Overseas and Home Defence Sub-committee) then reconsidered the period before relief for Hong Kong, asking Grasett whether it was possible to store enough provisions for the garrison and the population of Hong Kong Island to last 180 days. Grasett replied that the need to feed the large urban population and the hot and humid weather made storing provisions for 180 days impossible. He suggested that Hong Kong could effectively store provisions for only 130 days.[10] Grasett also mentioned that it was necessary to reinforce the garrison so that it could sustain a long siege. Ammunition storage should also be increased.[11] London again rejected Grasett's request for more troops, but agreed to send more ammunition if the situation in Europe allowed. By then, Hong Kong had over 22,000,000 rounds of .303 rifle and machine-gun rounds and more-than-normal high explosive shells for coastal guns.

Although the Port Defence Committee suggested that the garrison could not be relieved and could only be maintained intermittently by sea transport, Rear Admiral Thomas Phillips, by then the Deputy Chief of the Naval Staff, still suggested that Hong Kong should be defended to the last:

> Hong Kong is our most exposed outpost . . . we should do all we can to defend it without too many arguments; if it comes to war we should man the defences and fight as our forefathers did in many similar positions . . . I believe that an adequate British garrison and adequate defences should make that hidebound nation think very hard.[12]

Although the Royal Navy had conceded to the army and the RAF's position of abandoning the mainland, it did not entirely abandon the idea of using Hong Kong as a base. In early 1939, the RN Plans Division proposed buying the Aberdeen Dockyard and the surrounding land to develop underground magazines, a refuelling facility and a tanker pier. Mid-year, the navy also planned to install temporary batteries at Bluff Head and on Aberdeen Island.[13]

In October 1939, two obscure cases occurred in Hong Kong that highlighted British concern over the state of Hong Kong defence. On 1 October, two Indian troopers from the 5th Battalion, 6th Rajputana Rifles (aged thirty-three and twenty-one) deserted to the Japanese 23rd Army, which was suppressing the guerrillas near Shenzhen. The deserters were sentries along the border post, who had contemplated deserting when they saw the arrival of the Japanese. Although the British had a detailed report on Japanese activities along the border between 1939 and 1941, this event may be found only in the Japanese sources.[14]

The deserters claimed that they were exhausted by the endless trench-digging work and that their colleagues in the battalion were "overawed" by Japanese military prowess and had the impression that they would be seen as "Asian brothers" by the Japanese. As the two men could not read maps, they were considered by the Japanese to be of limited value. They had no idea of the defence scheme, and could only recall that the British officers claimed there were "four Indian and three British regiments, ninety guns, twenty-five aircraft and fifty warships in Hong Kong." Although the Japanese found the information offered of little value, the men were released as they were seen as genuine sympathizers of Japan. The British issued a wanted order through the radio on 6 September; the British consuls at Guangzhou and the British-controlled Municipal Committee of Shamian (Shameen) also sent search parties for the deserters.[15]

When the Indian troopers had gone missing, two soldiers (aged twenty-one and twenty-three) from the 2nd Battalion of the Royal Scots also crossed the border and were arrested by the Japanese on 6 September. The deserters complained of the harsh life; one wished to "return to India to see his wife." According to their "intelligence," the garrison had six regiments, fifty anti-aircraft (AA) guns near a large military airport, thirty bombers, numerous mines, three 16-inch guns on Hong Kong Island and a 6-inch gun every half a mile along the coastline of the island. There was also an Anglo-French fleet of eight cruisers, seven submarines and thirty destroyers, gunboats and auxiliary vessels. The Japanese consul at Guangzhou believed that the two men were not spies, as the British were apparently very nervous about their desertion. They were duly returned to the British after interrogation.

It is interesting to note that the two Royal Scots troopers had not mentioned the Gin Drinker's Line, the Kai Tak Airport and the real facilities at Stonecutters and Hong Kong Island. They also stressed the large number of coastal guns on the island, apparently trying to convey the idea that "any frontal attack against the Island would be dangerous." The scale of defence mentioned by these men is strikingly similar to the Standard A defence proposed by the 1938 Joint Overseas and Home Defence Sub-committee, which was seen as strong enough to deter the Japanese. Moreover, the Rajputana Regiment was immediately sent elsewhere, but the Royal Scots stayed until December 1941. Inferring from above, it is possible that the two Royal Scots troopers were sent by Grasett or one of his intelligence staff such as Colonel Charles Boxer to flood the Japanese with fabricated information, in order to cover possible leakages by the Indian deserters. This episode reveals the precarious position of Hong Kong and the British attempt to hide its weakness.

The Fall of France and Its Impact

In October 1939, the main problem of Hong Kong defence remained unsolved, namely the inability of the British to send a fleet to Asia. After London had decided to extend the period before relief for Hong Kong to 130 days, the situation in Europe took another sharp turn. In May 1940, the German forces penetrated the French defences at Sedan and swept across northeastern France. When Italy joined the war on the Axis side in June, the fall of France became inevitable. Britain had to fight alone, less than a year after the outbreak of the war. Not only did the British lose their foothold on the European continent, their forces were also tied down in the Mediterranean. In May 1940, the COS submitted the report "British Strategy in a Certain Eventuality," outlining the possible strategy of fighting alone against Germany and Italy. The COS suggested that, while the British Empire could win a long war of attrition, it could not defend itself against a Japanese attack during the process:

> To counter Japanese action in the Far East, a fleet, adequately supported by Air Forces, is necessary at Singapore. What forces we can send can only be judged in the light of the situation at the time. It is most improbable that we can send any naval forces to the Far East. Therefore we must rely on the United States of America to safeguard our interests in the Far East.[16]

After the fall of France, the British Isles were under direct threat by Germany. As Italy was in the war and most French colonies turned over to the Vichy government, the situation facing the British Empire was grimmer than ever.[17]

The Japanese immediately seized the opportunity to cut China off from outside help. In June, Japan demanded that Britain and France close the Burma Road, the major source of military supplies for the Nationalist government. France immediately accepted. The situation in Hong Kong deteriorated rapidly; Grasett warned London that "important precautionary measures for defence of Hong Kong should be taken without delay." He proposed to "remove frontier bridges, move mobile guns into position and partially man defences" and to evacuate the "maximum number of white women and children" before "the last moment."[18]

In response to the situation, the Joint Planning Sub-committee (JPC) reiterated that Britain could not protect its Asian possessions without Chinese, American and Soviet support. The Americans' willingness to uphold the status quo, the JPC argued, would be crucial. As for Hong Kong, the JPC maintained that "we should retain our present garrison to fight it out if war comes."[19] To forestall a premature Anglo-Japanese war, which the planners had no illusion could be avoided, the JPC and the Chief of Imperial General Staff (CIGS) recommended that the government negotiate with the Japanese and even concede to their demand over the Burma Road:

> Even if Japan is not in the end fully satisfied, negotiation for a wide settlement

can be spread out over a considerable period ... by a wide settlement including the liquidation of our weak military detachments in North China and Hong Kong, we should strengthen our military situation in the Far East where we must be prepared for war with Japan in the long run.[20]

London decided to give in to the Japanese demand on 12 July, thus avoiding an early outbreak of war.[21]

Meanwhile, the Japanese military believed that the international situation was ripe for a takeover of European territories in Asia in order to force the Chinese Nationalists to surrender. In July 1940, the Japanese army and navy submitted the *Proposal to Settle the Current Situation in Accordance with the Changing International Situation* (世界情勢ノ推移ニ伴フ時局処理要綱) to their government. To end the "China Incident" that had dragged on since 1937, the military proposed to "eliminate attempts to support Chiang by a third party" and to "put forward the Southern Policy" (南進政策).[22] In short, they envisaged starting a war in Southeast Asia in order to end the war in China. However, the Japanese army and navy were divided among themselves as to how to implement the plan. The army urged for a limited war against Britain alone, but the navy pointed out that the United States would intervene.[23] Before this question was solved, the army had overthrown the cabinet of Admiral Mitsumasa Yonai, which had opposed to the plan of joining Germany, and replaced it with that of Fumimaro Konoe, a malleable aristocrat. In September 1940, Japan joined the Axis Powers with Germany and Italy, and occupied the northern part of French Indochina.

Soon after the British had closed the Burma Road, the JPC submitted an updated version of the Far Eastern Appreciation. The Appreciation of 1940 outlined the grave situation faced by the British Empire: France had fallen; Italy had joined the war; the British were fighting hard in the Aegean, the Mediterranean and the Atlantic; Japan had acquired Hainan, the northern part of Indochina and the airfields in Siam. Furthermore, the Japanese had surrounded Hong Kong and threatened Malaya and Singapore, the "keystone" of British security in Asia. The appreciation took an even gloomier view than its predecessor:

> Hong Kong is not a vital interest and the garrison could not long withstand Japanese attack. Even if we had a strong fleet in the Far East, it is doubtful whether Hong Kong could be held now that the Japanese are firmly established on the mainland of China; and it could not be used as an advanced naval base.
>
> In the event of war, Hong Kong must be regarded as an outpost and held as long as possible. We should resist the inevitably strong pressure to reinforce Hong Kong and we should certainly be unable to relieve it. Militarily our position in the Far East would be stronger without this unsatisfactory commitment.[24]

However, the JPC recommended holding Hong Kong, as abandoning it might damage British prestige in Asia and precipitate a Japanese attack:

> In describing the position in this way, we do not mean to imply that we advocate immediate demilitarisation of Hong Kong, which, if it were undertaken by itself, would involve an incalculable loss of prestige. We felt, however, that such an offer might be used in arriving at a general settlement.[25]

The British hoped for a "general settlement" that would allow them to shorten their defence perimeter in Asia. The JPC also pointed out that the Royal Navy had only one heavy and four light cruisers and a few light vessels in Asian waters.[26] If the Japanese had attacked at this juncture, the eastern empire would have crumbled much more quickly than it actually did.

In response, Prime Minister Winston Churchill suggested that, while Britain could make concessions such as closing the Burma Road, it could not tolerate a Japanese seizure of the Dutch Indies. If Japan approached the oil fields of the Dutch Indies, then Britain would have no choice but to fight Japan. However, he doubted "whether the Japanese would wish to run the risks of such an adventure while they are entangled in China."[27] Whitehall did not send the gloomy appreciation to Hong Kong, while it was distributed to Australia, New Zealand, Canada and the military commander in the East. When in August London ordered British forces in Asia to study defensive measures against a Japanese invasion, Hong Kong was not even notified. In effect, Hong Kong had no place in British defence planning in Asia, which centred on the "Malay Barrier" (the Malay Peninsula, Borneo and the Philippines) and Singapore. When the British battalions at Shanghai and Tianjin finally withdrew, they were not sent to Hong Kong but to Malaya.[28] Nor did the British send new planes to Hong Kong.[29]

While Churchill was convinced that Japan would not start another war, the United States started to impose immense pressure on Japan from the second half of 1940, which gradually forced it to decide between war and submission. Such a move proved to be fatal for Hong Kong and the British Empire. When Japan forced Britain and France to close the Burma Road, the Americans stopped oil exports to all other countries except Britain, in effect placing an oil embargo against Japan. In September 1940, the Americans implemented conscription and imposed the embargo of scrap metal against Japan. The stiffening American attitude revived British hopes of deterring Japan through Anglo-American cooperation. The Marquess of Lothian, the British Ambassador to the United States, pointed out:

> [It] is essential that the United States should make it perfectly clear to the Japanese in the next week or two that any threat to British and Dutch possessions

in the Far East will inevitably involve Japan in war with the United States. If the Japanese are convinced that this is true they will probably draw back.[30]

However, Anglo-American military cooperation in Asia remained limited until the last months of peace.

In the second half of 1940, the mood of decision-makers and men on the spot about Hong Kong became gloomier. The Colonial Office suggested demilitarizing Hong Kong to avoid a "bloodiest holocaust."[31] The "tightly packed" urban population was seen as the biggest obstacle to any effective defence:

> The vast majority of this population (of Hong Kong) may be fairly described as docile and law-abiding, but it is of extremely timid nature, and thus liable to panic in the event of heavy and continuous air raids, or of extensive rumour-mongering by enemy agents.[32]

As it was unable to remove the Chinese population from Hong Kong, the government could not help but to allow refugees to flee to the mountains, spreading disease to the garrison defending the hills. The fifth columnists might also exploit the chaos caused by air raids and tie down the police force. The Colonial Office estimated that 200 bombers would attack Hong Kong every day (clearly an overestimation). Such intensity of bombing exceeded even what was experienced by London during the Blitz. In September 1940, Governor Geoffrey Northcote reiterated the position of the Colonial Office:

> Kowloon cannot be defended for long against a strong attack from the North. Its water supplies would fall into enemy hands very quickly and before long it would be without food. Thereafter, the longer the Island were to be defended the vaster would be the death toll in Kowloon. How long could His Majesty's Government permit this to continue in order to hold a fortress which without command of the sea has no military value?[33]

Northcote believed that without adequate air cover, an early warning system and shelters, "colossal slaughter" would occur if the Japanese bombed the combustible urban area. He concluded with the following observations:

1. The whole defence scheme of Hong Kong rests on being relieved by the Navy in some three to four months. That basis has been altogether swept away.

2. Were Hong Kong to be attacked in force its fall would be merely a question of time; meanwhile the slaughter of civilians, mostly Chinese, would be prodigious; so would be the destruction of property.

3. It is still possible . . . to withdraw the greater part of the garrison for service elsewhere and to declare Hong Kong an open town in the military sense, as it is an open port in the commercial.

4. Admittedly this would mean some loss of "face," but not more so than if the defence were to collapse—for reasons stated above—not long after an attack had begun.

5. The demilitarisation of the colony would not make it any less an integral part of the empire, aggression upon which would constitute a *casus belli*. Nor would it make any more likely an attack upon Hong Kong by Japan, for it is inconceivable that in present circumstances the Japanese are being or would be deterred from anti-British measures by the military strength of the colony.

6. Conceivably the USA Government, following its "no change in the Pacific" principle, might be more inclined to guarantee Hong Kong if it were an open undefended port, than otherwise.

7. If that were so, Chinese apprehensions and resentment would be largely allayed; indeed, having regard to the use which Chungking makes of Hong Kong they might welcome the step.

8. If the government could be relieved of anxiety on the score of Hong Kong, *qua* fortress, the British position in the Far East would be clarified and a weak spot in Britain's war front would be repaired.[34]

Throughout Northcote's memorandum, there was no mention of Grasett and the Commander-in-Chief of the China Station, nor was the memorandum endorsed by them. It was very different from the report submitted by previous governors such as Clementi. As suggested above, Grasett was ordered not to disclose the decision to give up Kowloon, thus Northcote probably had no idea of the general defence scheme of the colony that had already abandoned Kowloon.

On the other hand, the COS suggested that Britain might be able to "adopt a firmer line" towards Japan as the Americans became more involved in the Pacific:

> From a military point of view these new factors [US intervention and Japan entering the Axis alliance] alter the situation but little. The presence of a belligerent United States fleet in Far Eastern waters, with the ability to operate from Manila, might increase the chance of preventing the fall of Hong Kong or at any rate harassing the attacking forces. Without full knowledge of the part which the USA will play and the naval strategy she will adopt, we see no reason to alter our opinion that, from a purely military point of view, Hong Kong remains an undesirable commitment . . .
>
> The question of its demilitarisation is thus largely a political one and in formulating our views we have consulted the Foreign Office . . .[35]

Abandoning Hong Kong, the COS argued, would discourage Chinese resistance and "[shake] the faith of the USA" in the British determination to resist aggression. Demilitarization might also allow the Japanese to take over Hong Kong through "rapid peaceful penetration." The COS concluded that the retention of Hong Kong would "cause the Japanese to hesitate before attacking" and that "the possible loss of prestige due to the fall of Hong Kong in war even with all its attendant horrors would have less serious result than the loss of prestige from its demilitarisation under present conditions."[36]

One may argue that the insistence of the COS in December 1941 on holding Hong Kong ignored the potential loss of life and property. On the other hand, both Churchill and the COS were convinced that no rational Japanese government would attack the Western powers before ending the China war. Thus, retaining Hong Kong was an important means by which the British could express their willingness to stand with the United States and China against Japan. Although the Japanese understood the undefended state of the British possessions in late 1940 through the SS *Automedon* Incident, during which the Japanese got hold of the Far Eastern Appreciation from a German U-boat, no action was taken, as the Japanese navy was convinced that it was impossible to avoid American intervention. Thus, the idea that Britain and the United States were "inseparable" delayed the Asian war for more than a year, allowing the Western powers to strengthen the defence of their possessions. If the British had abandoned Hong Kong earlier, the colony might be used by Japan and the faction of Wang Jingwei as a subversive base against the Nationalist government. As the British goal was to delay the coming of war, taking an overt step such as demilitarization was perhaps undesirable.

However, as the United States took an increasingly hard line against Japan, the chance of delaying war gradually diminished.

Peace through Deterrence: The Strategy of Sir Robert Brooke-Popham

The British decision to reinforce Hong Kong has long been seen as an ill-conceived one, based on a poor grasp of the situation in Asia and an irrational complacency founded on the idea of self-perceived racial superiority. Recently, as Christopher Bell, Kent Fedorowich and David Macri have pointed out, the decision may in fact be seen as rational, in the context of the events in 1941 prior to the Japanese attack.[37] Instead of blindly sending the Canadian reinforcements into a death trap, London was trying to encourage Chinese resistance and deter Japan.

Air Chief Marshal Robert Brooke-Popham, the new Commander-in-Chief of the Far East, arrived at his headquarters in Singapore in December 1940. He was determined to sweep away the gloomy mood prevailing in Asia. Firmness, he believed, was the way to delay and even prevent the war with Japan. Soon after his arrival, he cabled to London that "our object is to prevent war here . . . to prevent war policy must be firmness and confidence not repeat <u>not appeasement</u> [original underline].

Lack of firmness always interpreted here as weakness."[38] Thus, he argued that "comparatively small increase now in air and particularly fighter and long range bombers might make difference between peace and war."[39] In short, he believed that the psychological impact of any British reinforcement to Asia was as much, if not more, important as its size and capability.

Brooke-Popham also believed that Britain should encourage Chinese resistance through "closer relations with China" in order to "make the Japanese task of withdrawal as difficult as possible."[40] As for the United States, he believed that "Anglo-American cooperation is the most potent single factor in restraining Japan from further aggression." Thus, the United States should be "encouraged in every possible way to maintain their recent tendency to show a firm front to Japanese aggression and to coordinate joint measures for defence against any eventuality." He particularly noted that "policy of firmness on our part factors in influencing US policy."[41] The possibility of exerting too much pressure so as to force Japan into war, however, escaped his observation.

Throughout his tenure, Brooke-Popham tried to prevent war by asking London for more reinforcements and by exaggerating British military might in Asia. On 7 December 1940, he suggested the Ministry of Information adopt a "settled and positive" propaganda policy:

> British propaganda organisation in the Far East should aim at conveying [to] the people of the Far East that victory for British arms in the West is inevitable and that our defensive strength in this theatre is also formidable. Our local object is to convince them and also the Japanese that our military strength in this area is greater than it is and too great to be challenged successfully. The representative of the Ministry of Information will be able to make good use of all information . . . to mystify and mislead potential enemies, and to encourage fearful but potential friends.[42]

He also engaged in a campaign to "mystify" the Japanese. When he visited Hong Kong, he praised the "strength of the colony's defence" and suggested that "the only way we can ensure against an attack on Hong Kong is to convince any would-be attacker that such an operation would be too costly."[43]

The Ministry of Information worked hard to ensure that Asians and the Japanese had received the message. For example, the ministry distributed the propaganda film *Alert in the East*, which was essentially a showcase of the British forces in Asia. The defences of Singapore, Malaya, Aden, Darwin, Fiji and Hong Kong were all featured. Hong Kong was referred to in the film as the "Gibraltar of the East," while submarines (already withdrawn in 1940), torpedo boats, Bren gun carriers, 9.2-inch guns, and submarine booms were shown. It also showed a group of Chinese workers digging and demolishing rocky hills, hinting that elaborate land and underground defensive structures existed.[44] The film claimed that the RAF was now able to fly from Singapore to support the colonies. This lie actually expressed the greatest fear held by many, including Brooke-Popham, namely the inadequacy of air defence in Hong Kong and other Eastern colonies.

Brooke-Popham visited Hong Kong on the New Year's Eve, 1941. He has been remembered as a typical example of British complacency in Asia through his suggestion, in a letter to General Hastings Ismay, the Military Secretary to the War Cabinet, that the Japanese was "a sub-human species who posed no threat."[45] Privately, however, he was less sanguine. In a letter to the Permanent Under-Secretary of State for Air, Arthur Street, he noted that it was impossible to judge the capability of the Japanese by observing the few soldiers he had seen, and that Hong Kong lacked civilian air-raid measures and anti-aircraft defence.[46] Thus, Brooke-Popham immediately asked for reinforcements after the visit. It was very difficult to present his case to London, however. If he was too confident, London would not appreciate the need to reinforce at all. If he was overly pessimistic, then London might conclude that any reinforcement sent would be wasted.

He pointed out to the COS that the purpose of increasing the garrison to six battalions was not to defend indefinitely the Kowloon Peninsula but to ensure the policy of holding Hong Kong Island for 130 days could be carried out. He praised Grasett, his student back at the Imperial Defence College, for maintaining the state of defence, and suggested that the garrison could "put up good show" if attacked.[47] He then suggested that the situation in Asia had already improved sufficiently to allow a reconsideration of the Hong Kong policy. The political and diplomatic benefits of reinforcing Hong Kong were deemed the most important:

> Repercussions from early fall of Hong Kong would be very serious throughout Far East. Demonstration at present juncture of our determination to defend Hong Kong would encourage Chinese in their resistance to Japan and would be important feature in our policy of firmness towards Japan which is calculated to reduce likelihood of aggression by her.[48]

He suggested sending two more battalions to Hong Kong when more Indian troops arrived at Malaya. With only six battalions (and the HKVDC), he argued, the defenders could not launch any counterattack with more than two companies. Four more Supermarine Walruses should be sent, and the number of anti-aircraft guns and medium artillery should also be increased. He also recommended establishing "organisation necessary to render effective Chinese military operations either regular or guerrilla to relieve pressure on Hong Kong" through Major General Lancelot Dennys, head of the British military mission in China.[49]

Churchill did not share Brooke-Popham's views. In a minute to Ismay dated 7 January 1941, he wrote:

> This is all wrong. If Japan goes to war with us, there is not the slightest chance of holding Hong Kong or relieving it. It is most unwise to increase the loss we shall suffer there. Instead of increasing the garrison it ought to be reduced to a symbolic scale. Any trouble arising there must be dealt with at the Peace Conference after the war. We must avoid frittering away our resources on untenable positions. Japan will think long before declaring war on the British Empire, and whether there are two or six battalions at Hong Kong will make no difference to her choice. I wish we had fewer troops there, but to move any would be noticeable and dangerous.[50]

Churchill's idea was shared by the CIGS, General John Dill, who believed that it was too early to reconsider the Hong Kong policy. However, he acknowledged the need to increase the store of supplies and the number of reserves for a siege of 130 days.[51] On 13 January, the COS replied to Brooke-Popham:

> While fully appreciating the arguments for reinforcing the infantry garrison at Hong Kong ... we adhere to the decision which we made in November that the dispatch of infantry reinforcement to Hong Kong cannot be made in present circumstances ...
>
> We view Hong Kong as an undesirable military commitment but demilitarisation is not now possible in view of the effect such a course would have both in Japan and China. In the event of war with Japan the Fortress must therefore be held as an outpost for as long as possible. Even at its present strength the garrison might cause the Japanese to hesitate before committing themselves to an attack on the colony. An increase of the regular infantry garrison from four to six regular battalions would be unlikely materially to influence such a decision by the Japanese and could not affect the ultimate result. It would however increase the loss should the Fortress fall. As you say we have no good reason for basing plans on a relief of the garrison being possible ...[52]

Brooke-Popham countered that, as there were not enough police in the colony to control the vast population, the garrison might be forced to shoulder part of that responsibility. When London decided to deploy four battalions to Hong Kong, it had not envisaged this role. The garrison would be understrength if it had to play a role in internal security.[53] According to the Interim Defence Scheme of 1939, he argued, one of the four battalions of the garrison had to perform delaying action on the mainland to buy time for the implementation of civil defence measures (such as scuttling ships and boats in Victoria Harbour and relocation of vital supplies). The battalion on the mainland would conduct sabotage and delaying actions, and would briefly resist on the Gin Drinker's Line, before withdrawing to the island. Brooke-Popham and Grasett believed that the battalion could not stay on the mainland for more than forty-eight hours, as it had to preserve its strength for the defence of the island. They calculated that, if there were three battalions on the mainland, then the time of resistance could be lengthened to at most twelve days, allowing the defenders to prepare thoroughly for island defence, even if the Japanese suddenly attacked. In addition, if only four battalions were available, they could not rotate and rest throughout the campaign, and would be rendered ineffective much more quickly. With two more battalions, the garrison could launch local counterattacks and even raids against the mainland, which, according to Brooke-Popham, were major morale boosts.

As for the relationship between the size of the Hong Kong garrison and Japan's decision for or against war, Brooke-Popham used the example of Sarawak to show that a slight increase (one company) would be interpreted as a large-scale reinforcement. He reiterated that the situation had improved, as Australian reinforcements were reaching Malaya, and a joint defence plan was being formulated with the ANZAC and Dutch forces. He suggested that "to us out here it seems no longer a question of reducing our losses in Hong Kong but of ensuring the security of places that will be of great value in taking offensive action at a later stage of the war."[54]

Still, London was unwilling to commit before the situation in the Atlantic and the Mediterranean improved. The COS replied that "we fully appreciate the force of these arguments but have reluctantly come to the conclusion that we must adhere to our decision that Hong Kong must not be reinforced in present circumstances. Should the present discussions in Washington or any major change in the situation alter our estimate of the position we will consider."[55] The COS still conceived the Hong Kong problem as one of balancing "the moral advantage of a protracted defence against the disadvantages of the political pressure for a relief of the garrison and the sufferings of the civil population which would result from such a defence."[56] During this period, the only reinforcement received by the garrison was fifteen Bren gun carriers and a number of spare anti-aircraft gun barrels.[57]

In all, Brooke-Popham saw Hong Kong as a tool for deterring Japan and encouraging China. He was confident in Grasett, but the idea of reinforcement was not merely the product of his faith in the garrison's ability to hold Hong Kong. In retrospect, the reinforcement policy urged by Brooke-Popham and Grasett increased the losses suffered by the British and Canadians, which has caused much controversy, but it was perhaps a less irrational move than thought if put in context. In fact, as discussed below, the United States also jettisoned its policy of abandoning the Philippines and reinforced it with American troops.

Brooke-Popham's correspondence shows that he was trying to deter Japan through a coalition of the British Empire, China and the United States. To ensure that China and America would stand up against Japan, Brooke-Popham believed that Britain had to show its determination by reinforcing Asia. This policy might also encourage the Asian subjects in British possessions and deter potential Japanese collaborators. Reinforcing Asia and exaggerating British strength might also mystify Japan, and force it to think twice before choosing war. Indeed, Japan did not take action even with the knowledge of British weakness in the second half of 1940 because it was wary of American intervention. On the one hand, Brooke-Popham had to maintain a confident outlook to persuade London that reinforcements would not be wasted in an unwinnable fight. On the other, he had to ask London constantly for more troops, planes and ships to back his scheme. Brooke-Popham faced immense difficulties in trying to deter and defer the war against Japan, but his difficulties and efforts have largely been forgotten.

Collective Security: The Actions of Other Allied Powers

Even before the outbreak of the European War, observers had already realized that one way to protect Hong Kong was to form an alliance consisting of Britain, the United States, France and the Soviet Union. A contemporary Chinese magazine wrote:

> On the other hand, if the United States and the Soviet Union had taken up their responsibilities in the West and the North Pacific and cooperated with Britain and France, the position of Hong Kong would be much strengthened.[58]

As mentioned, the Americans gradually took a firmer line against Japan from 1940. In March 1941, Congress passed the Lend-Lease Act, which allowed the United States to provide arms and supplies to Britain. The act was extended to China in May and later to the Soviet Union after the German invasion.[59] Later, the U.S. Pacific Fleet was redeployed from San Diego to Hawaii, shortening the distance to mainland Japan by around one-third.

From the 1920s, the Philippines were to have been abandoned in American war plans against Japan (known as War Plan Orange). However, the Americans started to boost the defence of the Philippines from early 1941. The Philippine Scouts and the US garrison were both strengthened and provided with modern armaments and a construction plan of $1,500,000.[60] By November 1941, one anti-aircraft (AA) regiment, two tank battalions (with 109 M3 Tanks, enough to deal with modern Japanese tanks), eighty-one P-40E fighters, more than five hundred trucks, vehicles, self-propelled guns and artillery pieces, and six torpedo boats were sent. A division was also mobilized before Pearl Harbor. The most important items were the thirty-five B-17 four-engine heavy bombers and twenty-three long-range submarines. They were strategic offensive weapons that could threaten Taiwan and mainland Japan. The Americans had put much faith in the B-17s; they planned to send 165 of them before spring 1942 and increase the number of fighters to 240.[61] In July, the United States Army Forces in the Far East was formed, led by General Douglas MacArthur. Thus, although the Americans kept the Orange Plan, the US forces in the Philippines were substantially strengthened.

From the late 1930s, British planners had started to look to the United States when considering the defence of Asia. In late 1940, Britain sent a military mission led by Commodore Roger Bellairs (who had participated in the discussion of Hong Kong defence in 1930 as the Director of Naval Plans) to America. The COS instructed Bellairs to invite the U.S. Pacific Fleet to replace the British fleet as the backbone of the War Memorandum (Eastern). Hong Kong, however, was no longer seen as a suitable base.[62]

Bellairs highlighted the need to shore up American confidence by sending more British troops to Asia:

> The position might be considerably improved if we could give the Americans a firm promise that reinforcements to bring the garrison of Malaya to full strength would be sent by a certain date ... On this basis, we could say to the Americans that we realise the risk which we are running, and which we are asking them to share, but that the risk will be for a very limited period, at the end of which time the danger of Japanese action can be faced with confidence. Such a statement would also be reassuring to the Dominions of Australia and New Zealand ...[63]

Thus, by reinforcing Malaya, the British tried to cultivate "collective security" in Asia and to cooperate with China, the United States and the Dutch Indies. In February 1941, the COS again highlighted in another memorandum the need for the United States to adopt more active measures to deter Japan.[64]

However, the British found to their dismay that the Americans had yet to form a consistent Japan policy and were unwilling to use their fleet to replace the Royal Navy. The British mission "failed to convince the US Staff Committee the fundamental importance of the retention of Singapore, not only to the British Commonwealth, but to the joint effort of the Associated Powers in the prosecution of war against Germany."[65] Although the meeting demarcated the areas of responsibility for US and British forces, the British had to be responsible for their own colonies. The Americans also refused to put any US forces under British control. Only the U.S. Asiatic Fleet would join the British forces after the fall of the Philippines.[66] Still, the British remained convinced that one way to ensure American cooperation was to reinforce Asia. In April, the British promised the Americans that they would send a substantial naval force to Asia between late 1941 and early 1942, including one aircraft carrier, five battleships, a battle cruiser, four heavy and nineteen light cruisers, and thirty-seven destroyers.[67]

It was a prevailing idea among British, American and even Chinese officers that, if Britain and America could amass sufficient forces in the Pacific, Japan could be deterred. The report of an Anglo-American-Dutch staff officer meeting in Singapore, held in April 1941, observed: "[Japan's] knowledge that all Associated Powers would unite to resist aggression against one might prevent war."[68] Vice Admiral Chan Chak, the KMT representative in Hong Kong, noted in his diary after meeting American and British officers in Hong Kong in April 1941:

> During the conversation I tried to analyse the naval disposition of the enemy [Japan] . . . I suggested that the Japanese were able to dominate a large part of the Pacific because of their bases across the ocean and the inner line advantage they enjoyed. If the American fleet was able to place two-thirds of its battle fleet (eight to nine battleships) at Hawaii, and the British deploy one squadron of battleships (two to three ships) at Singapore, they were able to deter the Japanese main fleet from leaving their home waters . . .
>
> Now, six months later, the British and the American navies finally took this step to suppress Japanese aggression . . . [Chan was referring to the dispatch of two British capital ships, HMS *Prince of Wales* and HMS *Repulse*, to Singapore in November].[69]

The British also had some preliminary discussions with China, although these talks bore little fruit before Pearl Harbor. In February 1941, Major General Lancelot Dennys went to Chongqing as the head of a British military mission. A month later, the British cabinet decided to transfer one hundred P-40 fighters to China to support its war effort.[70] In the following months, the Nationalist government sent a military mission headed by General Shang Zhen (商震) to visit Brooke-Popham, who reiterated the decision to send fighters to China. In May, Chiang Kai-shek even offered to send Chinese troops to defend Hong Kong and Burma.[71]

The COS had some reservations about Chiang's scheme. The CIGS, General John Dill, suggested that, as the goal of the British government "has always been and must remain avoidance of war with Japan," any overt moves that precipitated trouble should be avoided. He warned that "support given to China must have its immediate object of strengthening of our defensive position on our own frontiers . . . discussion with the Chinese should be based on our general Far Eastern war plan, and not on the immediate tactical needs of China." It was because "China's future," he argued, "depends on our winning the war."[72] Instead of launching conventional attacks that might lead to costly defeats, the Chinese should stick to guerrilla tactics.

For this purpose, Henry Pownall, the Vice CIGS, proposed to send eight experts on guerrilla warfare to China "voluntarily" to survey the terrain and the Chinese armies.[73] Still, the War Office decided that they would be sent only after the outbreak of war.[74] Meanwhile, because of General Erwin Rommel's victories against the British in North Africa, the decision to send the P-40s to China was cancelled. Despite the apparent lack of success, however, Sino-British conversations before the war had improved relations between the Chinese and British officers on the spot, as Chan Chak's example suggests. This cordial relationship certainly proved useful during subsequent events.

Canadian Reinforcement and the Rapid Deterioration of US-Japan Relations

To the British, the situation in Asia was seemingly improved from the spring of 1941, at least on the surface. In March, Nomura Kichisaburō (野村吉三郎), the Japanese Ambassador to Washington, started to negotiate with Cordell Hull, the US Secretary of State. Although the Americans did not send their fleet to Singapore, they were willing to discuss joint defence plans. Meanwhile, more reinforcements reached Malaya. Above all, Japan was still bogged down in a costly China campaign, with no end in sight. These factors boosted the confidence of Brooke-Popham and Whitehall. Maberley Dening, the head of the Far Eastern Department of the Foreign Office, suggested in May 1941 that war might eventually be averted if the British were able to keep up the pressure through reinforcement and coalition building:

> [the COS does not] in fact adopt a gloomy view of the position, and even on the assumption that the United States remain neutral, our armed strength in Malaya is no longer negligible. In fact I entertain some hope that, if the Japanese do not attack within the next two months and our programme of reinforcement continues according to plan, they may hesitate to attack at all.
>
> There is a good spirit in Malaya which the Commander-in-Chief does much to encourage. If we find ourselves at war with Japan we shall be readier than we have been on other and less happy occasions. I suggest that if we could inspire the United States Government with some of our resolution and confidence, they would be less likely to regard yet another debacle as a foregone conclusion.[75]

Other countries also showed more resolve. In June, the Dutch Indies ended oil negotiations with Japan. The latter faced the prospect of losing another major source of oil supply. A month later, Japanese assets in America, Britain and the Dutch Indies were frozen after the Japanese occupied the southern part of Indochina. The Foreign Secretary, Anthony Eden, suggested that the government should seize the opportunity to issue a joint or parallel statement to Japan, warning the latter that "any further action inimical to our joint interests would lead to trouble."[76] Brooke-Popham, who continuously urged firmer actions, even proposed to terminate all trade with Japan, to eject Japanese vessels from British, American and Dutch ports, and expel all Japanese nationals.

These actions were considered too much by the shrewder COS, which suggested that the actions taken had already destabilized the Japanese economy and might force Japan to take action. Thus, it was an opportune time to give conditional concessions:

> We suggest that opportunity may occur to point out to Japan the fact that the action we have taken has been purely defensive and, if Japan were prepared to take action sufficient to allay our fears, we, in combination with the United States, would be ready again to make available those economic advantages that Japan is now denied.[77]

The COS also suggested that, "until we are assured of the military support of the USA in the event of war with Japan, we should take no action, save in the defence of our vital interests, which is likely to precipitate war."[78] A similar idea was also expressed by the British Ambassador to Japan.[79]

Some American planners also shared this view. In November 1941, Brigadier General Leonard Gerow of the War Plans Division warned against premature action against Japan:

> Most effective aid to China, as well as to the defence of Singapore and the Netherlands East Indies, is now being built up by the reinforcement of the Philippines. The safety of Luzon as an air and submarine base should soon be reasonably assured by the arrival of air and ground reinforcements. Strong diplomatic and economic pressure may be exerted from the military viewpoint at the earliest about the middle of December 1941, when the Philippine Air Force will have become a positive threat to Japanese operations. It would be advantageous, if practicable, to delay severe diplomatic and economic pressure until February or March 1942, when the Philippine Air Force will have reached its projected strength, and a safe air route, through Samoa, will be in operation.[80]

However, without a clear goal other than forcing Japan to abandon its war in China and aggressive policy, the Roosevelt administration imposed an oil embargo against Japan in August. Britain and the Dutch Indies soon joined the embargo. This move forced Japan to choose from three options: to start a war, back down or face the prospect of running out of oil.

In mid-1941, Japan still wavered between war and peace.[81] The army believed that Japan should first strike south to ensure the supply of raw material and oil, while the opinion of the navy was divided. The cabinet, led by Fumimaro Konoe, was indecisive. He was less sanguine about Germany's prospects after the first year of the Soviet invasion, but diehards such as Tōjō Hideki were convinced that Germany would win the war. In a last attempt to avert war, Konoe invited President Franklin Roosevelt to hold a summit to discuss outstanding issues. However, while the US government insisted on a Japanese withdrawal from China, none of the Japanese leaders, even Konoe, were ready to give in.

During a cabinet meeting in August, it was decided that, if there was no breakthrough in US-Japanese relations, then whether war should be declared would be decided during the meeting with the emperor in early October. As Herbert Bix has pointed out, Emperor Hirohito could have extended this arbitrary deadline if he had wanted to avoid war, but he was already distracted by issues such as whether Japan could win the war and the countermeasures against a possible Soviet invasion of Manchukuo. In mid-October, pressured by Tōjō and the hardliners, Prime Minister Konoe resigned. The emperor refused Konoe's pledge to appoint a royal as his successor and instead picked Tōjō. By then, Hirohito was already heading towards war.

During this critical period, the British continued to reinforce Asia. In summer, the number of Australian troops in Malaya reached one division; two Indian divisions were already there. As Franco David Macri has suggested, the situation in Asia was further complicated by the German invasion of the Soviet Union in June. As the Soviet military quickly crumbled in the face of the German onslaught, British and American leaders were anxious to keep the Soviets in the war. One way to prevent the Japanese from attacking the Soviet Union was to maintain the Chinese resistance against Japan.[82] As the Far Eastern Appreciation had suggested in 1937, the idea of holding Hong Kong as a means to maintain Chinese confidence became the most forceful argument for the reinforcement policy.

Meanwhile, the situation in Hong Kong remained tense. In 1941, a number of Japanese naval and air attacks against local shipping occurred. Grasett requisitioned six Chinese Maritime Customs vessels to augment the coastal patrol of Hong Kong in April. The Royal Navy warship even fired at a suspected Japanese submarine in July.[83] In the same month, Grasett left the colony for a new post. When he passed through Canada before reaching London, he shared his idea of reinforcing Hong Kong with Major General Henry Crerar, the Canadian CGS, and with James Ralston, the Minister of National Defence. After the fall of Hong Kong, however, the two men refused to admit that such a discussion had taken place.[84]

In August, Grasett relayed the idea to the COS, which reported the matter thus:

> Major General Grasett brought up again the question of an infantry reinforcement of the garrison which he suggests the Canadian Government might be

agreeable to provide … To have reinforced a year ago would have been to throw good money after bad. The situation is now so changed that in four and a half months relief might be possible [the COS was referring to the large naval contingent planned in April] and such reinforcement might well prolong resistance for a further considerable period.

The present policy is that Hong Kong is to be regarded as an outpost and held as long as possible. Though it has been decided not to send reinforcements, in the event of war, it was never intended that the forces available to the Commander should not be adequate for the task. We agree that, at present, the available forces are insufficient to implement the defence plan, which is to deny to the enemy the dry dock and harbour for 130 days.

A small reinforcement of one or two battalions would increase the strength of the garrison out of all proportion to its numbers, and would provide a strong psychological stimulus to the garrison and to the colony. It would show Chiang Kai-shek that, in spite of our wide commitments, we really intend to fight it out at Hong Kong, and would also have a salutary effect on the Japanese.

You will remember this policy was last reviewed in January 1941, when it was decided not to send any more reinforcements to Hong Kong. Since then, however, the position in the Far East has changed radically and Japan has shown a certain weakness latterly in her attitude towards Great Britain and the United States.

Recently the United States have displayed a greater interest in the Far East and have despatched small reinforcements to the garrison of the Philippines. Reinforcement of Hong Kong from Canada would thus be in alignment with United States policy while Canada would be accepting a wider commitment in Imperial defence, similar to that which has been assumed by Australia in Malaya. For these reasons, the Chiefs of Staff consider that a reinforcement of up to two battalions of infantry should now be made to the garrison of Hong Kong. If the Prime Minister approves, we suggest that Mr. Mackenzie [William Lyon Mackenzie King, Prime Minister of Canada] should be approached with a view to obtaining this reinforcement.[85]

Not all were impressed by the proposal. A Colonial Office official remarked:

I fancy this paper may provoke the wrath of the Prime Minister. Quite apart from the old decision that no further reinforcements were to be sent to Hong Kong, the Prime Minister may well ask why it is that Major-General Grasett has not said before that the troops under his command were inadequate for their limited task, which has always been the defence of Hong Kong for a given period of time.[86]

Citing the example of the heavy losses suffered by Australians during the Battle of Crete, Leslie Hollis, the senior assistant secretary in the War Cabinet, noted the problem of sending dominion troops to potential battlefronts.[87]

The proposal, however, was supported by many others. Anthony Eden wrote to Churchill on 12 September: "Russia, the United States, China, and the British Empire, to say nothing of the Dutch, are more than this probably over-valued military power is prepared to challenge. Our right policy is, therefore, clearly to keep up the pressure." Brooke-Popham wrote to General Hastings Ismay: "It was grand news about the Canadian troops and I wonder how far it was Grasett's eloquence that carried the day."[88] The Canadian reinforcement indeed encouraged the Pacific nations. Soon after Canada sent the reinforcements, Australia sent two more battalions to Timor and Ambon to boost the defence of the Dutch Indies.[89]

The Dominion Office formally invited the Canadian government on 19 September:

> In consultation with late General Officer Commanding who has recently arrived in this country we have been considering the defences of Hong Kong. Approved policy has been that Hong Kong should be regarded as an outpost and held as long as possible in the event of war in the Far East. Existing army garrison consists of four battalions of infantry and although this force represents the bare minimum required for the task assigned to it we have thought hitherto that it would not ultimately serve any useful purpose to increase the garrison.
>
> Position in the Far East has now however changed. Our defences in Malaya have been improved and there have been signs of a certain weakening in Japan's attitude towards us and the United States. In these circumstances it is thought that a small reinforcement of the garrison of Hong Kong, e.g. by or more two more battalions, would be very fully justified. It would increase the strength of the garrison out of all proportion to the actual numbers involved and it would provide a strong stimulus to the garrison and to the colony, it would further have a very great moral effect in the whole of the Far East and would reassure Chiang Kai-shek as to the reality of our intention to hold the Island. . . .
>
> His Majesty's Government in Canada will be well aware of the difficulties we are at present experiencing in providing the forces which the situation in various parts of the world demands, despite the very great assistance which is being furnished by Dominions . . . It is thought that in view of their special position in the North Pacific the Canadian Government would in any case be wished to be informed of the need for the reinforcement of Hong Kong and the special value of such a measure . . . It may also be mentioned that the United States have recently despatched a small reinforcement to the Philippines . . .[90]

This telegram led to some controversy after the war, as it was suggested that the British had deliberately misled Ottawa into sending troops to Hong Kong by hiding their decision to maintain Hong Kong as an "outpost."[91] By comparing the COS memorandum and the invitation from the Dominion Office, London had already shared the available information and arguments for reinforcement with Canada, although its interpretation of the situation was over-optimistic. The "outpost" policy was stated in the first paragraph of the Dominion Office's telegram to Ottawa, although the following paragraph started with a "however," which may or may not hint at a change in policy.[92]

The Canadian decision-makers were aware of the difficulty of defending Hong Kong. General Crerar had examined the issue from both the British and Japanese perspectives in detail when studying at the Imperial Defence College in 1934. He argued that, if Japan moved southwards, it would antagonize Britain, the Netherlands and the United States. He concluded that the safety of Hong Kong relied not only on the Royal Navy but also on the ability of the powers to act together.[93] Thus, he suggested in 1936 as secretary of the Joint Staff Committee of Canada, "Were there a definite alliance between Great Britain and the United States it is possible that this deterrent would more than compensate for the threat which the Japanese would constitute to Hong Kong."[94] Crerar possibly shared Brooke-Popham's idea that war could be averted through collective action.

As Kent Fedorowich has suggested, Ottawa's decision was also related to Canadian politics. Since the outbreak of the war, the Liberal government of Canada, led by Mackenzie King, was cool to the idea of overseas military commitment. Although this attitude had some initial support, it was soon criticized by the opposition as the war went on. His policy was also opposed by the Canadian military, which vented its discontent during his visit to Canadian troops in Britain in August 1941. Although Canada contributed immensely to the war effort economically, its military had had only a limited role during the first two years of fighting. This certainly affected Canada's position in the Commonwealth and among the democratic powers. When the British and American leaders signed the Atlantic Charter in Newfoundland, Mackenzie King was not even notified. In view of these events, it was natural for Mackenzie King, also known as the "world's champion fence sitter," to change his position towards the question of Canadian military commitment in the Allied war effort.[95] The decision was also the result of recent developments in the Soviet Union. As Franco David Macri points out, during the cabinet meeting that decided to accept the British request, Mackenzie King acknowledged the need to help and encourage the Soviet Union through "all means within her power," possibly including reinforcing Hong Kong.[96]

Ottawa formally accepted the invitation on 29 September. Churchill, who had dismissed the idea in January 1941, declared that he would approve the scheme "unless the Foreign Secretary demurs." Anthony Eden "warmly welcomed" the reinforcement.[97] On 8 October, the General Officer Commanding Hong Kong, Major General Christopher Maltby, was notified. Maltby, elated, asked whether Canada could send one more battalion and a headquarters to form a full Canadian brigade.[98] James Ralston approved of sending the battalions of The Royal Rifles of Canada (721 men) and The Winnipeg Grenadiers (828 men) and a brigade headquarters (94 men), led by Colonel John Lawson, Director of Military Training, to Hong Kong. The C Force (as it was officially known) left Canada on 27 October and arrived at Hong Kong on 16 November (more details about the two forces follow in Chapter 8).

At least to the men on the spot, the Canadian reinforcement was not a last-minute effort to boost Hong Kong defence; rather, it was the first step of a larger programme of deterrence. However, it was amid this strategic redeployment that Japan launched its attack against Britain and the United States.

Alerts before the War

Just as Britain and the United States were trying to reinforce Asia, Japan gradually steered its course towards war. Still, before November its actions were so ambiguous that Washington and London were unaware of the coming of war until the last few days; they were unable to act decisively when it was known that Japan had decided to act. This led to the situation of "surprise despite warning," as Richard Aldrich suggested.

When Maltby learned about the coming of the C Force, he decided to change the defence scheme and man the Gin Drinker's Line. Maltby was apparently convinced that he had time to readjust to the new plan (see Chapter 8). However, the situation deteriorated quickly from early November.[99] On 7 November, the British intercepted a telegram from the Japanese consul of Singapore to Tokyo, suggesting that all Japanese ships were scheduled to leave on 16 November and that he himself was leaving on the 11th. Two days later, the British consul at Saigon reported that over 50,000 Japanese troops were moving from Indochina to Siam and Cambodia.

On 5 November, the Japanese approved the final negotiation plan with the United States and the general war plan against the Allies. The operational orders for Malaya and Hong Kong were issued on 6 November. Tokyo finally decided on 15 November that, if the US-Japanese negotiation failed, war would be declared against the British Empire, the Netherlands and the United States. The Japanese special envoy to the United States, Kurusu Saburō, arrived only on the 16th. This was interpreted by London as a sign of the de-escalation of tension. On the other hand, the Hong Kong garrison and the Far East Combined Bureau spotted unusual Japanese activities in Guangdong and Humen. The British estimated that the Japanese were either redeploying to build up a new base in Siam or trying to attack Kunming.[100] In fact, however, it was a ruse, code-named "Kunming Operation" (昆明作戰), launched by the Japanese to hide their preparations against the Allies.

The Joint Intelligence Committee accurately estimated that the Japanese redeployment was a sign of an imminent attack against Siam, the Dutch Indies and even Malaya. On 25 November, the British intercepted the infamous "East Wind Rain" telegram; on the same day, the Japanese carrier group set sail to Pearl Harbor from their secret anchorage at Etorofu-tō.[101] It was not until 1 December that the Japanese finally decided to fight. After the interception of the "East Wind Rain" telegram, the British started to round up potential collaborators such as the nationalists in Malaya and to prepare for defence. The British also noticed a rapid build-up of Japanese air strength in Indochina. Still, Churchill and Eden were convinced as late as 2 December that the Japanese would not take action until spring 1942. The COS was still occupied with the issue of sending another Canadian battalion to Hong Kong.

By 3 December, however, it was realized that war was imminent. On that day, Marshal Plaek Phibunsongkhram, the Siamese Prime Minister, warned Britain of a Japanese invasion of Malaya through Siam. It was also found that the Japanese embassies in London and Washington had destroyed their cipher machines. The COS immediately dropped the matter of reinforcement and turned to the issue of Anglo-American cooperation. When the British consulate at Haiphong reported that Japanese transports were sighted at Cam Ranh Bay on 5 December, Maltby ordered the garrison to prepare for war and mobilized the HKVDC.[102] The police force was also mobilized.[103] On the afternoon of 6 December, the police station of Sheung Shui received a report about imminent invasion by three Japanese divisions.[104] Meanwhile, Japanese transports were sighted near Malaya, heading towards Kra Isthmus. As the direction of the Japanese transport was unclear, Brooke-Popham did not launch Operation Matador, a preliminary strike to seize Kra Isthmus that was supposed to prevent a Japanese invasion from the Malaya-Siam border. Although Brooke-Popham still told the press that war would not occur, he warned RAF Kai Tak of the impending attack. Amid the chaotic situation, the Hong Kong garrison was actually better prepared than in other places. On the evening of 6 December, all the anti-aircraft guns were operational; the troops were in position by the next morning.[105] When Japanese planes reached Hong Kong on 8 December, the garrison, if not the city itself, was ready.

Conclusion

Hong Kong was treated as an "outpost" when war broke out in Europe again in 1939. The New Territories and Kowloon Peninsula were to be abandoned, and the garrison would try to hold Hong Kong Island and deny the use of Victoria Harbour by the enemy. Although "the period before relief" was set at 130 days, the planners hoped only that the colony could lessen the pressure on Singapore, the keystone of British defence in Asia. Meanwhile, Japan tried in vain to end its costly war in China by trying to isolate the Nationalist government through a southern advance; however, it entered into a vicious cycle of starting a war in order to end another one. After the Japanese invaded French Indochina in mid-1940, they had almost encircled Hong Kong. The chance of relieving Hong Kong during a Japanese invasion was increasingly slim.

From 1940, the British took steps to cooperate with China, the Dutch Indies and the United States to forestall a Japanese invasion. Brooke-Popham adopted a Janus-faced policy of exaggerating the British military might in Asia, on the one hand, and pressing for reinforcements from London, on the other. The Americans jettisoned their previous policy of abandoning the Philippines and deployed strategic offensive weapons such as long-range bombers and submarines there. By September 1941, it seemed that the reinforcement policy had forced Japan to reconsider its expansionary policy. As Japanese decision-makers wavered between war and peace, London and the men on the spot became more optimistic about the situation. This attitude, and the need to support China and the Soviet Union, prompted London to accept Grasett's plea and to invite Canada to reinforce Hong Kong. However, as Churchill prioritized the Middle East and the Soviet Union over the Far East, British possessions in the Far East were still too weak to withstand the Japanese attack.

The diplomatic pressure imposed on the Japanese by the Roosevelt administration ultimately prompted Japan to take action much earlier than expected by the British. Unaware of the actual state of US-Japanese negotiations, Britain had little choice but to follow the American policy of increasing pressure, which eventually forced Japan to choose between war and capitulation. For Hong Kong, this diplomatic and strategic blunder by Washington and London meant that the garrison was caught in the middle of a strategic and operational readjustment. This partly explained the collapse of Hong Kong defence during the subsequent battle.

7

HONG KONG BEFORE THE WAR

Regrettable as it may sound[,] there was perhaps no British Colony which had been inviting disaster for quite so long as Hong Kong. This was due to poor class and corrupt Government Administration, many old and atrophied Civil Servants, almost total lack of control by the Police, graft, loose living, drink and pleasure loving in every respect, the civilian population both white and coloured had for many years indulged in wishful thinking and had persuaded themselves in a complacent manner that no Japanese would ever come and take Hong Kong.[1]

—War Diary, 1st Battalion, the Middlesex Regiment, 1942

Hong Kong Unprepared?

The idea that the British had abandoned Hong Kong and its fall in December 1941 was largely due to negligence and incompetence was deep rooted. It has been suggested that little was done to prepare Hong Kong against the Japanese onslaught, in terms of both military and civilian defence. It was also alleged that the British failed or refused to enlist the assistance of the more than one million Hong Kong Chinese residents. As the quotation from the war diary of the Middlesex battalion above reveals, this idea was even shared by the defenders themselves. However, while such an idea was to an extent accurate, it was by no means a complete picture. As suggested in the previous chapter, the British government changed its policy and decided to reinforce Hong Kong as part of a larger scheme to shore up the Allied powers' position against the Japanese. In Hong Kong, although the colonial government, led by Governor Geoffrey Northcote who believed that the city would be easily destroyed by air attack, was hardly enthusiastic about civil defence, his successors, the now-forgotten Lieutenant General Edward Norton and the well-known Sir Mark Young, launched a serious endeavour to boost the civil defence of the colony. This chapter first describes the internal situation of the colony, and then discusses the intelligence activities of the powers, its economic contribution to the British and Chinese war effort, and the civil defence preparations that sometimes led to controversies.

Overview of Internal Situation

According to the census conducted by the Air Raid Precaution Department in March 1941, the total population of Hong Kong was 1,659,337—or 600,000 more than that of 1937.[2] As Cai Rongfang, John Carroll, Philip Snow and others have pointed out, pre-war Hong Kong was a diverse society. Tension existed between the different ethnic and social groups; however, they also cooperated to varying extents.[3] Thus, the thesis put forward by Gerald Horne, who has argued that prevailing racial tensions were a deciding factor in the Japanese success during the Battle of Hong Kong, is inadequate for explaining the situation.[4] Underneath British colonial rule, pre-war Hong Kong also reflected the kaleidoscopic political situation in China. Different political forces, including the Chongqing Nationalists, the pro-Japanese Nationalist Party led by Wang Jingwei, the Chinese Communists, smaller political groups and Japanese intelligence services, were all active in Hong Kong.

Compared to other parts of China, Hong Kong was relatively peaceful during the interwar period. After the Seamen's Strike of 1922 and the Canton-Hong Kong Strike of 1925–1926, the colonial government introduced a number of reforms to alleviate the discontent of the Chinese. Prominent Chinese and Eurasian elites, such as Sir Robert Ho Tung, Sir Shouson Chow and Sir Robert Kotewall were co-opted into the establishment and given titles and seats in the Legislative Council. Later, Sir Andrew Caldecott reformed the Urban Council, taking some early steps to localize the junior civil service, so as to absorb the young Chinese elite. The government also introduced measures and legislation such as the Building Ordinance and the Labour Officer to improve the lives of the population. The government even explored the feasibility of providing public housing. Although the gap between the rulers and the ruled was wide, and the cooperation between the colonial government and the Chinese public was limited at best, it is going too far to suggest that the Chinese preferred the Japanese to the British.[5]

It is equally unsatisfactory to describe the Indian residents through a simple loyal/disloyal dichotomy. Most of the 7,000 or so Indians in Hong Kong worked as soldiers, policemen, watchmen and merchants. Throughout the 1930s, there were two Indian battalions stationed in Hong Kong (around 2,000 men in total). As the religious and ethnic compositions of the Indian community were as complex as those of the Chinese, its reaction towards the Japanese was also varied. From 1939, the Japanese had started to collaborate with the Indian Independence League to cultivate nationalist and anti-British sentiments among Indians in Hong Kong and other British colonies.[6] As mentioned, some soldiers of the Rajputana battalion were under the impression that they would be treated as friends by the Japanese. In early 1941, the Sikh gunners of the Hong Kong Singapore Royal Artillery Regiment refused to replace their turbans with steel helmets. The event was defused before any mutinous acts occurred. However, as will be suggested in Chapter 8, the two battalions in Hong Kong maintained effective resistance throughout the Battle of Hong Kong. The Canadian soldier George MacDonell noted the morale of the Rajput battalion:

> As we watched them assemble for parade, we were struck by their quiet, proud bearing and their smiling, happy faces . . . their spotless uniforms were pressed to knife edges and their glossy polished boots reflected their impeccable khaki dress. . . . After the inspection was complete, the colonel mounted his horse and, standing in his stirrups, addressed his men in their own language for about three minutes. . . . After the colonel completed his address, they suddenly, without any warning, lifted their rifles and gave three mighty cheers . . . One could sense immediately that those cheers were from a force totally loyal and totally committed to the will of their commander.[7]

A large number of Eurasians also participated in the Volunteer Defence Corps. All 117 members of the 3rd Company of the HKVDC, formed in 1934–1935, were Eurasian. They would play an important role during the coming battle.[8]

Before the Japanese invasion, the Chinese Nationalist government treated Hong Kong as a major base for its international activities. As early as 1937, KMT dignitaries such as T. V. Soong had already gone to Hong Kong.[9] By 1939, thirty-two KMT organizations were operating in the colony under tacit British approval. They were responsible for works such as coordinating imports, liaising with the British and Americans, espionage, fund-raising (include the printing of the KMT-issued currency, *fabi* 法幣), gathering support from overseas Chinese and anti-Japanese propaganda. Prominent KMT figures such as Du Yuesheng, T. V. Soong, Dai Li and H. H. Kung all stayed (some briefly) at Hong Kong.[10] Hong Kong was even the place where the Japanese tried to conduct secret peace talks with Chiang Kai-shek.[11] Although the colonial government allowed these activities in order not to antagonize China and the local population, it had to prevent these activities from becoming a pretext for Japan to attack Hong Kong. In addition to these organs, the colony also housed more than 700 KMT soldiers, known collectively as the "lone battalion" (孤軍), which had withdrawn to Hong Kong during the fall of Guangzhou. They settled in camps near Ma Tau Chung in Kowloon. Although the government wanted to repatriate them, no action was taken before the Japanese invasion.[12]

The Chinese Communists were also active here. Prominent Communist figures in Hong Kong included Liao Chengzhi (廖承志), Zeng Sheng (曾生) and Pan Hannian (潘漢年); their targets were mainly intellectuals and workers.[13] The CCP established the "Office of the Eighth Route Army" (八路軍駐香港辦事處) as early as 1938. Later, Zeng Sheng, the leader of the Hong Kong Seamen's Union, established Communist cells at Huiyang (惠陽) and Bao'an (寶安) in Guangdong Province. They gradually emerged as the East River Column (東江縱隊), a CCP guerrilla unit operating in Hong Kong and Guangdong. Pro-CCP volunteer associations raised funds and supplies for the guerrillas. Hundreds of young overseas Chinese joined the guerrilla force.[14] Strikes against Japanese ships were orchestrated by the Seamen's Union and the dock workers.[15] In addition, the Wang Jingwei party and other political forces were active in China (see below).[16]

British, Chinese and Japanese Intelligence Activities in Pre-war Hong Kong

During the interwar period, Hong Kong was a British intelligence centre in Asia. The earliest signal intelligence organization in Hong Kong was a listening post established by the Royal Corps of Signals in 1920. A year later, the commanders-in-chief of the China, East Indies, and Australian stations decided to expand the naval signal intelligence network in the British dominions in the Pacific.[17] In 1924, the Royal Navy cooperated with the Government Code and Cipher School to establish a listening station on the flagship of the China Station for intercepting Japanese naval communications. At that time, flagships were usually heavy cruisers (or, later, the standard Treaty-cruisers) with good communication capability. A radio listening station at Stonecutters was later established. The navy also relied on the British staff of the Chinese Maritime Customs Service to monitor Japanese shipping in Asia.[18]

Before 1934, the army and navy intelligence branches in Asia cooperated little with one another. The situation was somewhat improved when the Far Eastern Combined Bureau (FECB) was established, with Hong Kong as its headquarters. Originally, the navy had preferred Singapore, which was deemed safer. As the army wanted to preserve its Shanghai Intelligence Office, Hong Kong became the compromise location. The main functions of the FECB included providing early warning of war, military intelligence for general officers commanding in Asia, and general intelligence about Asia for the British government. The headquarters of the FECB was at the naval yard; the radio station at Stonecutters became its subordinate Y-Section. The station initially had a staff of twenty-nine men; an additional seventeen worked at HMS *Tamar*. Because of the secretive nature of the organization, the commanders of the FECB were officially referred to as staff officers of the China Station. In addition to signal intelligence, the FECB also relied on informers from the business community, the merchant marine and even smugglers. As some informers were unwilling to enter the naval yard, the FECB also had a special office in the main building of the Hongkong and Shanghai Bank.[19]

Although the FECB was a joint organization of the three services, actual cooperation among the services was difficult. The majority of the staff, including its head, was from the Royal Navy. Although army involvement increased steadily, the RAF was hardly enthusiastic. In 1938, the budget for the army in the FECB was £1,700; by comparison, a mere £100 was earmarked for the RAF. Still, the FECB had some major breakthroughs in decryption, despite the meagre staff who worked shifts around the clock. The Royal Navy had already decrypted the code of the Imperial Japanese Navy in 1935. The army broke the code of the Foreign Ministry of Japan, allowing the British to read cables between Tokyo and Japanese consulates in China and Hong Kong. However, the under-staffed FECB was unable to handle all Japanese communications. As Richard Aldrich has pointed out, this partly explains the inability of the FECB to obtain more information about the tactical capabilities of the Japanese military.[20] Generally speaking, the FECB provided accurate intelligence. For example, it warned the Nationalist government about an imminent Japanese invasion of Guangzhou. However, the warning was ignored by the Nationalists' intelligence branch in Hong Kong.[21] It was not until mid-1941 that the Japanese discovered their communications were being intercepted, as its carrier group was moving towards French Indochina. Thereafter, the Japanese introduced a new code, which was not entirely decrypted before December 1941.[22]

The major British espionage organization working in Hong Kong was the branch of the Secret Intelligence Service (SIS). For most of the interwar period, it was headed by Charles Drage, a retired naval commander who worked in the Hongkong and Shanghai Bank. The Hong Kong Police also had its own special branch for internal intelligence. The main targets of espionage were the Soviet Union, the Comintern and the nationalist movements in Asia. One of the major successes of the SIS in Asia was the arrest of Ho Chi Minh and the capture of the Communist archive in Hong Kong in 1931. After the outbreak of the Sino-Japanese War, the SIS in Hong Kong had only a staff of merely two men, responsible for liaising with the German advisers of the Nationalist Army and for bribing Chinese officers from the Wang Jingwei regime into providing the British with information about the Japanese military.[23] However, the service had little success beyond that. In January 1941, Brooke-Popham complained that the identity of most of the SIS agents in Hong Kong, Shanghai and Singapore had already been exposed and that the branches were ineffective in general.[24]

The Royal Navy also sent the submarines of the 4th Submarine Flotilla to mainland Japan from Hong Kong from 1939 to 1940 for intelligence purposes. The submarines were re-supplied by ships from the Blue Funnel and Glen Lines, which travelled between Hong Kong and Shanghai. One such mission was the excursion by HMS *Regulus* into the Shibushi Bay of Kagoshima. HMS *Regulus* was even able to get close to IJN *Nagato*, the flagship of the Imperial Japanese Navy, and to take pictures of its turrets and rangefinders. Although sources are lacking, it is possible that other submarines from the 4th Flotilla participated in similar actions. HMS *Regulus* also sneaked into the waters near Vladivostok to observe, without being detected, an anti-submarine exercise of the Soviet navy.[25]

After the outbreak of the Sino-Japanese War, the Nationalist intelligence organizations became more active in Hong Kong. The major KMT intelligence organs in Hong Kong included the Southwest Transport Company (西南運輸公司) formed by the Central Bureau of Investigation and Statistics (Zhongtong, 國民黨中央調查統計局), the Bureau of Investigation and Statistics (Juntong, 軍事委員會調查統計局), the Relief Commission (賑濟委員會) under Du Yuesheng, and the Rongji (榮記行) and Huaji (華記行) companies formed by Chan Chak, head of the KMT in Hong Kong. According to a Japanese report, the Hong Kong branch of Zhongtong was led by the old guard Tongmenghui member Chen Su, who had an office on Ashley Road in Tsim Sha Tsui. The Juntong branch was led by Major General Wang Xinheng, whose subordinates were mainly graduates from the Whampoa Military and the Central Political academies. Some were members of the Revival Society (復興社), which was loyal to Chiang Kai-shek. The organization consisted of different branches with duties such as surveillance, liaison, counter-espionage and radio interception. It was also equipped with a radio able to intercept Japanese wireless communications. The Relief Commission was to liaise with the KMT espionage network in Shanghai and to monitor the out-of-office politicians in order to prevent them from joining the Wang Jingwei government. The Rongji and Huaji companies were responsible mainly for liaison and propaganda work. As will be discussed in the next chapter, during the Battle of Hong Kong, Chan Chak was also responsible for communicating with the Hong Kong triads.[26]

The most important success of the KMT intelligence branches was the defection of Tao Xisheng and Gao Zongwu in 1940, who exposed the secret treaty between Wang Jingwei and the Japanese government.[27] The colonial government initially tried to restrain the KMT intelligence organizations; Dai Li, the head of Juntong, was even arrested and deported from Hong Kong in April 1940. However, as the Japanese turned increasingly aggressive, the British tacitly allowed the KMT to carry out many of its activities.[28]

Soon after the termination of the Anglo-Japanese Alliance, the Japanese launched espionage activities against Britain. During the 1920s and 1930s, at least one British officer, Frederick Rutland, RN, was identified as a Japanese spy; two more senior officers, Rear Admiral Lord Sempill and Colonel Francis Piggott, were also suspected.[29] In addition to spies in the British establishment, the Japanese also dispatched a large number of operatives to Hong Kong. As Hong Kong did not close its land boundary with the mainland until late 1940, the Japanese built up a spy network in the colony. The operatives were disguised as consulate staff, businessmen, migrant farmers and artisans. A Lieutenant Colonel Suzuki Kenji (鈴木卓爾), who ostensibly came to Hong Kong to learn English, was in reality the head of the Hong Kong Branch (香港機關).

From 1926, the Japanese started to compile the *Hong Kong Military Gazette* (香港兵要地誌), which contained major details about geography, the garrison, transport, population and other matters. In 1934, Maruyama Masao (丸山政男) wrote a report about ways to capture Hong Kong, with the long-winded title "A Study of Military Geography and Other Related Information for the Capture of the British Colony of Hong Kong" (為攻略英領香港之兵要地誌並作戰資料). Based on these works, the Japanese General Staff updated the *Hong Kong Military Gazette* in 1938. The new version discussed the defence and other aspects of Hong Kong in detail, such as politics, economy, population, transport, hygiene, media and communications. The Japanese also discovered the Gin Drinker's Line, which consisted of "concrete-built *tochika*" (トーチカ, pillbox in Japanese), noting the presence of four *tochika* south of the Shing Mun Reservoir that were linked with communication trenches and protected by barbed wire and camouflage. It also noted that the structure, which was later known as the Shing Mun Redoubt, was built in November 1936.[30] The *Military Gazette* also alleged that there were new batteries at Junk Bay, Devil's Peak, Stanley, Cape D'Aguliar, Pok Fu Lam and Tai Tam, as well as a new airfield at Kam Tin. As this list makes clear, the *Military Gazette* was not as accurate as subsequent works have suggested. With the exception of the Shing Mun Redoubt, the map published in the *Military Gazette* failed to locate the position of most pillboxes of the Gin Drinker's Line. It wrongly suggested that there were three 18-inch guns and six anti-aircraft (AA) guns at Stanley, even mentioning a fanciful seaplane base at the Shing Mun Reservoir.[31] Although the *Military Gazette* accurately recorded the size of the garrison, it contained no information about its defence scheme.

With the aid of the Italians, the Japanese corrected some errors of the *Military Gazette*. An encrypted telegram from the Japanese 23rd Army noted that Gennaro Pagano di Melito, the Italian consul in Hong Kong and a retired officer of the Regia Marina (Royal Italian Navy), had passed on some "information about the defence of Hong Kong and its garrison" and provided "professional analysis" to the Japanese in April 1939.[32] As the telegram was sent neither by diplomatic nor naval cable, it was possibly missed by the Y-Section, thus the leakage was not known to the British.

With the above information, the Japanese produced another *Hong Kong Defence Map* in August 1939 to a scale of 1:25,000. Although the map was still inaccurate in some instances, it was able to show the fire direction of the pillboxes of the Shing Mun Redoubt, exposing the absence of frontal fire cover.[33]

The Italians were involved in another major intelligence leak. In June 1939, the Commander-in-Chief of the China Station, Admiral Percy Noble, conferred with the French at Saigon about military cooperation. The FECB later intercepted a Japanese consular report about the consensus between British and French officers over the indefensibility of Hong Kong. According to Richard Aldrich, the information came from a spy within the Hong Kong government who worked for the Italians.[34]

Before Italy became a belligerent party in 1940, the colonial government and the garrison could do little to stem Japanese and Italian espionage activities, as it was wary of antagonizing the Japanese. Only key figures were deported, such as Lieutenant Colonel Suzuki Kenji. From early 1940, the Hong Kong Branch became more active, approaching the triads. Lieutenant Colonel Okada Yoshimasa (岡田芳政), the successor of Suzuki, sent Lieutenant Sakata Shigemori (阪田誠盛) to liaise with the triads. Sakata, who had a Chinese alias Tian Sheng (田盛), had studied at Peking University. In October 1940, the Hong Kong Branch planned to launch a putsch to disrupt British rule. If it succeeded, a pro-Wang Jingwei army (with the grandiose name of "The Autonomous Group Army for the Salvation of the Chinese People" 中華人民自治救國集團軍), led by Xie Wenda (謝文達),[35] would "liberate" Hong Kong. However, Tokyo finally rejected the plan. Meanwhile, the pro-Wang Jingwei supporters in Hong Kong also operated newspapers, trying to sway public opinion and denounce both the Chongqing KMT and the colonial government. One of the more important of these newspapers was the *South China Daily* (南華日報).[36]

On 12 October 1941, Lieutenant Colonel Okada was ordered to mobilize the triads when the Japanese attacked Hong Kong. The Hong Kong Branch was to 1) prevent British destruction of the main roads; 2) direct Japanese troops through road signs and guides; 3) interrupt British troop movements by destroying British trucks in Kowloon; 4) destroy power plants and water sources; 5) conduct subversive activities such as distributing leaflets and bombing public areas; 6) take action against "prominent government officials and their families," "Chongqing public figures," and "ordinary citizens"; and 7) sever the internal and external communications of Hong Kong.[37] In mid-December, the Hong Kong Branch was renamed the Asia Prosperity Branch (興亞機關).

Although Okada claimed that his fifth column had prevented the British from destroying bridges and roads and cutting the water supply of Hong Kong Island, the actual damage caused by the fifth columnists was in question. As will be revealed in the next chapter, many of these claims were exaggerated and some (such as cutting the water supply) were fabrications. In all, although the Japanese were unable to obtain defence schemes and to decrypt British radio communications, they gathered some useful intelligence in Hong Kong, such as the presence of the Gin Drinker's Line, the knowledge of which shaped the Japanese plan against Hong Kong.

Economic Contribution of Hong Kong during the Early Stages of the War

Hong Kong contributed much to the Allied war effort during the early phase of the Second World War. As it was the only port available to Chinese Nationalists, a substantial amount of war materials and supplies reached the Nationalists through Hong Kong. They were transported to centres of resistance such as Wuhan and Changsha through the Guangzhou-Hankou Railway, until these cities were captured in late 1938. Before the fall of Guangzhou in December 1938, 60 to 70 percent of goods imported by the Nationalists passed through Hong Kong.[38] Parallel to this flow of military supplies was a lucrative smuggling business between China and the world. Some of it was even controlled by KMT agents in Hong Kong who were responsible for the import of war materials. For example, Lin Shiliang, a confidential assistant of H. H. Kung, the brother-in-law of Chiang Kai-shek, was accused of smuggling goods for personal profit. The Kung family was also implicated.[39]

Even before the fall of Guangzhou, numerous Chinese refugees fled to Hong Kong. Although they added much pressure to the colony in hygiene and housing terms, they also provided much cheap and skilled labour for the burgeoning industrial sector.[40] When the European War broke out, the industrial and economic potential of Hong Kong was mobilized to support Britain's war effort.

The shipbuilding industry of Hong Kong, one of the largest in Asia, contributed to the Allied war effort. Before the war, Hong Kong had already been able to construct vessels of more than 10,000 tons. In early 1941, the British government formed the Eastern Group Supply Council, consisting of representatives from Hong Kong, India, Malaya, Ceylon, Australia, New Zealand and East Africa, to coordinate the industrial mobilization of the Eastern colonies. The council recommended that Hong Kong should make use of its readily available manpower and shipbuilding industry. Before the fall of Hong Kong, the Taikoo and Whampoa docks had built ten 7,000-ton "Empire Ships" for the Ministry of War Transport. They were standardized transport ships built by private yards, similar to the Liberty Ships of the United States. Only three ships survived the war; five were captured by the Japanese (Table 23).

Table 23   Hong Kong-built Empire ships

Name	Builder	Tonnage	Launch	Commission	Note
Empire Almond	T*	6,860 t	7/1941	9/1941	Survived
Empire Blossom	T	6,603 t	12/1941	1942**	Captured and sunk in 1943
Empire Dragon	W*	6,854 t	12/1941	1942**	Captured and sunk in 1944
Empire Haven	T	6,603 t	4/1941	6/1941	Survived
Empire Wall	W	–	–	–	Captured and broken up in 1945
Empire Starlight	W	6,854 t	4/1941	7/1941	Sunk in 1942
Empire Pagoda	W	6,854 t	–	1942**	Captured and sunk in 1944
Empire Moonbeam	W	6,849 t	3/1941	6/1941	Sunk in 1942
Empire Moonrise	W	6,854 t	6/1941	8/1941	Survived
Empire Lantern	W	6,854 t	5/1941	12/1942**	Captured and sunk in 1944

*   T: Taikoo Yard; W: Whampoa Yard

** Completed during Japanese occupation

Source: William Mitchell and Leonard Sawyer, *The Empire Ships* (London, New York, Hamburg, Hong Kong: Lloyd's of London Press, 1990)

Although Hong Kong lacked large arsenals for producing steel plates and naval guns, it built auxiliary warships such as mine-sweepers and patrol boats. When the Eastern Group Supply Council decided to build warships in Hong Kong, plans of the HMS *Bangor*-class minesweeper were sent to Taikoo and Whampoa yards. Actual work started in July 1941, with four ships being built: HMS *Lantau*, HMS *Lyemun*, HMS *Taitam* and HMS *Waglan*. However, they were captured by the Japanese (Table 24).[41] Vaughan Shipbuilding, a smaller yard, built four patrol boats (MMS95, 96, 123, 124) for the Royal Navy. These boats, all unfinished at the time of the British surrender, were destroyed.

After representatives from the Ministry of Supply had inspected the industrial potential of Hong Kong, the colonial government formed a committee to discuss ways of encouraging the development of industry. The government bought telephones, knitwear, utensils, glass plates, barbed wire, steel shovels and pumps from local producers. A company producing binoculars was encouraged by the colonial government to build a factory in Hong Kong with a capacity for producing 4,000 binoculars per month. The Ministry of Supply wanted the factory to be relocated to Burma, but the owner wished to take advantage of the abundant supply of skilled workers in Hong Kong.[42] The Royal Army Ordnance Corps (RAOC) also cooperated with the Hong Kong government to produce some of the military supplies locally.[43]

Table 24 Minesweepers built in Hong Kong, 1941

Name	Builder	Tonnage	Start	Commission	Note
HMS *Waglan* (J211)	T*	673 t	7/1941	1944	Became Patrol Boat 102 of the IJN; returned to the British and broken up in 1947
HMS *Taitam* (J210)	T	673 t	7/1941	1944	Became Patrol Boat 101 of the IJN; sunk in January 1945
HMS *Lyemun* (J209)	W*	673 t	7/1941	1943	Became Gunboat *Nanyo* of the IJN; sunk in December 1943
HMS *Lantau* (J208)	W	673 t	7/1941	1942	Became cargo ship *Gyosei Maru*, later renamed *Kagoshima Maru*, broken up in 1950

* T: Taikoo Yard; W: Whampoa Yard

Hong Kong also contributed financially to the war. The colonial government established a wartime budget in October 1939 that was mainly used for the defence of the colony itself, with surpluses remitted to London. Providing additional funds proved to be a challenge. The proposal to levy income tax was opposed by the chambers of commerce and the unofficial members of the Legislative Council. The government then formed the War Revenue Committee to find new sources of revenue. Property taxes, salary taxes and taxation on tobacco and alcohol were all considered; many were adopted by 1940. With the additional income, it was expected that Hong Kong could provide HK$6,000,000 (or £375,000) to Britain and an additional $2,400,000 for local defence. In addition, the Legislative Council donated $1,600,000 to Britain. Between April 1940 and January 1941, the new taxes had raised $6,000,000, but the expenditure of the Air Raid Precaution alone amounted to $12,000,000.[44] In all, the public donated more than $10,000,000 to China and Britain, with voluntary associations raising money from the public such as the Bomber Fund of the *South China Morning Post*, the British War Organization, the China Defence League and the British Fund for the Relief of Distress in China.[45]

The Hong Kong government also tightened the control of foreign exchange and trade to support the Allied war effort and China's war against Japan. Soon after the outbreak of the Sino-Japanese War, British banks in China transferred £300,000,000 silver specie from Shanghai and other branches to the United States to be converted into gold specie via Hong Kong. When war broke out in Europe, the gold reserve of the Hong Kong government was shipped to India by the cruiser HMS *Birmingham*. Only a portion of the reserve was sent back to maintain foreign exchange and international trade payments. The colonial government introduced the Defence (Finance) Regulations in 1939, establishing control over foreign exchange. Only eighteen banks were allowed to conduct currency exchange, including the major local Chinese and British banks. To avoid antagonizing the Japanese, the Yokohama Specie Bank was selected. As the amount of foreign exchange was controlled by the government, large-scale movements of Japanese capital or attempts to disrupt the Chinese or Hong Kong currencies were prevented.[46]

In July 1941, the Hong Kong government amended the Defence (Finance) Regulations, decreasing the number of foreign exchange banks to eleven. Following British and American example, Japanese assets in Hong Kong were also frozen. Two months before the war, representatives from China, Britain and the United States held a meeting in Hong Kong to discuss exchange controls and measures to prevent the Japanese from damaging the Nationalist currency, *fabi*. It was agreed that a fixed exchange rate should be introduced between *fabi*, the British pound and the US dollar.[47] To help China stabilize *fabi*, the government also allowed the Nationalists to print *fabi* covertly in Hong Kong.[48]

War Preparation by the Hong Kong Government

Contrary to the popular belief that the British were reluctant in recruiting the local Chinese for defence, the British began to recruit more Hong Kong Chinese for the defence of Hong Kong on a large scale as early as 1936. That year, Lieutenant Michael Calvert was sent to Hong Kong to increase the number of Chinese sappers (previously known as the Submarine Miners) to 250.[49] When war broke out in China, the British recruited Chinese gunners for the artillery units in Hong Kong. The first group of gunners passed out in 1938.[50] In all, around 250 gunners and 250 sappers were recruited and distributed among the local units by December 1941. A month before the outbreak of war, the War Office agreed to form the first Hong Kong Chinese regiment, known as the Hong Kong Regiment. It was designated as a machine-gun battalion led by British officers and Chinese NCOs. The slogan adopted to attract recruits was "Protecting One's Home" (保衛蘆舍). On 3 November, the regiment planned to recruit fifty NCOs, but more than six hundred men applied.[51] From mid-November, the regiment began to recruit troopers. The physical requirements for the recruits were that they had to be 170 cm in height, 60 kg in weight and 86 cm in chest size. By the time the Japanese attacked, a platoon-sized unit was formed, led by Major H. W. Mayer from the Middlesex battalion. Hundreds of Chinese also served in the Royal Army Ordnance Corps, Royal Army Service Corps (RASC), Royal Navy Volunteer Reserves, and various British military units in Hong Kong. In all, according to the calculation of the Royal Corps of Signals, there were 1,073 Hong Kong Chinese serving in the British Commonwealth forces in Hong Kong by 8 December 1941.[52]

After the war started in Europe, the Hong Kong government revived conscription, but only for British residents. Most recruited residents were sent to the HKVDC or the Naval Reserves. The HKVDC started to recruit Chinese from the 1920s, but they were not employed as combat soldiers and did not receive equal allowances until 1937.[53] In May 1940, a militia consisting solely of those too old to serve in the regular forces was formed. Led by Harry Owen-Hughes, the manager of the Union Insurance Society, it was known as the Hughesiliers or the Methusaliers, after Methuselah.[54]

When Japanese forces were about to take Guangzhou in September 1938, the Hong Kong government took steps to prepare for war by amending the Emergency Regulations Ordinance of 1922, which empowered the police to arrest suspicious personnel, expel those without regular work and ban all seditious assemblies. The government also acquired the power to censor Chinese newspapers and journals, form Special Constables, demolish squatters' dwellings, control harbour activities and fix commodity prices.[55] In November 1938, all British residents were registered.

In August 1939, when war in Europe seemed imminent, London proclaimed the Order in Councils of Emergency Powers and Emergency (Colonial Defence) Powers, to further empower the colonial authorities. The Hong Kong government extended censorship to all publications.[56] On 26 August, Governor Northcote introduced the Defence Regulations of 1939 to the Legislative Council. It was more comprehensive than previous ordinances, allowing the government to control all forms of communication, port activities, import and export, propaganda and property other than land.[57] The regulations were further amended in spring 1940, when the government improved the security of sensitive areas such as military facilities, fuel stores and public works. Taking pictures of these facilities was no longer allowed; suspicious personnel were monitored. The police and military were empowered to requisition houses and vehicles and to search private homes.[58] The government also banned the export of nickel coins and products made of nickel, as nickel could be used to make bullets. The import of wireless communication devices was also banned.[59]

As the government had more wartime responsibilities, many of its officials had extra duties. For example, the secretary of China affairs was concurrently the director of intelligence; the chairman of the Urban Council was also the food controller; the crown solicitor was the director of evacuation; and the commissioner of police was the controller of land transport and chief security officer.[60] A number of new organizations were also formed (Table 25):

Table 25   New departments of the Hong Kong government, 1937–1941[61]

Name	Formation Date	Duty
Air Raid Precaution Department	1937	(Discussed below)
Foreign Exchange Office	9/1939	Exchange control
Labour Advisory Board	3/1940	Improve working conditions; prevent union activities
War Taxation Department	4/1940	Manage wartime taxes
Food Control Office	4/1940	Control food stores
Immigration Department	11/1940	Immigration control
Price Board	1941	Price control
War Supplies Board	1941	Manage wartime transport
Information Department	1941	Propaganda
Fisheries Research Station	1941	Increase local food production

As the British were rightly convinced that future enemies would target populated cities such as London, they saw civil defence organizations such as the Air Raid Precaution Department (ARP) as imperative for reducing the number of air raid casualties. During the Sino-Japanese War, the Japanese had a record of using terror bombing raids against unprotected Chinese cities. Since Hong Kong was seen as vulnerable to air attack, its government formed its own ARP.

From January to December 1939, the ARP recruited 120 Air Raid Precaution training officers, who each received fifty hours of theoretical and practical training about civil defence. These officers in turn trained 6,650 personnel, including 2,400 Air Raid Precaution wardens (the plan had been to train 9,600; the scheme was almost completed by December 1941), 1,500 policemen, 300 fire-fighters and 1,000 members of the St. John Ambulance Brigade. The ARP also distributed 180,000 leaflets and 200,000 booklets in Chinese and English entitled *The Protection of Your Home against Air Raids*. From 1938, blackout exercises were conducted once a season and irregular daytime exercises also took place. The ARP commandant, Wing Commander A. H. S. Steele-Perkins, boasted that Hong Kong could black out in two to three minutes. However, the actual results of the exercises suggested otherwise.[62] The ARP also built more than 800 Air Raid Wardens posts, each manned by six ARP wardens. There were plans to construct 1,600 of them in the town. In May 1940, the ARP School was operational, with the goal of training more ARP wardens.[63]

Originally, the colonial government had had no intention of building air raid shelters, largely because of Northcote's conviction that Hong Kong should be abandoned before the Japanese attacked. After the war scare, Lieutenant General Edward Norton, the acting governor during Northcote's sick leave, ordered the ARP to design and build shelters in urban areas. Steele-Perkins travelled to Chongqing to study the effectiveness of shelters. Although Chongqing was under heavy air attack, incurring casualties, the life of the city was relatively ordered. This experience convinced Steele-Perkins that shelters were an effective means of reducing air raid casualties and maintaining the order of the colony during air attacks.[64] In late 1940, a team of KMT signal intelligence experts was also sent to Murray Barracks to provide air raid early warning for Hong Kong.[65]

Norton, who did not share the idea that civil defence was useless, introduced numerous measures such as expanding the police force, establishing the Special Constables (a kind of auxiliary police force), an independent Fire Department, an Immigration Department and a War Supplies Board. After the Legislative Council passed the Civil Defence Ordinance in July 1941, the government encouraged the public to participate in civil defence organizations such as the Auxiliary Medical Services. Positions such as Distribution Officer (for food distribution), Officer in Charge of Communal Kitchens, and Evacuation Officer were created to prepare for food distribution and evacuation of the families of the civil servants and the soldiers during the war time.[66]

The Hong Kong government invested a large sum of money in the ARP. By September 1940, the ARP had spent $8,068,293; another $4,000,000 was spent in 1941.[67] As the ARP expanded rapidly without adequate supervision and was given the power to skip around normal government procedures, numerous cases of abuse and corruption occurred. The most well-known cases involving the ARP were the Hongkong and Shanghai Bank and Mimi Lau cases. The first took place in summer 1941, when the Hongkong and Shanghai Bank Main Building was ordered to black out. When the bank did not receive the agreed compensation, it reported to the government. The engineer of the Department of Public Works responsible for the payment shot himself before the investigation took place. To investigate alleged corruption and abuse within the ARP, the government appointed Puisne Judge Paul Cressall to form a board of inquiry. More cases surfaced, the most famous being the case involving Miss Mimi Lau (Lau Kam Ling), a starlet, clerk in a local steelworks, and close friend of Steele-Perkins, the ARP commandant. It was alleged that Lau had used her relationship with Steele-Perkins to secure shovel and helmet contracts for her company at a higher price.[68] It was also found that some contractors outsourced their work to shelf companies to exploit the government loophole of a 10-percent profit for all contracts. It was also discovered that half of the breeze blocks provided by a company were of inferior quality.[69] Despite censorship, the investigation dominated the headlines of Chinese and English newspapers until November, as more cases surfaced after another suicide attempt by an ARP official. Although Cressall finished his investigation in November, he was unable to finish the report, as he died in captivity in 1944. The manuscript of the report remains missing.

The English newspapers devoted overwhelming attention to the relationship between Mimi Lau and Steele-Perkins. As the latter was about to serve as the ARP commandant in Calcutta, he was a suitable scapegoat for blame that should have been placed on both the ARP and the Department of Public Works, which was responsible for the construction of air raid shelters and the procurement of breeze blocks. In the confusion, an unfounded rumour emerged that Mimi Lau had been responsible for the government's decision to buy inferior breeze blocks. Prisoners-of-war and civilian internees called the blocks "Mimi Laus."[70] The prevalence of this myth revealed the government's ability to influence the media; it also reflected the potential distrust between British and Chinese. Mark Young, the new governor, formed an Anti-Corruption Bureau in mid-November, three weeks before the outbreak of war.[71] The unchecked power of the government during the period of emergency was criticized; Sir Lo Man Kam, an unofficial member of the Legislative Council, questioned the government's use of the emergency legislation to demolish squatters' homes.[72]

As Kent Fedorowich has pointed out, the colonial government's decision to evacuate British women and children from Hong Kong led to much controversy. As early as June 1939, the British government started to devise plans for the evacuation of the families of British colonial officials and servicemen. When war became a real possibility after the fall of France a year later, Whitehall authorized the colonial government to implement the evacuation. By early August 1940, around 3,500 British women and children were evacuated. However, the unfair arrangements, such as the exemption of the families of senior officials while non-European and Eurasian family members were forced to stay in Manila instead of Australia, led to much resentment among the garrison, the British expatriate community and the Legislative Council. An Evacuation Representation Committee was formed among expatriates to lobby for the return of their family members. Facing much pressure from the community, the colonial government temporarily suspended the scheme soon after the war scare receded in late 1940. The Chinese community also resented the absence of evacuation plans for the Chinese, whose tax money was used to support the evacuation.

Right before the war, Mark Young still contemplated evacuating the Chinese in Hong Kong. He reported to the Colonial Office on 2 December:

> It is considered politically most desirable to give to the Chinese population an equal opportunity with Europeans to leave Hong Kong under prevailing conditions. Very grateful if you could waive immigration regulations for those Chinese who wish to go to Singapore. Number will not be large and all possible enquiries will be made to ensure that those leaving are reputable and of some financial standing. Grateful for most immediate reply since three ships leave almost immediately.[73]

Although both the colonial government and London stressed the need to evacuate loyal Chinese so as to avoid being seen as racially discriminating, British colonies in Asia, especially Australia and Singapore, refused to accept Chinese evacuees. Facing attack from both British and Chinese residents, the colonial government was hard pressed over the evacuation issue until the Japanese actually attacked.[74] Meanwhile, some prominent Chinese who were rich enough left Hong Kong before the war. Sir Robert Ho Tung, the leading Eurasian merchant, left the colony a few days before the outbreak of war, after being warned by the staff of the Japanese consul.[75]

Conclusion

By 1941, Hong Kong was a diverse and international society. As a result of the political turmoil in China and the Sino-Japanese conflict, it was also an arena in which various political forces from China planned and implemented their conflicting movements and schemes. As will be discussed, even during the Battle of Hong Kong, different factions struggled behind the scenes for control of the colony. Although Hong Kong was lost to the Japanese in 1941, it had rendered much economic support to both the British Empire and China. Between the outbreak of the Sino-Japanese War and the fall of Guangzhou, Hong Kong was the major seaport for Chiang Kai-shek's Nationalist regime. In addition, it was seen as a symbol of British support for the Chinese war effort. Although their full potential was never seen, the light and shipbuilding industries of Hong Kong contributed to the war against Germany.

As Hong Kong was in a difficult, if not desperate, geopolitical position, its government prepared for its civil defence despite pleas by the governor and the Colonial Office to demilitarize the colony. Although cases of corruption and wastage occurred in the process, some of the works, such as the air raid shelters and the Air Raid Precaution Department, did assist the colony and its garrison to resist the Japanese invasion. Compared perhaps to other British and Allied possessions in Asia, Hong Kong was better prepared, despite its ultimate fall.

8

THE FALL OF HONG KONG, DECEMBER 1941

Every day that you are able to maintain your resistance you help the Allied cause all over the world, and by a prolonged resistance you and your men can win the lasting honour which we are sure will be your due.

> —Winston Churchill to the Hong Kong Garrison, 20 December 1941

Hong Kong was very valuable to China as a port of access and had they not been convinced of our determination to stand and fight for its defence, and been taken into our confidence and given opportunities to inspect the defences and discuss plans for defence, the effect on their war effort would in all probability have been serious. A withdrawal of the troops in Hong Kong coinciding with the closing of the Burma Road might have had a marked effect on Chinese determination to fight on. Our policy for the defence of Hong Kong . . . played an important part at a critical period in China's war effort.[1]

> —Air Marshal Sir Robert Brooke-Popham, Commander-in-Chief, Far East, 1948

At 16:18 [Tokyo time, 25 December 1941] . . . we received a message about a white flag being hoisted in the Victoria Barracks . . . Suspecting that it was an enemy trick, we were filled in nervousness. After an hour, the enemy surrendered unconditionally; we were ordered to march into the Victoria Barracks. The soldiers were all relieved, and shouts of *"banzai!"*, *"banzai!"* could be heard throughout the Island.[2]

> —Reminiscence of a Japanese soldier of the 38th Division after the war

The Larger Context of the Hong Kong Operation of 1941

The defence of Hong Kong met its ultimate challenge after a century of planning and revision. The Japanese saw the capture of Hong Kong not only as a blow to the British in Asia but also as a means of accelerating the end of the war in China, as it would deprive Chiang Kai-shek of a window to the world and offer Japan a potential base from which to conduct subversive activities against him. During the battle, the Japanese High Command repeatedly raised concerns about the progress of the operation, and was anxious to finish it before the Chinese were able to reinforce Hong Kong. Moreover, it started the Third Changsha Campaign to support the siege. On the other hand, as the British saw Hong Kong as a symbol of their support for Chinese resistance, they reinforced the colony and courted the Chinese for joint defence. As discussed, the British commander in Asia cited the reinforcement of Hong Kong as a means of encouraging China and as part of an attempt to deter Japan. Maintaining Hong Kong, as David Macri has suggested, was a means for keeping the Soviet Union on the side of the Allies. Thus, the Battle of Hong Kong was by no means an isolated battle of a beleaguered garrison. It was actually a hallmark battle of the struggle involving Britain, Japan, China, the United States and even the Soviet Union in Asia. After the Battle of Hong Kong, the Japanese tried to use the ex-British colony as a convoy base and a political base against the Chinese Nationalists, but both attempts failed in the face of the counterattack of the Allies.

This chapter deals with the Battle of Hong Kong in 1941. It covers the ill-fated Canadian reinforcement, the planning of both sides, the different phases of the battle and an analysis of the battle.

The Arrival of Brigadier Lawson and the Second Canadian Reinforcement

On 27 October 1941, Brig. Lawson, the commander of the Canadian reinforcement to Hong Kong (C Force) and his second-in-command Lt. Col. (later Colonel) Patrick Hennessy arrived in Vancouver to board the ships to Hong Kong. The loading process was chaotic; the motor transports of C Force even failed to catch the ship.[3] The C Force was carried by SS *Awatea*, which was escorted by HMCS *Prince Robert*. Seasickness was a big problem for the C Force at sea. Lawson wrote in his diary on 30 October: "Sick up to 40, mostly seasick."[4] Training was also affected by the prevailing seasickness.[5] The first lecture to the troops, held on 2 November, disclosed the destination of the C Force.

The C Force arrived at Honolulu on 2 November. No soldier was allowed to disembark or to wear insignia. *Taiyo Maru*, a Japanese passenger ship, was in the neighbouring berth. When the C Force left the harbour on 3 November, some of the soldiers shouted "See you in Manila" from the deck. Lawson suspected that the incident gave the Japanese clues about the reinforcement, but apparently the Japanese had no knowledge of the event.[6] Lawson was aware of the imminence of war. On 12 November, he wrote, "[Winston Churchill] says UK will declare war if Japs do so against us. Wish he would let us get to Hong Kong first."[7]

The Canadian reinforcement was warmly welcomed by Governor Mark Young and the garrison commander Maj. Gen. Christopher Maltby when it arrived in Hong

Kong on 16 November. The troops, led by a band, marched along Nathan Road to the Sham Shui Po Barracks. Lawson immediately set to work. On 17 November, he had a "quick look around"[8] on the island with Maltby and discussed the defence scheme with the officers of the China Command. He also cabled the Canadian General Staff to discuss sending more men to Hong Kong.[9] He then toured the island with his battalion commanders.[10] He also relocated his headquarters (HQ) from Wan Chai Gap to Wong Nai Chung Gap to get a better access to different parts of the island.

Little attention has been paid to the empty entries of Lawson's diary. The first blank was between 21 November and 1 December, during the manning exercise of the garrison. Lawson was fully occupied; he also had to keep it secret. Rifleman John Beebe described what the garrison did in those three weeks before the battle:

> We lost no time in getting down to work, taking up our posts on guard duty at the permanent dugouts and shelters . . . we got familiar with the lay of the land during our three-day sessions on guard duty. In the following two weeks we got to know the place even better and to like it very well. We drilled hard every morning for two or three hours . . .[11]

Brigade training was scheduled for 8 December but as the war actually started on that day, the entries between 4 and 10 December were also left blank. In other words, the blanks of Lawson's diary actually suggest that the garrison was fully occupied by the redeployment and the exercises.

Lawson also brought with him the hope of more reinforcement. Two days after his arrival, Maltby cabled Brooke-Popham about the possibility of Canada sending a third battalion so that the garrison could stay longer on the Gin Drinker's Line. Brooke-Popham reported to the War Office:

> Brigadier Lawson straight from Canadian War Office suggests we ask Canada to complete Force C Hong Kong to an Infantry Brigade Group . . . If suggestion approved modified establishments personnel and vehicles suitable for Hong Kong will be wired direct to Defence. Lawson says "they will be thrown at us" . . .[12]

Brooke-Popham stressed the "salutary effect on Japan and strong psychological stimulus to Garrison and Colony" of further reinforcement.[13] With Kai Tak more secure, a fighter squadron could be deployed to cover the ground forces. He also suggested that an absence of air cover for the Canadian troops might lead to political controversy, and that the Americans might want to use Kai Tak as an "emergency landing ground" and to help the garrison.[14] Lawson even claimed that such reinforcement would be "thrown at" him from Canada.[15]

The COS discussed the issue on 26 November. The Vice CIGS, Maj. Gen. Archibald Nye, questioned the feasibility of holding Kai Tak and asked whether Canada's intention of sending more troops was based on the assumption that the Gin Drinker's Line could be held for an extended period of time.[16] Still, another COS meeting decided to allocate an additional four heavy and sixteen light anti-aircraft (AA) guns to Hong Kong, bringing the total number of AA guns available to twenty heavy and eighteen light guns.[17] On 1 December, the COS agreed that "the way now seemed clear for an approach to be made to the Canadian Government for the provision of the balance of an Infantry Brigade Group for Hong Kong."[18] As London gave the green light for the second batch of Canadian reinforcements, the Port Defence Committee further raised the AA standard to forty-eight heavy and sixty light guns.[19] The COS accepted this recommendation on 3 December,[20] but the issue was dropped as it was found that the Japanese were already on the move.

In other words, the defence of Hong Kong could have been considerably improved in the coming months after the arrival of the C Force. Another battalion would have been sent, and the anti-aircraft defence would also have been improved. Whether these improvements could have made a difference is not clear, as the Japanese attacked on 8 December, sealing the fate of the garrison.

British Redeployment in November 1941

The arrival of the Canadian reinforcement allowed Maltby to revise his plan. Originally, three battalions would be concentrated on Hong Kong Island, leaving only one battalion on the mainland for delaying action. The New Territories and Kowloon would be given up. Maltby explained in 1945 his decision to change the plan:

> At the outbreak of the war with Germany the garrison consisted of three infantry battalions and one machine gun battalion, which permitted the employment of only one infantry battalion on the mainland. The role of this latter battalion was to cover a comprehensive scheme of demolitions, and to act as a delaying force from the frontier back to Kowloon, the role of the garrison being to deny the use of the harbour to the enemy rather than for use of our own fleet.
>
> With the arrival of two battalions of Canadians, certain alterations were made to this plan. I visualised that the enemy might well only blockade me from the landward side, and that one battalion only there might very well enable them with a comparatively weak force to drive it back, and thus I would have been forced to give up the valuable area of Kowloon, with its stores, docks and supplies, and a population estimated at about 3/4 million, in the face of a comparatively small offensive. Moreover, and this was my chief reason, I would hand over to the enemy the high ground behind Kowloon and thus he would

> obtain ideal positions for artillery observation points for their direction of
> artillery fire on to the Northern shores of the Island and its defences.[21]

In short, the garrison was to deny the enemy the use of Kowloon Ridge as an artillery observation post and to gain time for the garrison to either rescue or demolish the supplies in Kowloon. As Maltby was aware of "the inherent shortcomings of linear defence and two serious gaps (Smugglers Pass and Customs Pass[22]) in that defence," he only intended to use the line to delay the Japanese advance for a short period. However, he also noted that he "saw no reason why the period between their crossing of the frontier and the evacuation of the mainland by my forces should not extend to a period of seven days or more," unless the Japanese launched a major offensive against the line.[23]

Maltby admitted that he had miscalculated when he expected the Japanese would land at the south shore of Hong Kong Island after taking the New Territories and Kowloon. Based on this assumption, he constructed a double-layered defence "ring." The infantry garrison was divided into two brigades, with the Mainland Brigade fighting a delaying action in the New Territories and along the line and the Island Brigade guarding the south shore of the island. Once the line was penetrated, the Mainland Brigade would retire to the island.

According to the new plan, the Mainland Brigade consisted of the 2nd Battalion, The Royal Scots (2RS, under Lt. Col. S. E. H. E. White); the 2nd Battalion, The 14th Punjab Regiment (Punjab, under Lt. Col. G. R. Kidd); and the 5th Battalion, The 7th Rajput Regiment (Rajput, under Lt. Col. J. Cadogan-Rawlinson), with Brig. Cedric Wallis in command. Its headquarters was at the northern end of Waterloo Road, adjacent to Cornwall Street. It consisted of the "Forward Troops" and the garrison along the Gin Drinker's Line.

The Forward Troops were deployed in two groups near the border. The one on Tai Po Road was comprised of C Company of the Punjab (hereafter in the abbreviated form "C/Punjab"), two Royal Engineers (RE) sections and armoured cars of the HKVDC. It was to destroy the bridges and tunnels along the Tai Po Road and the Kowloon-Canton Railway. The Forward Troop of Castle Peak Road consisted of detachments from the 2RS, two RE sections, and five Bren Carriers and two armoured cars of the HKVDC. It was to destroy the bridges along Au Tau and Castle Peak roads. After the demolition operations, the RE sections would destroy the immovable stores and facilities in Kowloon, while C/Punjab would take positions on the Monastery Ridge near Shatin under the cover of the armoured cars.

The 2RS occupied the left sector of the line. Three of its four companies held the line stretching from Shing Mun Redoubt on its right to Texaco Peninsula on its left. The infamous Shing Mun Redoubt protected the right flank of the battalion. The reserve company was at Golden Hill and the battalion HQ at the "Skeet Ground."[24] The battalion generally faced northwest, where the enemy attack was expected. In the middle of the line was the Punjab battalion. Its three front-line companies were deployed along the line from Shing Mun Valley to the Rajput position near Chuk Kok. It was also facing northwest, to prevent penetration from the direction of Shing Mun River towards the Line of Passes. However, the Shing Mun Valley created a gap between Shing Mun Redoubt and D/Punjab. This gap was plugged by a company (D Coy) from 5/7 Rajput. The right wing of the line was held by the 5/7 Rajput. Its front stretched from Chuk Kok to Fu Yung Pit along Tate's Pass, Sleepers' Hill and Wong Kang Tsai. The reserve company stayed at the junction of Jat Incline, Clear Water Bay Road and Anderson Road, and HQ at Customs Pass. The battalion was to prevent enemy landings in Port Shelter from outflanking the line. As the pill-boxes of this section were more scattered, it was more thinly defended compared to the other sections. The whole "Kowloon Line" was supported by the 1st Hong Kong Regiment, the Hong Kong Singapore Royal Artillery (1 HKSRA) that had three batteries: 1st and 2nd Mountain Batteries (1, 2 Mtn. Bty.) and 25th Medium Battery (25 Med. Bty.).

The Island Brigade was responsible for the defence of the south shore of Hong Kong Island before the fall of Kowloon. Commanded by Lawson, it consisted of the 1st Battalion, The Middlesex Regiment (Middlesex, under Lt. Col. H. W. Stewart); The Royal Rifles of Canada (RR, under Lt. Col. W. J. Home) and the Winnipeg Grenadiers (Winnipeg, under Lt. Col. J. L. R. Sutcliff). The brigade faced south, leaving the north shore largely undefended. The five companies of the Middlesex (A, B, C, D and Z, formed by personnel from the battalion HQ) defended the pill-boxes along the coast, with headquarters at Leighton Hill.[25] The Winnipeg battalion held the high ground in the southwestern part of the island, including Shouson Hill, the area between Pok Fu Lam and Kellett Bay, Aberdeen, Little Hong Kong. D/Winnipeg, the battalion reserve, was at the north of Wong Nai Chong Gap with the Island Brigade HQ. The Royal Rifles held the southeastern part of the island, including Windy Gap in the D'Aguilar Peninsula, Tai Tam, the Stanley Peninsula, Mount Parker, Sai Wan Hill and Lyemun. Supposedly well protected by the coastal guns and rugged terrain, the RR was scattered over a large area but ran the risk of being slow to respond to enemy landing.

The Hong Kong Volunteer Defence Corps (HKVDC), which was more familiar with the ground, was used to defend the key positions of the colony. Its companies held Kai Tak (1st), Stonecutters (3rd), Pottinger Gap and Big Wave Bay (2nd), High West (4th), Mount Davis (5th), the north shore of the island (6th), and Magazine Gap, Wan Chai Gap and Middle Gap (7th). Its gunners served in various coastal and anti-aircraft batteries. Its HQ was at the East Wing of the Government House in Lower Albert Road. The famed "Hughesiliers" or Hughes Group occupied the North Point Power Station.

The small Royal Navy flotilla was to play an active role throughout the battle. On 8 December, there were three destroyers in Hong Kong. However, only HMS *Thracian*, a World War I-veteran, was left after the outbreak of war.[26] The other two left for Singapore to support the ill-fated Z Force under Vice Admiral Tom Philips. Four gunboats—*Cicala*, *Moth*, *Tern* and *Robin*—were built between 1915 and 1934 and armed with QFs and machine-guns.[27] Hong Kong also boasted of its eight motor torpedo boats (MTBs). Two of them had been purchased by the Hong Kong government from the Chinese Torpedo Academy when the outbreak of the Sino-Japanese War prevented their delivery.[28] The navy also had the minelayer HMS *Redstart*, the gate vessels *Barlight*, *Aldgate* and *Watergate*, disarmed gunboat HMS *Cornflower* and HMS *Tamar*, some patrol boats, and a number of vessels from the Police and the War Department.[29] As Admiral Tyrwhitt, the Commander-in-Chief of the China Station during the late 1920s, had envisioned (see Chapter 5), this coastal fleet utilized the cover provided by the coastal guns, mines and anti-submarine boom to support every stage of the land operation.

In October, Maltby redeployed his troops according to the new plan. He inspected the line with his battalion commanders and ordered them to keep the plan in secret. Working parties were also sent to renovate the line, which had been left idle for three years.[30] From 11 November, the battalions of the Mainland Brigade entered the line and the artillery was also in position.[31] The Punjab, which was designated as the mainland battalion before Maltby changed his plan, knew the ground best. As mentioned, Maltby initiated a manning exercise for the two brigades between 21 November and 1 December, but before he was able to shore up his battalions through another brigade exercise scheduled for 8 December, the war had already started.[32]

Japanese Planning and Deployment

The Japanese had considered taking Hong Kong as early as 1936, when the Washington and London naval treaties lapsed. The ideas of fighting against the British and taking Hong Kong first appeared in the revised version of the Imperial Defence Policy in 1936. When Emperor Hirohito questioned these contents, the Chief of General Staff, Field Marshal Prince Kan'in Kotohito (閑院宮載仁親王), claimed they were merely "precautions for emergency."[33] The first operational outline against Hong Kong, appearing in early 1940, stressed the need to take the city to support the Japanese operation in China, as well as the need for the army and the navy to cooperate.

After the fall of France in June 1940, the Japanese tried to seal Hong Kong off from the mainland by capturing Bao'an and Shenzhen. A "blockade line" was set up between Bao'an, Shenzhen and Shataukok in an attempt to cut off the Hong Kong–China border. A month later, the General Staff sent Capt. Sejima Ryuzou to study the detail of the Hong Kong operation. One-and-a-half divisions and heavy artillery, he suggested, were needed for the operation. The Japanese forces should adopt a methodical approach by first taking Kowloon and the New Territories before approaching Hong Kong Island. As it was impossible to force the island to surrender through blockade, a potentially hazardous landing operation was necessary.[34]

In October 1940, the 38th Division was earmarked for attacking Hong Kong. Formed in August 1939, it was among the eleven divisions raised to support the war in China. Its three infantry regiments (228th, 229th and 230th, hereafter in the abbreviated form, e.g. "229 Rgt.") came from Nagoya, Toyohashi and Shizuoka. Supporting the infantry regiments was the reinforced 38th Artillery Regiment. The division had been active in Guangdong since October 1939 and had participated in a number of minor engagements against regular KMT forces and Communist guerrillas. Accompanying the division was the 1st Artillery Group commanded by Maj. Gen. Kitajima Kineo (北島驥子雄) that consisted of heavy artillery pieces from Manchuria, including a number of 240-mm howitzers and 150-mm cannons. The two units and other smaller artillery detachments were under the operational control of the 23rd Army. However, as the British position gradually improved in late 1940, the 38th Division was redeployed to Guangzhou, leaving only Kitajima's force at Shenzhen.

It was almost another year before the 38th Division returned to the Hong Kong–China border. On 3 September, the 23rd Army ordered Lt. Gen. Sano Tadayoshi (佐野忠義), the commander of the 38th Division, to prepare for an invasion against Hong Kong. The 23rd Army HQ was to assist the operation by liaising with the navy and providing general direction and intelligence, as well as artillery and air support. The division HQ was responsible for operational planning and command.[35] The Japanese High Command expected to take Hong Kong with one division in twenty to thirty days.[36]

The 38th Division trained its troops in Xianrenling near Foshan between 17 and 24 September. Much attention was paid to the attacking of pillboxes. The training was supervised by Maj. Gen. Ito Takeo (伊東武夫) of the 38th Infantry Group, which was responsible for the operational control of the infantry regiments. However, the training was cut short as the division was sent to participate in the Second Battle of Changsha, but more training in Foshan, Sanshui and Zhongshan followed in October.[37]

In October 1941, the Japanese finalized their operational plan, first drafted in 1940. The 38th Division would first encircle the British forces near the border, by advancing quickly along Castle Peak Road and Tai Po Road, and by taking the Gin Drinker's Line from the west through a methodical battle supported by heavy artillery. As it was expected that the British would deploy most of their troops along the line, the Japanese paid little attention to the battle on Hong Kong Island except for a decision to land on the north shore, as the south shore was protected by coastal batteries (Figure 21). Sano was requested to avoid unnecessary damage to the City of Victoria because of its potential usefulness. The Kempeitai was also ordered not to harass the Chinese population, as the city was seen as a potential political centre from which to topple the Chongqing regime.[38]

The High Command and the 23rd Army stressed the need to end the operation quickly, with minimal losses, as the division was earmarked to join the Southern Army for the Java operation afterwards. It was expected the Hong Kong operation would end in less than twenty-five days, with the following timetable:

- D+3 days: Reaching Tai Mo Shan
- D+9 days: Attack on Gin Drinker's Line to begin
- D+12 days: Taking Gin Drinker's Line and Kowloon
- D+17–19 days: Ready to land on Hong Kong Island
- D+22–24 days: Taking Hong Kong Island

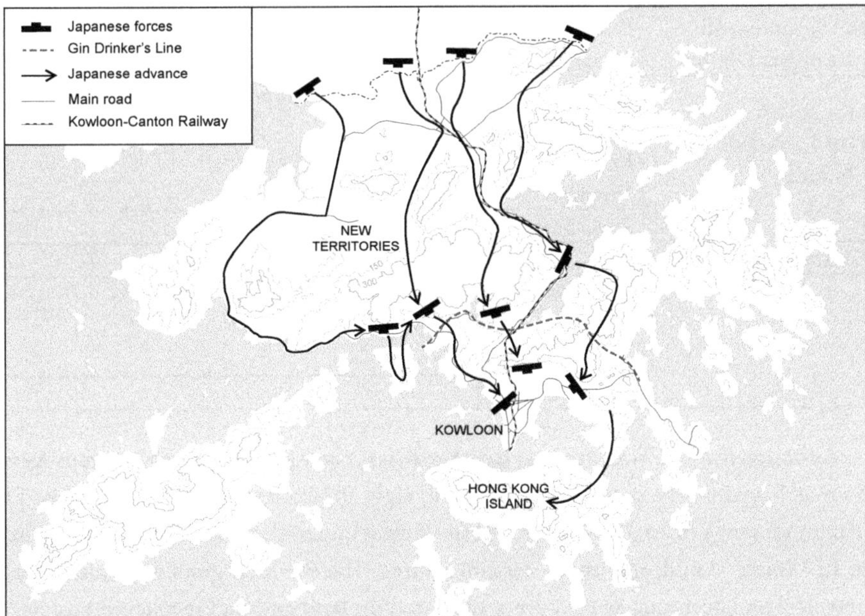

Figure 21   Japanese plan against Hong Kong, 1941[39]

The Japanese had assumed that effective resistance of Hong Kong would end soon after the fall of the Gin Drinker's Line. The 23rd Army even suggested that only three days would be sufficient to take Hong Kong Island. Ironically, while the Japanese deployed their heaviest field guns and prepared in detail for the attack against Kowloon, the fact that the island had been seen as a fortress by the British for a century was discounted. This shows the incompleteness of the Japanese intelligence work in Hong Kong.

The invading forces were supported by the 2nd China Expeditionary Fleet (第二遣支艦隊, 2CF), which was to blockade all the sea communication of Hong Kong, cut submarine cables, destroy the British naval forces and bombard land targets. It had a small naval infantry detachment that was responsible for landing on Tsing Yi, Stonecutters, and Hong Kong Island (this was not carried out). Commanded by Vice Adm. Niimi Masaichi, the 2CF was a small fleet that operated along the southern half of the China coast. It was divided into three forces:[40]

Units	Name	Type
Main body		
	IJN *Isuzu*	Light cruiser
	Tsuga	Destroyer
	Kawanishi E7K Seaplane x 2 Yokosuka B3Y Torpedo bomber x 3	
Monitor Force		
2nd Squadron, 6th Destroyer Flotilla	*Ikazuchi* *Inazuma*	Destroyer
11th Torpedo Boat Flotilla	*Kasasagi* *Kiji* *Kari* *Hiyodori*	Torpedo boat
	Tosho Maru	Patrol ship
Canton Force		
	IJN *Hashidate* IJN *Saga* IJN *Uji*	Gunboat
	Minesweeper x 2	

Although the 2CF was stronger than the Royal Navy in Hong Kong, its ships were no match against the coastal batteries. The eight 9.2-inch guns on the island had a maximum range of 26,700 metres, but the largest gun of the 2CF (the 140-mm guns of IJN *Isuzu*) could only reach 19,100 metres. The 9.2-inch guns were also more powerful and accurate, as they were mounted on land and had registered targets.[41]

This discrepancy of firepower, and the inability of the Japanese air forces to cause real damage to the batteries, explains the negligible role played by the Japanese navy during the battle.

The Battle of Hong Kong 1941

The Japanese Close In, 5–8 December

When the decision for war finally reached the 23rd Army on 5 November (Singapore time GMT+7.5 hours, same in the chapter[*]), Lt. Gen. Sakai Takashi was appointed as the army commander; the final preparations against Hong Kong started the next day. The 38th Division moved south from Humen on 4 December after concentration. In order not to attract Chinese or British attention, its units moved only at night and were widely scattered. By 7 December, the division was in position, except the 228 Rgt., which was still near Bao'an.[42]

By then, the British troops had just returned to the barracks from the manning exercise, with only the 2RS and the Rajput remaining on the Gin Drinker's Line. The 1 HKSRA was also in position, with each gun having 200 rounds ready and another 400 being stored in the magazines of Kowloon West Fort and Ma Tau Kok.[43] On 6 December, the police at Sheung Shui received a message about Japanese troop movements near Shenzhen. The RAF also received an alert from the Far East Command at night.[44]

Maltby then ordered the garrison on a war footing on the morning of 7 December. All troops, including the Forward Troop, were already in position by evening. When the Fortress HQ intercepted a message from Tokyo Radio indicating the imminence of war at 04:45 on 8 December, all troops were informed within an hour. At the same time, the Royal Engineers blew up the bridges along Shenzhen River. Two hours later, the state of war was confirmed.[45]

The Battle for the Mainland, 8–12 December

Two hours after the Japanese troops had landed in Kota Bharu of Malaya and an hour after the Japanese carrier task force attacked Pearl Harbor, the 23rd Army and the 2CF were ordered to invade Hong Kong by the secret code "hara-saku" at

---

[*]   At that time, the Japanese adopted the Chūō Hyōjunji (Central Standard Time), which was GMT+9. Thus, all the times mentioned by the Japanese documents should have 1.5 hours deducted from them. Although the Hong Kong government introduced a new winter time (GMT+8.5) in September 1941, all the major British documents about the battle still adopted the GMT+7.5 standard.

02:21, 8 December. The Japanese planned to launch a pincer attack against British forces along Shenzhen River after launching an air attack against Kai Tak. The pincers would take control of Castle Peak Road and Tai Po Road, encircling the British forces in between and taking the bridges at Tai Po. The main body of the 38th Division would then march south at noon to crush the British pocket and then occupy Shek Wu Hui and Fanling. The whole plan was, however, based on faulty intelligence. The Forward Troop in the area had withdrawn soon after destroying the frontier bridges and roads even before Kai Tak was hit.

At 05:50, Col. Habu Hideji (土生秀治) left the Guangzhou airfield with the 45th Air Regiment and its escort the 10th Independent Fighter Squadron, under Col. Takatsuki Hikari (高月光). Twenty-five minutes later, all twenty-seven Ki-32 bombers of the 45th Air Regiment entered the airspace of Hong Kong. They circled around and descended over Kai Tak.[46] At the same time, three seaplanes of the Imperial Japanese Navy left Sanzao Island (三灶島) and their signals were picked up by the KMT listeners at the Murray Barracks.[47] The RAF Kai Tak was defended by the 5th Anti-Aircraft Regiment of the HKSRA and the 1st Company of the HKVDC. The airfield itself was divided into two sections, with the eastern part used by the RAF and the western part by civilian airlines. As the RAF had already confirmed the outbreak of war at 06:30, the machine-gun positions were manned and ready when the Japanese planes arrived.[48]

The Japanese planes, approaching Kai Tak at 4,200 metres, were initially unable to spot any planes on the ground. They were also out of the range of the British machine-guns. When Col. Habu actually saw some planes at Kai Tak, he ordered the attack. Releasing their bombs from 2,000 metres, the Japanese bombers' accuracy was appalling. Most of the bombs fell on nearby Kowloon City. Only one dud bomb hit the airfield; the patrol vessels in Kowloon Bay were also unscathed.[49] It was the strafing of the escort fighters that caused the real damage; some of them descended to some eighteen metres from the ground.[50] Despite the British machine-gun fire, one Vildebeest torpedo bomber, two Walrus reconnaissance planes and eight civilian planes were destroyed beyond repair. However, two Vildebeests were still operational.[51] The Sham Shui Po Barracks was also attacked, but only a few engineers were wounded as the Canadian troops had already left the barracks for their positions.

When the Japanese flanking forces of 1st Battalion, 230 Rgt. (hereafter in the abbreviated form, e.g. "I/230") and III/229 entered Futian and Shataukok respectively at 07:30, the British Forward Troop had already gone. The Japanese decided to stick to the original plan even though the flanking forces were unopposed. At noon, the rest of the 38th Division marched towards Shek Wu Hui in two columns. By then, the British had completed the demolition of Tai Po Road and had been working on demolition along the Kowloon-Canton Railway. When the Japanese

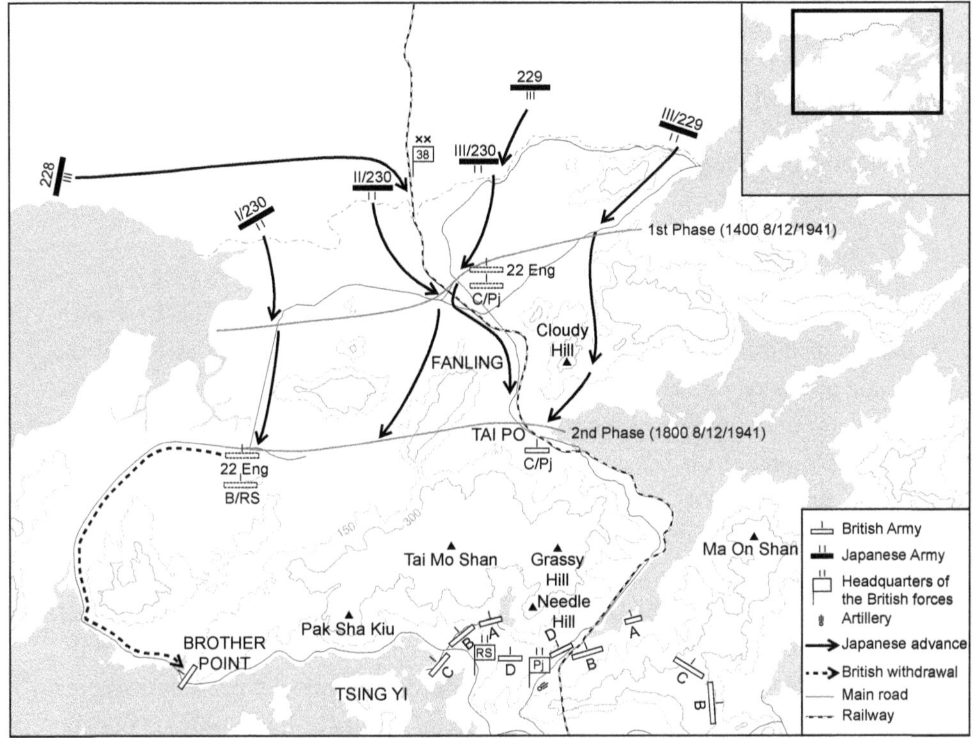

Figure 22   Japanese invasion of Hong Kong, 8 December 1941

gradually rolled south, they were ambushed by the Forward Troop under Maj. G. E. Gray on Tai Po Road near Tai Po Market in the afternoon. Gray's forces withdrew to the Monastery Ridge and joined the Punjab at Shatin and Tai Wai in the evening. On Castle Peak Road, the Forward Troop under Maj. S. Burn engaged the Japanese in Yuen Long and Ping Shan. After achieving its objectives, the unit returned to Lai Chi Kok at night (Figure 22).[52] Because of the British demolition works, many of the roads of the New Territories were destroyed; the heavy weapons of the Japanese forces were thus lagging behind.[53]

Although the British destroyed the roads and bridges and ambushed the Japanese vanguards, the Japanese reached Shek Kong and Tai Mo Shan by evening. When the HQ of the 38th Division reviewed the situation at night, it adopted a methodical approach to attacking the Gin Drinker's Line. The 230 Rgt. would approach the left sector of the line from Yau Kom Tau, Pak Sha Kiu and Tai Mo Shan. The 228 Rgt., which had arrived late, was to be deployed between Grassy Hill and Cove Hill, to approach the line from the north. The 229 Rgt. would roll south along Tai Po Road and land in Ma On Shan across from Tide Cove. A battalion-sized detachment (I/230) was to land at Tsing Yi. A general attack was to be launched only after the heavy guns had finished a preparatory bombardment, but they were nowhere near the front line by 9 December.[54] From 8 to 9 December, before the Japanese had launched their attack, the prominent Chinese figures had already been withdrawn from Kai Tak. Escapees included Soong Ching-ling and Soong Ai-ling (referred to elsewhere in this chapter as "the Soong sisters").[55]

The Fall of the Shing Mun Redoubt, 9–10 December[56]

As the fall of the Shing Mun Redoubt between 9 and 10 December led to an early collapse of the British resistance in Kowloon, the event was seen as one of the turning points of the battle. This section attempts to reconstruct the event and to discuss its ramifications by the critical use of both British and Japanese sources.

On 9 December, the Japanese were behind schedule. Although the 38th Division took the area between Shenzhen and Tai Mo Shan in two days, the success of the British demolition operations had delayed deployment of the heavy guns as they were all stuck in the road. Without heavy guns, it was deemed impossible to attack the Gin Drinker's Line. The HQ of the 38th Division postponed the general attack to 14 December. However, a series of fateful decisions by the commander of the 228 Rgt., Col. Doi Sadashichi (土井定七), and his subordinates not only disrupted the Japanese plan but also decided the course of the battle. It was only at 06:30 on 9 December that the 228 Rgt. had entered Hong Kong. After being delayed further by road congestion, the regiment had not by the afternoon arrived at its intended position between Grassy Hill and Needle Hill. Before that, Doi had already reconnoitred the Shing Mun Valley, and found that he could not simply cross the river to reach his intended target, Hill 303, as the banks of Shing Mun River were impassable by any sizeable units. The only alternative was to cross the dam of the Shing Mun Reservoir and move across Smugglers' Ridge. He also noted that there was little enemy activity in the area. Although Doi contemplated launching a surprise night attack to take Hill 303 through the dam, he hesitated because it was located within the boundary of the neighbouring 230 Rgt. By then, none of his units were in position; the artillery was still stuck by the destroyed bridges (Figure 23).[57]

South of the dam was the Shing Mun Redoubt held by A Company of the 2RS. Its commander, Capt. C. R. Jones, had assumed command only on 30 October. He was disliked by both Maltby and Wallis but supported by White, his battalion commander.[58] The three platoons of the company defended the redoubt and the surrounding area. Regular patrols were sent to cover the western area of the reservoir; they would be withdrawn at night to avoid being ambushed.[59] The redoubt was defended by the 8th Platoon. Jones set up his HQ at the observation post of the

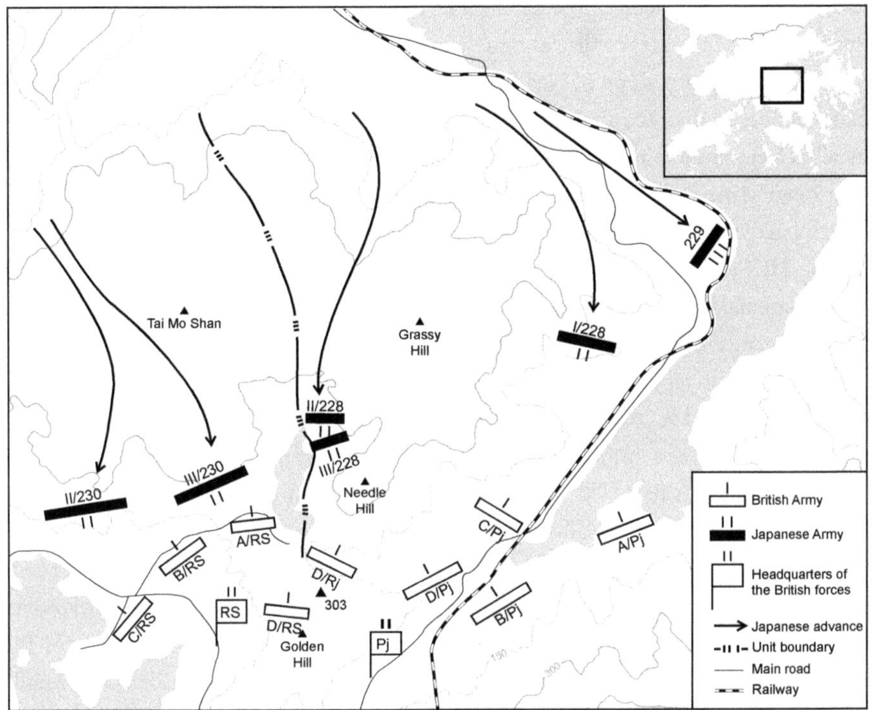

Figure 23   Situation near Shing Mun, 9 December 1941

redoubt. In all, three officers and thirty-nine other ranks were in the redoubt on 9 December, including Capt. Jones, 2nd Lt. J. S. R. Thompson of the 8th Platoon, 2nd Lt. Wilcox of the 2 Mtn. Bty. and two Indian signalmen.[60] According to the postwar reports, Wallis, White and Jones agreed that the troops should stay outside the pillbox at night to avoid being surprised.[61] Thus, not all the troops were inside the tunnels and pillboxes when the Japanese attacked.

The redoubt was protected by a ring of double-layered barbed wire, while another line of barbed wire cut the redoubt into two sections.[62] Around thirty anti-personnel mines were planted along the western approach of the reservoir, whence the enemy was expected to come. Indeed, even the Japanese had planned to attack from this direction, as they wanted to maximize the effectiveness of their artillery. It was planned that the 230 Rgt. was to infiltrate Tai Mo Shan and Sheung Kwai Chung from the west. The 228 Rgt. would attack directly from Cove Hill, Grassy Hill and Needle Hill towards Shing Mun River.[63] In short, the Japanese had no intention of attacking the redoubt from the east.

In the early morning of 9 December, the Japanese were found south of Tai Mo Shan and near Tsuen Wan, as well as near Telegraph Pass and Chuen Lung. Later in the day, more were seen in the catchment west of the reservoir. On the other hand, the area east of the reservoir was largely quiet, with only "slight movement" spotted on the southeastern slope of Needle Hill.[64] Although it was possible that the British had discovered the reconnaissance party led by Col. Doi, their attention was drawn by what happened in the west. In the afternoon, when Japanese troops were spotted near Lead Mine Pass, the British bombarded the area, but nothing was found by the search party sent afterwards.

The 2RS was possibly unaware of the approach of the 228 Rgt. The Z Force, a British special force nearby, saw the 228 Rgt. being shelled at Lead Mine Pass. C. M. McEwan, a member of Z Force, noted in his diary that he and his colleagues thought that the Japanese "would never come" through the pass. Thus, Z Force did not report to the HQ of the 2RS until night. By then, it was already too late.

After Doi had reconnoitred the Shing Mun Valley, another scout party was sent by Maj. Nishiyama Ryo (西山遼), the commanding officer of III/228, to study the feasibility of crossing the valley. The conclusion of the second party was similar to that of Doi. It also noted that the defence on Hill 303 was weak, and that Hill 255, south of the dam, was an ideal stepping stone for taking Hill 303.[65] The third reconnaissance party, led by Lt. Wakabayashi Tōichi (若林東一), commander of the 10th Company, III/228, also drew the same conclusion. Doi and Nishiyama finally decided to overthrow the original plan and send III/228 to attack across the dam at night. None of them were aware of the fact that they were attacking the Shing Mun Redoubt from an unexpected direction.[66]

Jones clearly was not expecting an attack. He was away from his headquarters for most of the day, busy conferring with White and commanders of the neighbouring units about patrol routes and coordination. After inspecting his platoons, Jones returned to the redoubt and at 20:00 sent Thompson to lead a patrol to the south slope of Needle Hill. Thompson was later criticized for failing to spot the approaching Japanese. However, Thompson had no chance to do so as the Japanese troops arrived at the south slope of Needle Hill long after Thompson's patrol had left. When at 22:30 Thompson returned from the southeast to the redoubt, the Japanese were still defusing the demolitions on the dam.[67]

Meanwhile, III/228 passed through the undefended dam and assembled beneath Hill 255. In other words, the forty-two defenders of the redoubt were facing the attack of an entire battalion.[68] As the Japanese were approaching, Jones was listening to Thompson's report and received a signal telling him that Z Force had arrived in the locality of his company. He then sent Pvt. Wylie to lead Z Force to the observation post of the redoubt. Wylie, who expected to return quickly, kept the key to the observation post with him. By then, all doors were locked at the redoubt as a blackout measure. Thus, unwittingly, Wylie locked Jones and the others up inside the observation post.[69]

The Japanese were spotted by L/Cpl. J. Laird as they were cutting the outer ring of the barbed wire. After a brief exchange of fire, Laird alerted PB 401, the nearby pillbox, and then reported to the observation post. As the crew of PB 401B were unable to fire at the incoming Japanese down below, they locked themselves up in the pillbox. Still, PB 401A was captured when the Japanese discovered the airshafts over the concrete tunnels and swarmed in the redoubt. PB 402 and the machine-gun position nearby pinned the Japanese down on Hill 255 and inflicted some casualties, but they were eventually silenced by the Japanese 9th Company of III/228. Sgt. R. Robb, the most senior personnel outside the observation post, tried to organize a counterattack of eighteen men, which was soon overwhelmed. The Japanese also noted that they engaged with Robb and his men in a "grenade battle" near Hill 225.[70] Robb was later blamed by Wallis and Maltby for not "staying put and fighting it out," but it seems that he could do little to retrieve the situation with merely eighteen men.

At 23:35, Jones reported the situation to White. As the phone was plugged to Bde HQ at that moment, Wallis spoke to them directly and noted the situation. By then, Lt. Wakabayashi's 10th Company of III/228 had already trapped Jones inside the observation post.[71] White ordered the 2 Mtn. Bty. to fire at Shing Mun River, stopping the advance of II/228. D/Rajput also fired at the Japanese above the redoubt with its Lewis light machine-gun and mortars. However, all was in vain— the Japanese were already in control of the redoubt and were attacking the observation post. After waves of grenade attacks, the Japanese demolished the door of the observation post, killing the Indian signalmen and wounding everyone inside. Jones, Thompson, Wilcox and other survivors, eighteen in total and mostly wounded, surrendered to the Japanese at 01:00 after brief fighting. After taking the observation post, Lt. Wakabayashi's troops also took PB 403. PB 402 was captured at the same time and PB 401B fell only the next morning, with its three occupants captured.

Although Wallis had contemplated an immediate counterattack, White proposed waiting for dawn, as the situation remained obscure and the ground was too difficult for a night attack. As the strength of the Japanese forces taking the redoubt was unclear, both Maltby and Wallis agreed to wait. D/Winnipeg was sent from the island to reinforce Kowloon, but Wallis did not use it for the counterattack, due to its inexperience.

After taking the redoubt, Col. Doi sent two telegrams to the divisional HQ, both received in a fragmented state. The HQ gathered from the fragments that Doi had entered the boundary of 230 Rgt. to attack Hill 303 without authorization and was stranded by fierce fighting.[72] Gen. Sano ordered Doi to withdraw to Needle Hill "for the sake of the division."[73] As the British had not counterattacked, Doi refused to leave the redoubt. It was not until dawn that Sano had a clear idea of what had happened. However, the army commander, Lt. Gen. Sakai, was alerted. He flew to the front and threatened to court-martial Doi and others who were responsible. Maj. Gen. Kuribayashi Tadamichi, the Chief of Staff of the 23rd Army, tried to speak up for Doi but was relieved by Sakai from active staff duty.[74] Sakai also postponed the general advance to 16 December. Although the incident soon blew over, the battalion played no active role on the front until the end of the campaign.

On the morning of 10 December, Wallis urged White to retake the redoubt. However, as it was estimated that there were as many as a hundred Japanese troops in the Shing Mun Redoubt, White insisted that he had no troops to spare for such an operation.[75] Wallis considered using D/Rajput for the counterattack, but he faced the same problem of White as his troops, other than a green Canadian company, were already committed to defending the Gin Drinker's Line. As such, Maltby and Wallis decided to send the 2RS back to a new position near Golden Hill. As the British were retreating, the guns at Stonecutters and Kowloon pinned Doi's troops down at the redoubt. The Japanese replied by shelling Stonecutters and the British position near Tide Cove. In all, however, only a few pillboxes were damaged and PB 211 was destroyed.[76]

The Loss of the Golden Hill Line, 11 December

By the evening of 10 December, the 2RS had withdrawn to the new line covering both the northern and southern slopes of Golden Hill and extending to Castle Peak Road. However, a gap existed between D/2RS, defending the northern slope, and the rest of the battalion; the telephone line between the battalion HQ and B and C companies was not completed that night. One of the remaining two platoons of A/2RS was sent to regroup at the Kowloon Reservoir, while the other joined D/Rajput.[77]

The Japanese soon advanced at midnight, 11 December, according to their original plan. When II/230 reached Sheung Kwai Chung at 01:30, they found that the British had already withdrawn. Its commander, Maj. Wakamatsu Mansoku (若松滿則), urged his superior, Col. Shoji Toshishige, to press on. Shoji, who had in mind the events of the previous night, declined. Nevertheless, Wakamatsu took the initiative and moved on. His decision led to a repeat of what happened at the Shing Mun Redoubt, which had overthrown the plans of both sides. At around 05:30, II/230 attacked Golden Hill with two companies. D/2RS launched a fierce bayonet counterattack near Hill 361 (southwest of Golden Hill) that killed one of the Japanese company commanders.[78]

Even so, by around 08:30, the Japanese controlled Hill 361. Meanwhile, on the southern slope, the B and C companies of the 2RS were under heavy infantry assault and bombardment: their line eventually collapsed. The commanders of the two companies, Capt. F. S. Richardson and Capt. W. R. T. Rose, were killed during the action. It was not until 09:10 that the 2RS HQ learned about the attack. Bren Carriers were immediately sent to provide support, but all they could do was to cover the retreat of the B and C companies. At one point, Castle Peak Road was defended only by a single platoon of A/2RS.

Although the British briefly suppressed the Japanese advance with their artillery fire, it was increasingly difficult to contain the breach. At 10:45, Col. L. A. Newnham, Maltby's Chief of Staff, arrived at Lai Chi Kok with armoured cars. He told the remaining troops, now led by Maj. Burns, that "there must be no going back from this locality under any circumstances."[79] D/Winnipeg was also sent to plug the gap. Newnham spent some time directing D/Winnipeg to defend a line east of Piper's Hill, to contain possible enemy penetration. By noon, the situation had been stabilized, mainly because the Japanese had ceased their advance.[80] However, the left flank of the Gin Drinker's Line was shattered. A gap was wide open in Kowloon Reservoir and the flank and rear of the Indian companies still holding along Shing Mun River were exposed. Wallis, realizing the danger of further penetration, ordered some of his artillery to withdraw from the front and warned his battalions that a general evacuation from Kowloon was imminent.

The success of Wakamatsu threw the Japanese commanders into confusion once again. This time, however, the Japanese decided to exploit the capture of Golden Hill. A meeting was held between the staff officers from the 38th Division and the 23rd Army in the afternoon, in the presence of the liaison officer of the General Staff. The liaison officer brought news about the rapid success of Japanese forces in Malaya, prompting the 23rd Army to take bolder action. At 15:00, the HQ of the 23rd Army ordered resumption of the advance.[81]

Evacuation of Kowloon, 11–13 December

When Newnham reported the situation in Lai Chi Kok to Wallis and Maltby, they all realized that the left section was untenable. At 12:00, 11 December, Maltby ordered the evacuation of Kowloon. The guns were to move first. Almost all the howitzers were evacuated except one gun of the 2 Mtn. Bty., which was destroyed by shell fire as the section went from Tai Wai to the Lion Rock Tunnel, only to discover that the tunnel had been demolished by the Royal Engineers and that they had to retrace their steps.[82] Despite this ordeal, the 2RS withdrew in good order and left

Kowloon at around 19:30 from the Kowloon City ferry pier. The armoured cars of the HKVDC left at the Jordan Road vehicular ferry pier. D/Winnipeg covered their retreat and left from the city pier at midnight. After demolishing the Kai Tak airfield, the 1st Company of the HKVDC also left Kowloon.

In the right sector, the Rajput took up prepared positions near Ma Lau Tong and Hai Wan Hill to cover the general retreat, after briefly engaging the vanguard of the 229 Rgt. near Tate's Cairn. The Punjab, after an exhausting march of 32 kilometres and thirty-six hours of combat without adequate food and rest, reached Yau Tong through the Line of Passes and Anderson Road on the morning of 12 December without losses. Part of the regiment was evacuated at 02:00. The battalion HQ, however, went along Clear Water Bay Road without noticing the junction towards Anderson Road and entered Kowloon. It then fought its way in Kowloon against the fifth columnists and Japanese vanguards and was evacuated after covering the retreat of civilians from the Star Ferry Pier at Tsim Sha Tsui. Wallis set up his HQ at the Hai Wan defence line to oversee the retreat and the last stand of his Mainland Brigade. Much of the evacuation work was done by Royal Navy torpedo boats. To cover the retreat, HMS *Thracian* went to Picnic Bay and destroyed a number of suspicious junks there. HMS *Tamar*, the long-time receiving ship at the Royal Naval Dockyard, was scuttled.

The 1st HKSRA Battery of Stonecutters covered the retreat of the 2RS with its fire, despite being heavily shelled by the Japanese. The West Fort of the island had been hit over fifty times by noon. When the order of withdrawal was received at 15:00, the battery and the 3rd Company of the HKVDC destroyed the facilities at Stonecutters and withdrew to Hong Kong Island. However, most of the movable guns, searchlights and heavy equipment could not be unloaded and had to be scuttled with the ships, as there were no suitable cranes.

By the morning of 12 December, most of the Mainland Brigade had withdrawn to Hong Kong Island (Figure 24). The previous night, Maltby had ordered the Middlesex battalion to man PBs 40 to 55 along the north shore of the island, from Aldrich Bay to Causeway Bay. The spare clerks, cooks and support troops of the battalion, led by Maj. S. F. Hedgecoe, formed a makeshift detachment to hold the pillboxes and the Taikoo Police Station.[83]

The Japanese, who had planned a general advance to capture Kowloon Ridge on 12 December, were unaware of the withdrawal. The three regiments started a three-pronged attack on Kowloon Ridge on the night of the 11th. At midnight, the Japanese landed on the deserted Tsing Yi Island, but could not find the 9.2-inch guns indicated by intelligence. The landing had previously been delayed because of the presence of HMS *Cicala*.[84] Although 229 Rgt. had spotted the Rajput troops,

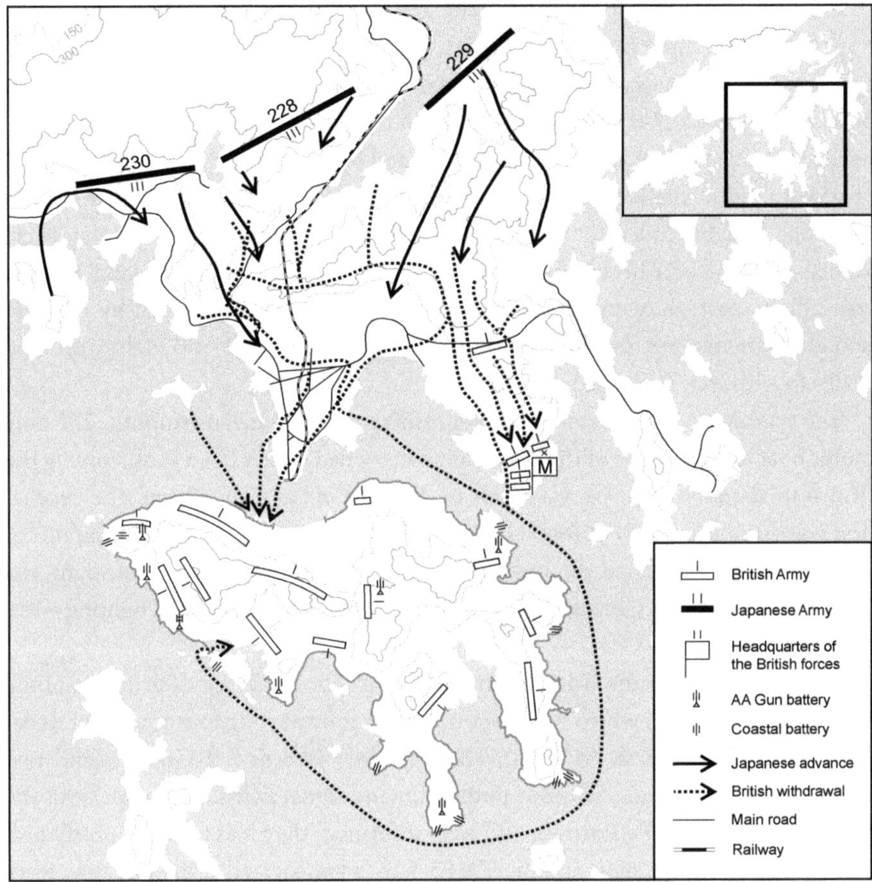

Figure 24   Evacuation of the Mainland Brigade, 11–13 December 1941

it was unaware of the withdrawal and failed to cut off the British troops. 230 Rgt. moved south and captured Eagle's Nest around midnight, while 228 Rgt. captured Beacon Hill before dawn. The III/228, which had taken the Shing Mun Redoubt without authorization, was kept behind the advancing 230 Rgt.[85]

At 06:00, 12 December, the first Japanese troops entered Kowloon, led by Maj. Nogumo of the 230 Rgt. They encountered the remnants of the Punjab HQ and the 2RS, but failed to prevent their withdrawal. They also opened fire on civilians and mobs on sight. The fall of Kowloon was known to all when the Japanese hoisted a flag above the Peninsula Hotel. The 38th Division HQ then moved into the China Light and Power Headquarters Building, at the junction of Waterloo Road and Argyle Street.

On the right flank, the advance of the 229 Rgt. was slowed down by the booby traps set by the Rajput troops. It was not until 13:30 that the regiment reached Chin Lan Chu. Its concentration was disrupted by British bombardment, directed by observers on Black Hill.[86] The sluggishness of the 229 Rgt. gave the Rajput a much-needed respite.[87] The Rajput was also supported by the 1 Mtn. Bty., which was supplied with 1,000 shells from the island. At 14:30, the Japanese assaulted the Ma Lau Tong line, but failed to penetrate it. Although the Japanese were beaten back, Wallis's position was becoming untenable. The logistics of the Mainland Brigade was falling apart, as many of the trucks, ships and barges controlled by Chinese non-combatants were deserted or even sabotaged.[88] Thus, at 21:00 Maltby ordered Wallis to withdraw from the mainland.

The evacuation from Devil's Peak Peninsula was by no means smooth. The only motor boat for the mules of the mountain battery had earlier been sunk, forcing the British to abandon their pack animals on the pier of Sam Ka Village. The evacuation was completed only at 09:00 on 13 December. HMS *Thracian* and the motor torpedo boats also ferried the Indian troops to the island. The previous night, the Japanese had reached Cheung Kwan O, but they failed to disrupt the fighting withdrawal of Wallis.[89]

The biggest loss to the British during the evacuation was the destruction of the police launch *Jeanette*, which was responsible for transporting four tonnes of dynamite from Green Island. At 22:00, 12 December, *Jeanette* left Green Island two hours ahead of schedule, without putting on any signal lights. Although both the harbour-master and the Fortress HQ were informed, they had failed to notify pillboxes along the north shore in time. PB 63, which was located at the vehicular ferry pier, opened fire on *Jeanette* and detonated its explosives at about 22:50, killing all hands on board.[90] This incident vividly revealed the anxiety felt by British troops after the fall of Kowloon.

The Underground Front

While the Hong Kong garrison was busy fighting the Japanese, it also faced the problem of fifth columnists. It had to be supported by the KMT and the triads to maintain order on the island. As mentioned, the Japanese had established contact with the triads long before the invasion. Before the battle, the triads were somewhat divided over whether they should cooperate with the Japanese or the British and the KMT. Some chose to work with the Koa Kikan, while others cooperated with Chan Chak, the KMT representative in Hong Kong. There were also fence-sitters who only wished to fish in troubled waters.

While the Hong Kong Police had had a long history of dealing with the triads, the Internal Security Scheme of the Police, "a bulky volume" that "required much time and patience to digest the amendments and cross references," paid little attention to the problem. The British were also not given time to revise it after the civilian defence exercises held between 26 and 29 November.[91] The Japanese fifth columnists had some success in Kowloon. Triad members known as the "Victory group" (勝利友) guided Japanese troops across Tai Mo Shan and sabotaged trucks and boats in Kowloon. They also sniped at British troops and civilians at Sham Shui Po, Mong Kok and Yau Ma Tei. To an extent, their action disrupted the British attempt to hold the Devil's Peak Peninsula.

At 19:00, 11 December, F. W. Shaftain, head of the Crime Investigation Department, received a report indicating that the Japanese-controlled triads were about to attack Europeans on the island.[92] Shaftain alerted the commissioner of police, J. Pennefather-Evans, and suggested buying off the triads. Pennefather-Evans gave twenty thousand dollars to Shaftain, who "after hours of futile endeavour" and "in desperation," contacted Lt. Col. S. K. Yee (余兆麒), Chan Chak's subordinate, for help.[93]

Yee sought out Zhang Zilian (張子廉) and Situ Meitang (司徒美堂). Zhang Zilian was one of the five leaders of Wushengshan (五聖山), a branch of the Hong Society (formed in Shanghai in 1923), and a prominent figure of the Constant Club (恆社), which had been founded by Du Yuesheng (杜月笙) in 1932. Situ Meitang was the head of Zhigongdang (致公黨), which supported the war against the Japanese.[94] Zhang called up five triad representatives and met them in Chan Chak's office. Shaftain invited these representatives to attend a meeting in the commissioner's office, which ended in a fierce argument. The representatives insisted that they were merely mediators and held no responsibility for ensuring that the triads would back down. The police officers, on the other hand, refused to let them leave the office unless they acted immediately.

Yee and Zhang eventually managed to calm the quarrel down by holding a discussion between them and the representatives alone.[95] Together they called on a "Central Government agent" named Mr. Wong, who provided a list of over 200 triad heads. The police and Chan Chak's forces then carried out "a large number of raids"; the triad leaders were "picked up and escorted to" Cecil Hotel.[96] Yee and Zhang then presided over a secret meeting with these captured heads. The triads demanded a sum of money far beyond what the British could provide. Eventually, Yee and Zhang managed to reach an agreement with the triad leaders: the cooperation of the triad societies was won "at the cost of the substitution of 'protection racket' on Chinese civilian."[97] An anonymous police reported that "the influence of the Central Government held in check some 60,000 Triad Society members, who did not commence to exact payment for their restraint until after the evacuation of Kowloon, and the surrender of the Island."[98] This event, however, was covered up after the war. Neither Shaftain nor Pennefather-Evans would allow the details of the meeting to be revealed, as the Hong Kong government had practically been blackmailed by triads. Shaftain even made up a story claiming that Zhang "came to the rescue and undertook to deal with this aspect" and that the debt to him was "discussed and settled" after the war.[99]

An Argentinian Who Tried to Establish a Neutral Zone

The consular representative of the Argentine Republic, Ramon Lavalle, tried to establish a neutral zone in occupied Kowloon during the battle. Lavalle, who was at his home at 38 Kadoorie Avenue, witnessed random shootings and lootings in Kowloon as the Japanese entered the city. He approached Maj. Nishiyama[100] of III/228 for help when he saw Japanese soldiers entering the houses of Kadoorie Hill looking for women. Nishiyama refused to control his troops and to help the local hospital, which was running out of food.[101]

On 14 December, Lavalle again urged Nishiyama for help, proposing to establish a neutral zone demarcated by Nathan Road, Waterloo Road, Argyle Street and Prince Edward Road. The area included three hospitals and one church, in addition to the Portuguese and Argentine consulates. Lavalle was again refused. Travelling around Kowloon in search of food with a pass issued by the Japanese, Lavalle witnessed the Japanese shoot at Chinese civilians who entered "restricted areas" without warning.[102] Lavalle recorded what he saw in Kowloon and testified against Japanese officers during the war crime trials in 1946.

First Peace Mission, 13 December

The 23rd Army HQ assumed that the garrison would fight to the last on the Gin Drinker's Line. With the fall of Kowloon, it believed that the British were about to surrender. On 10 December, the Japanese started to drop propaganda leaflets urging the Indians and the Chinese to surrender. The defenders were unmoved. The Japanese then ordered a unilateral ceasefire and sent a delegation, led by Lt. Col. Toda, to the island on 13 December. Accompanying Toda were Mrs. C. R. Lee, the wife of the Colonial Secretary's secretary, a Russian woman who was about to give birth, and Mrs. Lee's two dachshunds.[103]

Lt. Col. Toda handed a note to Mark Young through Maj. Charles Boxer, who brought this reply from Young:

> Governor and the C-in-C Hong Kong has the honour to acknowledge the receipt of a letter addressed to him by His Excellency Lt. Gen. Takashi Sakai and to return the following reply.
>
> He acknowledges the spirit in which this communication is made but he is unable in any circumstances to hold any meeting or parley on the subject of the surrender of Hong Kong.[104]

When Winston Churchill received a report from Maltby, he insisted on further resistance:

> We are all watching day by day and hour by hour your stubborn defence of the port and fortress of Hong Kong. You guard a link long famous in world civilization between the Far East and Europe. We are sure that the defence of Hong Kong against barbarous and unprovoked attack will add a glorious page to British annals.
>
> All our hearts are with you in your ordeal. Every day of your resistance brings nearer our certain victory.[105]

During the ceasefire, Maj. Oyadomari, the Director of Operations of the 38th Division, took a reconnaissance trip along the coast from Tai Kok Tsui to Ngau Tau Kok, to investigate the British positions on the island. He realized that the shore between North Point and Braemar Point was the most suitable landing site.[106]

Gunnery Duel across Victoria Harbour, 13–16 December

As the British refused to surrender, the Japanese bombarded the island with their heavy artillery.[107] Eight Type 45 240-mm howitzers of the 1st Artillery Group, the largest of the invading Japanese force, were deployed at Shek Li Pui Reservoir, Kowloon Hospital and Tai Shek Ku.[108] Sixteen Type 89 150-mm howitzers were deployed at Tai Wai, with eight of them targeting the area between Mount Davis and Mount Nicholson, and the rest pointing at the area between Mount Nicholson and Chai Wan. Eight 150-mm mortars, originally deployed at Kowloon Reservoir, were moved to Ho Man Tin Hill to escape from British counter-battery fire. Six more 150-mm guns were deployed at Kadoorie Hill and Crocodile Hill. The 38th Artillery Regiment deployed its guns at Ma Tau Kok, Hung Hom and Tsim Sha Tsui. Smaller guns were deployed at Crocodile Hill, Hai Wan Hill, Black Hill and Devil's Peak.[109]

The British reorganized the defence of the island. It was estimated that the Japanese would land in four areas: Lyemun to Quarry Point, North Point to

Bowrington, Victoria City, and Kennedy Town. The coastline between North Point and Victoria City was seen as more vulnerable, as it was close to Kowloon and could easily be covered by Japanese artillery fire. The area between Lyemun and Quarry Point was seen as a less likely landing place, as it was littered with abandoned vessels.

On 12 December, Brig. Lawson, the commander of the Island Brigade, discussed with Maltby the reorganization of the garrison into two brigades, each responsible for half of the island, divided by a line running from PB 52 through Tai Hang Village, Jardine's Lookout, Wong Nai Chung Reservoir, Violet Hill, Stanley Mound and Chung Hom Kok. The deployment plan was as follows (Figure 25):

West Infantry Brigade
> Brigadier John K. Lawson
> Headquarters: Wong Nai Chung Gap
> - Punjab: Victoria City
> - Winnipeg Grenadiers
>   - A Coy: Little Hong Kong; B Coy: Pok Fu Lam; C Coy: Bennet's Hill; D Coy: Wong Nai Chung Gap; E Coy: Wan Chai Gap[110]
> - Middlesex
>   - A Coy: PB 1–11 (Sandy Bay to Aberdeen Island); C Coy: PB 12–20 (Brick Hill to Repulse Bay); Z Coy: PB 58–72 (~14/12) (Kennedy Town to Wan Chai) Northwest coast (14/12 ~17/12)
> - HKVDC
>   - 4th Coy: High West, Victoria Gap and Mount Kellet; 5th Coy: Mount Davis; 6th Coy: Northern shore of Hong Kong Island; 7th Coy: Magazine Gap, Wan Chai Gap and Middle Gap
> - Royal Scots: Causeway Bay

East Infantry Brigade
> Brigadier Cedric Wallis
> Headquarters: Tai Tam R.A. Plotting Room
> - Rajput
>   - A Coy: Shau Kei Wan and Aldrich Bay; B Coy: Braemar Point; C Coy: Taikoo Dockyard; D Coy: North Point
> - Royal Rifles
>   - A Coy: Windy Gap, D'Aguilar Peninsula; B Coy: Stanley Mound; C Coy: Chai Wan Pass; D Coy: Obelisk Hill
> - Middlesex
>   - B Coy: PB 21–30 (West Bay to Red Hill); D Coy: PB 31–39 (Tai Tam Bay to Pakshawan)

- **HKVDC**
  - 1st Coy: Vicinity of Tai Tam Reservoir; 2nd Coy: Pottinger Gap and Big Wave Bay; 3rd Coy: Jardine's Lookout

The scheme later led to much controversy. First, the division of the Canadian forces was seen as counterproductive. During the ensuing battle, Lt. Col. W. J. Home, the commander of the Royal Rifles (RR), did not work well with Wallis. According to Lawson's diary, he had made the decision to split the Canadian contingent jointly with Maltby. Wallis, on the other hand, was seemingly not consulted, as he received the order soon after he returned from the mainland.[111] In accordance with the new scheme, the Royal Navy withdrew from the Royal Naval Dockyard to share the Aberdeen Industrial School with the RAF, withdrawn from Kai Tak. HMS *Moth*, which was being refitted in the dry dock, was scuttled. Four river steamers were sunk in the western entrance of Aberdeen, leaving only the southeastern entrance open.[112]

At 14:30, 13 December, the Japanese artillery shelled Mount Davis and the Jubilee Battery. Although only two duds actually hit and no casualties were caused, the top gun of Mount Davis Fortress, particularly useful for landward firing, was hit

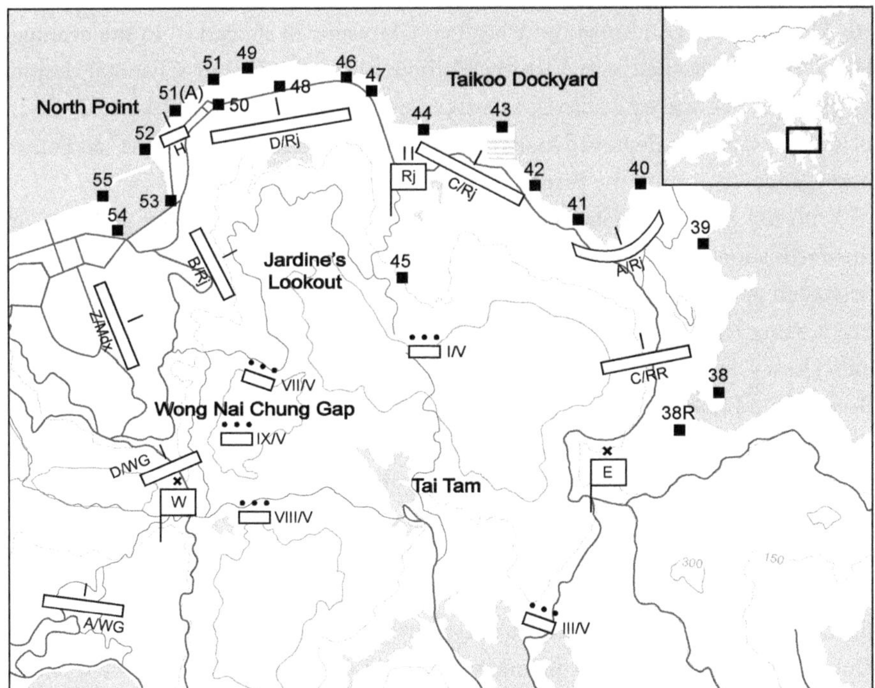

Figure 25   British defence of Hong Kong Island East, 14–18 December 1941

by a dud 240-mm shell and was put out of action due to bore damage. The bombardment also caused a fire in Kennedy Town that was not put out for hours.

On 14 December, the British set up a Counter-Battery HQ at Wong Nai Chung Gap, under the command of Maj. G. E. S. Proes of the 4th Med. Bty. Although the Fortress HQ ordered that all firing reports and suspicious Japanese battery positions should be reported directly to the Counter-Battery HQ, the garrison was not familiar with the new system and the HQ remained ineffective throughout the battle. Moreover, as most of the Japanese artillery was deployed in the built-up area in Kowloon (and some of it near hospitals), the British often decided not to reply even if the Japanese positions were found.

The Japanese started to bombard the island systematically from the 14th. On that day alone, 3,660 shells of 240-mm to 150-mm calibre were expended.[113] The Belcher Battery, Pakshawan Battery, Mount Davis Fortress and Magazine Gap were all hit. The two 4.7-inch QFs of the Belcher Battery were destroyed, but the latter two batteries were unscathed. The Indian gunners of the Belcher Battery withdrew from the destroyed battery and joined the infantry garrison. A main cable running between the Fortress HQ and Magazine Gap was hit, severing telephone communication between Fortress HQ and the southern half of the island for twenty hours.

The British actively responded to the attack. Japanese positions at Stonecutters, Ho Man Tin, Ma Lau Tong and Chiu Lan Chu were all shelled.[114] In the evening, HMS *Thracian* dashed into Victoria Harbour through Sulphur Channel, despite its previous damage by a shovel, to attack Japanese-controlled vessels at Kowloon Bay.[115] The Japanese deployed loudspeakers to play "Home, Sweet Home" and other propaganda, to prompt the British to surrender, without effect.[116]

With the help of collaborators, the Japanese located most of the pillboxes on the north shore. On 15 December alone, PBs 52, 51A and 51 in North Point were destroyed and PB 49 was severely damaged. PB 47 in Braemar Point and PB 40 in Ah Kung Ngam were constantly shelled. However, the Japanese were unable to inflict heavy damage on the batteries except the Pinewood Anti-Aircraft Battery. The British found that the Japanese were unable to shell new positions accurately even though they had full control of the sky.[117]

One hope for the beleaguered defenders of Hong Kong, was the Chinese reinforcements. When the Japanese attacked, the British sent Lt. Col. Harry Owen-Hughes, HKVDC, the commander of the Hughesiliers, to Chongqing to coordinate the rescue effort with the Nationalist Chinese. However, it was soon found out that the Chinese were unable to launch a sizeable rescue effort until early January 1942.[118] During the Japanese bombardment, Maltby told the garrison news of the Chinese reinforcement. He was told on 14 December by Adm. Chan Chak (who confirmed the news with Yu Hanmou) that the Chinese forces under Yu were approaching Pinghu, Lilang and Danshui. Although Maltby questioned the impact of the reinforcement, he distributed propaganda about this after Harry Owen-Hughes had confirmed the news of the Chinese reinforcement. He reported to London on 15 December:

> Morale civil population still shaky owing to continued difficulty over rice distribution but otherwise things are getting under better control ... We are circulating propaganda about proximity Chinese Govt. troops advance in order to bolster morale but realize they cannot be expected to exert any real influence before early January.[119]

The expectation of reinforcement partly explained the garrison's stubbornness when the Japanese attacked the island. However, this led to some bitterness against Maltby after the war. RSM E. C. Ford of the Royal Artillery criticized this decision in his memo, written on 31 December 1941:

> No power on earth can ever forgive the General and his staff for wilfully and knowingly spreading false reports of the close proximity of Chinese Soldiers. It is the first time in History that British Empire forces have had to be sustained on lies.[120]

In the evening, the Pakshawan Battery briefly exchanged fire with the Japanese forces on Devil's Peak; the British motor torpedo boats also engaged the 11th Torpedo Boat Flotilla of the 2CF near Tai O. No damage was caused on either side.[121] That day, the 23rd Army sent over six air raids and over eighty bomb runs against Aberdeen. However, the results were minimal at best.[122]

On 16 December, the Japanese launched the largest air attack against Hong Kong. At 07:30, aircraft from the 23rd Army attacked Hong Kong Island. Two planes were shot down by the anti-aircraft guns at Wong Nai Chung and Brick Hill. From 11:30 to 12:55, eighteen G4M bombers of the Kanoya Air Group and twenty-six G3Ms of the 1st Air Group attacked the island. The first group dropped nine 800-kg bombs and thirty-six 250-kg bombs on Aberdeen, Shau Kei Wan, Lyemun Barracks and Sai Wan Battery. The attack damaged the Aberdeen Police Station and claimed MTB 08 and a tug. A bomb also destroyed the gate of the Aberdeen dock, forcing the British to beach HMS *Thracian*. Its guns were unloaded to join the defence. The second group concentrated on Mount Davis Fortress, dropping seventeen 800-kg bombs, eighteen 250-kg bombs and thirty-four 60-kg bombs. Most bombs, however, missed their targets; the battery remained operational.[123] At least 150 civilians were killed or wounded during the attack.[124] The Japanese Army had also summoned eighteen Ki-21 heavy bombers of the 14th Army Air Group to attack Mount Davis Fortress and Belcher Battery, with only minimal effect.[125]

Throughout the day, the British positions along the north shore were shelled; the plotting room of Mount Davis Fortress received a direct hit from a dud. Although no casualties were caused, the remaining 9.2-inch guns had to rely on the position-finder for firing. The height-finder of Sai Wan Battery was also destroyed. By the end of the day, half the pillboxes between Lyemun and Bowrington were destroyed. Crews moved to alternative positions but their communications were often cut by shell fire.

Although the three-day bombardment brought little real damage, it helped wear down the defenders and, more importantly, disrupted the British defence along the north shore. The Hong Kong government and Chan Chak had cracked down on the triad riot instigated by the Japanese, but sporadic fifth columnist activities still harassed the British defence. The position of the defenders on the island remained difficult, even if the Japanese had yet to launch a full-scale attack.

Second Peace Mission and Plan of Landing

Soon after the failure of the first peace mission, the Japanese planned an amphibious operation against Hong Kong Island. The Japanese decided to launch a general assault against the island on 18 December. Another peace mission, after three days of bombardment, would be sent before the actual assault. A group of swimmers from the 38th Division, led by two officers who were Olympic athletes, was gathered on the 13th to receive special training to swim across the harbour. However, the plan was dropped as many of them were killed by British bombardment as they were going to Tide Cove to receive training.[126]

At 00:30, 17 December, the Japanese shelled the north shore of the island randomly for thirty minutes. In the morning, the City of Victoria received a "warning bombardment" for two hours. It was accompanied by air attacks against Shau Kei Wan and Wan Chai. The Peak and Garden Road were also attacked, with the goal of intimidating the governor.[127] After the bombardment, Lt. Col. Toda returned to the island with a second note. He received the following reply:

> The Governor and Commander-in-Chief of Hong Kong declines most absolutely to enter into any negotiation for the surrender of Hong Kong and he takes this opportunity of notifying Lt. Gen. Takaishi Sakai [*sic*] and Vice Admiral Masaichi Niimi that he is not prepared to receive any further communication from them on the subject.[128]

Lt. Col. Toda claimed that he was "genuinely surprised and disconcerted" by the reply, telling Boxer that the Japanese would "attack indiscriminately" in the coming battle.[129] On the other hand, the British saw the second peace mission as a sign of Japanese weakness. The Fortress diary noted:

> This second delegation coming within four days of the first suggests that the Japanese felt none too comfortable about the task facing them. This may be due to the Chinese threat to their communications, the losses we have inflicted, an attack on our morale or a combination of all three.[130]

This attitude possibly explains why no special measures were taken before the Japanese landing. Indeed, the British even reduced the troops on the north shore by sending Z/Middlesex back to Leighton Hill. During the truce that lasted until 16:00, the British repaired the telephone lines damaged during the bombardment.

On the afternoon of the 17th, Maj. Gen. Sano and Lt. Gen. Kitajima issued the orders for the operations on the island. The Japanese would land between North Point and Braemar Point, as the coastline there had a more gentle relief. A smaller force would land at Lyemun Peninsula. The idea of landing at the Western District was dropped, due to the presence of the sea wall and to the fact that the landing force would be isolated. To ensure the troops could scale any sea wall if they should encounter one, Sano chose to land at high tide. To retain the element of surprise, the first landing wave would be carried by collapsible boats. The reinforcements would be carried by the faster but noisier *daihatsu* or *shohatsu*.

In all, a two-pronged attack was planned (Table 26). The main body, known as the "Right Column," would land at North Point and Braemar Point. It was to occupy the high ground east of Tai Hang Village and Jardine's Lookout, and then push westward towards High West. The "Left Column" would land at Aldrich Bay and Shau Kei Wan. After reaching Violet Hill, it would swing west towards the Peak and High West. The boundary of the two columns ran along the eastern corner of Taikoo Dockyard, Tai Tam Reservoir, Wong Nai Chung Gap, Aberdeen Reservoir, and the junction of Harlech Road, Lugard Road and Hatton Road to the east of High West. It should be noted that no attempts were planned to separate the garrison by taking Wong Nai Chung Gap. Instead, Wong Nai Chung Gap was used for assembling the troops before they swept across the western half of the island. The divisional artillery was divided into the Left and Right groups. The Left Group covered the area between North Point and Aldrich Bay, the Right Group from Sai Ying Pun to Braemar Point. After the infantry had established a beachhead, the Left Group would land on the island. The Kempeitai of the 23rd Army was responsible for arresting Chongqing officials such as Adm. Chan Chak and Chinese dignitaries such as the Tiger Balm magnate Aw Boon Haw (胡文虎).[131]

Table 26   Japanese plan against Hong Kong Island, 18 December 1941

Army HQ: Tai Po

Divisional HQ: Ma Tau Wai

HQ of 38th Infantry Group (operational control of the infantry regiments): Tai Shek Ku

Right Column	Right Wing (*Shoji butai*)	Left Wing (*Doi butai*)
Maj. Gen. Ito Takeo	230 Rgt. (less I/230 Bn.)	228 Rgt. (less III/228 Bn.)
	First Wave: III/230 Bn.	First Wave: II/228 Bn.
	Target: North Point	Target: Taikoo
	Second Wave: II/230 Bn.	Second Wave: I/228 Bn.
	Target: North Point	Target: Braemar Point
	5th Ind. Rapid Firing Gun Bn.	
Left Column	229 Rgt. (less I/229 Bn.)	
Col. Tanaka	First Wave: III/229 Bn.	
Ryosaburo	Target: Aldrich Bay	
	Second Wave: II/229 Bn.	
	Target: Ah Kung Ngam	
	5th Coy, 10th Ind. Mtn. Gun Rgt.	
	2nd Ind. Rapid Firing Gun Bn.	
Division reserves	I/229 Bn.	
	III/228 Bn. (Kowloon East Defence Force)	
	I/230 Bn. (Kowloon West Defence Force)	
Landing support unit	20th Ind. Eng. Rgt.	
	3 x *daihatsu* landing craft	
	18 x *shohatsu* landing craft	
	200 x collapsible boat	

The Japanese commanders were extremely optimistic about the coming operation. They expected that the landing force would reach High West and the Royal
Naval Dockyard less than twenty-four hours after the landing. It was assumed that
the British would be ready to surrender once the Japanese had landed.[132]

On the evening of 17 December, the Japanese shelled the north shore of the
island until nightfall.[133] To draw British attention, the flagship of the 2CF, IJN
Isuzu, steamed out with a destroyer and two torpedo boats to bombard Aberdeen
from the south of Lamma Island under cover of darkness, hitting the Aberdeen
Industrial School with a single dud. The 229 Rgt. sent two scout parties to recon-
noitre the north shore. The first was spotted and repulsed, but the second one, led
by Lt. Masushima Zenpei (増島善平), commanding officer of the 12th Company
of III/229, landed near Taikoo Dockyard and the abandoned PB 41 and PB 42.[134]
Masushima found that the beach southwest of Aldrich Bay[135] was not mined and

was defended only by simple barbed wire and two outposts. What Masushima had found was a gap between the A and C companies of the Rajput battalion, which was thinly spread along the coastline between North Point and Aldrich Bay. PB 40, which had spotted Masushima and his party, could have reported the incident, but its communication was cut by shell fire.[136] Lt. Masushima left the island from the jetty outside PB 42; although he was fired on by PB 40 again, he and his party returned unscathed.

This daring reconnaissance mission allowed the Japanese to refine their landing operations. The coastline between North Point and Braemar Point was found to be thinly defended. Although Aldrich Bay was too narrow and surrounded by British positions, an alternative position large enough for a sizeable landing party was found. This gave the Japanese a great advantage during their landing the next day.

Japanese Landing on Hong Kong Island, 18 December

On 18 December, the Japanese continued their air and artillery attack against Hong Kong Island. Eleven ships in the harbour were sunk by both sides; the Japanese bombardment set fire to the oil depot in North Point. Although Sano expressed some concern about it, the thick smoke created by the fire would partly hinder the British line of sight during the coming battle.[137] At noon, the 18-pounder guns at Braemar Point were destroyed, leaving no artillery for counter-landing in the sector. The Japanese shifted their attention to Causeway Bay in the afternoon, leaving King's Road littered with damaged trucks and debris.[138] Lyemun Barracks, Shau Kei Wan Police Station, Taikoo Dockyard, North Point, Aldrich Bay, Sai Wan and Stanley were all hit. Communication between the Rajput and the East Brigade HQ was cut. The battalion HQ also briefly lost contact with its B and D companies. A rubber factory in Shau Kei Wan and a paint factory in Braemar Point were both hit and set on fire. Smoke carried by the easterly wind further reduced the visibility of the British troops and disabled the searchlight position on Watson Road in North Point.

Lt. Col. J. Cadogan-Rawlinson, commander of the Rajput, discussed the situation with Capt. H. R. Newton of D/Rajput and Maj. J. J. Paterson of the Hughesiliers. They agreed that the growing intensity of bombardment could be a sign of imminent attack and that the smoke offered much advantage to their opponent.[139] At dusk, the 229 Rgt. was spotted coming down from Hai Wan Hill. At 18:30, the Japanese began the preparatory bombardment, targeting the area defended by the 2RS and the Rajput. PBs 40, 41, 42 and 43, all near the landing site, were heavily shelled. By then, Sai Wan Battery had been put out of action.[140]

The Japanese landing force started to board the landing crafts and disembarked at 19:20 as the barrage moved inland. Their right flank was protected by two *sho-hatsu* armed with machine-guns. The fire at North Point, Braemar Point and Taikoo Dockyard, having previously caused much hindrance to the British, now illuminated the incoming Japanese troops. The II/228 was first spotted by PB 43, PB 44 and D/Rajput at approximately 20:00.[141] Cadogan-Rawlinson, who was immediately informed, instructed C/Rajput to send two platoons to protect the battalion HQ and ordered the searchlight at North Point to point in the direction of Aldrich Bay. The searchlight position of Lyemun Fort was also turned towards the incoming 229 Rgt. At the same time, all pillboxes and alternative positions in the vicinity opened fire, catching the Japanese in the crossfire.

However, there was not enough time to stop the landing. At around 20:15, III/230 landed at North Point near modern-day Provident Centre; five minutes later, II/228 was ashore near Taikoo Dockyard. The III/229 landed at Aldrich Bay at 20:28. Sakai and Sano toasted each other when they saw three red flares fired by the successful assault waves.[142] After the Japanese landed, fierce fighting erupted along the north shore. D/Rajput received the full weight of III/230 and fell back towards the Braemar Hill Reservoir.[143] The Japanese penetrated its line and pushed south to the west of the reservoir. The pillboxes along the coast inflicted some losses on the Japanese, but were silenced one by one.[144] C/Rajput held the high ground south of Taikoo Dockyard until midnight, but lost contact with the battalion HQ. Cadogan-Rawlinson and his HQ retreated when the Japanese threatened to surround them.

On the left, III/229 landed at the southwestern corner of Aldrich Bay. Although they were engaged by heavy machine-gun fire from the pillboxes and alternative positions, they managed to land on the beach and suppress the British resistance. It appears that the Japanese landed in the gap between C/Rajput and A/Rajput, thus they met with relatively light resistance. The Japanese soon breached the defence and continued to move south towards Mount Parker. A/Rajput, despite being cut off from the remainder of the battalion, managed to maintain communication with the battalion HQ until 23:00.[145]

An hour after the landing of the first wave, II/230 and the HQ of the 230 Rgt. landed at North Point and moved west along King's Road. The I/228 landed at Braemar Point with the regiment HQ and moved south towards Mount Butler. The II/229 and its regiment HQ landed at Ah Kung Ngam. They reached Lyemun Fort, which was in fact a magazine without guns situated in the gap between A/Rajput and C/RR. A/Rajput was slowly pushed south by II/229. Coping with such tremendous odds, the Indians continued their stiff resistance until the first few hours after midnight; some of them later withdrew to the south while others joined the forces in Pakshawan Battery.[146] After capturing the fort and Sai Wan Battery, south of the fort, which was held by the 5th AA Bty., the Japanese advanced towards Pakshawan Battery, defended by the 4th Bty. of the HKVDC under Capt. K. M. A. Barnett. The gunners launched counterattacks and resisted until 21 December, when Barnett ordered the gunners to surrender. Before that, the Chinese gunners were ordered to take off their uniforms and go into hiding.[147]

As soon as the Japanese landed, the garrison acted accordingly. As Chan Chak pointed out, the British planned to draw a line between Causeway Bay and Jardine's Lookout, to contain any intrusion into the city.[148] The first to move was a platoon of the Middlesex battalion led by a HKVDC armoured car, which was sent to North Point. Wallis ordered the 6-inch howitzers at Chai Wan to fire at Taikoo, to suppress Japanese movements; Lawson deployed his "flying columns" at 22:40. Three platoon-sized "columns" were deployed at the summit of Jardine's Lookout, the gap between Jardine's Lookout and Mount Butler, and Stanley Gap.[149] He also sent A/Winnipeg to Mount Butler. These moves were, according to Chan Chak, who had been informed of the British counter-landing plan beforehand, preliminary steps to an immediate counterattack at dawn before the Japanese had firmly established a beachhead.[150]

The situation was dire for the British (Figure 26). By midnight, the Rajput was facing six battalions (approximately 6,000 men in total)—its line was about to break. The Japanese controlled the shoreline from North Point to Lyemun and had captured Sai Wan Battery. The British positions at Mount Butler, Mount Parker, Braemar Hill and the urban area of North Point were all under heavy assault. However, the British maintained spirited defence. B/Rajput, which was on Tai Hang Road, swung towards Braemar Hill Reservoir and attacked the flank of 230 Rgt. to support D/Rajput, which was fighting desperately against four Japanese battalions at the north of Braemar Hill Reservoir. C/RR launched two counterattacks against Sai Wan Battery, supported by artillery, but it failed to drive back the 229 Rgt. The determined British resistance had thrown the Japanese forces into confusion. It was not until 22:50 that the Japanese Left Column could establish contact with the divisional HQ, and the Right Column was not able to do so until 03:00. The three regiments were fighting alone without knowing the whereabouts of the others.[151] Like Cadogan-Rawlinson, Col. Doi of the 228 Rgt. had also lost control of most of his subordinates for the night. The three Japanese regiments slowly attacked in three separate directions, with 230 Rgt. moving south into Wong Nai Chung Gap, 228 Rgt. moving southwest towards Quarry Gap and 229 Rgt. moving southeast around Mount Parker. All attempts to establish communication between the three regiments failed.[152]

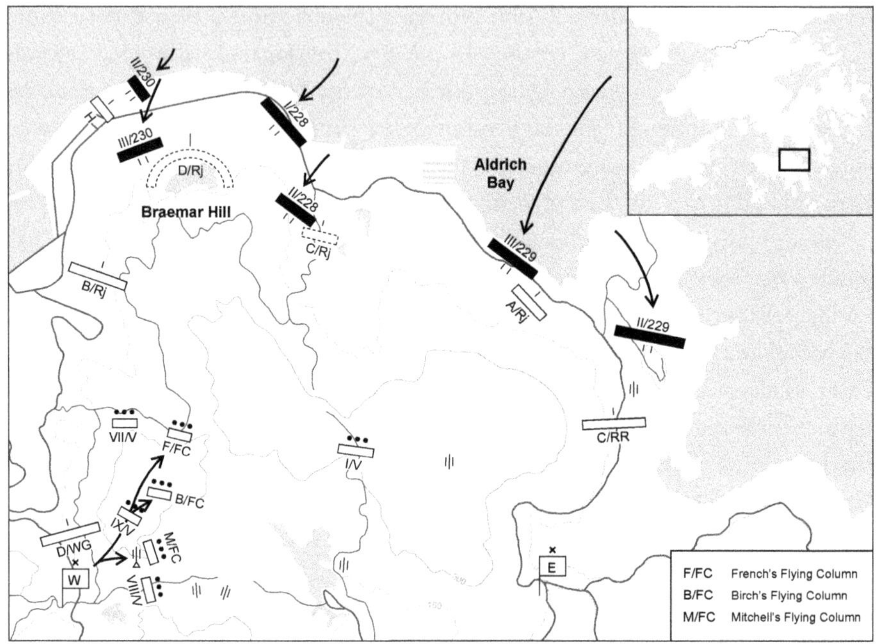

Figure 26   Japanese landing on Hong Kong Island, 18 December 1941

A focal point during this phase of the battle was the North Point Power Plant, held by the Hughesiliers. The unit consisted of British expatriates over fifty-five years old and nationals from Allied or neutral countries. It was led by Maj. J. J. Paterson of Jardine's Matheson & Co. In all, there were four officers and sixty-six other ranks in the power plant, including naval personnel from Taikoo Dockyard, technicians from the China Light Company from Kowloon, and eight officers and men from the Free French. Some of them had seen extensive military service. Paterson had served in the Imperial Camel Corps in Palestine during the First World War. Capt. R. Egal and Lt. F. M. Jacosta,[153] the two French officers, had fought in the Great War. Jacosta had also participated in the Spanish Civil War. A number of local dignitaries were also found in the unit, including T. A. Pearce of the Jockey Club and Baron Edward des Voeux, the secretary of the Hong Kong Club.[154] Although the power plant was heavily shelled, Paterson noted that morale of his unit was high, in no small part due to the encouragement of Egal and Jacosta.

The Hughesiliers had opened fire at the invading Japanese troops, but they were cut off from other British units soon afterwards. When the Middlesex convoy sent by Lawson was advancing along King's Road near the Standard Oil Depot, it was ambushed by the Japanese, who knocked out the HKVDC armoured car. Some survivors of the platoon then joined the Hughesiliers at 01:00. Paterson refused

Jacosta's suggestion of withdrawal, as he worried that the men would be ambushed; he thought their presence might help disrupt the Japanese advance. The Hughesiliers then raided and destroyed the quick-firing gun that had ambushed the Middlesex convoy. The defenders also shot a number of Japanese officers in the vicinity, forcing the Japanese to send I/229 from the mainland to surround the power plant.[155] As ammunition was running out and the situation grew desperate, the Hughesiliers tried to break out the next morning, with des Voeux, Jacosta and Pearce killed during the fighting along Electric Road. The survivors continued to resist in buildings nearby until the Japanese threatened to set fire to the houses at 16:30 the next day.[156] Around three hours before that, the Middlesex platoon remaining at the power plant surrendered, after expending most of its ammunition.[157]

In retrospect, the resistance of the Hughesiliers at the power plant and that of the Rajput at Tai Hang had deflected the advance of 230 Rgt. towards the south instead of in the intended westward direction, thus unwittingly driving the Japanese towards Wong Nai Chung Gap through Sir Cecil's Ride.

The Battle of Wong Nai Chung Gap

The British HQ, which assumed the Rajput was still resisting, responded to the Japanese landing by concentrating its mobile forces, including B/Punjab and A/Winnipeg, near Tai Hang, Mount Butler and Jardine's Lookout, the last of which was held by the 3rd Company of the HKVDC. Before dawn on 19 December, Lawson, who had sent all his "flying columns" and A/Winnipeg to the front, had only three sections from 3rd Coy/HKVDC and the reduced D/Winnipeg to guard the north and south entrances of Wong Nai Chung Gap Road, with another section of 3rd Coy/HKVDC screening Sir Cecil's Ride. Holding the house of Dr. Li Shu Fan (White Jade) near the southern entrance of the gap was the platoon-sized Hong Kong Chinese Regiment.[158] The defenders were widely scattered; the Ride was left undefended when D/Winnipeg moved to its daylight position. Worse, A/Winnipeg was soon lost in the mountain trail, losing contact with the units around it and failing to reach Mount Butler on time. Still preparing for his counterattack in the morning, Lawson asked A/2RS and a company of the Royal Engineers to move into the gap.[159] On the east, after the failed attempt to retake Sai Wan Battery, Wallis struggled hard with his reduced brigade to prevent the 229 Rgt. from reaching Tai Tam.

Meanwhile, the Japanese continued their advance in the eastern half of the island. The 230 Rgt., which had lost contact with other units, engaged with 3rd Coy/HKVDC near Jardine's Lookout. Its commander, Col. Shoji, decided to flank his enemy up on Jardine's Lookout, advancing southwards along Sir Cecil's Ride. The

Japanese column began to lengthen on the narrow path of the Ride. The Japanese troops slowly advanced under cover of darkness and sneaked through the gap left by the reduced D/Winnipeg, without noticing other garrison troops around them. Moving southward along Sir Cecil's Ride, the 230 Rgt. unwittingly went straight into Wong Nai Chung Gap.[160] Col. Shoji then split his battalions into two directions, one (III/230) moving south-westward into Wong Nai Chung Gap with the goal of taking Mount Nicholson, another (II/230) turning eastward towards Jardine's Lookout to outflank The Volunteers (Figure 27).[161]

The 228 Rgt., although ambushed by Rajput troops near Mount Butler, reached Gauge Basin with its supporting artillery.[162] The II/228 also reached the top of Jardine's Lookout from the east and drove one of Lawson's flying columns down the hill. Later, it pushed the reinforcing A/Winnipeg southward from Jardine's Lookout.[163]

At around 06:30, 230 Rgt. was finally spotted by the units around the road junction in Wong Nai Chung Gap; they immediately opened fire. The British finally realized that the Japanese had already entered the gap, where they were soon covered by fire from both sides. PB 1, commanded by Lt. B. C. Field of the 3rd Company, HKVDC, poured devastating fire on the closely packed columns of III/230 waiting at the end of Sir Cecil's Ride. However, PB 1 was unable effectively to train its guns at II/230 to the southeast. According to the Japanese, PB 3, which was near Black's Link, opened fire and was soon silenced by III/230 with the support of rapid-firing guns.[164] The III/230 also engaged intensely with the D/Winnipeg and the West Brigade HQ. The British guns at Racecourse also poured fire on the 230 Rgt., which was practically surrounded by the British in the gap. Lawson, who was under direct attack, ordered the 2RS to reinforce his position at 07:00. A/2RS, which was already moving towards the gap, reached Stubbs Road some thirty minutes later.[165] Despite suffering casualties, the numerically superior Japanese troops captured Wong Nai Chung Gap Police Station in the early morning and slowly came to control the gap.

Maltby sent the following telegram to the War Office at 08:36: "Situation very grave (;) deep penetration made by enemy. All cipher book and drums destroyed…"[166] Still, the British resisted with much vigour. At 08:45, six motor torpedo boats, previously sent by Maltby as part of the counterattack, went into Victoria Harbour from Sulphur Channel to attack the Japanese landing crafts. The first pair (MTBs 07 and 09) surprised the Japanese and sank three collapsible boats. The second pair (MTBs 11 and 12) came under heavy fire; MTB 12 was disabled and beached near the shore of Kai Tak airfield during the attack. Despite the order to withdraw, MTB 26 from the third pair dashed into the harbour and attacked. It was also disabled and captured outside North Point, with all its seven crew killed.[167]

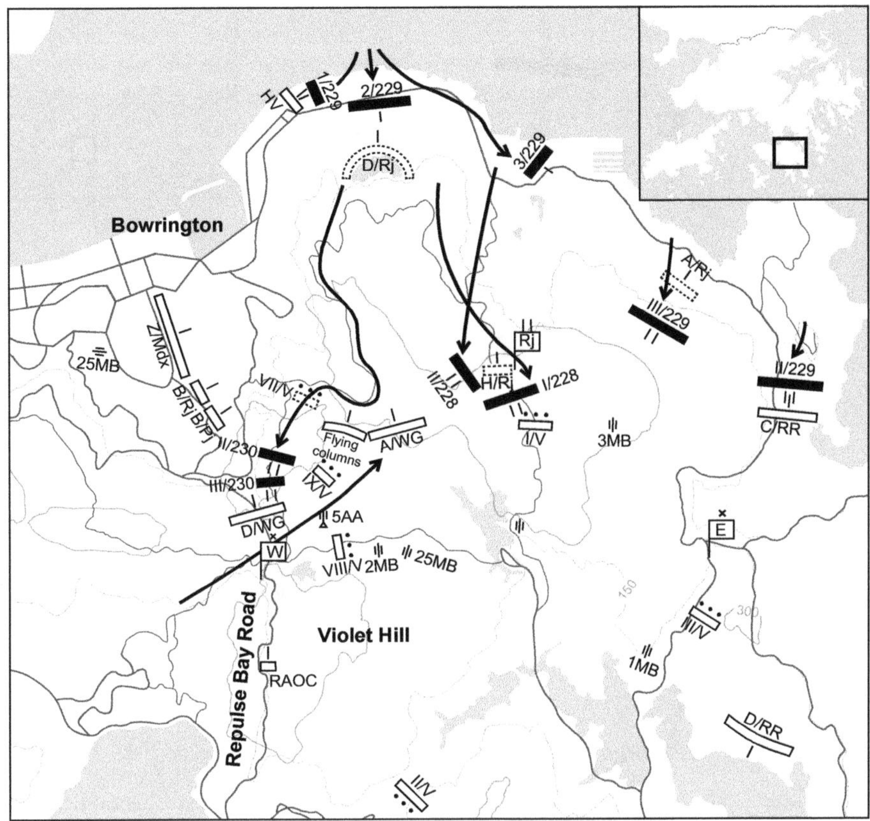

Figure 27   Japanese penetration, early morning, 19 December 1941

This daring attack inflicted some twenty casualties on the Japanese, causing much confusion and anxiety to their commanders.[168]

During the battle for Wong Nai Chung Gap, the Japanese gained a distinct advantage, as part of the III/230 and a company of the 5th Rapid Firing-Gun Battalion (equipped with Type 94 37-mm light guns) had taken Wong Nai Chung Gap Police Station, which could command all roads leading to the gap from the south. The Japanese then established a strong line supported by rapid-firing guns to secure the position.[169] By 07:00, the northern and southern entrances of the gap were already controlled by the Japanese, with the headquarters of the West Brigade, the West Fire Command and D/Winnipeg trapped inside. The Japanese continued to assault the HQ of D/Winnipeg despite sustaining heavy casualties.[170] During the ferocious battle, the commander of II/230 was also wounded when he tried to lead a charge against the British position in the gap.[171] A/2RS was moving towards the West Brigade HQ but was held up in the northern entrance of the gap, suffering heavy

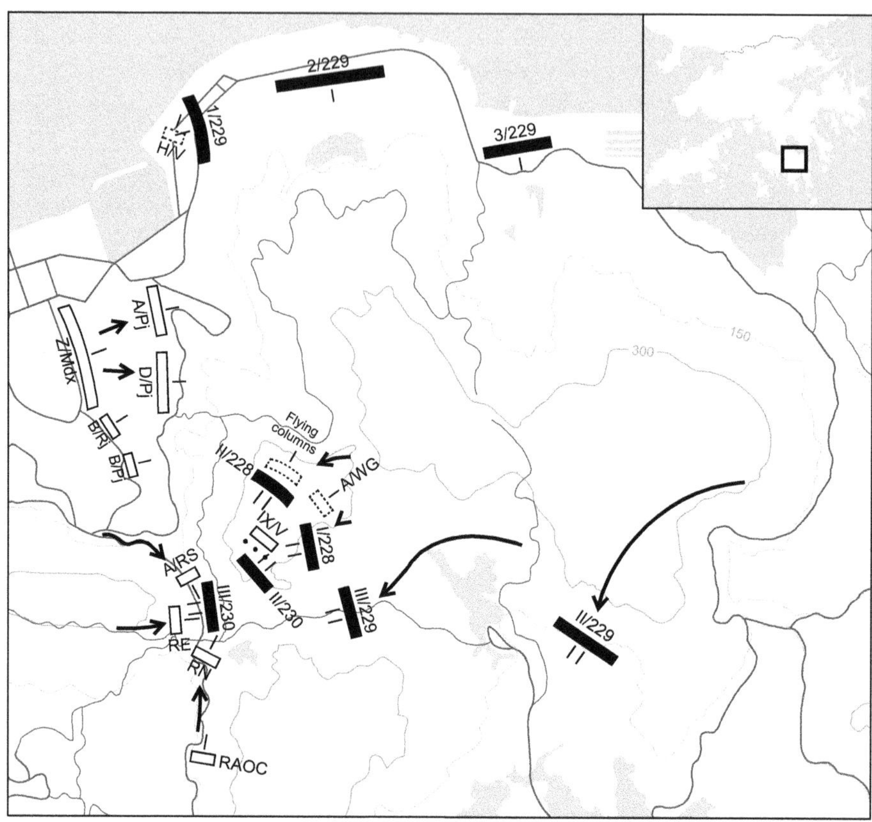

Figure 28   Battle of Wong Nai Chung Gap, 08:30–12:00, 19 December 1941

casualties from Japanese rapid-firing guns. The Royal Engineers from the south, which was a mixed contigent of British and Chinese sappers, was also beaten back. At about 10:00, Lawson decided to break out with his staff. He said his last words to Maltby, "I'm going outside to fight it out."[172]

Before Lawson left his HQ, he sent Capt. H. A. Bush to the HQ of D/Winnipeg across Wong Nai Chung Gap Road to cover the evacuation. However, instead of following Bush, Lawson and his men turned southward, probably towards a trail leading to Black's Link. They were spotted and killed almost instantaneously by the soldiers of the 230 Rgt.[173] In the east, Wallis was hard pressed by the 229 Rgt., which was thrusting into Gauge Basin. Wallis ordered the destruction of the Collinson, Bokhara and Chung Hom Kok batteries, and pulled back his infantry and mobile artillery to the Stanley Peninsula.

Although the West Brigade had lost its commander, British reinforcements were being poured into the gap. The first to arrive was a naval company consisting of personnel from HMS *Thracian* and HMS *Tamar*, led by Cdr. A. L. Pears. When approaching the gap from Repulse Bay Road, it was ambushed by Japanese forces. Some survivors withdrew to Postbridge, a house at the junction of Wong Nai Chung Gap Road and Repulse Bay Road.[174] It enjoyed a commanding position over the gap, the police station and the reservoir, and was held by the Royal Artillery and the Royal Naval Volunteer Reserve (RNVR).[175] The defenders held Postbridge until evening and had a clear view of the battle. Near Postbridge, the Hong Kong (Chinese) Regiment also continuously exchanged fire with the Japanese in White Jade.[176]

From 11:00 to 12:00, the British reinforced the defenders of the gap and North Point from two directions. The A and D/Punjab pushed towards Braemar Hill to relieve D/Rajput, which had already been destroyed, with its commander killed. A/2RS finally pushed into the gap. Under devastating artillery fire from the 230 Rgt., part of the company reached within 180 metres from Lawson's HQ by 12:25.[177] As it was already pinned down, White urged the Winnipeg Grenadiers to reinforce the gap (Figure 28).[178]

By noon, PB 1 and PB 2 had resisted for hours against hundreds of Japanese soldiers. Of the nine defenders of PB 1, one was killed and seven were wounded before noon. All three Vickers machine-guns were damaged, but were still firing. Capt. Field was wounded three times throughout the day. L/Cpl. Hung Kai Chiu, who briefly replaced Field, directed the defenders of the two pillboxes against repeated assault.[179]

At 14:15, Maltby issued Operation Order No. 6, ordering a general counterattack. The Fortress HQ assessed the situation as follows:

> The infiltration of the enemy after the landings at Lyemun, North Point and Taikoo had been rapid during the morning 19 Dec 41. Small parties of the enemy keeping to the high ground had reached Tai Tam and Wong Nei Chong Gaps [sic]. Given the recapture of Wong Nei Chong Gap it seemed possible to restore the position by retaking Jardine's Lookout, Mount Butler and Mount Parker. The strength of the enemy could not be ascertained but it seemed doubtful if it exceeded two battalions. Elsewhere certain sub-units were maintaining their ground stubbornly and particularly the defence of the Hong Kong Electric Power House by a party of elderly civilians, cut off in an exposed position, proved a fine example.[180]

The Operation Order No. 6 read:

> At 1415 hrs 19 Dec 41 an order was issued from Fortress HQ directing an attack to take place at 1500 hrs in an Easterly direction to the line (incl) Middle Spur–Wong Nei Chong Reservoir–Clements Ride [sic] to join with objective reached by 2/14 Punjabs on Tai Hang Village and Braemar Reservoir now being delivered. The 2/14 Punjabs were to exploit in a Northerly direction and relieve the Hughesliers [sic]. Left flank of troops on Mount Cameron were to

attack on axis Middle Gap–Wong Nei Chong Reservoir–Gauge Basin. 2RS to
be directed on to include Jardine's Lookout (Excl Tai Hang Village). All troops
to advance at 1500 hrs.[181]

A four-pronged attack was planned. A and D/Punjab were to advance towards Tai
Hang and Braemar Hill Reservoir. The 2RS was split into two parties, with the first
(C and D companies) attacking Jardine's Lookout from the west via Stubbs Road
and the second party (B and HQ companies) joining X/Winnipeg (comprising the
personnel of Battalion HQ) and the Royal Engineers to break into the gap from the
south. The East Brigade would also send a detachment of a hundred Royal Artillery
gunners (British, Indian, and Chinese) from Repulse Bay Road to support the operation. The goal was to retake the gap and Jardine's Lookout and to link up with the
beleaguered (actually destroyed) Rajput battalion (Figure 29).

It seems that the Fortress HQ lagged considerably behind the events. The Rajput
battalion was largely destroyed, while the Hughesiliers were trapped and running
out of ammunition. Instead of two battalions, the Japanese actually had seven battalions on the island. Two of them were in the gap, two were between Stanley Gap
and Jardine's Lookout, two were at Tai Tam, and another was at North Point. Thus,
the British were throwing seven companies against twenty-one. This misjudgement
wasted a considerable number of troops that might have been useful for the defence
of the western high grounds during the later stages of the battle.

Before the attack, the commanders at the front had already discovered that
something had gone wrong. Lt. Col. Kidd of the Punjab conferred with Lt. Col. H.
W. Stewart of the Middlesex and Capt. R. G. Course of B/Rajput. They found that
D/Rajput had withdrawn to the rear of B/Rajput and its commander was missing.
They were also unaware of the whereabouts of A and D/Winnipeg, which were
struggling on the southern slope of Jardine's Lookout.

The British attacked notwithstanding. A and D/Punjab reached Leighton Hill
at around 15:45. They met stubborn resistance from III/230 as they were trying to
take the northern part of Jardine's Lookout, and were driven back in the late afternoon. To the south, C and D/2RS attacked Jardine's Lookout and entered the gap,
supported by four Bren Carriers and seven heavy machine-guns. The attack was led
by D/2RS, which had fiercely contested Golden Hill earlier. D/2RS reached the
deserted West Brigade HQ, but was pinned down by heavy machine-gun and mortar
fire. By dusk, the two companies returned to the petrol station on Stubbs Road.

On Black's Link, HQ Coy and B/2RS attacked the gap with X/Winnipeg, sup-
ported by a single Bren Carrier. The two companies of the 2RS were held up by
Japanese fire, but X/Winnipeg reached the HQ of D/Winnipeg. Its commander,
Capt. E. Hodkinson, found the Japanese had occupied the police station and

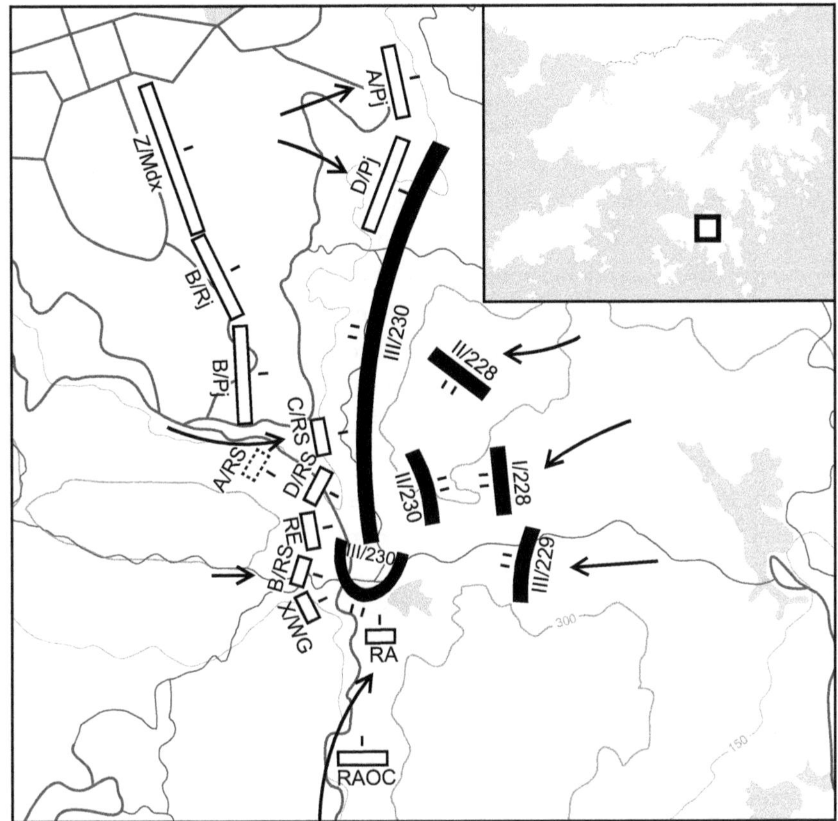

Figure 29   British counterattack on Hong Kong Island, 15:00–04:00, 19–20 December 1941

reported to Maltby that he was to attack Mount Parker after clearing up the station at 17:00.[182] The Indian gunners from the East Brigade, led by Lt. Col. J. C. Yale, Maj. E. W. De V. Hunt and Maj. L. J. Feilden and escorted by two armoured cars, were again ambushed by the Japanese from the police station, while advancing along Repulse Bay Road in the evening. Although the gunners overcame the rapid-firing guns and reached the gap at midnight, Feilden was killed and Yale was wounded and missing.[183] Hunt rallied the remaining gunners to join Hodkinson to take the police station, but they were also beaten back, with the armoured cars being knocked out.[184] After Hunt was also killed later that night, only thirteen gunners returned to Stanley.

Although the 230 Rgt. was attacked by the Punjab and the 2RS, it was able to hold Jardine's Lookout. Meanwhile, II/228 pushed A and D/Winnipeg southward. While D/Winnipeg was eventually dispersed, a large part of A/Winnipeg, led by CSM J. R. Osborn, fell back to Stanley Gap. During the fierce fighting, the

Canadians continued to retreat; Osborn was killed in the late afternoon when he threw himself on an exploding grenade. He was posthumously awarded a Victoria Cross in 1946.[185]

At 17:30, Capt. Field ordered the wounded men from PBs 1 and 2 to be evacuated via Tai Hang Road, and asked for reinforcement from the Fortress HQ. Soon after the evacuation, II/228 attacked the two pillboxes with full strength. Field received his fourth wound and withdrew to PB 2 with L/Cpl. Hung. Field and the soldiers remaining in PB 2 surrendered upon request. As they left, L/Cpl. Hung was hit badly by a sniper. He decided to remain inside PB 1 and helped himself to what was left of the medical supplies. He was, however, never seen again.[186] Of the twenty-one men under Field's command, six were killed, five wounded and one missing. Postbridge held out until around 22:00, when the engineers from the III/229 destroyed its main gate. Most of its defenders withdrew to "the Ridge" to continue their resistance, while the naval personnel returned to Aberdeen. As the 229 Rgt. approached Aberdeen, the British dug in near the northern ridge of Brick Hill. Cdre. Collinson scuttled all vessels except HMS *Cicala* and the surviving motor torpedo boats.[187]

The fighting on 19 December inflicted heavy losses on both sides. The British garrison had been bloodied, and a number of senior officers including Lawson were lost. The newly formed Hong Kong (Chinese) Regiment, which had only around fifty soldiers, was also routed out when it was retreating towards Repulse Bay the next day.[188] The Japanese had expected a walkover after landing, but things went badly wrong. Only the unintended capture of Wong Nai Chung Gap Police Station by III/230 saved the Japanese from further trouble. The Japanese had paid a high price for the eastern half of the island. The 230 Rgt. alone sustained some 600 to 800 casualties on the 19th.[189] Col. Shoji had to apologize for the heavy casualties and the extra logistical work they entailed. It took two days for Japanese medics to retrieve all the dead and wounded of the 230 Rgt.[190] The other two regiments, however, suffered only lightly.

Failed British Counterattacks

After midnight on 20 December, sporadic British counterattacks, mostly uncoordinated, were launched against the Japanese forces at Wong Nai Chung Gap. These futile attacks further dissipated the strength and energy of the defenders. At 01:00, C and D/2RS resumed the drive into the gap from the north. D/2RS even reached the police station, but was again driven back.[191] A and D/2RS attacked the police station again an hour later but to no avail. The Japanese inside the station, many of them artillerymen, were equipped with hand grenades as they had no rifles. These grenades effectively halted the British counterattack.[192] Another attempt by the HQ Coy/2RS also ended in failure.[193] After three failed attempts, the 2RS withdrew to the western side of the gap.

Near Jardine's Lookout, C/2RS reached Sir Cecil's Ride and saw over 500 Japanese troops there at around 04:00. The Royal Scots then retreated westward, as they could not tackle so many enemy troops. Meanwhile, the HQ of D/Winnipeg, forty strong, was still holding out. Other British forces passing through the gap failed to notice their existence. An attempt made by an HKVDC engineer to establish communication between the HQ and nearby units also failed.

At dawn, the gap became no man's land. The Japanese held the east and south sides with the northern entrance covered with fire, while the 2RS controlled the western slope. The Middlesex was still holding Leighton Hill, while the remnants of the Rajputs defended Broadwood Road. The Punjab was on Tai Hang Road. To their south, A and D/Winnipeg were dispersed and X/Winnipeg was ordered to regroup at Middle Gap after suffering heavy casualties.[194] Wallis, whose force was greatly reduced, had established himself in the Stanley Peninsula.

The Japanese mainly advanced on the southern front in the morning. After taking Postbridge, the 229 Rgt. continued its western drive and approached the golf course of Deep Water Bay, along the catchment of Violet Hill. However, following the trail of the catchment, they reached the vicinity of the Repulse Bay Hotel, southeast of their intended destination. A company of the regiment got lost and reached The Twins; the other reached Shouson Hill on its own initiative.[195] The commanding officer of the 229 Rgt., Col. Tanaka Ryosaburo (田中良三郎), stayed in the garage of the hotel at the moment but was unaware of the fact that the main building of the hotel was occupied by around 250 British civilians and soldiers, commanded by 2nd Lt. R. L. Grounds.[196]

At 07:40, Grounds reported the situation to Maltby, who was conferring with Wallis about retaking the gap from the south. Realizing the possibility of his brigades being separated, he instructed Wallis to send A and D/RR and two platoons of the 2/HKVDC to advance along Repulse Bay Road to the gap, followed by B and HQ companies of the RR. C/RR would hold Palm Villa to block any Japanese advance to the south along Tai Tam Road. Twenty minutes later, after Grounds reported to Maltby, the British guns on Stanley Mound fired at Repulse Bay and Violet Hill. At around 08:00, Grounds led his men to storm the garage, later joined by Canadian and HKVDC troops. Although Grounds was killed, the Japanese were evicted and forced to burn the cipher books and radio set in haste.[197] The RR and HKVDC continued to press forward along Repulse Bay Road, but were later forced to withdraw to Eucliff and the hotel.

Meanwhile, the 9th Company of the 229 Rgt., which had gone astray, reached the old anti-aircraft battery on Hill 143, south of Shouson Hill, previously occupied by C/Middlesex until the day before. When the Japanese vanguard pushed further west, however, they were ambushed by C/Middlesex. In the morning, C/Winnipeg, supported by Bren Carriers, was moving along Island Road from Bennet's Hill. It clashed head on with the 9th Coy; although the Canadians fell back, one-fourth of the Japanese troops had become casualties.[198]

In response to the Japanese advance on the southern front, the British continued to pour troops to the south. After deploying most of Wallis's troops to Repulse Bay Road, Maltby sent A/Punjab to Wong Chuk Hang with the goal of retaking the southern slope of Shouson Hill. At around 11:00, D/RR advanced again into the gap from The Twins via Violet Hill, supported by a single 3-inch mortar with twenty-four rounds. Although it was able to inflict some losses on a supply column of III/229 near Repulse Bay Gap, its progress was slow, as the troops were unfamiliar with the ground. A/RR was dispersed and took up strong positions in the mansions along Repulse Bay Road.

Sometime before noon, Col. P. Hennessy, the highest ranking officer of the C Force after Lawson went missing, was mortally wounded at the Peak by a Japanese shell. He was succeeded by Col. H. B. Rose of the HKVDC. At noon, Gen. Sano decided to move his HQ to Braemar Point to get a better idea of the situation. He was under fire when crossing the harbour and had to run for cover while landing. Eventually, he established his HQ at the house of Chen Shulin, the son of the KMT warlord Chen Jitang.[199] The Right Artillery Group also landed on the island with I/230. [200]

At around 13:30, Maltby ordered the West Brigade to attack eastward again. The goal was the anti-aircraft position in the gap.[201] The plan, however, was thwarted, as the fresh I/230 had pushed into Tai Hang Village and forced Z/Middlesex, the Rajput and B/Punjab to retreat to a new line stretching from Leighton Hill to Tai Hang Road. In the afternoon, Wallis ordered A and B/RR to take the gap with the Bren Carriers led by Maj. C. R. Templer, the commander of 30th Coast Battery. It was also supported by HMS *Cicala*, which helped to suppress the Japanese near the coast of Deep Water Bay. However, Templer's troops also failed to retake the police station.

One of the reasons for the stubborn British resistance was the expectation of a Chinese relief column. When Maltby was told about a "Chinese air raid" against Kowloon, he asked Adm. Chan Chak for more information on 20 December. Chan claimed that 60,000 Chinese troops were about to attack Shenzhen. Although Maltby estimated that the Chinese could not attack until early January, he sent the following message to all units at 16:00:

> There are indications that Chinese Forces are advancing towards the Frontier
> to our aid. All ranks must therefore hold their positions at all costs and look
> forward to only a few more days strain.[202]

Chan noted in his diary that he had received a phone call from Yu Hanmou, the commander of the Chinese forces in Guangdong, claiming that his troops had reached Longgang and Henggang, with their vanguard approaching Shenzhen.[203] In fact, the vanguard of Chinese relief forces, which consisted of two divisions and a brigade (158th, 159th and Independent 9th Brigade) and supported by seven corps near Shaoguan, were still near Huizhou (惠州) and unable to interfere, due to the presence of the "Araki Column," consisted of the 66th Infantry Regiment of the Imperial Japanese Army's 51st Division and various smaller units of the 23rd Army.[204] The Chinese planned a full scale attack against Shenzhen in early January.[205]

After taking Tai Hang, the Japanese advanced along the northern half of the front. The I/228 had originally planned a night attack against Mount Nicholson, held only by 2RS after X/Winnipeg had withdrawn in the morning. Covered by heavy fog, a

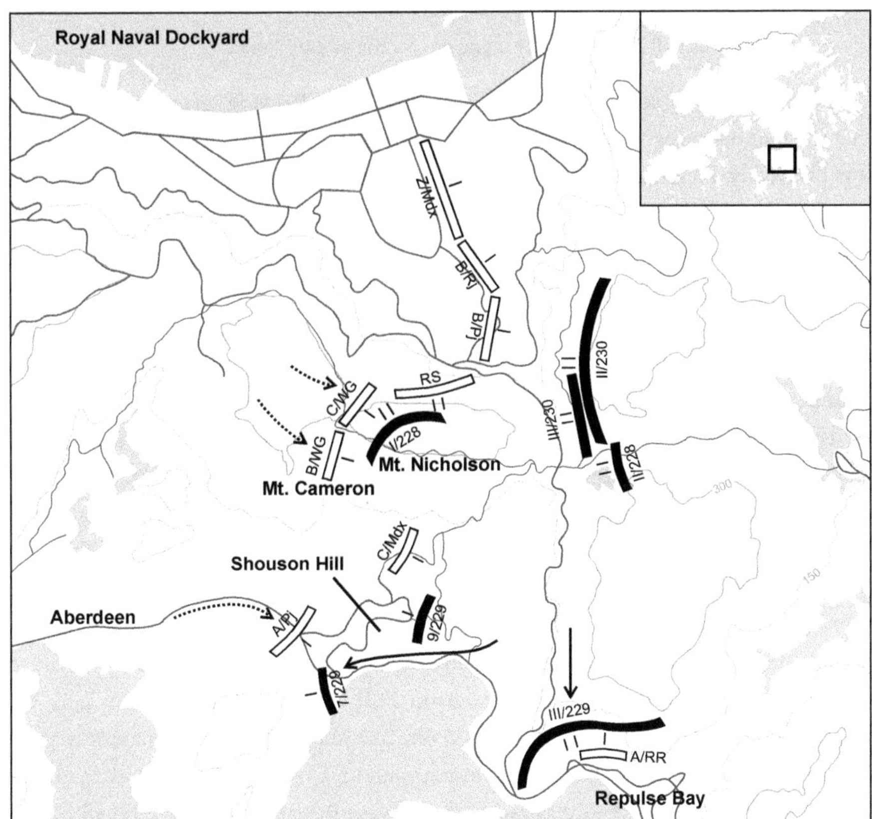

Figure 30   Japanese advance renewed, morning, 21 December 1941

company of Japanese troops seized the opportunity to reach the southern slope of Mount Nicholson without being detected and attacked the flank of D/2RS, forcing the latter to withdraw. By 20:00, I/228 had taken Mount Nicholson, cutting the line of West Brigade in half, but the British had little idea of the extent of the breach. The Fortress HQ still noted at 22:15 that "if a relief party is sent from higher slopes on East Mt Nicholson they might engage and hold this party of enemy" (Figure 30).[206]

After the failures of 19 and 20 December, the British reconsidered their approach. At around 22:30, 20 December, Wallis conferred with Newnham and Maltby in detail about the operation. Wallis pointed out that it was useless to attack from Repulse Bay Road without adequate artillery support, as the road was dominated by the Japanese at Violet Hill and Middle Spur. Wallis proposed the alternative route of Tai Tam Tuk and Gauge Basin, from which he might be able to disrupt the rear of the Japanese forces. Accordingly, Maltby issued the following instructions to Wallis:

- Hold what you have i.e. Repulse Bay Hotel
- Do what you can to get Wong Nei Chong Gap [*sic*] via Gauge Basin
- Use your Bren gun carriers boldly in reconnaissance
- Boldness will pay especially if you get on the enemy's rear.[207]

Col. Rose, the new commanding officer of the West Brigade, proposed to Maltby that the two brigades be coordinated to attack at dawn. However, as the East Brigade was not ready, Newnham let the West Brigade attack first at 07:00, followed by the East Brigade two hours later. The attacking force of the West Brigade was B and C/Winnipeg. They were to advance through Middle Gap to retake Mount Nicholson, and then push forward into the gap. The East Brigade would use the RR and the HKVDC to attack along Tai Tam Road and reach the gap from the east through Tai Tam Reservoir.[208] A/Punjab would also attack in the south to retake the eastern part of Shouson Hill.

The Winnipeg Grenadiers attacked on time at 07:00, with whatever scarce artillery support the British could muster. During the two-hour assault, I/228 was hard pressed; both sides engaged in hand-to-hand and grenade fighting. Two of the Japanese squads were annihilated, showing the intensity of the battle.[209] Although the Canadians had taken the top, they were eventually driven back by the more numerous Japanese. All officers of B/Winnipeg were killed, along with seven NCOs and twenty-nine soldiers. The Japanese lost at least fifty soldiers.[210] Before A/Punjab attacked, the 229 Rgt. controlled Shouson Hill and held a top overlooking the Repulse Bay Hotel. A/Punjab was wiped out in a charge against the Japanese position on Shouson Hill. The battalion commander, Lt. Col. Kidd, was found dead near the hilltop. By then, all counterattacks of the West Brigade had failed. HMS *Cicala*, which had supported the British troops from Deep Water Bay for days, was repeatedly attacked by Japanese aircraft and field artillery. The gallant gunboat finally succumbed to four bomb hits by Japanese aircraft and was abandoned in the East Lamma Channel on the morning of 21 December.[211]

At 09:15, Wallis organized his attack into three columns and concentrated them at Palm Villa. The order of battle was as follows:

Advance Guard	Commander: Maj. T. MacAuley (RR)
	1st Coy/HKVDC; One section of 3-inch mortar; Bren Carriers, 1st Coy/HKVDC
Main Body	Commander: Lt. Col. W. J. Home (CO RR)
	HQ Coy/RR; C/RR; D/RR; 2nd Coy/HKVDC; 3-inch mortars
Flanking Force	Commander: Capt. W. F. Clarke (RR)
	HQ Coy/RR; 10 men, 1st Coy/HKVDC; 2 sections, D/RR

The three columns had different targets. The "Advance Guard" was to retake the junction of Tai Tam Road and Tai Tam Reservoir Road, or "Taitam Fork" as the British called it. The "Main Body" would then push into the reservoir and attack the gap from Gauge Basin. The "Flanking Force" would take Bridge Hill and Notting Hill and cover the flank of the Main Body.

Standing along the way of the East Brigade were the 2nd and the Machine Gun companies of I/229. They reached Taitam Fork on the evening of 20 December and were split in two. One group rested at the pumping station at the northern tip of Red Hill; the other was stationed north of Bridge Hill. The Japanese troops captured the European engineers and the Chinese mechanics inside the pumping station and used the boilers, still running, to dry their clothes. The next morning, the boilers ran out of fuel and stopped, cutting the supply of running water to the island. Unwittingly, the Japanese had dealt a devastating blow against the defenders.[212]

Wallis's attack went well at the beginning. The Flanking Force climbed up the ridge between Bridge Hill and Notting Hill and made contact with the Japanese. The Advance Guard, though briefly pinned down by fire from Red Hill, eventually drove the Japanese into the pumping station. Both sides then struggled for control of the pumping station, but the British were unable completely to secure Red Hill, which was in control by the Machine Gun Coy of I/229, which delivered effective fire on the British forces at Tai Tam Road. D/RR rushed up Bridge Hill to reinforce the British forces near the pumping station. On the other hand, elements of the 2nd Coy of I/229 also climbed to the same top from the opposite direction. The Japanese troops on Red Hill failed to stop the Canadians as they were protected by terrain. As the Canadians reached the top first, they poured deadly fire on the

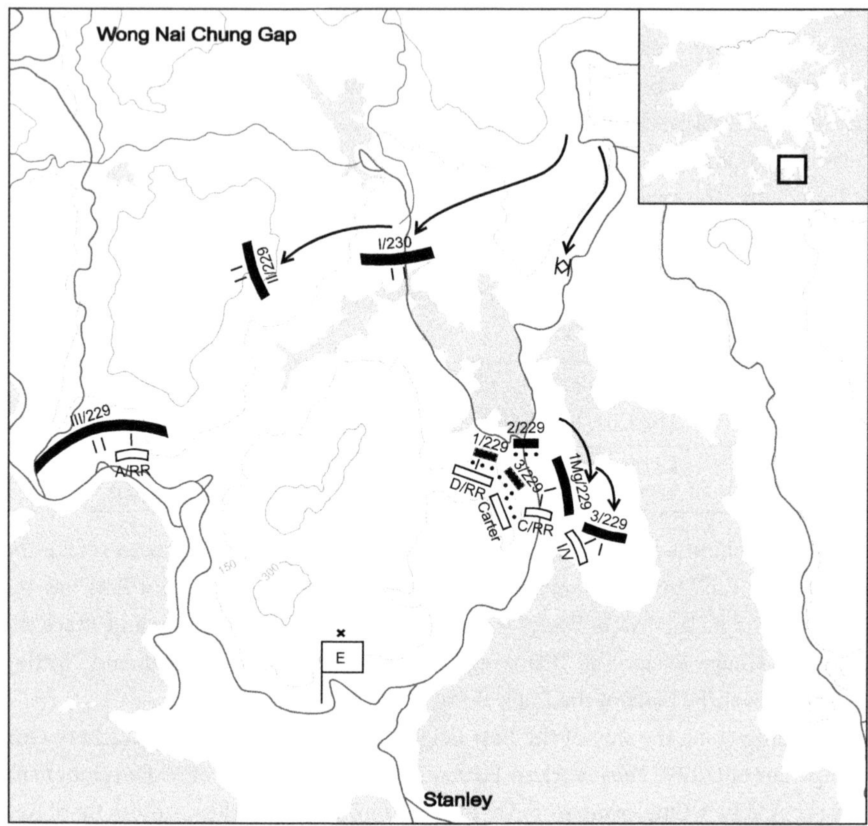

Figure 31   Wallis's counterattack, 21 December 1941

Japanese climbing uphill, killing thirty-six instantly, including the company commander, and severely wounding most of the rest (Figure 31).[213]

By 14:00, the Canadians took Bridge Hill. With the support of Bren Carriers, C/RR eventually reached Taitam Fork. However, the Japanese on Red Hill continued to disrupt the British advance; attempts to dislodge them failed. The Japanese, sensing an imminent breakthrough, deployed part of I/230 with Type 94 tankettes to the scene. The British Advance Guard was eventually forced to withdraw. Wallis, whose troops were ill-equipped against tanks, was forced to call off the operation at 18:00.[214]

While the East Brigade was struggling at Taitam Fork, the situation of the West Brigade deteriorated. North of Wong Nai Chung Gap, a gap was created after the failed counterattack in the morning. Part of the Punjab was redeployed to prevent a penetration towards Mount Gough, Wan Chai Gap and the Peak. The Fortress HQ also ordered the Winnipeg Grenadiers to hold Mount Cameron at all costs. In the southern section, the British could barely hold the Repulse Bay Hotel. The Japanese continued to make progress towards the southern part of Leighton Hill and pushed towards Middle Gap.

In all, the counterattacks from 19 to 21 December left the British garrison expended and exhausted. By noon of the 21st, the front line of the West Brigade went through Leighton Hill, Happy Valley, Wan Chai Gap, Mount Cameron and Little Hong Kong. The 2RS and the Winnipeg, which formed the centre of the line, had suffered heavy casualties. Only the B, C, D/Punjab; A, C, Z/Middlesex; and 4th, 5th, 6th/HKVDC of the West Brigade remained effective. The East Brigade had lost the Rajputs, although Cadogan-Rawlinson returned to the front and rallied the remnants of B and D/Rajput to fight at Leighton Hill. With the Rajputs fighting in the West Brigade, the effective units left for Wallis were the Royal Rifles, B and D/Middlesex, and 1st and 2nd/HKVDC. However, as the Japanese largely controlled the area near Shouson Hill, Wallis and his units were trapped on the Stanley Peninsula. The expected Chinese help, if it came at all, was seemingly too late to make a difference. In the late afternoon of 21 December, Maltby was told by the military attaché at Chongqing that the Chinese could not launch a sizeable attack before 1 January 1942.[215]

The Japanese were only a little better off. The advance of the 228 Rgt. towards Middle Gap was constantly disrupted by British resistance and the bombardment of the 9.2-inch guns of the Stanley Battery. The 230 Rgt. was still regrouping and recuperating from the heavy fighting on 19 December. The III/229, which had cut off the two British brigades, faced the British from the Repulse Bay Hotel, Repulse Bay Road and west of Shouson Hill. Its southern and western routes were blocked by A/RR, which had used the houses along Repulse Bay Road to form a series of positions. With their numbers, however, the Japanese could afford more mistakes; they could eventually wear the defenders down by their sheer number.

At 20:30, Wallis sent A/RR and a detachment consisting of Royal Army Service Corps and Royal Army Ordnance Corps personnel up to Wong Nai Chung Gap. The reconnaissance unit penetrated the gap without being spotted.[216] Maltby and Wallis then contemplated using the Royal Rifles to launch another night attack, but the idea was opposed by Lt. Col. Home, commanding officer of the RR, who believed that such an action would be a waste of lives and who requested an audience with Governor Mark Young. The controversy among the senior officers of the garrison lasted long after the war.[217]

Contemplation of Surrender, 21 December

On 21 December, even Maltby expressed much pessimism about the future of the garrison. He sent the following telegram to the War Office:

> Sitrep [situation report] to 1030 hours 21st December 1941. Enemy attacking westward across Mount Nicholson through Middle Gap … Troops very tired after long day's fighting and very wet cold nights. Although little of Hong Kong still in our hands, unable to reach food and ammunition store as position [Little Hong Kong] surrounded. Transport facility difficult. Royal Canadian Rifles attacking from Stream area through Tytam Tuk [*sic*] toward enemy rear but progress slow.[218]

Mark Young, who was aware of the grave situation and Maltby's attitude, sent another telegram to London in the afternoon, asking for permission to surrender conditionally:

> Enemy held key position on hills and G.O.C. advises that we are very rapidly approaching a point at which only remaining resistance open to us will be to hold for short time only a small pocket in centre of city leaving bulk of fixed population to be overrun.
>
> I feel it will be my duty to ask terms before this position is reached …[219]

When London received Mark Young's telegram, Lord Privy Seal Clement Attlee, Secretary of State for War Henry Margesson and CIGS Gen. Alan Brooke held a meeting. Winston Churchill had sent a telegram to Hong Kong earlier on 20 December:

> We were greatly concerned to hear of the landings on Hong Kong Island which have been effected by the Japanese. We cannot judge from here the conditions which rendered these landings possible or prevented effective counter attacks upon the intruders. There must however be no thought of surrender. Every part of the Island must be fought and the enemy resisted with the utmost stubbornness.
>
> The enemy should be compelled to expend the utmost life and equipment. There must be vigorous fighting in the inner defences and if the need be from house to house. Every day that you are able to maintain your resistance you help the Allied cause all over the world, and by a prolonged resistance you and your men can win the lasting honour which we are sure will be your due.[220]

Churchill's thoughts were shared by his war cabinet and the military. Gen. Alan Brooke felt that, although "resistance could probably not be continued for more than a few days and would be on a small scale," he maintained that "the psychological aspect was of overriding importance, particularly with an Oriental enemy." Thus, prolonging the resistance of Hong Kong would "gain an indirect military advantage in that the Japanese would judge our resistance in Malaya and elsewhere by the same standard."[221] He insisted that, even though it was "an unpleasant decision," the resistance should continue.

Walter Guinness, the Colonial Secretary, suggested that "the Governor should be empowered to surrender in view of the suffering which would be inflicted on the civil population."[222] Brooke, however, suggested that the suffering of the civilians had been considered when it was decided that Hong Kong should be held for four months. Whitehall then replied to Mark Young with the following telegram:

> Your message 0521 has been received. It crossed a message from the Prime Minister, who is temporarily out of reach, as follows: begins To C-in-C and Governor of Hong Kong. The eyes of the world are upon you; we expect you to resist to the end. Ends. In spite of conditions which you and GOC are facing the difficulties of which are clearly understood, HMG's desire is that you should fight it out as in the Prime Minister's message.[223]

King George VI, Henry Margesson, Alan Brooke and Lord Moyne also sent telegrams to encourage the garrison to continue the resistance. The Admiralty asked the War Office to remind Maltby to destroy all oil installations and stores before it was too late.[224] On 22 December, the British coastal guns destroyed the Texaco Oil Depot and the oil installations of the Royal Naval Dockyard. However, the Standard Oil Depot at Lai Chi Kok was not shelled, as it was deemed too close to the Lai Chi Kok Hospital.[225]

"Fight It Out"

By 22 December, the 23rd Army HQ became increasingly anxious about the progress in Hong Kong. The Vice Chief of Staff of the army was sent to the 38th Division HQ to "advise" on the operation. This was seen as a humiliation and exerted much additional pressure on the front-line officers.[226] To subdue the defenders quickly, the Japanese reorganized their artillery and set up observation posts on Jardine's Lookout and Mount Nicholson.

On the morning of 22 December, Maltby was told by Adm. Chan Chak that the Chinese reinforcements had fought against the Japanese forces near Shenzhen and Nantou. However, Chan Chak admitted in his diary that he had faked the news to Maltby, as Yu Hanmou had not contacted him since 20 December:

> Though we look forward to the counterattack, we received no news about this so far. I have to ask my staff Cai Zhongjiang and Chen Jianru to fake a few reports . . . Everyone (the British) was delighted about the news . . .[227]

As fighting subsided on the evening of 21 December, Wallis concentrated his troops on the Stanley Peninsula. Although the East Brigade was cut off and had no running water, it occupied a narrow and defensible front and could still utilize the water storage of the Stanley Battery. Most of the artillery and mortar ammunition of the brigade, however, were expended. An in-depth defence position was prepared along the peninsula as follows:[228]

Forward Area	Commander: Lt. Col. Home (HQ: Stone Hill) Position: along Palm Villa, Stone Hill, Stanley Mound and Stanley Gap Road Royal Rifles (minus A Coy and those in the Repulse Bay Hotel); 2nd Coy/HKVDC; One MG section of Middlesex at Palm Villa; One 2-pounder gun at Palm Villa
Supporting Area	Commander: Lt. Col. Wilcox (HQ: Stanley Prison) Position: along PBs 23, 24, 26, 27, 28, and St. Stephen's College B and D/Middlesex; 1st Coy/HKVDC; Prison Wardens Platoon HKVDC; Two 18-pounder guns for beach defence; One 2-pounder gun near Stanley Police Station; Two MG sections of Middlesex at Stanley Village Road
Reserve Area	Commander: Lt. Col. S. Shaw of 8th Coast Regiment 9.2-inch gun at Stanley Battery; 6-inch gun at Bluff Head Battery; Two 18-pounder guns; Two 3.7-inch howitzers
Brigade HQ	Stanley Prison

On 22 December, the Japanese made steady progress. The Canadian pockets in Wong Nai Chung Gap were finally overrun, although some survivors from the HQ of D/Winnipeg were able to sneak back to the British line.[229] The I, III/229 and I/230 had moved southward and approached the Stanley Peninsula from the northwest and northeast, despite the resistance of the Royal Rifles. Home urged a withdrawal from Stanley Mound but was refused by Wallis. The British forces had withdrawn from the Repulse Bay Hotel and the civilians inside surrendered. The Japanese spared the civilians, but massacred the Canadian troops captured near Eucliff. In the north, the Japanese approached Mount Cameron, Little Hong Kong and Wan Chai Gap with artillery and air support, but they met fierce resistance from the Winnipeg Grenadiers all day.[230]

At 18:00, Maltby reported that his troops were divided and exhausted, but they intended to resist:

> The enemy has been able to land fresh troops, on north-east coast of Island and has been attacking continuously all last night and today with land forces, mortars, gunfire and dive-bombing.
>
> Yesterday counter attack from Stanley toward Ty Tam Tuk [*sic*] failed

although certain number of enemy killed at cost of about 100 Canadian casualties. Counter attack by Company of Winnipeg Grenadiers to retake Wong Nei Cheong Gap [*sic*] also failed in face of enemy concentrated mortar and light machine gun fire.

Our troops are very tired and have suffered heavy casualties including Canadian Brigadier Lawson believed killed Canadian Colonel Hennessy killed by shell fire and Colonel Kidd Indian Army missing believed killed.

Island now split in 3 parts. Isolated British Force in Stanley, Japanese on eastern half of Gap just west of Repulse Bay W/T Station still infiltrating and ourselves still in possession of Wireless apparatus though very weakly held adjacent to tip.

Small pockets of British remnants still holding out in isolated positions. Water and transport situation critical. Still unable to replenish ammunition supply as required. Hong Kong surrounded though still holding out. Much material damage by dive bombing, mortar and shell fire. Have successfully destroyed oil installations at Texaco Asiatic Petroleum Co. Ma Tau Kok but cannot repetition cannot destroy at Lai Chi Kok on account for proximity of large civil hospital.[231]

In the evening, the Japanese reorganized I/229 and I/230 into a "Stanley Force." At midnight, the 228 Rgt. finally captured Mount Cameron, forcing Maltby and Rose to deploy the reserves (the 4th Coy/HKVDC and the Royal Marines Detachment) at Mount Gough, Magazine Gap and Wan Chai Gap. By then, the West Brigade was fully committed, except for C/Punjab, which was defending the northwestern coast.[232] Throughout the night, British patrols and the guns at Stanley harassed the 228 Rgt.[233] Meanwhile, the Public Works Department (PWD) informed Maltby that, because the Tai Tam pumping station had ceased operating, the garrison and civilians had to rely on the "trickle of water" from the Pok Fu Lam Reservoir. The PWD concluded that "the town was now helpless."[234]

The Japanese exerted more pressure on the northern front the next day. The Japanese forces near Causeway Bay broke the depleted Rajputs and gradually approached Leighton Hill and Bennet's Hill. The defenders of the former were attacked from the east and north, and by 11:30 were gradually pushed to Gilman's Garage, at the junction of Hennessy Road and Johnston Road. An hour later, the front was on the line running from PB 55 to Percival Street and Leighton Hill, which was still holding out. At 11:40, II/230 reached the high ground east of St. Albert's Convent.[235] Naval parties from Aberdeen were sent to reinforce the defenders of Bennet's Hill, but the situation remained critical. Little Hong Kong, the only major magazine remaining in British hands, was surrounded by the Japanese.[236]

On the Stanley front, the Japanese also advanced steadily. On the morning of 23 December, Wallis counterattacked again with B/RR and eight Vickers heavy machine-guns of the B/Middlesex against I/230 at Stanley Mound, but was repulsed. After that, II/229 turned west from its position south of Wong Nai Chung Gap and moved towards Aberdeen, Brick Hill and Bennet's Hill. III/229 pushed southeastward towards Chung Hom Kok along Repulse Bay Road, pushing back the British along the way and reaching Headland Road at 15:30, despite harassing fire from the Bluff Head Battery. At night, Wallis contemplated a raid against the Japanese at Tai Tam Tuk with volunteers from Middlesex and the RNVR, armed with sub-machine guns and grenades, but the plan was jettisoned as only a single motor torpedo boat was available to help with the operation.[237]

In Stanley, Home again requested to speak with Maltby. According to Wallis, Home claimed that the Royal Rifles was no longer fit to fight and that further resistance was futile. Wallis and Lt. Col. Wilcox disagreed, arguing that the peninsula was defensible and they were "anyhow paid as soldiers to fight" and were "relieving pressure of the rest of the Island garrison" by tying down some of the enemy forces.[238] The next morning, Wallis spoke to Maltby; the former was urged to keep the RR fighting. Home was persuaded to take a rest. However, the tension within the British command would soon rise again.

On 24 December, the Japanese planned the final push to eliminate the garrison. After taking Bennet's Hill and Leighton Hill, the troops facing the West Brigade would all push westward with the goal of taking, on Christmas Day, the high ground northwest of Wan Chai Gap,[239] Hill 281 southeast of Mount Gough,[240] Mount Gough and Mount Kellet. The following day, the target would be the Peak and High West. In short, the Japanese had to overcome the mountains of the western part of the island one by one. The Stanley Force, which would attack from the 24th, was expected to occupy the peninsula in two days. To prepare for the final attack, III/228, the last fresh infantry battalion of the 38th Division, was sent to the island.

On the afternoon of 24 December, II and III/230 took Leighton Hill and concentrated near Wan Chai Gap, Magazine Gap and Mount Gough. The Z/Middlesex at Leighton Hill, after days of intense land and air attack and having been reduced to around forty officers and men, were finally ordered to withdraw behind Morrison Hill.[241] Earlier, the Royal Marines and the remnants of the Rajputs had dug in on Mount Parrish[242] and established a new line between Stubbs Road and Wan Chai.[243] After the fall of Leighton Hill, the left sector of the West Brigade had to fall back further to Percival Street, Leighton Road and Canal Road. Still, the resistance of the West Brigade continued as a daring convoy of Middlesex and 2RS soldiers extracted ammunition from beleaguered Little Hong Kong under intense Japanese fire in the late afternoon.[244]

The perimeter of the East Brigade continued to shrink under heavy pressure from the Stanley Force. On the morning of 24 December, Wallis reported to Maltby that a number of officers in the Royal Rifles had become increasingly pessimistic about the prospects of the garrison.[245] Maltby urged Wallis to hold on, and to remove the commander of the RR: "You will not chuck it unless you run out of ammunition, water or food. Do not talk of surrender. Put Col. Home [*sic*] into hospital."[246] Meanwhile, I/229 advanced along Tai Tam Road and pushed D/Middlesex to the neck of the peninsula. On the western side, III/229 captured the junction of Repulse Bay Road, Headland Road, Stanley Gap Road and Chung Hom Kok Road. By sunset, the Japanese had captured the high ground overlooking the peninsula and were able to lay an accurate barrage on the defenders at night. The Royal Rifles, except B/RR at Chung Hom Kok, which had not received the order of withdrawal, went to Stanley Fort and were relieved by 1st and 2nd Coy/HKVDC. At night, Wallis divided his position into three lines. The first was defended by 2nd Coy/HKVDC under Maj. H. R. Forsyth, with three 2-pdr guns. The second line went across St. Stephen's College. The last line was mainly defended by the gunners mentioned above.[247]

On Christmas Eve, Mark Young and Maltby sent their greetings to the garrison:

> From H.E. to Troops:
> In pride and admiration I send my greetings this Xmas Day to all who are fighting and to all who are working so nobly and so well to sustain Hong Kong against the assault of the enemy.
> Fight on. Hold fast for King and Empire. God Bless you all in this your finest hour.

> From Fortress H.Q. to Tps:
> Xmas Greetings to you all. Let this day be historical in the proud annals of our Empire. The order of the day is Hold Fast.[248]

To the men at the front, the evening of the 24th was the beginning of the end. The 230 Rgt. attacked Morrison Hill and broke into the tunnels beneath Mount Parrish that connected Stubbs Road and Kennedy Road. As such, the Rajputs' position was bypassed and the left and centre of the West Brigade separated. The Japanese entered the City of Victoria and directly threatened the Fortress HQ. In the southern sector, the Japanese also took Bennet's Hill and the Brick Hill AA Battery, driving the RAF personnel and Winnipeg Grenadiers back to Aberdeen.

It was at Stanley that the fighting was the fiercest. The I/230 attacked from Stanley Mound towards Stanley Village, but was pinned down by the Prison Wardens Platoon and D/Middlesex, defending Maryknoll until dawn. When they were finally surrounded, some of the Middlesex soldiers swam across Stanley Bay to join the B/RR at Chung Hom Kok, while others boarded a launch to rejoin the West Brigade to continue the fight.[249] The I/229 attacked along present-day Stanley Beach Road with tanks. Forsyth and the HKVDC held their fire until the Japanese closed in, destroying all three Japanese tanks.[250] However, the 2nd Coy of I/229, which was almost annihilated by the Canadians on Bridge Hill, outflanked the British through the Main Beach. It was briefly suppressed by the fire of PB 27, but succeeded in disrupting the British position. While leading a charge against this threat, Forsyth was mortally wounded. His last command was "Never mind about me, fight on, muster all the Thompson guns and grenades you can get and get in behind them."[251] After his death, the British position collapsed and the survivors fled to St. Stephen's College. Forsyth was recommended to be awarded the Victoria Cross due to his actions.[252] At 01:00, Wallis reported that "the enemy had succeeded in getting behind several of the Forward Defended Localities and some of the HKVDC were now being mopped up at the Stanley Police Station." Maltby simply replied: "Hold on to the last."[253]

After penetrating the right wing of the first line, I/229 assaulted the second line behind the main building of St. Stephen's College, which was used as a field hospital. The 2nd and 3rd companies of I/229 broke the right half of the line with flame-throwers and grenades. The first two lines of the left sector, attacked by I/230, held out until 08:30 on 25 December. During the fierce struggle for Stanley Village, most of the officers of B and D/Middlesex became casualties.[254] At 04:00 on 25 December, the 2nd Coy of I/229 massacred the wounded soldiers and nurses in St. Stephen's College. In all, at least a hundred unarmed men and women were killed.[255] At noon, D/RR launched a final counterattack against St. Stephen's College across the Stanley Cemetery. The Canadians drove the Japanese out of their positions through fierce hand-to-hand fighting but they were eventually outnumbered and driven back. During this thirty-minute action, there were twenty-six killed and seventy-five wounded. After that, the East Brigade was unable to launch any counterattacks.

British Surrender

On Christmas Eve, the Japanese shelled Victoria City all night and tried to persuade the British to give up. A ceasefire was arranged between 10:00 and 12:00, but the Japanese air force and some troops were unaware of the truce and continued to attack.[256] Mark Young decided to hold on after an emergency meeting. The Fortress HQ then set up roadblocks and laid mines on Kenney Road to prevent further penetration. When the Japanese renewed attack, they soon captured the naval hospital beside the Wan Chai Market, held by the Middlesex through the air-raid tunnels beneath Mount Parrish. The last reserves from the Punjab were sent to Wan Chai but they were also beaten back. New positions were set up at O'Brien Road and Murray Barrack.[257] The 2RS was also pushed back to Magazine Gap by the 228 Rgt.[258] At 14:30, the chief signal officer reported that communication between the Fortress HQ and the rest of the garrison would soon be cut. Soon afterwards, the Japanese took Wan Chai Gap and were about to capture Magazine Gap as well.[259]

Lt. Col. Stewart of the Middlesex reported at 14:50 that the line of O'Brien Road had been suppressed by crossfire from Kowloon and the Japanese forces in front of them. His position would be untenable in thirty minutes. Stewart suggested forming a new line in front of the Naval Dockyard, but this would leave the Fortress HQ unprotected. C/Middlesex, which had been surrounded in Shouson Hill for days, finally surrendered to the Japanese at 15:00. Thus, the last magazine was now in Japanese hands. By then, the West Brigade had only six howitzers and sixty rounds for each gun.[260]

At 15:15, Maltby reported to Sir Mark Young that the Japanese were now breaking up the West Brigade and entering the city. Maltby estimated that the Japanese would reach Victoria Gap no later than 18:00. By then, it would be too late to surrender, as communications would be paralysed.[261] Mark Young conferred with Colonial Secretary F. C. Gimson, Attorney General Greville Alabaster and Cdre. Collinson. All agreed to surrender. Mark Young then sent his last telegram to the Colonial Office:

> Military and naval commanders have now advised me that no further effective resistance can be made. I am taking action in accordance with that advice. Ends.[262]

The Japanese demanded an immediate ceasefire, and took Maltby and Mark Young to the Peninsula Hotel at dusk. However, this only marked the surrender of the West Brigade. Before he was taken, Maltby sent Lt. Col. R. G. Lamb, commander of the Royal Engineers, to tell Wallis the news. Wallis referred to Maltby's previous order and suspected Lamb of bringing a fake message. It was not until 01:30 that he was convinced, after receiving a message signed by Lt. Col. Stewart and carried by his aide-de-camp.[263] An hour later, the British forces at Stanley surrendered (Figure 32).

The British resistance was unexpectedly stubborn. The Japanese had planned to take the island in one day, but the battle lasted for a week. The timing of the British surrender also surprised the Japanese. When Mark Young refused to surrender at noon, the Japanese became anxious about the coming battle. The regimental history of the 228th and 229th regiments noted that, when the Japanese troops saw white flags being hoisted in the British positions, they were relieved to be spared another round of difficult fighting.[264]

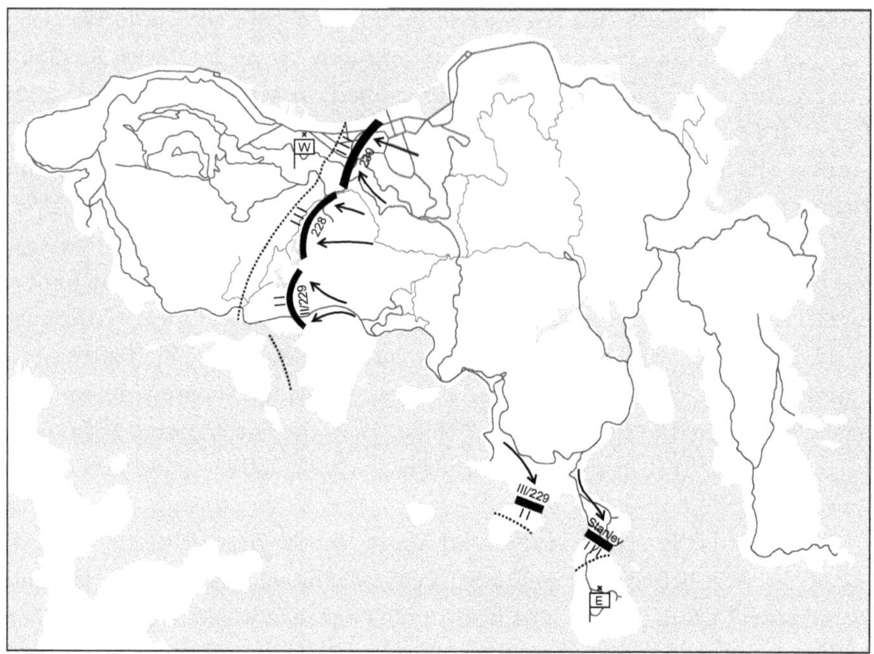

Figure 32   Final position, 15:00, 25 December 1941

The Breakout of Admiral Chan Chak

When the Japanese attacked Hong Kong, some KMT figures such as the Soong sisters escaped on a night flight from Kai Tak.[265] On 15 December, Sir Clark Kerr, the Ambassador to China, mentioned a Chinese committee to "explore ways and means of escape."[266] The "Chinese committee" was possibly the Temporary Joint Liaison Office of the All Chinese Organization (中國各機關駐港臨時聯合辦事處), set up earlier by Adm. Chan Chak.

In addition to getting the important Chinese figures out of the colony, Chan Chak also assisted Hong Kong's resistance. He conferred with Maltby and the civilian staff from the colonial government every morning from 9 December, keeping them informed about the Chinese reinforcement (although some of his information was inaccurate).[267] Chan also discussed with Robert Kotewall matters of refugee and food, and asked the Chinese banks in Hong Kong to support the war effort. At least 900,000 *fabi* was provided by Chan and his subordinates such as Henry Hsu through their network. Another HK$30,000 was borrowed from the Hongkong and Shanghai Bank to run the Joint Liaison Office.[268]

On the night of 11 December, Chan Chak's subordinate helped the Hong Kong government to crack down on the fifth columnist conspiracy on the island. The next day, Chan Chak established the ABCD Chinese Corps Hong Kong (香港中國抗戰協助團), with a nominal strength of 15,000 men. This group was formed by stranded triad members loyal to the Chongqing regime and led by Situ Meitang of the Hong Society and Zhang Zilian. They were to suppress any pro-Japanese triads and fifth columnists in Victoria City. Chan himself fought briefly against a group of fifth columnists near the Peak and helped destroy, with Henry Hsu and his aide-de-camp Yeung Chuen, a Japanese launch broadcasting a message urging surrender.[269] He also contacted the Communist East River Column to solicit support for the operation extracting Chinese dignitaries from the colony.[270]

When the Japanese landed, Chan Chak asked the British to arm 1,000 experienced men from his corps to join the fight. Maltby was apparently too occupied to respond; it was not until 22 December that he authorized Chan to form a "dare-to-die" squad armed with pistols and grenades.[271] According to police records, attempts to retrieve ammunition were repeatedly stopped by the Japanese up to the morning of 25 December, by which time it was too late to make any difference.[272, 273]

The idea of getting out of Hong Kong was first proposed by Kendall of Z Force, who was inspired by the motor torpedo boat attack on 19 December. Two days later, Lt. Comm. G. H. Gandy was ordered to leave with Z Force, Chan Chak and his staff on an MTB when the worst came.[274] After having settled his family and ordered the Joint Liaison Office to work underground, Chan handed his will to his brother and tried to break out.[275] At about the same time, S. K. Yee told David MacDougall (head of the Ministry of Information in Hong Kong) about the escape plan and invited MacDougall to join.[276] A number of officers were also ordered by Maltby to leave.[277]

At about 15:20, the Fortress HQ signalled the 2nd MTB Flotilla to "GO AT ONCE."[278] The rendezvous of the escape party with the MTB proved extremely difficult. Collinson ordered Gandy to leave as soon as possible, but Chan and his party had not arrived until late afternoon and did not board until the evening.[279] During the search for the MTBs, the party was constantly under fire and Chan was wounded.[280] When Chan finally came on board at around 21:00, he decided to go to the Dapeng Peninsula via Ping Chau to join Liang Rongyuan, the leader of a local guerrilla force.[281] That night, the sky was clear but the crescent moon was very dim.[282] The MTBs cruised at the speed of 22 knots around the southern shore of Hong Kong Island, but were discovered by IJN *Tsuga* and torpedo boat *Kasasagi* near Tathong Channel. The Japanese switched on the searchlight and trained their guns on the MTBs. Chan ordered all MTBs to go straight at the Japanese vessels to feint a torpedo attack. According to the Japanese record, the two Japanese ships thought that the MTBs were about to launch their torpedoes and took evasive action, allowing the MTBs to escape. The MTBs sailed northward and escaped near Ninepin Group.[283]

Commander Montague, who was ordered to assist Chan, left Hong Kong on C410 through Mirs Bay after he saw the MTBs leaving Hong Kong. When Chan Chak reached Nam O, he joined Montague and scuttled all vessels.[284] On 26 December, Chan met Liang Rongyuan and moved to Xinxu. They learned that KMT troops had reached Huiyang, Dansui and Bao'an before the British surrendered. As Changsha was also under Japanese attack (as a simultaneous operation with that of Hong Kong), the KMT forces turned around and moved north. Three days after reaching Xinxu, Chan's party arrived in Huizhou and returned to the area under KMT control.[285]

The Battle of Hong Kong: A Military Assessment

The Battle of Hong Kong was a bloody battle. According to Maltby, the British forces had 3,445 men killed, wounded or missing, or 31 percent of the total strength.[286] After the war, the Royal Signals estimated the number of deaths at 1,679, with around 12,000 men and women captured. More than 900 of the around 1,000 Hong Kong Chinese serving in the British forces were listed as "missing," as most of them were ordered by their officers to take off their uniforms and go into hiding.[287] On the other side, the IJA 38th Division lost 136 officers and 2,082 troopers (killed, wounded, or missing), or 9 percent of the total strength of the division. The 230th Regiment suffered most, losing 668 officers and men. The other two regiments also lost 29 and 30 percent of their officers respectively. The number of Japanese deaths would increase substantially in the months after the battle, as many of the wounded died later.[288]

It is unlikely that Hong Kong could have been saved in December 1941. Strategically, Hong Kong was in a dire, if not hopeless, position. It was within the Japanese area of control and was surrounded. Britain was busy fighting on different fronts and had few resources to spare. As the Japanese navy controlled the South China Sea, it was impossible for the British to reinforce Hong Kong in war. The only possible source of help was the Chinese, whose army had little hope of relieving the colony quickly. Although Hong Kong was a symbol of resistance and a considerable economic asset to both China and Britain, it could hardly survive under Japanese attack.

The Japanese forces attacking Hong Kong enjoyed much operational and tactical advantage. First, their superior numbers ensured that they could afford to make more mistakes than the British. They enjoyed superior firepower and control of the air. They had more guns and infantry support weapons (especially light artillery) than the British. The Japanese soldiers had recent combat experience and were adequately equipped, and they had relatively more time to prepare for the invasion. However, Japanese planning for the campaign was inadequate at best. The negligence shown by the Japanese staff officers was amazing, given the long time the Japanese had had to plan and gather accurate intelligence. As a result of their bias towards the mainland, the Japanese planned thoroughly for the attack against the New Territories and Kowloon, without knowledge of the British disposition of troops and overall planning. It was only because of the initiative of officers on the spot, much to the outrage of the high command, that the rapid Japanese victory on the mainland was enabled. The Japanese plan for the island was crude: no plan was made to separate two British brigades or to capture the reservoirs, although they were eventually done. As the Japanese themselves admitted after the battle, the landing was a "boar-like blind rush" (*chototsu-mōshin*), without adequate intelligence about the British or cooperation with the Japanese artillery.[289] This led to the unexpectedly heavy casualties suffered by the three regiments, especially in Wong Nai Chung Gap and Stanley. With artillery, naval and air support, the Japanese conquered the island largely because of their sheer numbers and the unexpected capture of Wong Nai Chung Gap.

On the other hand, the British faced decisive disadvantages throughout the campaign. They were inferior in number and not adequately equipped. The delay of the motor transport and Bren-gun Carriers of the C Force deprived the defenders of much-needed mobility and armour protection. The British also lacked mobile artillery pieces and had no air force whatsoever. As noted after the battle, the British field equipment was too heavy and conspicuous. However, the British utilized their resources effectively. For example, the coastal guns of Hong Kong prevented the Japanese navy from supporting the infantry, while the Royal Navy was involved in most major engagements of the campaign under cover of the coastal guns. The Royal Navy absorbed 20 percent of the Japanese air attacks against Hong Kong.[290] The coastal guns also played a similar role. The British caused some delay to the Japanese through the demolition operations in the New Territories; they withdrew to the island in good order, with minimal losses. The Canadian C Force, which was often seen as inexperienced, had inflicted heavy casualties on the Japanese forces on several occasions.

However, the British garrison made a number of crucial mistakes that possibly quickened the fall of Hong Kong. First, the fall of the Shing Mun Redoubt showed the lack of preparation by the various units and the danger of placing only three battalions along the Gin Drinker's Line during the early phase of the campaign. The garrison also failed to prevent a landing on the north shore. The battalions were, after the fall of Kowloon, still spread across the coastline of the island, as Maltby was convinced that the Japanese had the capability to land in the south. After the Japanese had landed and penetrated Wong Nai Chung Gap by chance, the garrison launched a series of uncoordinated counterattacks that not only weakened the defenders but also led to much loss of life and equipment. These failed counterattacks were important reasons why the British garrison was unable to check the Japanese advance. Contrary to the idea that the colonial government was unprepared for war, the measures such as the construction of the air raid shelters, recruitment of the Air Raid Precaution Wardens, and the expansion of police force (including the Special Constables) were largely able to maintain public order in Hong Kong until the Japanese landed on Hong Kong Island. However, this success was not without a price; the colonial authorities were forced to collaborate with the Hong Kong triads at the expense of the civilians.

9

HONG KONG UNDER THE JAPANESE OCCUPATION, 1942–1945

[After] I had left a report of a Japanese convoy leaving Hong Kong for the South reached Waichow with sufficient detail to be able to be telegraphed to Kweilin and passed on to the Americans, who flashed it to their submarines. They were able to intercept the convoy which was severely mauled . . . [1]

—Douglas Clague, an officer of the British Army Aid Group (BAAG)

Japanese Defence of Hong Kong and Allied Counterattacks

From January 1942 to early 1945, the Japanese used Hong Kong as a naval and logistics base in the Western Pacific. By nature, the strategic role of Hong Kong as the staging area for operations in the region had not changed, although the Japanese were advancing southwards instead of northwards like the British a century previously. During this period, Hong Kong was deep in the Japanese zone of control, despite the fact that the adjacent area of Guangdong was partly controlled by the Chinese Nationalists and Communists.

The Japanese only deployed a token garrison at Hong Kong. In February 1942, the Government of the Hong Kong Occupied Territory was formed, headed by Lieutenant General Isogai Rensuke (磯谷廉介). The Hong Kong Defence Force (香港防衛隊, HKDF) and Hong Kong Artillery Force (香港砲兵隊) were formed under the new administration. The 23rd Army defended the area north of Shenzhen River. The 2nd China Fleet, which played only a negligible role during the invasion, soon moved its headquarters to Hong Kong after the battle.

In January 1942, the IJA 38th Division had left Hong Kong for the Dutch East Indies. The HKDF had merely three battalions, supported by a number of batteries.[2] The battalions were deployed at Hong Kong Island, Kowloon and the New Territories. The latter two battalions were active only in the urban area, the Kowloon-Canton Railway area, and the posts at Lok Ma Chau, Shenzhen, Deep Bay and Frontier Road.[3] As the garrison was deemed too weak, 250 replacement troops from the 23rd Army stayed in Hong Kong.[4] The so-called Hong Kong Artillery Force was a glorified ad hoc battery consisting of 150 men and a number of captured British field pieces.[5]

Table 27　Order of battle of the 2nd China Fleet, January 1942[6]

Units	Name
Main body	IJN *Isuzu* (light cruiser)
11th Torpedo Boat Flotilla	Torpedo boat x 5
Flying Corps	Torpedo bomber x 3
Xiamen Base Force	*Kasashima* and two more patrol boats
	Small gunboat x 4
	32 smaller patrol and port service crafts
Hong Kong Base Force	IJN *Hashidate* (gunboat)
	IJN *Saga* (gunboat)
	IJN *Uji* (gunboat)
	Minesweeper x 2
	62 smaller patrol and port service crafts

The Japanese naval presence was even smaller than that of the Royal Navy in 1941. In early 1942, the larger ships of the 2nd China Expeditionary Fleet (2CF) such as the light cruiser IJN *Isuzu* and the torpedo flotilla were withdrawn (Table 27). Only three ocean-going gunboats and a number of patrol crafts were left to perform duties such as minesweeping, patrols of the outer islands and suppression of pirates and guerrillas. The 2CF was also responsible for the protection of shipping near Hong Kong, anti-submarine patrol and anti-air defence. It was clearly ill-equipped for these tasks.

The air defence of Hong Kong hardly improved with the change of owners. Until October 1942, its air defence consisted only of eleven guns. The air defence system was divided into two separate areas, with the army responsible for Kowloon and the navy Hong Kong Island. No central warning and command existed.[7] From January 1942, the 2CF protected shipping around Hong Kong, including the troopships carrying the 38th Division. In January alone, the gunboats and planes of the 2CF escorted 121 troop and cargo vessels.[8] As Japan had yet to adopt the convoy system, a large number of lone transports travelled around Hong Kong and in the South China Sea. This posed a lot of problems for the 2CF as it had only a few aircraft and ocean-going vessels. However, as the Allied air and naval forces had yet to operate in this area, the Japanese suffered only negligible losses from residual mines laid by the British.

After the war, except for the Anglo-Chinese servicemen who were told by their commanding officer to escape, the defenders were sent to prisoner-of-war (POW) camps in different parts of Hong Kong, such as Sham Shui Po, Ma Tau Chung and North Point. Civilian internees were sent to Stanley. Their suffering has been extensively recorded by Emerson, Banham and others. A substantial number of the POWs were shipped from Hong Kong; many died in the process. More than 800 of them perished on the Japanese freighter SS *Lisbon Maru* in October when the ship, which had no markings on its hull as to its purpose as a POW transport, was sunk by a US submarine.[9]

Hong Kong was again a battlefield when the Allies counterattacked from late 1942 on. Due to increasing Allied air activities in South China, the air defence of Hong Kong was placed on alert from June. The Japanese also restored HMS *Moth* and renamed it IJN *Sumo*.[10] Two months later, a Japanese cargo ship was sunk by a US submarine near Taiwan. Consequently, the air and naval units of the 2CF patrolled constantly near Hong Kong.[11] To prevent US submarines from entering Victoria Harbour, an anti-submarine boom was installed in East Lamma Channel.[12] As the Allied submarines could not disrupt Japanese shipping in the area because of their limited numbers and faulty torpedoes, Hong Kong was used by the Japanese as the staging point of the convoys heading for their South Pacific stronghold of Rabaul in late 1942.[13]

In October 1942, the American China Air Task Force (CATF) launched the first Allied air attack against Hong Kong. However, the Japanese had forewarning and deployed twelve Nakajima fighters at Kai Tak before the attack. On 25 October, twelve B-25 bombers escorted by P-40 fighters attacked the Whampoa Shipyard at Kowloon. During the ensuing dogfight, the CATF lost one bomber and one fighter.[14] The Japanese had one cargo ship sunk and eight dockyard buildings destroyed. Over fifty residents were killed or injured.[15] Another raid of six bombers at night against the North Point Power Plant was ineffective.[16] Thereafter, the CATF and its subsequent organization the 14th U.S. Army Air Force (14th USAAF) attacked Hong Kong intermittently but usually on a small scale.

From 1943, the Allies caused real disruption against Japanese shipping near Hong Kong with their air power and submarines. Although the Japanese gradually adopted the convoy system, many cargo ships still travelled alone; the 2CF did not have enough resources to protect them.[17] The Allied naval and air forces also received much help from underground resistance units such as the British Army Aid Group (BAAG) and the East River Column. The 14th USAAF usually ambushed Japanese ships found by the resistance fighters with one or a pair of fighter-bombers. As a 2CF report to Tokyo noted, even if the Japanese cargo ships could reach open sea without interference by Allied aircraft, they were constantly attacked by American submarines.[18] With the guerrillas and the BAAG controlling the coast and passing information about Japanese activities to the Allies, the South China Sea became increasingly dangerous for the Japanese.

In April 1944, the Japanese launched the Ichigo Offensive to destroy the Sino-American airfields in South China and to link up the Japanese forces from North to South China. The Chinese forces were pushed back at Hunan and Guangdong, forcing the 14th USAAF to abandon its anti-shipping campaign in South China. However, the Ichigo Offensive was unable to reverse the tide. By July 1944, the Americans had secured the Marianas; the British had also beaten the Japanese forces in Imphal. The 14th USAAF soon resumed its air attack against Hong Kong, fielding the latest P-51 fighters from December.[19] As Choi Cho-hong has suggested, the US military had contemplated retaking Hong Kong together with Chinese forces between 1943 and early 1944 (codenamed Operation Carbonado), but American planners finally chose the Philippines over Hong Kong because the Chinese position in South China was severely weakened by the Ichigo Offensive.[20]

After Task Force 38 (TF38) of the U.S. Navy had destroyed the Japanese air forces at Taiwan and then the main body of the Japanese navy during the Battle of Leyte Gulf in October 1944, Hong Kong was exposed to Allied attack. In November 1944, the Japanese High Command estimated that the Allies would land in South China. The Hong Kong-Guangzhou area was seen as the most probable target. This understanding led to the placing of both the Government of the Hong Kong Occupied Territory and the HKDF under the command of the 23rd Army. Lieutenant General Tanaka Hisakazu, commander of the 23rd Army, became the new governor in January 1945.[21]

While the Japanese were trying to reorganize their command structure in South China, the TF38 launched Operation Gratitude, a large-scale attack against Japanese shipping and airfields in Indochina, Hainan Island, Guangzhou, Hong Kong, Taiwan and the Ryukyu Islands. Admiral William Halsey, commander of the TF38, intended to destroy the remaining Japanese warships. However, as most of them had already withdrawn to mainland Japan or Singapore, he had to content himself with the destruction of Japanese supply lines to Southeast Asia. On 13 January 1945, Admiral Chester Nimitz, Commander-in-Chief of the Pacific Fleet, signalled Halsey that he could attack Hong Kong if more valuable targets were absent. The attack was postponed due to poor weather until 16 January.[22]

On that day, Hong Kong was subject to a sizeable air attack. According to the war diary of the Japanese vessel *Shin-i* (神威), over 120 planes attacked Hong Kong for eleven hours.[23] Due to poor weather and unexpectedly heavy Japanese resistance, the US aircraft sank only a cargo ship and a tanker and damaged several other tankers and vessels. The Kai Tak airport was disabled, with all planes there destroyed. Both Kowloon and Taikoo docks were badly hit. The village of Hung Hom, which was near Kowloon Docks, was devastated; hundreds of villagers were killed or wounded.[24] The TF38 lost forty-nine planes on that day in the Pearl River Delta and Hainan; *Shin-i* claimed that the Japanese shot down ten planes over Hong Kong.[25]

The Japanese High Command saw Operation Gratitude as the prelude to a landing and poured troops into South China. The main body of the reinforcements consisted of the 129th and 130th divisions. Their ancestor was the 19th Mixed Brigade, which had operated in South China since 1944. When this unit was dispatched from Japan to China, over half of its strength (2,700) was lost on the *Lima Maru* when it was sunk by a US submarine.[26] Thus, the two divisions consisted mainly of poorly trained reservists and replacements. Three more divisions were allotted to the 23rd Army until March, when U.S. Marines landed at Iwo Jima. By then, it was clear that the Hong Kong-Guangzhou area had been bypassed.[27]

The Japanese plan for the defence of the Hong Kong-Guangzhou area was called Operation Kō-ichigo (光一號作戰). In all, the 23rd Army had three divisions at its disposal (104th, 129th and 130th). The army was ordered to resist any Allied invasion without outside help. The 129th Division was ordered to hold the line from Hong Kong to Shantou (汕頭) and to "destroy the enemy landing forces at the shoreline."[28] Although the navy argued that it was necessary to hold some of the outer islands, the army insisted on concentrating at Guangzhou and Hong Kong. The army's opinion prevailed: most of the 23rd Army was concentrated around the two cities by May 1945.[29] If the Allied forces landed, the 129th and 104th divisions would first resist near Bias Bay and Starling Inlet before fighting delaying actions in the New Territories and the Gin Drinker's Line. Like the British garrison of 1941, the Japanese garrison in 1945 planned to fight their last battle on the hills of Hong Kong Island.[30] By the end of the war, the 23rd Army had 80,485 Japanese troops near Hong Kong and Guangdong, of which around 46,000 were combat troops (Table 28).[31]

By then, the Japanese faced the same problem that the British had faced during the interwar period: how to defend Hong Kong without naval supremacy. Fortunately for the Japanese, they had some control over the hinterland, although it was constantly disrupted by KMT regulars and CCP guerrillas. The Japanese responded to the situation by putting up field defences in different parts of Hong Kong. Although the general plan of defence has yet to be found, some underground dugouts have subsequently been discovered along the Line of Passes and on Hong Kong Island. When the HKSAR Government opened the Shataukok restricted area in March 2012, a number of trench systems, finished with concrete pillboxes and temporary artillery positions, were found near Shan Tsui. These positions were close to the Starling Inlet, the only beach large enough to land a division on within the boundary of Hong Kong. They were supported by another set of positions at Luk Keng (鹿頸). The Japanese navy also dug several caves on Lamma Island for their Shin'yō (震洋) suicide motorboats.[32] These facilities were never tested, as Japan surrendered in August 1945.

Table 28   Japanese army units near Hong Kong, August 1945

23rd Army		
HQ: 832		
Art. Elements: 1,188		
Eng. Elements: 704		
Comm. Elements: 1,851		
Logistic Elements: 15,781		
Aux. Troops: 4,582		

104th Division	129th Division	130th Division
HQ: 314	HQ: 510	HQ: 329
108th Rgt.: 3,787	91st Inf. Bri.: 5,588	91st Inf. Bri.: 5,432
137th Rgt.: 3,787	92nd Inf. Bri.: 5,588	92nd Inf. Bri.: 5,432
161st Rgt.: 3,787	129th Art. Rgt.: 777	130th Art. Rgt.: 0
104th Art. Rgt.: 1417	129th Eng. Rgt.: 401	130th Eng. Rgt.: 901
104th Eng. Rgt.: 424	Aux. Troops: 1,780	Aux. Troops: 2,637
Aux. Troops: 3,349	Total: 14,644	Total: 14,731
Total: 16,865		

23rd Mixed Brigade	8th Mixed Brigade	13th Mixed Brigade
HQ: 184	HQ: 177	HQ: 177
Inf.: 7,974	Inf.: 5,708	Inf.: 5,708
Art.: 992	Art.: 0	Art.: 0
Aux.: 353	Aux.: 111	Aux.: 111
Total: 9,503	Total: 5,996	Total: 5,996

31st Ind. Mixed Rgt.	Hong Kong Defence Force	Government of the Hong Kong Occupied Territory
2,262	HQ: 80	HQ: 94
	67th Bn.: 809	Dock Staff: 1,508
	68th Bn.: 809	Aux. Troops: 877
	69th Bn.: 809	Total: 2,479
	HK Art. Force: 627	
	Aux. Troops: 293	
	Total: 3,427	

The British Army Aid Group and the East River Column

After the fall of Hong Kong, both the Chinese and the British continued the war in Hong Kong until 1945. The most important of the underground resistance organizations were the British Army Aid Group (BAAG) [33] and the East River Column. The BAAG was established by Lieutenant Colonel Lindsay Ride, a professor at the University of Hong Kong and a medical officer of the HKVDC. He was the senior medical officer among the British POWs at Sham Shui Po Camp, which housed over 6,000 British and Canadian POWs. As the Japanese refused to provide adequate supplies to maintain the camp, Ride soon escaped from it with two British officers and a Chinese orderly through Lai Chi Kok, Piper's Hill and Siu Lek Yuen, before being rescued by the East River Column near Sai Kung. He was escorted to Guilin via Huizhou and Qujiang (曲江).

After reaching Guilin, Ride proposed forming an underground resistance group to help POWs in Hong Kong through escapees who knew the ground. His idea was endorsed by General Archibald Wavell (Commander-in-Chief of Southeast Asia) and General Lancelot Dennys (head of the British military mission to China). When Ride and Horace Seymore (Ambassador to China) promised that the BAAG would not engage in political activities with Chiang Kai-shek, the unit was established in Guilin in July 1942. Early members of the BAAG included Ronald Holmes, a Hong Kong government cadet and member of the Special Operations Executive (SOE), Douglas Clague, a Royal Artillery officer who had also escaped from the POW camp, and Chinese operatives such as Paul Tsui (later the first Chinese Administrative Officer) and Chan Kwok-wing.

The main role of the BAAG was to communicate with POWs in Hong Kong. The means of communication included leaving messages at the workplace of the POWs (such as the Kai Tak base) and smuggling messages into the camps via Chinese drivers. By January 1943, the BAAG had established contact with senior POWs such as Colonel Newham, Captain Douglas Ford of the 2nd Battalion of The Royal Scots (2RS) and Lieutenant Hector Gray of the RAF. However, while hatching a mass escape plan, they were apprehended in May 1943 and later charged with espionage and executed.[34] Also killed was Captain Mateen Ansari of the Rajput, who refused to turn himself in to the Japanese and tried to escape from the Indian POW Camp.[35] In general, the Indian POWs were unwilling to collaborate with the Japanese. Both the Indian National Army and the India Independence League failed to attract much support.[36] As Chan Sui-jeung has pointed out, the POWs were less willing to cooperate with the BAAG after this failure.[37] The BAAG also tried to rescue prominent civilians such as the Chief Manager of the Hongkong and Shanghai Bank, Sir Vandeleur Grayburn. However, Sir Vandeleur Grayburn was tortured to death by the Japanese in August 1943.

In addition to rescuing POWs and internees, the BAAG provided intelligence and weather reports to the Allied forces operating in South China. The BAAG also helped the Hong Kong residents who were driven into the mainland by the Japanese and smuggled skilled dockyard workers out of the city. This, according to Chan Sui-jeung, partly explains the inefficiency of the Hong Kong dockyards during the war. The BAAG also rescued hundreds of Chinese and Eurasian soldiers of the HKVDC and various branches of the British military, 128 of whom later formed the Hong

Kong Volunteer Company to fight in Burma with the Chindits, under the command of Brigadier Michael Calvert, who came to Hong Kong to recruit the Chinese Royal Engineers in 1936. Together with the East River Column, the BAAG penetrated into Kowloon and the New Territories to gather military intelligence. When news of the Japanese surrender had reached London, the BAAG agents Roger Lobo and Leung Yun Cheung relayed London's order to restore a British administration to Franklin Gimson, the interned Colonial Secretary. Members of the BAAG such as Ronald "Ronnie" Holmes (who briefly served as the Acting Colonial Secretary during the 1967 riot) and Paul Tsui worked in the transitional administrations and also the restored colonial government after the unit was disbanded in 1949.

Another major resistance group was the East River Column, a product of the cooperation between the KMT and the CCP after the Marco Polo Bridge Incident of July 1937. In August 1937, Zhou Enlai (周恩來) was appointed by the CCP to lead its activities in South China. By the end of the year, he had held secret discussions with the British about organizing branch offices of the Eighth Route Army and the New Fourth Army in Hong Kong. In April 1938, the CCP decided to establish a guerrilla unit in Guangdong as a means of expanding its influence in South China, particularly in the rural area. After the fall of Guangzhou in October 1938, CCP member Zeng Sheng established a guerrilla group at Bao'an. In 1940, the KMT tried to suppress the CCP guerrillas around the East Pearl River, reducing their strength to around a hundred men. The survivors were then reorganized as the 3rd and 5th brigades (*dadui* 大隊) of the Guangdong Anti-Japanese Guerrilla Force (廣東人民抗日游擊總隊), commanded by Zeng Sheng and Wang Zuoyao (王作堯), with Lin Ping (林平) as political commissar. The CCP guerrillas at the East Pearl River area consisted of around 1,500 men in late 1941.[38]

The CCP guerrilla unit infiltrated into Sai Kung, Shataukok and Yuen Long during the Japanese invasion of Hong Kong. In January 1942, these forces were reorganized as the Hong Kong-Kowloon Brigade (港九大隊), with Cai Guoliang as the leader. The guerrilla dispersed bandits in the New Territories and armed themselves with munitions abandoned by the British. They had rescued more than eight hundred pro-KMT and -CCP dignitaries and intellectuals from Hong Kong, including He Xiangning (何香凝, Liao Zhongkai's wife), Mao Dun (茅盾, writer) and Zou Taofen (鄒滔奮, journalist).[39] The guerrilla unit also helped POW camp escapees such as Lieutenant Colonel Ride to leave Hong Kong.

The Hong Kong-Kowloon Brigade was organized into logistics, intelligence, translation, medical, transportation, security, propaganda, international and political branches. The main fighting units of the brigade included the battalions (*zhongdui* 中隊) of Lantau, Shataukok, Sai Kung, Yuen Long and a naval battalion. In late 1943, a new urban battalion was formed to operate in Kowloon. When the East River Column was formally established in December 1943, the Hong Kong-Kowloon Brigade was incorporated as an independent unit. The unit was then placed under the control of the Second Division (第二支隊) of the East River Column in late 1944. Two major sources of money and supplies for the guerrilla unit were contributions by Chinese residents and the "custom duties" (or water-legs 水腳) from smugglers.

Throughout the war, the East River Column cooperated with the BAAG, although both were suspicious of each other at the beginning. The two organizations cooperated in gathering intelligence, guiding USAAF attacks and communicating with POWs. According to Chinese oral sources, the East River Column was even able to plant spies within the Japanese civilian and military administrations.[40] The column also rescued over a hundred Allied personnel with the BAAG, including POW camp escapees and thirty-eight USAAF and USN pilots whose planes were shot down near Hong Kong.[41] From October 1943, the USAAF sent a radio to work with the BAAG and the East River Column.[42] From Japanese sources, it appears the guerrilla unit tried to disrupt Japanese shipping near Hong Kong, damage facilities, distribute anti-Japanese propaganda and kill Japanese soldiers and collaborators (Table 29).

The Japanese occupation force could not effectively check the guerrilla menace. The HKDF seldom approached Sai Kung, the stronghold of the guerrillas, although it raided and destroyed the guerrilla base in Nam Chung of Shataukok in March 1943. The underground resistance forced the Japanese to be on constant alert and to limit their area of control to the urban area and the Kowloon-Canton Railway. The reason for the Japanese failure to suppress guerrilla activity was the inability of their different branches to cooperate. For example, it was not until November 1943 that the HKDF and the 23rd Army organized a joint expedition against the guerrilla forces. Even then, the expedition was conducted only along the Kowloon-Canton Railway. Between December 1943 and December 1944, the Japanese had captured only twelve rifles and two pistols during their anti-guerrilla operations.[43]

After the war, when the Hong Kong-Kowloon Brigade left Hong Kong, ninety-six of them stayed behind at the request of the Hong Kong government to act as village guards in Yuen Long, Sai Kung, Sheung Shui and Shataukok.[44] Most of the members of the brigade followed the East River Column to mainland China and participated in the Chinese Civil War.

Table 29   Guerrilla activities as recorded by the 2nd China Fleet, 1942–1945

Date	Event
12/1942	Attacks at Liusha (六沙), Nanao (南澳) and Xiachuan Island (下川島) against Japanese patrol craft and coastal shipping, four IJA soldiers killed
13/12/1942	Raid at Xiachuan Island, supplies looted
7/6/1943	The power plant at Fanling destroyed
8/6/1943	The Kowloon-Canton Railway damaged, infiltration of agents at Kai Tak
24/6/1943	Lighthouse on Beiding Island (北捉島) bombed
28/6/1943	Military road near Shenzhen bombed
11/1943	The 23rd Army and the HKDF engaged in a punitive expedition
27/12/1943	Patrol craft missing, possibly sunk by the guerrillas
3/1944	Attack on Japanese patrol craft near Bias Bay; raid at Sanmen (三門) and Guiling (龜令) Islands
4/1944	Japanese military police killed at Kowloon; railway bridge destroyed; anti-Japanese leaflets distributed
29/5/1944	300 Japanese soldiers laid siege to the Tung Chung Village on Lantau Island for four days with no result
25/7/1944	Japanese oil tanker attacked near Cheung Chau
9/1944	Japanese cargo ship looted while mooring near Hong Kong
30/9/1944	Japanese military police and patrol crafts attacked near Sai Kung and Lantau, with Japanese personnel captured
11/1944	Japanese patrol craft attacked
12/1944	BAAG agents disguised as fishermen detected while operating in Kowloon but escaped capture

Conclusion

Throughout the Pacific War, although Hong Kong briefly served as a strategic port for the southern expansion of the Japanese Empire, the city was of little military importance. Although the Japanese intended to use Hong Kong as a political base for their subversive activities against the Nationalist government, the attempt was largely a failure. The function of Hong Kong as a military port also steadily declined due to the inability of the Japanese to control the China coast. When the Japanese were on the defensive from 1944, Hong Kong was exposed to large-scale Allied attack. As it was no longer a vital asset in the war against Japan because of Allied successes elsewhere, it was largely left alone until the end of the war. This spared Hong Kong from destructive urban fighting such as that experienced in other major cities of the world including Berlin, Shanghai, Nanjing and Manila.

10

THE DEFENCE OF HONG KONG DURING THE EARLY STAGES OF THE COLD WAR, 1945–1960

Hong Kong would not be defended in war against a major power in occupation of the Chinese mainland.

—Cabinet decision on the defence of Hong Kong in 1946

The real defence of Hong Kong lies not in the strength of the garrison, which, even at its present level, could not repel an outright attack, but in the realisation by the Chinese that such an attack would precipitate a full-scale war.

—Cabinet Defence Committee on the defence of Hong Kong, 1955

The Cold War and British Strategic Contraction

It has been estimated that Britain lost one-fourth of its wealth during the Second World War.[1] A considerable part of the Eastern Empire, including Hong Kong, Singapore, Malaya, Burma and Brunei, had been occupied. As Britain was unable to offer much protection, Australia and New Zealand turned to the United States during the war. The British Raj finally became India and Pakistan in 1947. The British government was burdened with huge debt; the British economy was damaged by the loss of capital, investment and a large part of the merchant marine. Britain thus adopted a policy of strategic contraction after 1945. Military deployment around the world was replaced by a policy that centred on Europe and the Middle East and the development of nuclear deterrence. Although Britain maintained a sizeable military force in Asia up to 1958, its political and military influence in the area gradually declined. This change was reflected in the downgrading of the China Station into the Far Eastern Squadron. Although the squadron retained a number of capital ships during the 1940s and 1950s, it shrank in size during subsequent decades.

After the Second World War, defence planners for Hong Kong faced unprecedented problems, not only because of the changes illustrated above. Traditional opponents such as France, Russia and Japan were no longer threats. When the Nationalist government in China was replaced by the People's Republic of China (PRC) in 1949, the colony was seen as being less secure. During the period covered by this chapter, although the British maintained naval and air superiority in Hong Kong with the aid of the United States, they found it increasingly difficult to secure the land frontier. Thus, as the British were less able to deploy a large garrison in Hong Kong from the 1950s, they devised new ways of securing the colony, including maintaining Anglo-Chinese relations and persuading the United States to help defend Hong Kong.

Soon after the establishment of the PRC, Hong Kong became an outpost of the Western Bloc. Hong Kong was used by both sides of the Cold War as a political, intelligence, propaganda and economic base. Although the Americans believed that Hong Kong was indefensible in a conventional war, they were gradually persuaded by the British to support the status quo. At one time, even the use of atomic weapons was considered, although there were never firm commitments. On the other hand, the PRC decided not to take Hong Kong by force, as it increasingly saw the city as an important economic asset. Still, Hong Kong was seen as a potential flashpoint by all sides.

The tremendous change in military technology that occurred during the Second World War also affected the defence of Hong Kong. Conventional weapon systems such as warships, aircraft and armoured fighting vehicles became dramatically stronger, while electronic equipment such as radar became widely used. Above all, the emergence of atomic weapons challenged existing ideas of how wars between powers should be fought; it allowed the British to employ nuclear deterrence as a means of protecting themselves.

Post-war Hong Kong experienced rapid socio-economic change. The pressure caused by population increase and economic transformation, as well as internal and external political situations, led to large-scale social disruption during the 1950s and 1960s. The most serious incidents were the riots of 1956 and 1967, which had lasting impacts on the identity of Hong Kong and its subsequent development. While it is interesting to look at the role of the Hong Kong garrison during these events, it is perhaps more important to look at the impact (or lack thereof) of these events on British defence policies for Hong Kong.

This chapter focuses on the British defence policy for Hong Kong between the end of the Second World War and the early 1970s. It first discusses the British policy of deterrence in 1949, before turning to Anglo-American cooperation over the defence of the colony in the 1950s. It then looks at the changing defence policy and the role of the garrison during the riots of 1956 and 1967.

Continuing the Policy of Deterrence, 1946–1950

Immediately after Japan surrendered on 15 August 1945, the Colonial Secretary, Franklin Gimson, left the internment camp and formed a provisional administration. Two weeks later, Rear Admiral Cecil Harcourt arrived in Hong Kong with the British Pacific Fleet (BPF), to support British rule.[2] Although the Chinese Nationalists also sent troops to Hong Kong with the intention of occupying the territory, they abandoned their claim as they did not want to antagonize Britain and the United States while facing the possibility of a civil war with the Chinese Communists. A military administration replaced the provisional government until the return of Sir Mark Young in 1946. The British returned to Hong Kong over the protests of the Nationalists, largely because of their ability to deploy a sizeable naval force to East Asia for the first time since the 1930s. Although smaller in size than the U.S. Pacific Fleet, the BPF was substantially stronger than the previous China Stations and incomparably better than the meagre Chinese navy, which had to make do with captured Japanese naval vessels and donations from Britain and the United States.

However, the British could not maintain such a large fleet for long, due to the state of its post-war economy and the shift in its strategic focus. The cabinet decided in March 1946 that "Hong Kong would not be defended in war against a major power in occupation of the Chinese mainland."[3] The garrison, which had only three battalions, was responsible for internal security. In a statement presented by the Minister of Defence to parliament in February 1947, the British government would only "maintain forces in the Far East to provide garrisons for British Colonies, including Hong Kong and Malaya, and to assist in maintaining security."[4] Hidden in this vague statement was the intention not to hold Hong Kong in wartime.

Since 1947, the situation in China had changed drastically. The KMT had suffered a series of major defeats against the CCP; its rule on the mainland was crumbling. The replacement of the Nationalist regime with a Communist one added much uncertainty to the security situation of Hong Kong. The cabinet suggested in December 1948 that the garrison was "living near the edge of a volcano."[5] The situation in Central and South China grew steadily worse in 1949, when the People's Liberation Army (PLA) crossed the Yangtze River in March. The Commander-in-Chief of the Far East, General John Harding, Governor Sir Mark Young and the Chiefs of Staff Committee (COS) gathered in London to discuss the problem of Hong Kong. It was estimated that, although the PLA would not attack Hong Kong on a large scale, the colony faced three types of threats from the mainland, including:

- Internal unrest inspired by the Communist-dominated trade unions
- Large-scale influx of refugees by land and/or by sea
- External aggression by guerrilla bands[6]

Harding believed that a garrison of two brigades (six battalions) was required. However, as Malaya (where Communist insurgents threatened to penetrate the jungle) had diverted some British resources, reinforcement to Hong Kong could only be sent from elsewhere. Thus, the COS prepared an additional brigade in Britain for any emergency in Hong Kong. To guard against the influx of refugees and labour unrest, the number of police was increased substantially.[7]

In 1949, the British saw Hong Kong primarily as a "valuable centre of trade" that could not be held "unless the new Chinese government acquiesced in our continuance there." Thus, when it was suggested that Hong Kong "might be a centre of a South China bureau which transmitted Communist directives to neighbouring countries," action against the suspected Communist activities was opposed by some ministers. They argued that such action might "preclude the possibility of our entering into friendly relations with a Communist regime."[8] The idea that a friendly relationship with the new Chinese government should be maintained in order to preserve Hong Kong and British trade in China prevailed throughout the Cold War. In addition, it was realized that "the communist threat within Hong Kong could not be met by military force but only by measures of political warfare."[9] Thus, the Hong Kong government imposed "certain restrictions" on "overt political activities," and concentrated on an "endeavour to raise the standard of life in Hong Kong by social and economic measures so that it would be apparent that life under British rule was preferable to life in neighbouring areas dominated by communism."[10]

The problem of Hong Kong was reviewed in April 1949, when HMS *Amethyst*, a sloop stranded in the Yangtze River, exchanged fire with the PLA. The COS argued that, while "any strong Chinese Central Government is likely, in the long run, to desire to terminate the British occupation of Hong Kong," a British regime in Hong Kong "may well be considered to be useful to a new Communist Government, as an economic link with the outside world."[11] When the Hong Kong government swooped down on the Chinese Communist files at Fang Fang's (方方) home in April 1949, it was also found that the CCP had no plan of attacking Hong Kong.[12] Still, as Hong Kong might "become the stage for a trial of strength between Communism and the Western Powers like Berlin," the COS argued that the colony should be held, "even if Communist China declares war on Great Britain," unless the Russians intervened.[13] Unlike the mood in 1941, it was now realized that "it would be unwise to count on the support of public opinion in the United States" in the defence of Hong Kong.[14] In this context, the British had to protect the colony alone.

In 1949, the British revived the policy of deterrence that had failed in 1941. The COS concluded that, if Britain was able to deploy a strong enough garrison, "its presence would show our determination to hold the colony and should thus deter the Communists from open hostilities."[15] The CCP, as the COS argued, had yet to become a "major power." Thus, the reinforcement policy did not violate the policy of abandoning Hong Kong in a war against the power controlling mainland China.[16] It was also pointed out that, although the PLA was much better than its predecessors in terms of training, discipline, morale and the standard of its officers, it also lacked air, naval, motor and armour support, and was less well equipped and trained than the British forces. In addition, the PLA could not be effectively deployed across the boundary of the New Territories because of the narrowness of the front and the lack of communications.[17]

In short, the COS argued that Hong Kong was defensible and should be reinforced. Although the policy was similar to the one in 1941 that had failed, this time the British deployed a sizeable force. By mid-year, the forces stationed in Hong Kong included an entire division, tank detachments, more than twenty fighters, a cruiser squadron and a number of coastal defence vessels.[18] The COS also recommended sending one aircraft carrier, a flotilla of destroyers, sixteen Hornet jet-fighters and an additional Gurkha brigade.[19]

The new plan drew the main defensive line from Deep Water Bay to Tolo Harbour, including the heights at Lam Tsuen and Snowdon. The new line, with a length of twelve kilometres, was more than ten kilometres further to the north than the Gin Drinker's Line of 1941.[20] This arrangement shows the confidence of the British in their air and naval superiority. Narrowness was not the only advantage enjoyed by the new line. As its flanks were secured by the sea, the attackers would be forced to attack uphill from the plains of Fanling and Sheung Shui with massed infantry. The garrison could also utilize its tanks and fighter-bombers. Thus, the British believed that the defenders could contain an attack of two to three PLA divisions (40,000 men).[21] Consideration of the water supply for Hong Kong also influenced this plan, as it was suggested during a cabinet meeting that, if the New Territories was also defended, its water supply "should be sufficient to meet the requirements of the population and of the increased garrison, provided that control was maintained over consumption."[22]

In June 1949, the Minister of Defence, Albert Alexander, visited Hong Kong. He found that, although the garrison was confident that a Chinese attack could be repulsed, the relation between the General Officer Commanding Hong Kong, Lieutenant General Francis Festing, and Governor Alexander Grantham was tense. The disgruntled governor complained that the measures urged by the military were harmful to the development of the colony, which he believed would be returned to China sooner or later:[23]

> Immigration control, registration of the population, compulsory military service and many of the elementary security measures which are in force in most states today would, to all intents and purposes, kill our trade in order to make the defence of its corpse more effective.[24]

However, Albert Alexander had the idea that, while the governor's power and function should remain unchanged, the view of the military commander should prevail whenever there was "a clash of opinion between the governor and the commander."[25] Grantham insisted that he should be given the right to protest to the Colonial Office if such a situation occurred, otherwise he would immediately resign. Although his request was granted, London instructed him that he should report to the Defence Committee of the cabinet before turning to the Colonial Office.

Alexander was satisfied with the military preparations. The new Hong Kong Defence Force, reformed in March 1949, was expanded into a force of over 2,000 men consisting of Chinese, English, Eurasian and Portuguese soldiers. Alexander was confident that Hong Kong could be held with additional men and equipment, especially new technologies such as the early warning and fighter control radar:

> The circumstances in 1949 are wholly different from those of 1941, the memory of which still lives in Hong Kong. There is no doubt today of our control of the sea; we shall have an integrated scheme of land defence including air support on an adequate scale; and we shall have fighter defences backed by an early warning system which, even taking into account the limited depth and size of the territory, should be able to deal effectively with such air attack as it is likely to meet. I consider that under these conditions the defence can succeed against the probable scale of attack. So far as I have doubts they concern such things as water, food and fuel . . .[26]

Thus, the British were confident of not only their numerical but also their technical superiority, a feeling that had persisted from the beginning of colonial rule.

Alexander stressed the need to look for non-military means of holding Hong Kong. To prevent Hong Kong from succumbing to an economic blockade by the PRC, Grantham was trying to increase the volume of trade with other countries; Alexander suggested that it was "one of the most important things that the civil authorities can do to help prepare Hong Kong to meet the Communist challenge."[27] He proposed expanding the Special Branch of the Hong Kong Police and increasing propaganda work. He argued that the Chinese residents were subjected to the "influence of heavy communist propaganda" that could only be resisted by "judicious counter propaganda." The relative prosperity and stability of Hong Kong, he suggested, should be placed in "contrast with the daily lessening of freedom under a police state in China and the lower standard of life there."[28]

While Hong Kong was seemingly secure because of the military build-up, the British reconsidered their Hong Kong policy in mid-1949. The Foreign Office and the Colonial Office were asked to devise a long-term policy.[29] Two months later, they submitted a memorandum suggesting that Britain should negotiate the future of the colony only with a Chinese government that was "friendly, democratic, stable, and was able to control the entire country."[30] The issue should not be raised as yet. Prime Minister Attlee deleted the word "democratic," to leave room for future discussion.[31] The realization that Hong Kong and the China trade could not be sustained in the face of a hostile Chinese government led partly to the British decision to recognize the PRC in December 1949. Foreign Secretary Ernest Bevin suggested, "recognition is no more than an acceptance of a fact, which its withholding would not alter . . . the effects of a negative policy on our long-term relations with China as well as our trading interests in China need no elaboration." Governor Grantham also favoured early recognition, "in view of the very large Chinese population in Hong Kong and the New Territories."[32] Afterwards, the British pulled troops out of Hong Kong, despite the outbreak of the Korean War. The troops were sent either to Malaya or to Korea to support the United Nations' campaign to hold the southern part of the Korean Peninsula.[33]

As the British expected, the PRC had no plan to take Hong Kong by force. In October 1949, the CCP had already decided to leave Hong Kong alone for the time being. Zhou Enlai, the Premier of the PRC, adopted the policy of "take a long-term view and make full use of Hong Kong" (長期打算，充分利用). One of the aims of this policy was to prevent Britain from unreservedly supporting the American position on Taiwan and East Asia.[34] The US government also found that, although the British were willing to support the status quo in Asia (such as the existence of the Republic of China in Taiwan), because of Hong Kong they were less willing to back the anti-communist policy of the United States in Asia.[35] The Chinese policy was largely maintained from the 1950s to the end of the period discussed.[36] It is apt to suggest that the British policy over Hong Kong was influenced less by ideology than by a shrewd calculation of interest. During the Korean War and the subsequent period, British control of Hong Kong was threatened by a potential Sino-American war. It seemed possible that the situation in 1941, in which overt American policy had pushed the British into an unwanted war, would repeat itself.

Anglo-American Cooperation on Hong Kong Defence, 1950–1960

From the early 1950s, Britain increasingly relied on the United States to defend Hong Kong. Nonetheless, while the United States was unwilling to commit itself to this purpose, it used Hong Kong to pressure Britain to support its stand over Indochina and Jinmen (Kinmen or Quemoy). Hong Kong became increasingly important in the overall American strategy in Asia.[37] Thus, although its garrison had decreased steadily, Hong Kong was strategically no less important to Britain, the United States and China.

While in 1949 the British were confident of their ability to hold Hong Kong, the Americans were less sanguine. The U.S. Joint Chiefs of Staff (JCS) told President Harry Truman that the British were over-optimistic.[38] As early as June 1949, the JCS had suggested that Hong Kong was irrelevant to US strategy as it lay outside the anti-communist island chain that consisted of Japan, Okinawa, Taiwan and the Philippines. Moreover, public opinion would not allow the use of American troops to defend a British colony.[39] Thus, the JCS suggested that, unless the US government prepared for a total war against China and the Soviet Union, the colony should be abandoned.[40]

This attitude was little changed when the Korean War broke out in June 1950. During the war, Hong Kong assumed its traditional role as a staging area for British expeditions in Asia. As many as fourteen artillery regiments and battalions went to Korea via Hong Kong.[41] Over 130,000 US troops also rested in Hong Kong in 1953.[42] As the North Korean invasion of the South was checked by the United Nations, the Chinese sent troops to the Korean Peninsula in November, turning the war into an international conflict. Meanwhile, the situation in the Taiwan Strait remained tense, with the PRC's attempt to cross the strait thwarted only by the presence of the US 7th Fleet. The situation threatened to escalate into an open Sino-American conflict. The Americans urged the British to dispatch part of the Hong Kong garrison to the Korean Peninsula. It was proposed within the British government that Hong Kong could be defended by American troops, but the idea was seen as politically unfeasible.[43] When the 27th Brigade left for Korea in July 1950 and the garrison was reduced to two brigades, the COS could only resurrect Brooke-Popham's approach in 1941, by ordering the garrison to "deter Communist China from attacking Hong Kong by giving the impression that there would be strong opposition."[44]

During the Korean War, the Americans remained reluctant to commit to Hong Kong defence.[45] When in 1951 the United States discussed with Australia and New Zealand the formation of an Asia-Pacific alliance against the Communist Bloc, Hong Kong and Britain were left out.[46] From the British perspective, the uncompromising attitude of the United States towards China might lead to a repeat of the situation in 1941; while the Americans were unwilling to provide real assistance, they agitated the Chinese and made war more likely. When the United States imposed an embargo against China in spring 1951, the COS flatly suggested that the repercussions of such a move "ranged from more increased tension to an expansionist war by China in Southeast Asia which might well lead in its turn to a general war."[47] As in 1941, since the British were unable to meet their global military commitments alone, they had no choice but to follow the United States in imposing an embargo against China.

The British then revisited the idea of inviting the United States to be a partner in Hong Kong defence. As early as 1951, the British had suggested treating any Chinese attack against Hong Kong as an action against Britain itself, expecting the Americans to intervene.[48] By then, the military advantage enjoyed by the garrison over the PLA had disappeared. While the PLA was equipped with Soviet jet-fighters and heavy tanks, the Royal Navy's control of Hong Kong waters was now less assured because of the departure of major units back to Europe. The garrison was also reduced, as it was a financial drain for the British government. In June 1952, the military expenditure for Hong Kong was £10,700,000, or one-twelfth of the total military budget.[49] Lord Cherwell, the Paymaster General, urged cutting the overseas garrison "ruthlessly."[50] As the British had been paying since 1945 for the Hong Kong garrison mostly from their own coffers, they were more than willing to reduce it to save money.[51] In 1952, the COS recommended a small garrison for internal security duty only.[52]

After the Korean War, the United States became more interested in Hong Kong. In April 1953, the National Security Council (NSC) proposed that the United States "should assist in strengthening the free world vis-à-vis the Soviet orbit" by "maintenance of the offshore defence positions (Japan, Ryukyu, Formosa, the Philippines, Australia and New Zealand)" and by promoting a "strong, expanding and viable economy" in Asia.[53] As for China, the ultimate goal was to "eliminate the threat from that country to Free World security," either through the development of China into an "independent, stable, self-sustaining, non-Communist government" or through detaching her from the Soviet orbit.[54] As for Hong Kong, if it was attacked by the PRC, the NSC recommended the United States to assist in relief and evacuation and to "consider such military assistance for the defence of Hong Kong as may be appropriate in the light of our own commitments and capabilities at the time." The NSC also recommended the government consider "what further actions should be taken against Communist China at Hong Kong."[55]

Because of Hong Kong's peculiar location, the Chinese, British and Americans all saw it as a useful strategic asset, although none would risk a general conflict over its control. As the US Staff Study pointed out in 1957, the PRC had extensive activities in Hong Kong:

> The Communists are conscious of the influence of Hong Kong on British policy, and may hope to exploit the colony as a means to extracting concessions, and of driving a wedge between the United States and the United Kingdom. Hong Kong is also useful to them as a centre for espionage and subversive activity. Sizeable resources have been devoted by the Communists to extending their control of Hong Kong's movies and other media, as a means of influencing the overseas Chinese. Despite the decline in Hong Kong's importance as an entrepot for trade with Communist China, the colony retains some economic value for the Communists. . . . [as] a useful source of foreign exchange, derived mainly from agricultural produce which could not be easily sold elsewhere.[56]

The PRC agents were active in Hong Kong; some even penetrated the Hong Kong government, as the case of the senior policeman John Tsang (Siu-Fo) shows. Tsang reached the rank of Assistant Superintendent of Police before being identified as a spy and sent back to China in 1961.[57] On the other hand, the KMT also saw Hong Kong as an area for espionage activity: in 1955, a bomb was planted on the aircraft *Kashmir Princess*, which was to carry Chinese Premier Zhou Enlai. Zhou did not board the flight after being notified of the plot, but the bomb killed sixteen men on board. It was also suggested in 1960 that "the foreign exchange gained from Hong Kong has risen to the point where it covers most of the adverse balance in Communist China's trade with Western Europe."[58]

During the Cold War, the Americans saw Hong Kong not only as "a neutral bridge, show window, and refugee heaven," but also a source of political and economic information on China.[59] Hong Kong continued to play its pre-World War II role as a British intelligence centre in Asia. The RAF 367 Signals Unit was responsible for post-war signal intelligence works; a listening post was established at Tai Po Tsai and then at Little Sai Wan. In the 1950s, 300 National Service personnel were selected to receive advanced Chinese-language training to serve as listeners in Hong Kong. They were replaced by civilian personnel from the Government Communication Headquarters (GCHQ) only from the early 1960s. The role of the listening station was to intercept all radio broadcasts and wireless communications from mainland China and to pass the information on to other intelligence agencies.[60]

Information about China, including the interceptions of RAF Little Sai Wan, was translated into English by the US consulate in Hong Kong or other organizations such as the Union Research Institute (友聯研究所), which was established in 1955 and funded by the Asian Foundation.[61] Numerous publications appeared, such as *Foreign Broadcast Information Service-China, Survey of the China Mainland Press,*

Selections from China Mainland Magazines, Current Background, Joint Publications Research Service, Summary of World Broadcasts, and *Communist China Yearbook,* published by the Union Research Institute. The *China News Analysis,* edited by the Jesuit László Ladány, was also seen as an important source of information. Ladány stayed in China from 1939 to 1949, and published the *Analysis* from 1953 to 1982 on a weekly basis.[62]

Like the PRC, the Americans also saw Hong Kong as an important propaganda base. The Staff Study of 1957 suggested that "the USIS [U.S. Information Service] office in Hong Kong has in recent years placed major emphasis on the production of news periodicals, books, movies, radio scripts, and other anti-Communist materials directed at the overseas Chinese.... [Overseas Chinese] look to the colony as a non-Communist source of supply for typical Chinese foodstuffs and other products, as well as cultural materials, movies, and news of the homeland." Hong Kong was also "a show window for the people on the mainland, presenting them through the evidence of their senses with an example of law and order maintained without terror, and relative material abundance produced without regimentation."[63] From 1958 to 1961, the United States annually spent over US$5,800,000 in Hong Kong, of which $5,000,000 was spent on the P. L. 40 (US aid to Hong Kong residents) and the refugee programme.[64]

The United States seemingly became more interested in Hong Kong's defence. The Commander-in-Chief of the U.S. Pacific Fleet, Admiral Arthur Radford, argued that, with US naval and air support, the British could hold Hong Kong. He suggested that Hong Kong was "the only remaining beachhead in friendly hands on the mainland of China" and "a useful point of contact with anti-Communist elements in Communist China."[65] He even proposed to Governor Grantham devising an Anglo-American plan to defend the colony.

Radford's attitude encouraged the British, who wanted to place Hong Kong within the US defence framework. However, President Dwight Eisenhower only used the Hong Kong problem to solicit British cooperation. In April 1954, Eisenhower proposed joint action to protect Vietnam, which was increasingly under communist threat. Eisenhower wrote to Churchill:

> The coalition we have in mind would not be directed against Communist China. But if, contrary to our belief, our efforts to save Indochina and the British Commonwealth position to the south should in any way increase the jeopardy to Hong Kong, we would expect to be with you there.[66]

Later, the US government proposed forming a Southeast Asia Treaty Organization (SEATO) to resist the potential communist threat. The Foreign Secretary, Anthony

Eden, suggested that, while SEATO might help protect Hong Kong, he believed that its target was ultimately China. Supporting the US position would, Eden argued, jeopardize the ongoing negotiation between China and the Western powers taking place in Geneva over Vietnam and Korea. Thus, Eden recommended that his government not follow the United States over the issue.[67]

Although Hong Kong fell outside the protection of the SEATO, after the Geneva Conference the British decided to maintain only a minimal garrison there. In order not to alert China and the United States, Churchill insisted that the decision be kept secret and even ordered the Colonial Secretary not to disclose it to Grantham.[68] In July 1954, the COS recommended that the government "rely on indirect means to prevent [Hong Kong] from being attacked."[69] Although the COS did not specify the "indirect means," inviting US support was probably one such means. Soon after the formation of SEATO in September 1954, the British finally made some headway in persuading the Americans to commit themselves. Walter Smith, the US Assistant Secretary of State, orally promised that US assistance would be forthcoming if Hong Kong was attacked.[70]

However, the Americans remained ambiguous over the issue. In January 1955, the PLA seized Yijiangshan Island (一江山島) and bombarded the KMT-controlled islets of Jinmen and Mazu (Matsu) off the Fujian coast. The United States passed the Formosa Resolution, which pledged to use US military force to defend Taiwan. President Eisenhower even claimed that he was prepared to use atomic weapons to fulfil his pledge. To enlist British support, Eisenhower wrote to Churchill again, promising to stand with the British in Hong Kong irrespective of public opinion. However, the United States had only evacuation plans for Hong Kong. Eisenhower again used Hong Kong in exchange for Churchill's support over the US position at Jinmen and Mazu. Admiral Felix Stump, Redford's successor, put it simply: "Hong Kong is an offshore island which is indefensible without immediate US naval and air support. As such it might be a useful *quid pro quo* to secure more courageous British support for a firm US policy with respect to the defence of Kinmen and Matsu."[71] Roger Makins, the British Ambassador to the United States, also told London that, as the Americans now saw Hong Kong as one of the offshore islands, Britain should stand by the United States so that American intervention would be forthcoming if trouble arose in Hong Kong.[72] However, Churchill chose to follow the existing policy of maintaining a friendly relationship with the PRC, and refused to support the US position. Consistent with his approach between 1940 and 1941, Churchill focused on Europe and the Middle East and tried to avoid an unnecessary war in Asia.

As the Taiwan Crisis receded in mid-1955, the COS changed the role of the garrison: to "demonstrate British determination to defend the colony against attack; to impose sufficient delay to allow reinforcements to cover an orderly evacuation and to show the Chinese that an attack on the colony would mean war; and to maintain internal security."[73] This recommendation was opposed by the Colonial Office, which suggested that, if the garrison had only one brigade, the planned evacuation operation might fail as there would not be enough manpower to resist the PLA, arrange the evacuation and maintain internal security. The Colonial Office also suggested that, as "the life of Hong Kong depends on confidence," a further reduction in garrison size would shatter such confidence and jeopardize the development of the colony. The confidence in Britain of other Asian countries, especially Malaya and Singapore, would also be affected. Worse, the reduction might prompt the Chinese to invade. These arguments were similar to those employed by the COS between 1940 and 1941, when it urged the maintenance of the Hong Kong garrison.

In its reply to the Colonial Office in November, the Defence Committee obliquely explained its intention of drawing US support to protect Hong Kong:

> The real defence of Hong Kong lies not in the strength of the garrison, which, even at its present level, could not repel an outright attack, but in the realisation by the Chinese that such an attack would precipitate a full-scale war.[74]

As a full-scale war between China and Britain would invariably involve the United States and might lead to the use of atomic weapons, the British used this position as a new deterrent to protect Hong Kong.

As the Americans detected the British intention to reduce their military presence, they again became more active over Hong Kong defence. From then on, the British held the initiative, as they could reduce their commitment, on the one hand, and pressure the Americans to guarantee the security of the colony, on the other. In early 1956, Stump revived the idea that Hong Kong could be held, during a conference between Australian, New Zealand and American military representatives. He ordered the installation of radar that could be used to direct US carrier-borne aircraft in Hong Kong. He even sent a staff delegation to hold unofficial talks with the British about defending Hong Kong. Two months later, an outline of the defensive plan was drafted, which envisaged British forces absorbing the initial attack before counterattacking with US naval and air support. The British laid down several "assumptions" for future discussion:[75]

- The UK intends to resist aggression against Hong Kong in whatever form it may come.
- The US is not prepared to see Hong Kong fall into Communist hands.

- There would be continuing and close alignment of Anglo-American policies permitting cooperation in planning for the defence of Hong Kong.
- Both governments are prepared to see nuclear weapons used in the defence of the colony.

The final assumption marked the first mention by Britain and the United States of the use of atomic weapons in defending Hong Kong.

These talks did not yet change the official US policy. In July 1957, Eisenhower approved the NSC 5717 Paper, which highlighted the use of Hong Kong as an intelligence and propaganda base. However, the paper also stated that it was impossible to defend the colony, and it was "not in the US interest to undertake military operations to perpetuate the existence of the colony." If the PLA actually attacked, US forces would participate only in the evacuation operation.[76]

Still, the British continued to reduce the garrison. Although the governor and the General Officer Commanding Hong Kong suggested that at least seven battalions were needed to maintain internal security, London had already decided in 1957 to reduce the garrison again. The Ministry of Defence first suggested that the government should "substantially reduce" the garrison in the draft of a policy paper for parliament, but the line was deleted in the eighth proof of the draft, possibly because the government was unwilling to disclose the decision.[77] The reductions in 1957 and 1958 focused mainly on the Royal Navy. The naval facilities were scheduled to be closed gradually or to be transferred to Singapore.[78] The decision allowed the government to save £1,500,000 per annum and to reduce 4,500 dockyard staff.[79] In 1958, the Royal Navy's strength in Asia consisted merely of a squadron of frigates and the Hong Kong Flotilla. All coastal guns were decommissioned in 1956.[80] The RAF garrison at Kai Tak was reduced to three Venom fighters and one Vampire.[81]

The British increasingly stressed the importance of US support and atomic deterrence. In April 1958, a top-secret memorandum with the title "The Effects of Anglo-American Interdependence on the Long-term Interest of the United Kingdom" was submitted by the Foreign Office after Prime Minister Harold Macmillan visited Washington. The memorandum suggested that Macmillan had "engaged the interest" of the Americans "in the defence of Hong Kong."[82] It stressed the importance of relying on the United States, as Britain needed time to recover from the impacts of the Second World War and decolonization, and suggested introducing means of "political consultation to Far Eastern problems" and "military consultation" between the United States and the United Kingdom.[83] In 1961, Alec Douglas-Home, the Foreign Secretary, wrote that, as the British were unable to defend Hong Kong through conventional means, effort should be made to "encourage the Chinese to believe that an attack on Hong Kong would involve US nuclear retaliation."[84] By then, nuclear deterrence had become one of the major means for the British to defend Hong Kong.

Even with prospective US support, the British were sober about the future of the colony. In the *Future Policy Study 1960–1970*, drafted by the Ministry of Defence in 1960, Hong Kong was seen as a "danger-point where trouble might break out any time." To protect Hong Kong, Britain should "live with China" and "try to reach an accommodation with her on any points on which this might be possible," through an attitude that was "reasonable but firm, realistic but not provocative."[85] The report stressed the impossibility of retaining Hong Kong indefinitely, even with US support:

> Without the leased territories the colony is not viable; the lease expires in 1997 and we cannot hope to negotiate an extension of it. Nor is there any prospect of our being able to transfer sovereignty to an independent Hong Kong, or fit it into any eventual solution for Formosa. We might in due course consider making a public declaration to the effect that we would stay until 1997 then withdraw altogether. But, in the foreseeable future, such a declaration would be unwise. We should not even prepare for any new move because this would destroy the confidence on which our present position rests and might preju-dice the outcome of any joint Anglo-United States review of Western policy in the Far East. Our position in Hong Kong may be expected to give us some influence over the Americans when they are ready to reconsider their policy towards Communist China and Formosa. Meanwhile, we have no choice but to remain in Hong Kong and should, without provoking the Chinese, show that we intended to do so.[86]

This realization further reinforced the determination of the British to minimize the military deployment in Hong Kong before 1997.

As the British steadily decreased their military presence, while insisting that any attack against Hong Kong would be equal to the declaration of a full-scale war, the United States gradually showed less reluctance to use military force in securing Hong Kong. In December 1959, the US Operations Coordinating Board proposed revising the NSC 5717, because of the "stiffer British attitude regarding their deter-mination to maintain control" and the increased importance of the colony as "an industrial and financial centre in the Fast East" with "potential effect on US eco-nomic policy for that area."[87] Six months later, the US government replaced the NSC 5717 with NSC 6007 as the basis of its Hong Kong policy. It suggested that, if the PRC attacked, the US government would act "in the light of British determination to resist and the circumstances prevailing." The NSC also proposed considering the use of military deployment, high-level statements and a display of US military might to support the British. The British intention of drawing US support was also understood:

> In anything short of a global or regional conflict in which British resources
> would be stretched to the breaking point, it is believed that the British would
> resist—by forces of arms, if necessary—any Chinese Communist demands for
> the return of the colony. The British are thought to calculate that their resist-
> ance to an all-out Communist attack, while not sufficiently powerful to prevent
> loss of the colony, might generate a larger conflict which the Communists
> would not desire. The British willingness to resist thus constitutes a deterrent.[88]

Thus, by 1960, the United States had been transformed from a bystander into a
partner in the British policy of deterrence. This deterrence policy allowed Britain to
steadily reduce its military commitment, even though the internal situation in Hong
Kong was at times in flux.

The Post-Korean War Garrison

Because of post-war reconstruction and an absence of threats, the problem of the
military contribution to Britain did not resurface until 1949. In 1950, the colony
was asked to pay HK$16,000,000 towards reinforcing the garrison. This amount
was around 6.27 percent of the total government expenditure of that year.[89] From
1953, the colonial government had to pay for the reconstruction of the local
forces as well as the maintenance of British regular forces in Hong Kong. The total
amount spent on defence was about HK$20,000,000–$30,000,000 per annum (of
which around 90 percent was military contribution) until 1965, when the British
demanded an increase in military contribution under a five-year scheme. Despite
the protests of the Hong Kong government, it was finally agreed by the two sides
that Hong Kong had to pay £3,925,000 per annum, with another £2,400,000 for
the four financial years between 1967 and 1971, to fund capital works programmes
for the military. It was agreed that the works would be reverted to the Hong Kong
government without additional charge when the military had relinquished them.[90]
As Britain had substantially decreased its military deployment in Hong Kong after
1958, Hong Kong again became a contributor to imperial defence in the 1960s, a
situation unseen since the 1880s.

After the end of the Korean War, the British cut down the size of the garrison
to two brigades (six battalions), a small Hong Kong Flotilla, and a detachment of
the RAF equipped first with jet-fighters and then with helicopters. To augment the
reduced garrison, the recruitment of locals was restarted as soon as 1946. The army
unit became the Hong Kong Military Service Corps (HKMSC) in 1962; according
to the regimental history of the unit, over 6,000 Hong Kong Chinese served in this
unit from 1962 to 1997. The first Chinese officer of the unit, Lieutenant Cheung
Kwok Tong, received his commission (a Governor's Commission) in 1975 and a

Table 30   Military expenditure of the Hong Kong government, 1949–1970 (in millions, HKD)

Year	Military Spending	Total Government Spending
1949	0.05	159.73
1950	16.05	181.08
1951	0.70	251.26
1952	1.68	275.15
1953	31.80	310.51
1954	29.65	354.74
1955	27.94	371.97
1956	21.98	401.69
1957	22.68	465.75
1958	25.63	530.04
1959	24.39	587.50
1960	34.07	707.79
1961	30.85	843.27
1962	33.93	949.16
1963	29.24	1,113.08
1964	31.81	1,293.01
1965	31.76	1,436.59
1966	62.58	1,765.70
1967	65.86	1,804.98
1968	88.59	1,872.97
1969	88.21	2,032.18
1970	87.91	2,478.20

Sources: *Hong Kong Annual Report*, 1949–1972.

Queen's Commission two years later. In all, thirty-four Hong Kong Chinese in the HKMSC received commissions in the British Army.[91] Serving in the HKMSC, the Royal Navy, the Royal Hong Kong Auxiliary Air Force, and other regular units was seen as a better (thus more competitive) choice than serving as a policeman, as it offered higher pay and a better image.

During the 1960s and 1970s, the major land units included the 48th Gurkha Brigade, the 51st Infantry Brigade, the Hong Kong Regiment (The Volunteers) and a number of armoured and artillery elements. After the withdrawal of the 51st Infantry Brigade, the garrison was reduced to four battalions, including the Gurkha Field Force (a brigade-sized unit) and the Hong Kong Regiment (The Volunteers).[92] The need to protect Hong Kong and maintain its public order allowed the British to retain a larger Gurkha contingent with the support of the Hong Kong government; these units played a significant role during the Falklands War of 1982.

The role of the garrison was limited to demonstrating the British intention to hold Hong Kong and to public relations. Its role was defined in a Ministry of Defence memorandum in 1969:

> To assist the police to control the frontier and to maintain law and order throughout the colony . . . man exposed positions covering areas in which violent disturbances can occur . . . carry out patrols in the remote areas of the New territories [*sic*] and help the Hong Kong Government to deal with the subversion in the small scattered villages . . . act with fairness, discipline and determination . . . [in order to] gain and hold the confidence of the population.[93]

Figure 33   Cartoon mocking the inability of the British to hold Hong Kong, 1967[94]

To maintain confidence, larger vessels of the Royal Navy also paid regular visits, while the RAF maintained a detachment of helicopters at Kai Tak.[95] As boosting and maintaining public confidence was a priority, the discipline of the British forces during the post-war period was considerably better. Punishment for misconduct became harsher. For example, a sergeant was demoted and denounced publicly for killing a cat in 1958.[96] At the beginning of the period, social segregation and racial discrimination still existed between Chinese and British servicemen in Hong Kong; however, as Anglo-Chinese soldier L/Cpl. Phillip Thompson observed, this situation gradually improved because of an influx of more open-minded officers from the 1960s.[97] Segregation measures were gradually abolished; British and Chinese servicemen worked well together.[98]

The situation in Hong Kong was largely peaceful except during the 1956 and 1967 riots. From August 1953, RAF fighter patrols were no longer armed with live ammunition.[99] However, the minesweeper HMML 1323 was shelled in September 1953 by a Chinese gunboat near Hong Kong with the loss of three seamen.[100] In response, two destroyers and twelve de Havilland Hornets were dispatched to the scene as a show of force.[101] Although no subsequent incidents occurred, the Royal Navy established the "Emergency Destroyer" system of placing one operational destroyer or frigate at the Naval Dockyard every day until the 1960s.[102]

A considerable number of Hong Kong citizens participated in the protection of their home, not only as regular soldiers but also in the militia and auxiliary units. This certainly gave the participants and the public a sense of citizenship and belonging, if not an identity as British subjects. From 1949 to 1951, the Hong Kong government introduced additional legislation, including the Compulsory Service Ordinance, Naval Volunteer Reserve (General Reserve) Ordinance, Essential Service Corps Ordinance and the Royal Hong Kong Defence Force Ordinance. British males were required to join the reconstituted Hong Kong Defence Force (later The Royal Hong Kong Regiment (The Volunteers), a battalion-sized unit) after 1951; Chinese were also accepted into the unit. Chinese residents aged sixteen or above could join the Auxiliary Medical Services, Reserve Fire Brigade, Auxiliary Police, Essential Service Corps, Civil Aid Services and the RAF/RN Reserves.[103] In March 1959, there were 17,903 Hong Kong residents serving in the Defence Force, the civil defence units and other volunteer units (Table 31). In addition, there were around 1,000 regulars from the Hong Kong Chinese Training Unit (predecessor of the previously mentioned Hong Kong Military Service Corps), several hundred Hong Kong Chinese serving on Royal Navy vessels, and a small number of RAF guardsmen and auxiliaries. Before 1958, the Royal Naval Dockyard also hired around 5,000 Chinese workers and technicians to service Royal Navy vessels.

Among the above services, the Civil Aid Service and the Auxiliary Medical Service were predominantly Chinese. More than half the strength of the Hong Kong Defence Force (later renamed The Hong Kong Regiment (The Volunteers) [HKR] and, after 1967, The Royal Hong Kong Regiment (The Volunteers) [RHKR]) was made up by Chinese, a situation wholly different from that in 1941. Among Hong Kong Chinese serving in the HKR/RHKR, Captain James Chan's (陳益中) experience was typical. The son of a government clerk and himself worked in a government clinic, Capt. Chan served in the Despatch Service of the Civil Aid Service before joining the HKR in 1966. After two weeks of basic training, he received four months of formal training including courses on firearms, leadership skills, basic medical knowledge, map reading and drills. He was then chosen as a radio operator

Table 31   Hong Kong Defence Force, civil defence units, as well as auxiliary forces strength and nationality, 1959[104]

Units	British	Others	Chinese	Total
Civil Aid Service	50	68	4,799	4,917
Aux. Medical Service	110	161	3,079	3,350
Reserve Fire Brigade	21	9	528	558
Essential Service Corps	1,119	701	2,478	4,298
Police Reserves	207	271	1,210	1,788
HK Defence Force	102	245	410	757
Naval Reserves	74	16	113	203
RAF Auxiliaries	36	39	59	134
Light Forces	5	6	22	33
Recon Platoon	14	19	21	54
Intelligence Platoon	1	5	14	20
Staff Duties	19	1	0	20
Home Guard	6	47	20	73
HQ Staff	41	16	8	65
				16,270*

* excluding other smaller contingents

because of his English-language skills. After three more weeks of advanced training, he became a lance corporal. Three years later, he was commissioned, finally withdrawing from service in 1972 with the rank of captain. Members of the RHKR received no fixed salary and were given only subsidies during the monthly training and large exercises that took place twice a year.[105] During the riots of 1956 and 1967, the unit saw extensive service.

In addition to the British garrison, Hong Kong also boasted a peculiar form of informal protection offered by the U.S. Navy, which saw the colony as a stopping and resting point. This brought a small economic boost for the colony, particularly during the Vietnam War.[106] Major US warships such as the USS *Oriskany* and USS *New Jersey* also called at Hong Kong.[107]

As the post-war garrison was reduced, the Hong Kong government was finally able to take back military land in the urban area. The Royal Naval Dockyard, which had served the China Station from the 19th century, was finally closed in 1958, with only a portion of land retained by the military. The Kowloon Naval Dock had been returned earlier. The Whitfield Barracks was returned in 1967, while the Sham Shui Po Camp was transferred to the civilian authorities soon after. The RAF also surrendered the land for its communication centre near modern-day Choi Hung, which became a public housing estate (Choi Hung Estate).[108] However, the Hong Kong government had to pay most of the defence cost of the colony after the 1957–1958 reductions.[109]

The Final Tests: The 1956 and 1967 Riots and Aftermath

Hong Kong experienced rapid economic development during the Cold War. The period also witnessed sometimes intense clashes of ideologies and interests among residents, many of whom had settled in the colony as a result of the political turmoil in China. These clashes not only tested the civilian government but also the garrison. The riots in 1956 and 1967 were the most serious incidents; the latter riot was the direct result of political chaos in the PRC during the Cultural Revolution. However, though the two events were serious in terms of human and material losses, social disruption and political implications, they had little impact on the ongoing British military withdrawal. As these events have been discussed in detail in other works, the following section focuses mainly on the role of the military.

The immediate cause of the 1956 riot was the removal by Resettlement staff of pro-KMT propaganda materials from the Lei Cheng Uk Estate before the Double Tenth day of 1956. The long-term causes included socio-economic hardship among working people, widespread activity by triads with close relations to the Chinese political parties, and the feud between pro-KMT and pro-CCP unions. The northwest corner of Kowloon was, by then, both a developing industrial area and a hotbed of union and triad activities. The actions of the Resettlement staff caused much resentment among the pro-KMT residents and led to a riot on the morning of 10 October. Squads of police were deployed on Castle Peak Road and in the Lei Cheng Uk Estate, but the riot spread southwards and reached Sham Shui Po, Mong Kok and Tai Hang Tung at night.[110]

Although the police controlled a large part of Castle Peak Road, they were unable to contain small-scale outbreaks in the inner streets. Organized rioters set up road-blocks in different parts of Kowloon and extorted money by forcefully selling KMT flags to vehicles. Pro-KMT unionists and triads also attacked pro-CCP unionists and their offices and clinics in Tsuen Wan. Buildings that had displayed PRC flags on 1 October were set ablaze. The police at Tsuen Wan, seventy of them in total, were isolated because Castle Peak Road was not cleared. They had to withdraw into the police station to guard the firearms.[111] At 1:00 p.m., the rioters attacked and burned a taxi carrying the Swiss consul, wounding him and killing his wife. As the situation was no longer controllable by police, the military was called in. Three battalions in Kowloon were mobilized and authorized to shoot any rioters. Spontaneous looting and arson also occurred at Kwun Tong, Ho Man Tin and Hung Hom. On the evening of the 11th, the government put Kowloon under curfew; the police and troops patrolled the street. When the situation in Kowloon calmed down during the next day, the police arrested 6,000 suspected rioters at the resettlement estates in Kowloon with the support of the troops, who withdrew only after the curfew was lifted on 16 October.[112]

The riot, which lasted around two days, killed fifty-nine people and injured over four hundred. Forty-four deaths were caused by shooting; at least eight men were killed at Tsuen Wan by the mobs. The garrison suffered 17 wounded, and the police 107. The government estimated that the losses caused by the riot, including the destruction of the Garden Bread Factory, reached $4,770,000.[113]

The PRC government criticized the colonial authorities for failing to maintain order. Governor Grantham worried that the PRC might demand an immediate takeover.[114] Although the Americans highlighted the connection between the KMT and the triads in Hong Kong, there is no evidence to prove that the KMT had deliberately planned the incident. The official report of the Hong Kong government suggested that the riot was an attempt by opportunistic triads, with few political implications, to expand their power amid a dispute between officials and residents of the Lei Cheng Uk Estate.[115]

Although the riot brought little social improvement, the Hong Kong Police actively augmented its ability to suppress riots of a similar kind. These measures proved to be useful during the 1967 riot. Emergency Units of fifty to sixty men were trained in the Police Training Contingent, which was established and headed for a time by Peter Godber. The goal was to form a number of flexible and fast-responding units with adequate equipment for containing and crushing riots in urban areas. Each member of the Emergency Units would receive two months of training in the contingent. One of the instructors was Lieutenant Les Guyatt of the British Army, who brought military tactics into the training.[116]

In the 1960s, despite considerable economic development and improvements in standard of living, social tensions remained. The protest in 1966 against the increase in the fare of the Star Ferry was only one of the many manifestations of this tension. Meanwhile, the situation in China became extremely volatile because of the Cultural Revolution. Key government organs of the PRC such as the Foreign Ministry were influenced by the wave of extremism. By 1966, chaos and xenophobia in China gradually spread across the border, reaching Macao and Hong Kong. From November to December 1966, a large-scale disturbance occurred in Macao that ultimately led on 3 December to a shooting incident in which eleven people were killed. The PRC government condemned the Portuguese colonial authority; Guangdong closed its border with Macao and stopped its water supply. The Portuguese were forced to make an apology and to expel KMT personnel and organizations from Macao. As Gary Cheung Ka-wai has suggested, the success of the leftists in Macao brought much pressure to bear on the leaders of the PRC agents in Hong Kong.

They felt that they had to take some action or else they would be criticized by the lower cadres for being timid. Thus, from early 1967, the CCP cadres in Hong Kong started to take a harder line against the colonial authority.[117]

From early 1967, a series of labour disputes broke out; a riot also occurred in the Kowloon Walled City. On 6 May, a labour dispute at the Hong Kong Artificial Flower Works in San Po Kong escalated into a clash between police and workers. Twenty-one workers were arrested. The leftist newspapers claimed that the event was part of an Anglo-American plot against the PRC; leftist unions and organizations mobilized their members to gather at the factory. A week after the initial clash, six hundred riot police tried to disperse the crowd, employing tear gas and wooden bullets. A thirteen-year-old boy was killed.[118]

Although the action revealed the improved ability of the police to handle large-scale disturbances, the event escalated into a political struggle between PRC agents and the colonial authority. On 12 May, the Hong Kong and Kowloon Committee for Anti-Hong Kong British Persecution Struggle (港九各界同胞反對港英迫害鬥爭委員會) was formed, with an explicit anti-colonial agenda. Small-scale attacks intermittently broke out in Kowloon. A procession supporting the leftists in Hong Kong was organized in China. The Foreign Ministry of the PRC and the New China News Agency (Xinhua News Agency) both criticized the British; the former openly supported the "struggle" in Hong Kong. On the other hand, the Hong Kong government estimated that the disturbance was not a deliberate attempt by the PRC to take over. Thus, it was firm in public but tried to communicate with the leftists. With apparent support from the mainland, the leftists took a firmer line by staging protests every day in front of the Governor's House. In fact, both sides looked for ways to defuse the situation. Jack Cater, the Assistant Colonial Secretary, told the leftist representative that if the protests were carried out peacefully then the British would not employ force to disperse them.[119] Although doves from both sides were trying to calm things down, the situation was so tense that conflict was difficult to avoid.

On 22 May, a procession marching towards the Governor's House was stopped by the police. A clash again broke out. The police accused the protesters of feigning their wounds, while they blamed the police for the injuries.[120] After the clash, a curfew was introduced in Hong Kong Island: all public gatherings were banned. The leftist unions threatened a general strike involving public transport and the essential services. Although Zhou Enlai privately disapproved of the actions of the leftists, the PRC publicly supported their actions. In early June, the *People's Daily* published a series of columns supporting the anti-British movement.[121] The Hong Kong government took a firm line against the leftists. On 23 June, the police raided the headquarters of one of the leftist unions, meeting fierce resistance. Three workers were killed, and dozens of workers and policemen were wounded. Although the leftist unions were able to mobilize as many as 50,000 workers to join their strike, the result was limited and their actions alienated the public.[122]

The situation was the most intense in the summer. From June onwards, the Guangdong authorities started publicly to support the anti-British movement. Loudspeakers chanted anti-British slogans along the border; the trains running across the border had similar slogans written on them. On 8 July, the police post at Shataukok was attacked by automatic weapons; five policemen were killed. Four of them had been killed before being authorized to return fire.[123] The news briefly shocked London. During a cabinet meeting, Prime Minister Harold Wilson instructed contingency plans to be devised if Hong Kong was untenable.[124]

Soon after this incident, the Gurkhas were dispatched to the Northern Districts. However, no further incidents occurred along the border. Although the Hong Kong government had planned for the worst, it remained firm in suppressing the riot. The curfew for the northern part of the island was continued from 11 July, while the Acting Colonial Secretary, Richard Holmes, who had served in the BAAG, declared that the government would take active measures. The same day, The Volunteers was mobilized, while the police searched the leftist offices at Wan Chai at night. Two days later, the police raided several leftist headquarters.

The Hong Kong Regiment was first deployed at Lau Fau Shan, then redeployed on village patrol in various parts of the New Territories such as Sai Kung, where the bombs being planted on the streets of Hong Kong were allegedly made.[125] From 29 July, the regiment also engaged in anti-intimidation duty, namely to protect the tram drivers who refused to join the strike. The situation was initially tense, as the HKR was finding as many as forty-eight bombs in a morning. The duty was carried on until October.[126] As Captain Chan Yik Chung suggested, however, the soldiers were, in general, calm as the British officers had already told them that Beijing was unlikely to take overt action. The British understanding of Beijing's attitude probably explains the decisive actions taken by the Hong Kong government against the leftists.

In August, the riot led to numerous casualties. Supported by the helicopter from HMS *Hermes*, the police raided a leftist stronghold on the island. From August on, the rioters planted real and fake bombs across Hong Kong. The bombs killed not only British bomb experts and policemen, but also a secondary-school boy, a seven-year-old girl and her two-year-old brother. In all, the British military disposed of over 8,000 bombs. On 22 August, Red Guards looted and burned the British embassy in Beijing. Two days later, Lam Bun, a broadcaster of the Commercial Radio Hong Kong, was burned to death by the leftist mob. Tension, however, gradually receded afterwards as the PRC government apologized for the incident in Beijing, although the leftists in Hong Kong continued to plant bombs across the colony. The Hong Kong government finally lifted the curfew in December 1967. In all, fifty-two men, women and children were killed, and more than eight hundred were wounded. More than two thousand suspected rioters were arrested, including some students.

Although the riot delayed the withdrawal of British military forces, it did not stop the trend. In 1968, London decided to withdraw from Malaya (where the civil war had ended) and Singapore; the bases in the two former colonies were handed to the local governments.[127] After the 1967 riot, the garrison of Hong Kong was kept at a minimal level, although additional plans were devised to augment the garrison in an emergency. In 1971, the Ministry of Defence devised Operation Galaxy, a plan of shipping four battalions (including one Gurkha battalion) from the United Kingdom to Hong Kong entirely by air. The troops and their equipment would be sent by Vickers VC 10 and Lockheed C-130 Hercules via Singapore to Hong Kong within 75–77 hours. The plan especially arranged propaganda elements to move with the troops.[128] In addition, to prevent the leftist unions from paralysing the essential services and military facilities, the British also prepared Operation Halibut, a plan of sending 1,340 military engineers and technicians to Hong Kong within 124–183 hours.[129] After the riot, the RAF permanently deployed helicopters at Hong Kong to boost the responsiveness of the garrison and the police. As Hong Kong remained largely peaceful during subsequent decades, the main duty of these helicopters was search and rescue, for example, delivering a pregnant woman from Lantau to Hong Kong Island. This was certainly an effective way of building up trust and of winning hearts and minds among the residents.[130]

Conclusion

The Second World War was followed by the Cold War, decolonization and the strategic contraction of the British Empire. Hong Kong was at the forefront of all these developments. Although PRC decision-makers never seriously contemplated taking Hong Kong by force, the colony was seen as a potential flashpoint by both blocs of the Cold War. It remained as a military base for British and American forces, and was also a considerable economic asset for Britain and the PRC. Both sides also saw it as a propaganda, intelligence and political asset. As the British could no longer deploy large field forces, they continued the policies of deterrence and Anglo-American cooperation that were adopted before the Second World War. Although the Americans were ambiguous about whether they would defend Hong Kong with military force or even nuclear weapons, they certainly understood the British intention and were willing to cooperate in their deterrence policy. As China remained uninterested in starting a war over Hong Kong, the years after 1949 were marked by continuous peace, with only short periods of tension and unrest such as in the riots of 1956 and 1967. After the 1967 riot, British military presence was kept minimal; the role of the garrison shifted to border patrol, disaster relief and imaging. By then, Hong Kong was no longer militarily important for Britain.

11
CONCLUSIONS

The Strategic Role of Hong Kong and Its Defence

The strategic role of Hong Kong and its defence constantly changed according to the internal situation of Britain, imperial need, economic situation, technological change and changes in policymaking mechanisms as well as in policymakers. Changing international relations and the political situation in China provided opportunities for and imposed limitations on decision-makers. Hong Kong had been a beachhead of British military penetration in East Asia in the 19th century. The British military forces that participated in the two Opium Wars, the Crimean War, the Anglo-Satsuma War and the Boxer War all passed through Hong Kong. Victoria Harbour provided shelter not only for British merchantmen but also for the warships of the China Station. The warships were supplied, repaired and serviced by the dockyards at Hong Kong, which were some of the largest ones in Asia. Although more forward outposts were later founded, such as Port Hamilton and Weihaiwei, they lacked the location advantage and the infrastructure to sustain large naval and military forces. From 1841 to 1970, Hong Kong emerged as and remained a major shipping node, not only for South China but for the whole of Asia.

As other European powers (later joined by Japan and the United States) extended their influence and, later, actual military presence in Asia during the second half of the 19th century, plans for the defence of Hong Kong were constantly revised and upgraded. Contrary to the view that planners in London were unwilling to spend money on the defence of Hong Kong, untried and often expensive military technologies were employed, despite the constant argument over who was to pay the bill. The Brennan torpedo was only one of the more awkward examples of this trend. Before the First World War, the first line of defence was the Royal Navy, which had maintained a sizeable China Station able to project power throughout Asia. Brute force alone was not enough, however. The prestige of the British Empire, sustained by its size, wealth, industrial might and naval preponderance, also counted. In addition, from 1902 to 1922 Hong Kong was also guaranteed by the Anglo-Japanese

Alliance, which allowed the British to maintain a small garrison during the first decades of the 20th century.

Nonetheless, the extension of the boundaries of Hong Kong in 1898 complicated the defence problem. From 1899, the colony had a lengthy land boundary with mainland China; planners were constantly troubled by the prospect of an enemy occupying Kowloon Ridge that could command Victoria Harbour and the north shore of Hong Kong Island. To protect the dockyard facilities, it was necessary to extend the defence perimeter to include Kowloon Ridge. The realization of this fact shifted the attention of British planners from coastal defences to defence against attacks from the border or the New Territories. Before the First World War, the British believed that the most threatening potential enemy of Hong Kong was not France and Russia but Japan. Though a British ally, she was the most powerful military power in Asia, possibly the only one that could deploy large land forces against Hong Kong. Eventually, the Kowloon defence line, first advocated by local commanders in the early 1910s, was built during the First World War. However, planners were forced to abandon the idea of holding a line across Kowloon Peninsula, as urban development rendered such a line indefensible.

After the First World War, the strategic importance of Hong Kong to the British Empire did not decline. After the termination of the Anglo-Japanese Alliance in 1922, Hong Kong was seen by the Royal Navy as an important advance base against Japan. Although the plan against Japan was partly a means by which the Royal Navy could demand more resources from the British government, the need to hold Hong Kong against a Japanese invasion before the arrival of the British main fleet led to continuous debate throughout the interwar period. This period also witnessed the establishment of an independent Royal Air Force, which was itself hungry for more resources. As the so-called Ten Years Rule had limited British military spending, debates over the defence of Hong Kong became battlegrounds for limited resources among the armed services. The situation of Hong Kong was further complicated by its peculiar geography, by which suitable sites for large air bases could be found only in the northern part of the New Territories, dangerously close to the boundary with China and the beaches suitable for enemy landing. Thus, Singapore, which was closer to Britain and commanded the vital sea-lane of the Malacca Strait, was seen by the British as a more suitable site for the main naval base. However, although Singapore received the highest priority, Hong Kong was not abandoned: from the early 1930s, a sizeable reorganization of the colony's defence, including the construction of the notorious Gin Drinker's Line, was carried out.

In the late 1930s, as Britain was threatened simultaneously by Germany, Italy and Japan, the Royal Navy shifted its attention to the Mediterranean Sea. From then on, the factors of the defence of Hong Kong changed fundamentally. The garrison was no longer expected to hold Kowloon Ridge to protect the harbour facilities, as the British main fleet would not arrive within ninety days. The colony was now seen as an "outpost" and the garrison only expected to hold Hong Kong Island. This led to another reorganization of Hong Kong defence, most importantly the relocation to Hong Kong Island of all coastal guns on the mainland and Stonecutters. The work on the Gin Drinker's Line was stopped; it was relegated as a delaying line whose main purpose was to buy time for the garrison to prepare for the defence of Hong Kong Island.

After the outbreak of the Second Sino-Japanese War in 1937, the British increasingly turned to a policy of deterrence by trying to forge an alliance between Britain, China and the United States. The British were placed in an embarrassing position, as they had to support the Chinese war effort without antagonizing Japan. Meanwhile, Hong Kong became an important window through which China received foreign materials and munitions until the fall of Guangzhou in late 1938. By then, Hong Kong was deep inside the Japanese area of control; the Japanese were able to attack the colony directly from the land frontier. For this reason, Hong Kong was continuously seen as an "outpost" during the early part of the Second World War. In 1940, Brooke-Popham arrived in Singapore as the Commander-in-Chief of the Far East. He believed that international cooperation, a stronger British attitude and more reinforcements might deter Japan. This coincided with an improvement of the situation in the Middle East, leading to a rethinking of the British defence policy in Asia. By then, Hong Kong was seen as a place where British determination to resist possible Japanese aggression could be showcased, in order to encourage China and the United States to form a united front. The result was the dispatch of the two ill-fated Canadian battalions to Hong Kong.

After the Second World War, Hong Kong became a dormant front of the Cold War after the Chinese Communists took over mainland China. The Chinese Communists saw Hong Kong as an important economic asset and cultivated their political influence there. The Americans, who had become the leaders of the Western camp, saw Hong Kong as an important political, intelligence and propaganda outpost. The economic development of Hong Kong was augmented in order to form a contrast with the backwardness of mainland China. The British initially deployed a substantial garrison, but gradually withdrew forces as they were needed elsewhere, such as Malaya and Korea. From then on, the British turned to the United States for the protection of Hong Kong, mainly by showing their intention of turning any Chinese Communist attack into a general conflict. Although the Americans remained ambiguous, the situation in Hong Kong remained largely peaceful from 1949 to 1970, despite internal unrest in 1956 and 1967.

Making Defence Policies

From the 1860s, the British started to conceptualize the defence of Hong Kong in an imperial context. Hong Kong was no longer seen as an isolated locality but the "eastern fortress" of an imperial network linked by steamships. This understanding emerged in parallel with the establishment of military-civilian institutions that collected and assessed intelligence, devised and revised defence schemes, and disseminated information. These institutions included the Colonial Defence Committee, Committee of Imperial Defence and the Chiefs of Staff Committee. Meanwhile, the bureaucratic infrastructure of the army and navy expanded considerably so that colonial defence could be regularly reviewed and upgraded according to latest information collected. Not all of this behind-the-scenes work was realized in actual structures built or plans devised, but the idea that the British neglected the defence of colonial Hong Kong is open to challenge. These institutions and policy mechanisms were the real strengths of Britain, in addition to its material advantages such as wealth and industrial capacity. It should be noted that financial factors were not always the primary consideration of British decision-makers when planning the defence of Hong Kong and related strategies.

The understanding of Hong Kong as part of the imperial network led to the regularization of the military contribution to Britain from the colony, as well as the decline of the influence of the Hong Kong government and the Colonial Office over defence policy. During the 1860s and 1870s, governors had played a considerable role in the making of defence policies. Hennessy, for example, pressed the idea of a Chinese regiment and almost succeeded. As late as 1926, the governor still had some say on defence issues as the chair of the Local Defence Committee. However, such influence declined with the formation of specialized planning organizations such as the Chiefs of Staff Committee and the Joint Planning Sub-committee. Thus, throughout the interwar period, the Hong Kong government received only limited information about military arrangements. As mentioned, Northcote even subtly complained that he had little idea of the garrison's plan in 1938. During the Battle of Hong Kong, Mark Young was ordered not to surrender by London until General Maltby made it clear on 25 December 1941 that further resistance was impossible. After the war, the final clash between the Hong Kong government and the military ended in London's decision that the view of the military should prevail whenever there was a difference of opinion between the governor and the commander over defence issues.

Military and Urban Development

The military history of Hong Kong is closely related to the city's urbanization. During the early days of colonial rule, the military occupied the central part of the City of Victoria. Throughout subsequent decades, the colonial government tried in vain to persuade the services to move away from prime land to make way for urban expansion. After the annexation of Kowloon and Stonecutters in 1861, the military obtained a considerable amount of land in the former and practically occupied the latter after a lengthy discussion with the civilian government. At the turn of the 20th century, the naval dockyard and army facilities still occupied the central part of the Central District, while the two services established more facilities on the other side of the harbour. After the First World War, the Royal Air Force acquired the reclaimed land at Kai Tak and some of the surrounding areas (paid by the Hong Kong government) to establish an air base. Throughout the interwar period, the problem of finding a larger piece of land for a bigger air base proved to be insurmountable. The extensive use of land by the military was in a sense a form of indirect military contribution, a fact that the colonial government repeatedly pointed out in its efforts to counter London's demands for more money.

On the other hand, urban development presented a new defence problem for the garrison. The defence perimeter of the garrison was gradually enlarged as a result of urban expansion and the emergence of new facilities such as Taikoo Dockyard on the eastern part of Hong Kong Island. Urban expansion sometimes forced the garrison to abandon its plans and to adopt new defence positions. For example, as a result of development in Kowloon during and after the First World War, planners had to consider constructing permanent defences along Kowloon Ridge. It was during the period of strategic contraction after the Second World War that the military gradually returned the land to the colonial government. The closure of the naval dockyard in 1958 marked not only the end of Hong Kong as a major British naval base but also the decline of military influence on the city's development.

The Garrison and Hong Kong

In the first decades of British rule, the garrison consisted of Englishmen, Scots, Welsh, Irish and Indians from different parts of the subcontinent. Members of the garrison significantly outnumbered the European population of Hong Kong. Thus, it was natural that the garrison had a considerable impact on the life of the colony. Previous works have detailed the sporting and social activities of the officers and men. Other than parades, sporting matches, races and balls, the garrison was involved in many events in Hong Kong history, especially when disaster struck. The garrison aided the civilian authorities in typhoons, fires and epidemic outbreaks. It also helped suppress piracy near Hong Kong and South China, although the main purpose was to protect British shipping; the problem of piracy was only solved by the end of this period.

To sustain the garrison, the Hong Kong government paid a regular military contribution to Britain from 1865 on. The financial implications of this contribution, such as the high-premium and low-rent policy, may still be felt today. The need to maintain the health of troops was one reason for the early hygiene legislations and the construction of permanent barracks and hospitals in Hong Kong. To cater for the sexual needs of the garrison, a series of VD-policing legislations and regulations were introduced. These measures were subjected to continuous attack from moralists at home and on the spot; they were eventually abolished. Indeed, they were never as effective as their advocates claimed.

The experience of the troops stationed in Hong Kong was highly diverse at different times. For the early garrison, a tour of duty in Hong Kong was highly risky; the death toll was high. As Hong Kong developed, it gradually became a much better place for soldiers, especially during the interwar period, as the global drop in the price of silver greatly enhanced their buying power. The emergence of places such as Wan Chai as red light districts also provided much opportunity for soldiers and sailors to spend their surplus income. For those who enjoyed sports and sailing, Hong Kong was a great place to stay, as the memoirs and contemporary writings of soldiers reveal. Before the Second World War, the European soldiers lived in a largely separate world from their Chinese and Indian colleagues. The rigid class structure of the Victorian and Edwardian periods also ensured that officers and men lived in separate spheres. After the Second World War, however, racial and class barriers gradually broke down; the number of Chinese serving in the British military increased significantly. In addition, the long history of Indian military service in Hong Kong must not be overlooked. Indian sepoys were among the first recruited; they formed a significant part of the garrison until the end of the colonial period. Indian soldiers fought with determination during the Japanese invasion; after the war, the Gurkhas were responsible for the security of the colony for decades. The story of their experience in Hong Kong certainly deserves further study.

Summary

This book suggests that Hong Kong was strategically important in the history of East Asia from the mid-19th century to the 1970s. Hong Kong was also an indispensable part of the history of British imperial defence until the practical end of the British Empire. The British used Hong Kong first as a strategic springboard for extending their influence in Asia, later as a means for maintaining a presence when they were forced to shift focus back to Europe and the Middle East. The long presence of a sizeable British armed force was by no means irrelevant in the history of Hong Kong, despite the city being more commonly known for its economic development. Thus, without an adequate appreciation of its military past, it is impossible to understand fully the history of the ex-colony and its role in the international relations of the 19th and 20th centuries.

Appendices

Appendix I: Bibliographical Review

This book is built upon the rich literature about the military history of Hong Kong. It is, above all, inspired by the comprehensive study by Brian Farrell, John Miksic, Malcolm Murfett, and Chiang Ming Shun on the military history of Singapore, a place that shared much similarity with Hong Kong in terms of historical experience.[1] Although a comprehensive study of the military history of Hong Kong is needed, there are numerous works on the garrison, on military structures and battles. For example, Kathleen Harland's *The Royal Navy in Hong Kong* and Commodore Peter Melson's *White Ensign—Red Dragon* chronicle in great detail the life and operation of the Royal Navy in Hong Kong, from the establishment of the colony to the handover.[2] Gerald Graham's *China Station* discusses in detail the often problematic British naval presence in the China seas.[3] Donald Oxley's *Victoria Barracks*, Alan Harfield's *British and Indian Armies on the China Coast* and Dennis Rollo's *Guns and Gunners of Hong Kong* all record the Army's presence.[4] Gordon Alderson's *History of Royal Air Force Kai Tak* provides a complete narrative of the RAF's history well until the 1970s.[5] The book *Second to None* by Phillip Bruce narrates the illustrious history of the Hong Kong Volunteer Defence Corps (later, Hong Kong Regiment) from its inception in 1854 to disbandment in 1995.[6]

Among these works, Dennis Rollo's *Guns and Gunners* comes close to being a military history of Hong Kong. It traces the history of the coastal and anti-air batteries and the Royal Artillery units in Hong Kong throughout the colonial period. However, as it looks exclusively at the artillery, many gaps remain in the narrative of Hong Kong military history, especially in the planning and policy aspects.[7]

As the largest battle ever fought in Hong Kong, the Japanese invasion of December 1941 and the subsequent resistance operations have received much attention. Two of the early and more popular English works on the topic are *The Fall of Hong Kong* by Tim Carew and *Hong Kong Eclipse* by George Endacott, who passed away before his work was completed.[8] In addition, as two Canadian battalions participated in the battle and suffered much hardship as captives, the Canadian government's decision to dispatch the battalions and their operations during the battle have been intensively debated. From the 1980s, a school emerged in Canada, championed by Carl Vincent's *No Reason Why* and the documentary *The Valour and the Horror*, suggesting that, with full knowledge of the desperate position of Hong Kong, the British misled the Canadians into sending reinforcements to the colony, while the Canadian military and government showed great negligence in handling the affair.[9] Subsequent works such as *C Force to Hong Kong* largely follow this discourse.[10] The thesis was not challenged until a new generation of scholars from Britain and Canada—such as Christopher Bell, Galen Roger Perras and Kent Fedorowich—critically examined British and Canadian archival sources concerning the events.[11] Recently, Franco David Macri's work about the international situation before the outbreak of the Pacific War and Hong Kong's role in Allied strategy has shed much new light on the events preceding December 1941.[12]

A new wave of works about the Battle of Hong Kong have appeared in the last two decades, the most important being *Not the Slightest Chance: The Defence of Hong Kong* by Tony Banham, *The Battle for Hong Kong* by Colonel Oliver Lindsay and *The Damned* by Nathan Greenfield.[13] They have exhausted the British archival and oral sources and presented a complete picture of the battle from British and Canadian perspectives. However, the contexts of the battle have received relatively little attention, and Japanese sources have been largely overlooked. Philip Snow's *The Fall of Hong Kong* tries to put the battle and the Japanese occupation in a larger historical context, and his work reveals the complexity of pre-war Hong Kong society.[14] Nonetheless, even Snow does not discuss the role of Hong Kong in British strategic planning and imperial defence policy. There are also a number of Chinese works about Hong Kong during the Second World War, such as *The Fall of Hong Kong* (香港淪陷) and *The Dramatic Story of Hong Kong's Anti-Japanese Resistance* (香港抗日風雲錄) by Xie Yongguang.[15] As for the resistance movement during the occupation, *BAAG: Hong Kong Resistance* by Edwin Ride (a descendant of Lindsay Ride) and *East River Column* by Chan Sui-jeung meticulously study the two organizations and the lives of the resistance fighters during and after the war.[16]

There are a number of studies about the military events of Hong Kong during the colonial period. Through a detailed study of the novel *The Back Door*, Gillian Bickley in *Hong Kong Invaded* discusses the prevailing fear among residents of Hong Kong about its defence during the late 19th century.[17] Patrick Hase's *The Six-Day War of 1899* reconstructs the "small war" fought in the New Territories in 1899.[18] A number of articles in *Modern Chinese Naval History: New Perspectives*, edited by Lee Kam Keung, and another compilation by Ma Yau-woon deal with Hong

Kong-related issues such as the Royal Navy vessels captured by the Japanese during the Battle of Hong Kong.[19] The *Journal of Royal Asiatic Society Hong Kong Branch* also features a number of articles about local military history and heritage.[20] As for the military history of Hong Kong during the Cold War, Mark Chi-kwan's *Hong Kong and the Cold War* uses British and American sources to illustrate the changing consideration of Britain and the United States towards the strategic function and defensibility of the colony.[21] From the 2000s, Lai Wai Chung, Ho Chi Wing and their research team have used aerial photographs and fieldwork results to study the surviving military structures of Hong Kong. They have reconstructed the layout of the Gin Drinker's Line, which is supported by archival research conducted by the authors of this work.[22] Rob Weir's work, in turn, has rediscovered the "Kowloon landward defence line" built during the 1910s.

This work is aided by numerous works on British military history. For example, Donald Schurman's *Imperial Defence* and subsequent works such as *Far Flung Lines* outline the emergence of the concept of imperial defence and the institutions responsible for the formation of British defence policies.[23] David Edgerton and George Paden have challenged the thesis of irreversible decline of the British military after the First World War and highlighted the real strengths and weaknesses of the British war machine during the interwar period.[24] Richard Aldrich's *Intelligence and the War against Japan* reconstructs the British intelligence apparatus in Asia during the interwar period and discusses in detail the reason for the failure of the British to react decisively when Japan attacked in December 1941.[25]

Appendix II: British Command Structure in Hong Kong

The British Army and Royal Navy have had a long history of cooperation. The policies of the two forces were coordinated by cabinet committees such as the Colonial Defence Committee, on which the two services had almost equal representation. Before the RAF Far East Command was established in 1930, the army and navy had separate command structures in Asia. It was not until the late 1940s that the three services came under the same Commander-in-Chief of the Far East.

Royal Navy units in China and Hong Kong were controlled by the East Indies and China Station before the establishment of the China Station in 1865. The local naval force, responsible for the defence of the colony rather than the larger area, was organized as the Hong Kong Flotilla. The areas under the China Station's responsibility included not only Hong Kong and the China coast, but also the waters stretching from Singapore to Vladivostok. Soon after the outbreak of the Pacific War in December 1941, the Eastern Fleet was formed; its commander, Vice Admiral

Thomas Philips, also commanded the China Station. The Eastern Fleet was forced to withdraw into the Indian Ocean after the destruction of HMS *Prince of Wales* and the fall of Singapore; it did not re-enter the Pacific until 1944. After the war, the China Station was not revived. The highest Royal Navy command in Asia was the Far Eastern Squadron. The Hong Kong Squadron, however, was revived and existed until the 1990s.

The command structure of the British Army in Asia was similar to that of the Royal Navy. After the Opium War, the Eastern Expeditionary Force was abolished. The Hong Kong garrison was commanded by the GOC British Forces in Hong Kong. Between 1854 and 1869, as British forces were active in different parts of China, the command was renamed China and Hong Kong Command. It was further expanded to cover the Straits Settlements and became the GOC British Troops in China, Hong Kong and the Straits Settlements until 1889, when defence schemes were created by the individual colonies. After the leasing of Weihaiwei in 1898 and the Boxer War of 1900, the British garrisoned at Beijing, Tianjin, Weihaiwei and Shanghai. In 1904, the China Command was split into two, with the above-mentioned garrisons reorganized under a North China Command. The units in Hong Kong and Shanghai were organized into a South China Command. Both commands reported directly to the War Office. When most of the units under the two commands were sent elsewhere during the First World War, the two commands merged in 1915 and became the China Command. The arrangement was reversed only in 1925–1932, when the situation in China required increased British military presence. Thus, in 1941, the formal title of Major General Christopher Maltby was GOC British Troops in China.

After the Second World War, the command system was again changed. A new command, British Forces in Hong Kong, was established, headed invariably by a general officer of the army. This reflected the small British naval presence in the Western Pacific and the decreased importance of Hong Kong as a naval base.

Appendix III: British Army Commanders at Hong Kong, 1843–1960

Name	Chinese Name	Rank	Terms
General Officer Commanding, British Forces in Hong Kong			
George D'Aguilar	德己立	Maj. Gen.	1843–1848
William Staveley	士他花利	Maj. Gen.	1848–1851
William Jervois	乍畏	Maj. Gen.	1851–1854
General Officer Commanding, British Troops in China and Hong Kong			
Robert Garrett	賈勵	Maj. Gen.	1854–1857
Thomas Ashburnham	亞士本含	Maj. Gen.	1857–1858

Name	Chinese Name	Rank	Terms
Charles van Straubenzee	士都本	Maj. Gen.	1858–1859
James Hope Grant	克靈頓	Maj. Gen.	1860–1861
John Michel	米曹	Maj. Gen.	1861–1862
Charles Staveley	士他花利	Maj. Gen.	1862–1863
William Brown	布朗	Maj. Gen.	1863–1864
Philip Guy	佳菲臘	Maj. Gen.	1864–1867
James Brunker	布倫嘉	Maj. Gen.	1867–1869

General Officer Commanding, British Troops in China, Hong Kong and the Straits Settlements

Name	Chinese Name	Rank	Terms
Henry Whitfield	威菲路	Maj. Gen.	1869–1874
Francis Colborne	哥布倫	Lt. Gen.	1874–1878
Edward Donovan	唐樂文	Lt. Gen.	1878–1882
John Sargent	沙真	Lt. Gen.	1882–1885
William Cameron	金馬倫	Lt. Gen.	1885–1889

General Officer Commanding, British Troops in China and Hong Kong

Name	Chinese Name	Rank	Terms
James Edwards	愛德華茲	Maj. Gen.	1889–1890
George Barker	白加	Maj. Gen.	1890–1895
Wilsone Black	布力	Maj. Gen.	1895–1898
William Gascoigne	加士居	Maj. Gen.	1898–1903

General Officer Commanding, British Troops in South China

Name	Chinese Name	Rank	Terms
Villiers Hatton	克頓	Maj. Gen.	1904–1906
Robert Broadwood	樂活	Maj. Gen.	1906–1910
Charles Anderson	晏打臣	Maj. Gen.	1910–1913
Francis Kelly	祁利	Maj. Gen.	1913–1915

General Officer Commanding, British Forces in China

Name	Chinese Name	Rank	Terms
Francis Ventris	雲地利	Maj. Gen.	1915–1921
George Kirkpatrick	祁柏卓	Maj. Gen.	1921–1922
John Fowler	科拿	Maj. Gen.	1922–1925

General Officer Commanding, British Troops in South China

Name	Chinese Name	Rank	Terms
Charles Luard	盧押	Maj. Gen.	1925–1929
James Sandilands	山打倫	Maj. Gen.	1929–1932

General Officer Commanding, British Troops in China

Name	Chinese Name	Rank	Terms
Oswald Borrett	波老	Lt. Gen.	1932–1935
Arthur Bartholomew	巴度苗	Maj. Gen.	1935–1938
Edward Grasett	賈乃錫	Maj. Gen.	1938–1941
Christopher Maltby	莫德庇	Maj. Gen.	1941

General Officer Commanding, British Troops in Hong Kong

Name	Chinese Name	Rank	Terms
Francis Festing	菲士廷	Maj. Gen.	1945–1947
George Erskine	區士覲	Maj. Gen.	1947–1948
Francis Matthews	馬調士	Maj. Gen.	1948–1949

General Officer Commanding, British Forces in Hong Kong

Name	Chinese Name	Rank	Terms
Francis Festing	菲士廷	Lt. Gen.	1949

Name	Chinese Name	Rank	Terms
Robert Mansergh	孟沙	Maj. Gen.	1949–1951
Geoffrey Evans	伊雲士	Maj. Gen.	1951–1952
Terence Airey	魏宜禮	Maj. Gen.	1952–1954
Cecil Sugden	蘇登	Lt. Gen.	1954–1955
William Stratton	史德頓	Lt. Gen.	1955–1957
Edric Bastyan	巴斯田	Lt. Gen.	1957–1960
Roderick McLeod	麥堅樂	Lt. Gen.	1960–1961
Reginald Hewetson	許偉信	Lt. Gen.	1961–1963
Richard Craddock	賈禮達	Lt. Gen.	1963–1964
Denis O'Connor	區金諾	Lt. Gen.	1964–1966
John Worsley	華智禮	Lt. Gen.	1966–1968
Basil Eugster	余智韜	Lt. Gen.	1968–1970

Appendix IV: Commanders of China Station, 1865–1941

Name	Chinese Name	Rank	Terms
George King	佐治京	Vice Adm.	1865–1867
Henry Keppel	加普	Vice Adm.	1867–1869
Henry Kellett	奇力	Vice Adm.	1869–1871
Charles Shadwell	沙維	Vice Adm.	1871–1874
Alfred Ryder	賴德	Vice Adm.	1874–1877
Charles Hillyar	曉義雅	Vice Adm.	1877–1878
Robert Coote	古德	Vice Adm.	1878–1881
George Willes	威利士	Vice Adm.	1881–1884
William Dowell	道維	Vice Adm.	1884–1885
Richard Hamilton	咸美頓	Vice Adm.	1885–1887
Nowell Salmon	沙文	Vice Adm.	1887–1890
Frederick Richards	李察士	Vice Adm.	1890–1892
Edmund Fremantle	飛文度	Vice Adm.	1892–1895
Alexander Buller	布拿	Vice Adm.	1895–1897
Edward Seymour	西摩	Vice Adm.	1897–1901
Cyprian Bridge	比力治	Vice Adm.	1901–1904
Gerard Noel	路維	Vice Adm.	1904–1906
Arthur Moore	摩亞	Vice Adm.	1906–1908
Hedworth Meux*	藍敦*	Vice Adm.	1908–1910
Alfred Winsloe	溫士勞	Vice Adm.	1910–1913
Martyn Jerram	謝南	Vice Adm.	1913–1915
William Grant	賈蘭	Vice Adm.	1916–1917
Frederick Tudor	都鐸	Rear Adm.	1917–1919
Alexander Duff	達夫	Vice Adm.	1919–1922

Name	Chinese Name	Rank	Terms
Arthur Leveson	李維信	Adm.	1922–1924
Allan Everett	艾華禮	Rear Adm.	1924–1925
David Anderson	安達臣	Rear Adm.	1925
Edwyn Alexander-Sinclair	冼克萊	Vice Adm.	1925–1926
Reginald Tyrwhitt	特韋希	Vice Adm.	1926–1928
Arthur Waistell	偉思圖	Vice Adm.	1928–1931
Howard Kelly	祁利	Vice Adm.	1931–1933
Frederic Dreyer	戴爾	Adm.	1933–1936
Charles Little	李度	Vice Adm.	1936–1938
Percy Noble	紐寶璐	Adm.	1938–1940
Geoffrey Layton	李頓	Vice Adm.	1940–1941
Tom Philips	湯菲力	Vice Adm.	1941

* His original name was Hedworth Lambton.

Notes

1 Introduction

1. From Chow Kai Wing, "Shijiu shiji Zhongguo waijiaoguan lun Xianggang zai haifang shang de zhongyaoxing" [The Importance of Hong Kong in Coastal Defence according to the Chinese Diplomats of the 19th century], *Jindai Zhongguo haifang guoji yantaohui* (Hong Kong: The Chinese University of Hong Kong, 1998), p. 4.
2. "Hong Kong Defence Scheme, Revised to June 1910," CAB 11/57, p. 8.
3. Chow, "Shijiu shiji Zhongguo waijiaoguan lun Xianggang zai haifang shang zhi zhongyaoxing," p. 4.
4. "Hong Kong Defence Scheme, Revised to June 1901," CAB 11/57, p. 14.
5. Not to be confused with the Lin Fa Shan of Lantau Island.
6. "Notes on the Garrison Required," WO 32/5316, p. 9.
7. "Hong Kong Defence Scheme, Revised to June 1910," CAB 11/57, p. 4.

2 A British Foothold in China, 1839–1861

1. A balanced reappraisal of the Opium War was written by Julia Lovell in 2012. See Julia Lovell, *The Opium War: Drugs, Dreams and the Making of China* (London: Picador, 2012). In 1808, during the Napoleonic War, the British also tried to seize Macao but abandoned the scheme because of Portuguese and Qing opposition. See Frederic Wakeman, Jr., "Drury's Occupation of Macau and China's Responses to Early Modern Imperialism," *East Asian Studies*, No. 28 (2004), pp. 27–34.
2. Yu Shengwu and Liu Cunkuan, *Shijiu shiji de Xianggang* [Hong Kong in the 19th century] (Beijing: Zhongguo shehui kexue chubanshe, 2007), p. 27.
3. Gerald Graham, *The China Station: War and Diplomacy 1830–1860* (Oxford: Clarendon Press, 1978), pp. 12–14.
4. Susanna Hoe and Derek Roebuck, *The Taking of Hong Kong: Charles and Clara Elliot in China Waters* (Hong Kong: Hong Kong University Press, 2009), p. 151.
5. Alan Harfield, *British and Indian Armies on the China Coast, 1785–1965* (London: A and J Partnership, 1990), p. 11.
6. Ibid., p. 28.
7. John Carroll, *A Concise History of Hong Kong* (Lanham, MD: Rowman & Littlefield, 2007), p. 20.
8. Peter Melson, *White Ensign—Red Dragon: The History of the Royal Navy in Hong Kong, 1841–1997* (Hong Kong: Edinburgh Financial Publishing [Asia], 1997), p. 6; Denis

Rollo, *The Guns and Gunners of Hong Kong* (Hong Kong: The Gunners Roll of Hong Kong, 1991), p. 8.

9. Rollo, *Guns and Gunners of Hong Kong*, p. 10.

10. Harfield, *British and Indian Armies on the China Coast*, pp. 41–2; Rollo, *Guns and Gunners of Hong Kong*, p. 10.

11. Harfield, *British and Indian Armies on the China Coast*, pp. 39, 47.

12. Melson, *White Ensign—Red Dragon*, pp. 6, 26.

13. Based on the map in Rollo, *Guns and Gunners of Hong Kong*, p. 10.

14. Harfield, *British and Indian Armies on the China Coast*, p. 43.

15. Phillip Bruce, *Second to None: The Story of the Hong Kong Volunteers* (Hong Kong, New York: Oxford University Press, 1991), p. 4.

16. Christopher Munn, *Anglo-China: Chinese People and British Rule in Hong Kong, 1841–1880* (Hong Kong: Hong Kong University Press, 2009), p. 60.

17. Patricia Lim, *Forgotten Souls: A Social History of the Hong Kong Cemetery* (Hong Kong: Hong Kong University Press, 2011), pp. 251–5.

18. Frank Welsh, *A History of Hong Kong* (London: HarperCollins, 1997), p. 261.

19. "Hong Kong Annual Administration Report, 1869," in R. L. Jarman, *Hong Kong Annual Administration Reports, 1841–1941*, Vol. 1 (Farnham Common: Archive Editions, 1996), p. 351.

20. Norman Miners, *Hong Kong Under Imperial Rule: 1912–1941* (Hong Kong: Oxford University Press, 1987), p. 191.

21. "Hong Kong Annual Administration Report, 1869," in Jarman, *Hong Kong Annual Administration Reports, 1841–1941*, Vol. 1, p. 351.

22. *Irish University Press Area Studies Series, British Parliamentary Papers. China, Vol. 28* (Shannon: Irish University Press, 1971), pp. 553–4.

23. Quoted from George Endacott, *A Biographical Sketch-book of Early Hong Kong* (Hong Kong: Hong Kong University Press, 2005), p. xvii (Introduction by John Carroll).

24. Kanwal Vaid, *The Overseas Indian Community in Hong Kong* (Hong Kong: Centre of Asian Studies, the University of Hong Kong, 1972).

25. Quoted from Wong Kam C., *Policing in Hong Kong* (Farnham, Surrey; Burlington, VT: Ashgate, 2012).

26. Lim, *Forgotten Souls*, p. 255.

27. Graham, *The China Station: War and Diplomacy 1830–1860*, p. 267.

28. Rebecca Berens Matzke, *Deterrence through Strength: British Naval Power and Foreign Policy under Pax Britannica* (Lincoln: University of Nebraska Press, 2011), pp. vii–viii, 105–53.

29. Ibid., pp. 254–75, 296–7.

30. Rollo, *Guns and Gunners of Hong Kong*, p. 11.

31. *The Navy List: Corrected to the 20th June, 1848* (London: John Murray, 1848), pp. 115–54.

32. Paul Kennedy, *The Rise and Fall of British Naval Mastery* (London: A. Lane, 1976), p. 180.

33. Douglas Sellick, *Pirate Outrages: True Stories of Terror on the China Seas* (Fremantle, WA: Fremantle Press, 2010), pp. 64–5; A. D. Blue, "Piracy on the China Coast," *JRASHK*, Vol. 5 (1965), pp. 74–5.

34. Sellick, *Pirate Outrages*, pp. 70–4.

35. Melson, *White Ensign—Red Dragon*, pp. 20–3; for a detailed account of the Water Police, see Iain Ward, *Sui Geng: The Hong Kong Marine Police 1841–1950* (Hong Kong: Hong Kong University Press, 1991).

36. Rollo, *Guns and Gunners of Hong Kong*, pp. 15–7.

37. Bruce, *Second to None*, p. 5.

38. Ibid., p. 12.

39. Graham, *The China Station: War and Diplomacy 1830–1860*, pp. 291–2.

40. Bruce, *Second to None*, p. 11.

41. Rollo, *Guns and Gunners of Hong Kong*, p. 21.

42. Ibid., p. 23.

43. Bruce, *Second to None*, p. 25.

44. Ibid., pp. 25–6, 37–40.

45. Graham, *The China Station: War and Diplomacy 1830–1860*, pp. 285–6.

46. Cai Rongfang, *The Hong Kong People's History of Hong Kong* (Hong Kong: Oxford University Press, 2001), p. 34.

47. Bruce, *Second to None*, p. 32.

48. Harfield, *British and Indian Armies on the China Coast*, p. 84.

49. Ibid., pp. 143–5.

50. Government of India, *Frontier and Overseas Expeditions from India*, Vol. 4 (Government of India, 1911), pp. 443–4.

51. Harfield, *British and Indian Armies on the China Coast*, p. 149.

3 Hong Kong in an Imperial Defence System, 1861–1883

1. Alan Harfield, *British and Indian Armies on the China Coast, 1785–1965* (London: A and J Partnership, 1990), pp. 147–8.

2. Matthew Perry, *Narrative of the Expedition to the China Seas and Japan, 1852–1854* (Mineola, NY: Dover Publications, 2000).

3. Kemp Tolley, *Yangtze Patrol: The U.S. Navy in China* (Annapolis: Naval Institute Press, 1971), p. 26; Robert Johnson, *Far China Station: The U.S. Navy in Asian Waters, 1800–1898* (Annapolis: Naval Institute Press, 1979), p. 126.

4. Yu Shengwu and Liu Cunkuan, *Shijiu shiji de Xianggang* [Hong Kong in the 19th century] (Beijing: Zhongguo shehui kexue chubanshe, 2007), pp. 87–8.

5. See the map in Denis Rollo, *The Guns and Gunners of Hong Kong* (Hong Kong: The Gunners Roll of Hong Kong, 1991), p. 23.

6. Tang Kaijian, Shao Guojian and Chen Jierong (eds.), *6000 Years of Hong Kong History, Prehistory to 1997* (Hong Kong: Qilun, 1998), pp. 143, 147.

7. *The Hong Kong Government Gazette*, 10/9/1864, p. 324.

8. "Question," 6/3/1865, HC Deb 06 March 1865, *UK Historical Hansard*, Vol. 177, p. 1119. From UK Parliament website, http://hansard.millbanksystems.com/commons/1865/mar/06/question-5#S3V0177P0_18650306_HOC_25

9. "Report on Contagious Disease Ordinance," 11/3/1880, *Irish University Press Area Studies Series, British Parliamentary Papers: China*, Vol. 25 (Shannon: Irish University Press, 1971–1972), p. 551.

10. Phillip Bruce, *Second to None: The Story of the Hong Kong Volunteers* (Hong Kong, New York: Oxford University Press, 1991), pp. 38–9.

11. "Annual Return for the 2nd Battalion, 9th Regiment of Foot, Station, Hong Kong," 1/11866, *Irish University Press Area Studies Series, British Parliamentary Papers: China*, Vol. 28 (Shannon: Irish University Press, 1971–1972), p. 444.

12. James Norton-Kyshe, *The History of the Laws and Courts of Hong Kong from the Earliest Period to 1898* (Hong Kong: Vetch and Lee, 1971), pp. 103–4.

13. *Irish University Press Area Studies Series, British Parliamentary Papers: China*, Vol. 28, p. 90.

14. Donald Mackenzie Schurman, *Imperial Defence, 1868–1887* (London; Portland, OR: Frank Cass, 2000), p. 5.

15. A recent study of the transformation of the military during this period is James Hevia, *The Imperial Security State: British Colonial Knowledge and Empire-Building in Asia* (Cambridge: Cambridge University Press, 2012).

16. John Charles Ready Colomb, *The Defence of Great and Greater Britain: Sketches of Its Naval, Military and Political Aspects (1880)* (London: Eilbron, 2005), p. 106.

17. "Observations," 26/5/1865, HC Deb 26 May 1865, *UK Historical Hansard*, Vol. 179, p. 906. From UK Parliament website, http://hansard.millbanksystems.com/commons/1865/may/26/observations#S3V0179P0_18650526_HOC_61

18. Rollo, *Guns and Gunners*, p. 35.

19. Ibid.

20. Schurman, *Imperial Defence*, p. 50.

21. Ibid., p. 54.

22. "Report of a Colonial Defence Committee on the Temporary Defences of the Cape of Good Hope, Mauritius, Ceylon, Singapore and Hong Kong," 4/1878, CAB 7/1, p. 1.

23. Ibid., p. 1.

24. Ibid., p. 13.

25. Ibid.

26. Ibid., pp. 13–4.

27. Based on the description of "Report," 4/1878, CAB 7/1.

28. Steve Tsang, *A Modern History of Hong Kong* (Hong Kong: Hong Kong University Press, 2004), p. 65.

29. "Governor Hennessy, C. M. G., to the Right Hon. Sir M. E. Hicks Beach," 11/5/1878, "Further Correspondence Respecting the Defences of the Colonies," CAB 7/1, p. 89.

30. Ibid.

31. Ibid., pp. 98–9.

32. "Governor Hennessy, C. M. G., to the Right Hon. Sir M. E. Hicks Beach," 18/5/1878, "Further Correspondence," CAB 7/1, pp. 106–7.

33. "CO to WO," 30/6/1878, "Further Correspondence," CAB 7/1, p. 106.

34. "Admiralty to CO," 27/6/1878, "Further Correspondence," CAB 7/1, p. 105.

35. *Irish University Press Area Studies Series, British Parliamentary Papers: China*, Vol. 28, p. 90.

36. "Governor Hennessy to Sir M. Hicks Beach," 6/3/1880, CAB 7/4, p. 302.

37. "Governor Hennessy, C. M. G., to the Right Hon. Sir M. E. Hicks Beach," 24/5/1878, "Further Correspondence," CAB 7/1, p. 125.

38. "Governor Hennessy, C. M. G., to the Right Hon. Sir M. E. Hicks Beach," 16/7/1878, "Further Correspondence," CAB 7/1, p. 173.

39. "Foreign Office to Colonial Office," 17/10/1878, "Further Correspondence," CAB 7/1, pp. 194–5.

40. "WO to CO," 8/1/1879, "Further Correspondence," CAB 7/1, p. 2; "CO to WO," 8/2/1879, "Further Correspondence," CAB 7/1, p. 10; "WO to CO," 19/4/1879, "Further Correspondence," CAB 7/1, p. 23.

41. "Governor Hennessy, C. M. G., to the Right Hon. Sir M. E. Hicks Beach," 22/7/1878, "Further Correspondence," CAB 7/1, p. 132.

42. "Governor Hennessy, C. M. G., to the Right Hon. Sir M. E. Hicks Beach," 15/7/1878, "Further Correspondence," CAB 7/1, p. 173; "Governor Hennessy, C. M. G., to the Right Hon. Sir M. E. Hicks Beach," 16/7/1878, "Further Correspondence," CAB 7/1, p. 173; "Answer of Governor Pope Hennessy," 16/12/1879, CAB 7/4, p. 301.

43. "Report of a Colonial Defence Committee on the Temporary Defences of the Cape of Good Hope, Mauritius, Ceylon, Singapore and Hong Kong," 4/1878, CAB 7/1, p. 16.

44. Ibid.

45. Schurman, *Imperial Defence*, p. 86.

46. Ibid., p. 89.

47. "Third and Final Report of the Royal Commissioners Appointed to Inquire Into the Defence of British Possessions and Commerce Abroad," 1882, CAB 7/4, pp. 28–9.

48. "War Office Memorandum on the Defences of Hong Kong," 21/10/1879, revised in 23/12/1880, CAB 7/4, pp. 341–3.

49. "Report of Local Committee on Defences of Hong Kong," 11/10/1881, CAB 7/4, pp. 330–5.

50. "Colonel Crossman, R. E. to the Inspector-General of Fortification, on the Defence of Hong Kong," 24/10/1881, CAB 7/4, pp. 316–21.

51. Based on the description of "Colonel Crossman, R. E. to the Inspector-General of Fortification, on the Defence of Hong Kong," 24/10/1881, CAB 7/4.

52. "Third and Final Report of the Royal Commissioners Appointed to Inquire Into the Defence of British Possessions and Commerce Abroad," 1882, CAB 7/4, p. 15.

53. Ibid., pp. 15–7.

54. Peter Melson, *White Ensign—Red Dragon: The History of the Royal Navy in Hong Kong, 1841–1997* (Hong Kong: Edinburgh Financial Publishing [Asia], 1997), p. 35.

55. "Governor Hennessy to Sir M. Hicks Beach," 6/3/1880, CAB 7/4, p. 302.

56. Tang, Shao and Chen (eds.), *6000 Years of Hong Kong History*, p. 207.

57. "Governor Hennessy to Sir M. Hicks Beach," 16/3/1880, CAB 7/4, p. 306.

58. "Colonel Gordon to Governor Sir J. P. Hennessy," 4/7/1880, CAB 7/4, pp. 309–10.

59. "WO to CO", 30/6/1880, "Further Correspondence," CAB 7/1, p. 308.

60. Launched in 1870; 6,100 tons, armed with ten 9-inch RMLs.

61. Launched in 1877; 5,600 tons, armed with two 10-inch RMLs and seven 9-inch RMLs.

62. John Beeler, "Steam, Strategy and Shurman: Imperial Defence in the Post Crimean Era, 1856–1905," in Greg Kennedy and Keith Neilson (eds.), *Far Flung Lines: Essays on Imperial Defence in Honour of Donald Mackenzie Shurman* (London: Frank Cass, 1997), p. 44.

63. *Brassey's Naval Annual, 1887* (Portsmouth: J. Griffin & Co., 1887), pp. 135–9.

4 Hong Kong Defence during the Age of Empires, 1883–1919

1. "Naval Commander-in-Chief to Governor," 25/11/2908, CAB 38/17/4, p. 22.
2. "Dai ichi kantai Honkon, Kamon, Shōsanho nikeru chōsa hōkoku" [The First Fleet's Report on Hong Kong, Xiamen, and Xiangshanpu], 1910, Kaigunshō kōbun bikō (KKB), The National Institute for Defense Studies Archive (NIDS), Japan Center for Asian Historical Record (JACAR), Ref: C06092361800.
3. *Jane's Fighting Ships of World War I* (London: Studio Editions, 1990).
4. Ming K. Chan and John Young, *Precarious Balance: Hong Kong between China and Britain, 1842–1992* (Hong Kong: Hong Kong University Press, 1994), pp. 17–9.
5. Donald Dyal et al., *Historical Dictionary of the Spanish American War* (Westport, CT: Greenwood Press, 1996), p. 161; Robert Johnson, *Far China Station: The U.S. Navy in Asian Waters, 1800–1898* (Annapolis: Naval Institute Press, 1979), p. 258.
6. Chan Lau Kit-ching, *China, Britain and Hong Kong 1895–1945* (Hong Kong: The Chinese University Press, 1990), pp. 19–106.
7. Spencer Tucker, *The Encyclopedia of Spanish-American and Philippine-American Wars: A Political, Social, and Military History*, Vol. 1 (Santa Barbara: ABC-CLIO, 2009), p. 291.
8. For the development of the planning branches in the Royal Navy during the period, see Shawn Grimes, *Strategy and War Planning in the British Royal Navy, 1887–1918* (Woodbridge: Boydell, 2012), pp. 7–41.
9. David French, "The British Army and the Empire, 1856–1956," in Greg Kennedy (ed.), *Imperial Defence: The Old World Order, 1856–1956* (Abingdon: Routledge, 2008), p. 99.
10. *Brassey's Naval Annual, 1902* (Portsmouth: J. Griffin & Co., 1902), p. 438.
11. "Despatch Respecting Military Contribution, Presented to the Legislative Council, by Command of His Excellency the Governor, on 30th April, 1891," *Hong Kong Government Sessional Papers*, 1891, p. 193.
12. Norman Miners, *Hong Kong Under Imperial Rule: 1912–1941* (Hong Kong: Oxford University Press, 1987), p. 103.
13. Ibid., p. 105.
14. "Financial Returns," *The Hong Kong Government Gazette*, 1892–1917.
15. Frank Welsh, *A History of Hong Kong* (London: HarperCollins, 1997), p. 263.
16. Miners, *Hong Kong Under Imperial Rule*, pp. 193–4.
17. "Vice-Admiral to Governor," 11/4/1896, CO 129/271, slide 644.
18. Welsh, *A History of Hong Kong*, p. 265; Miners, *Hong Kong Under Imperial Rule*, p. 196.
19. "Dai ichi kantai Honkon, Kamon, Shōsanho nikeru chōsa hōkoku," 1910, Kaigunshō kōbun bikō (KKB), The National Institute for Defense Studies Archive (NIDS), Japan Center for Asian Historical Record (JACAR), Ref: C06092361300.
20. "WO to CO," 26/7/1879, *The Hong Kong Government Gazette*, 16/10/1880, p. 819.
21. "Report on the Victoria Gaol," *Hong Kong Government Sessional Papers*, 1901, p. 25.
22. "Report on the Victoria Gaol," *Hong Kong Government Sessional Papers* (1901–1908); "Report of the Superintendent of Prison," *Annual Report* (1909–1913).
23. John Carroll, *A Concise History of Hong Kong* (Lanham, MD: Rowman & Littlefield, 2007), pp. 42–3.
24. Yang Bafan and Yang Xing'an, *Yang Quyun jia zhuan* (Hong Kong: Xintian chuban, 2010).

25. Harfield, *British and Indian Armies on the China Coast*, pp. 174–7; Donald Oxley (ed.), *Victoria Barracks, 1842–1979* (Hong Kong: British Forces Hong Kong, 1979), pp. 44–5.

26. Oxley (ed.), *Victoria Barracks*, p. 46.

27. Alan Harfield, *British and Indian Armies on the China Coast, 1785–1965* (London: A and J Partnership, 1990), pp. 315–6.

28. Harfield, *British and Indian Armies on the China Coast*, p. 206; *The Royal Engineers Journal*, Vol. 56 (1942), p. 96.

29. *The Star*, 8/9/1900; "Hong Kong Coy Royal Engineers," China 1900, WO 100/95;

30. Kathleen Harland, *The Royal Navy in Hong Kong, 1841–1980* (Hong Kong: Royal Navy 1981), pp. 20–38.

31. Peter Melson, *White Ensign—Red Dragon: The History of the Royal Navy in Hong Kong, 1841–1997* (Hong Kong: Edinburgh Financial Publishing [Asia], 1997), p. 45.

32. Harfield, *British and Indian Armies on the China Coast*, p. 187.

33. *Brassey's Naval Annual*, 1899.

34. Denis Rollo, *The Guns and Gunners of Hong Kong* (Hong Kong: The Gunners Roll of Hong Kong, 1991), p. 49.

35. Ibid., pp. 46–7.

36. Map based on the description in Rollo, *Guns and Gunners of Hong Kong*, pp. 46–7.

37. Ibid., pp. 50–2.

38. "Report on the Defences of Hong Kong, by Lieutenant-Colonel C. H. Fairfax Ellis, R. A. and Lieutenant-Colonel G. Barker, R. E.," 30/7/1886, CAB 11/57.

39. "Despatch Respecting the Proposed Defence Works," 1/1886, *Hong Kong Government Sessional Papers*, 1886.

40. "Hong Kong: Report on the Blue Book and Departmental Reports for 1889," *Hong Kong Government Sessional Papers*, 1889; "Hong Kong: Report on the Blue Book and Departmental Reports for 1892," *Hong Kong Government Sessional Papers*, 1892.

41. Rollo, *Guns and Gunners of Hong Kong*, pp. 54–5.

42. "Hong Kong: Report of Local Joint Naval and Military Committee of April 1894," 27/7/1894, CAB 11/57; "Hong Kong: Report of Local Joint Naval and Military Committee of July 1895," 27/7/1894, CAB 11/57.

43. Edwyn Gray, *Nineteenth-Century Torpedoes and Their Inventors* (Annapolis, MD: Naval Institute Press, 2004), pp. 157–9.

44. "The Brennan Torpedo," *UK Parliament Hansard*, 10/7/1890; "The Brennan Torpedo," *UK Parliament Hansard*, 27/6/1892; "The Brennan Torpedo," *UK Parliament Hansard*, 3/5/1894; "The Brennan Torpedo," *UK Parliament Hansard*, 1/7/1897.

45. *Brassey's Naval Annual*, 1887 (Portsmouth: J. Griffin & Co., 1887), p. 497.

46. Gray, *Nineteenth-Century Torpedoes and Their Inventors*, p. 160.

47. "Hong Kong: Defence Scheme, Revised to May 1894," 5/1894, CAB 11/57, pp. 40, 43.

48. Rollo, *Guns and Gunners of Hong Kong*, pp. 70–1.

49. Map based on the description of Rollo, *Guns and Gunners of Hong Kong*, pp. 70–82.

50. For a detailed survey of the Pottinger Battery, see Lawrence Lai et al., "A Survey of the Pottinger Battery, Devil's Peak, Hong Kong," *JRASHKB*, Vol. 47 (2008), pp. 91–114.

51. "Revision of Fixed Defences: Memorandum by the Colonial Defence Committee," 7/3/1907, CAB 11/57, p. 1.

52. "Advanced Report (No. IX of Committee on Armaments) of Hong Kong," Appendix of "Revision of Fixed Defences: Memorandum by the Colonial Defence Committee," 7/3/1907, CAB 11/57, p. 1.

53. The guns at Stonecutters East would be reserved for training purposes.

54. "Advanced Report (No. IX of Committee on Armaments) of Hong Kong," Appendix of "Revision of Fixed Defences: Memorandum by the Colonial Defence Committee," 7/3/1907, CAB 11/57, p. 1.

55. Rollo argued that it was. Rollo, *Guns and Gunners of Hong Kong*, pp. 78–9.

56. Map based on the descrption of "Revision of Fixed Defences: Memorandum by the Colonial Defence Committee," 7/3/1907, CAB 11/57.

57. "Report of Local Committee: Hong Kong; Remarks by Colonial Defence Committee," 4/1/1888, CAB 11/57.

58. "Reply to Defence Circular: Hong Kong," 7/1889, CAB 11/57, p. 1.

59. Ibid., p. 1.

60. Ibid., p. 1.

61. Ibid., p. 2.

62. Nicholas Papastratigakis, *Russian Imperialism and Naval Power: Military Strategy and the Build-up to the Russian-Japanese War* (London, New York: I.B. Tauris, 2011), p. 86.

63. "Report of Local Committee: Hong Kong, Remarks by Colonial Defence Committee," 25/11/1889, CAB 11/57.

64. Ibid.

65. "Covering Letters of the Defence Scheme," 5/1894, CAB 11/57.

66. Gillian Bickley suggested that the work was possibly written by the editor of the *China Mail*, the officers of the Hong Kong Regiment or the militiamen of the Hong Kong Defence Corps. Gillian Bickley, *Hong Kong Invaded! A '97 Nightmare* (Hong Kong: Hong Kong University Press, 2001), pp. 8–10.

67. Ibid., pp. 35–84.

68. Ibid., p. 22.

69. Ng Chi-wah, "*Backdoor* and Coastal Defence of Hong Kong," in Lee Kam Keung et al. (eds.), *Modern Chinese Naval History: New Perspectives* (Hong Kong: Hong Kong Museum of Coastal Defence, 2004), p. 264.

70. "Hong Kong Defence Scheme, Revised to June 1897," CAB 11/57, p. 5.

71. "GOC China and Hong Kong to Governor of Hong Kong," 18/6/1897, CAB 11/57.

72. Papastratigakis, *Russian Imperialism and Naval Power*, pp. 187–8.

73. Peter Wesley-Smith, *Unequal Treaty 1898–1997: China, Great Britain and Hong Kong's New Territories* (Hong Kong: Oxford University Press, 1980), p. 11.

74. "Hong Kong: Extension of Boundaries, Memorandum by the Colonial Defence Committee," 12/11/1896, CAB 11/57; "Hong Kong: Extension of Boundaries," 3/5/1898, CAB 11/57.

75. "Hong Kong: Extension of Boundaries, Memorandum by the Colonial Defence Committee," 12/11/1896, CAB 11/57.

76. *Despatches and Other Papers relating to the Extension of the Colony of Hong Kong, Hong Kong Government Sessional Papers*, 1899, pp. 3–6. http://sunzi.lib.hku.hk/hkgro/view/s1899/1610.pdf

77. "Translation of Written Statement of Ng K'i-ch'eung, dated 21st April, 1899," in *Despatches and Other Papers relating to the Extension of the Colony of Hong Kong*, p. 46.

78. *Despatches and Other Papers relating to the Extension of the Colony of Hong Kong*, p. 6.

79. Patrick Hase, *The Six-Day War of 1899: Hong Kong in the Age of Imperialism* (Hong Kong: Hong Kong University Press, 2008), p. 184.

80. Robert Groves, "Militia, Market and Lineage: Chinese Resistance to the Occupation of Hong Kong's New Territories in 1899," *JRASHKB*, Vol. 9 (1969), 45–7; this is the number of guns captured by the British after the battle. See also Liu Cunkuan (ed.), *Zujie Xinjie* (Hong Kong: Sanlian shudian [Hong Kong], 1995), p. 52.

81. *Despatches and Other Papers relating to the Extension of the Colony of Hong Kong*, p. 6; Liu (ed.), *Zujie Xinjie*, pp. 95–6.

82. "Disturbances in New Kowloon," *Singapore Free Press and Mercantile Advertiser*, 12/4/1899.

83. Melson, *White Ensign—Red Dragon*, p. 41.

84. "Enclosure No. 2 in Governor's despatch of the 7 April, 1899," in *Despatches and Other Papers relating to the Extension of the Colony of Hong Kong*, p. 12.

85. Groves, "Militia, Market and Lineage," p. 55.

86. "Report by Lieut.-Colonel O'Gorman on the Military Operations in the Chinese Hinterland," in *Despatches and Other Papers relating to the Extension of the Colony of Hong Kong*, p. 60.

87. Lieutenant Keyes later captured four torpedo destroyers of the Qing during the Boxer War. He eventually became Deputy Chief of the Naval Staff and Commander-in-Chief, Mediterranean Fleet.

88. HMS *Fame* was equipped with one 12-pounder QF and five 6-pounder QFs. Melson, *White Ensign—Red Dragon*, p. 42.

89. Liu (ed.), *Zujie Xinjie*, p. 100.

90. "Report by Lieut.-Colonel O'Gorman on the Military Operations in the Chinese Hinterland," p. 61.

91. Hase, *The Six-Day War of 1899*, pp. 76–7.

92. "Report by Lieut.-Colonel O'Gorman on the Military Operations in the Chinese Hinterland," p. 63; "Colonial Secretary's Minute of the 24th April, 1899," in *Despatches and Other Papers relating to the Extension of the Colony of Hong Kong*, p. 45.

93. "Lockhart's Letter to the Governor," 19/4/1899, in *Despatches and Other Papers relating to the Extension of the Colony of Hong Kong*, p. 38.

94. Hase, *The Six-Day War of 1899*, p. 116.

95. Ibid., pp. 114–6.

96. "Hong Kong: Boundaries and Defence of New Territory: Memorandum by the Colonial Defence Committee," 23/1/1899, CAB 11/57.

97. "Hong Kong Defence Scheme, Revised to June 1901," CAB 11/57, pp. 12, 14.

98. Ibid., p. 12.

99. Ibid., p. 12.

100. Ibid., p. 15.

101. Ibid., pp. 21–7.

102. Ibid.

103. "GOC South China to WO," 14/3/1912, CAB 38/22/38, p. 2.

104. "Hong Kong Defence Scheme, Revised to June 1903," CAB 11/57, pp. 2–5.

105. "Hong Kong Defence Scheme, Revised to June 1907," CAB 11/57, pp. 7–9.

106. "Naval Commander-in-Chief to Governor," 25/11/2908, CAB 38/17/4, p. 16.

107. Ibid., p. 19.

108. Ibid., p. 21.

109. Broadwood commanded the 57th Division during the First World War; he was killed in action in 1917 during the Battle of Passchendaele. He was probably the only GOC Hong Kong that was killed in action.

110. "GOC to Governor," 7/12/1908, CAB 38/17/4, p. 23.

111. Ibid.

112. "Naval Commander-in-Chief to Governor," 11/12/2908, CAB 38/17/4, p. 23.

113. "Hong Kong—Standard of Defences: Memorandum by the Colonial Defence Committee," 10/1/1911, CAB 38/17/4, pp. 1–2.

114. "Extract from the Report of the Inspector-General of the Forces," 15/3/1910, CAB 38/17/4, p. 24.

115. "Hong Kong—Standard of Defences: Memorandum by the Colonial Defence Committee," 10/1/1911, p. 2.

116. Ibid., p. 6.

117. Ibid., p. 12.

118. Ibid., pp. 7–8.

119. Ibid., p. 8.

120. Ibid., pp. 7–9.

121. Edward Spiers, *The Army and Society, 1815–1914* (London: Longman, 1980), p. 266.

122. "Hong Kong—Standard of Defences: Memorandum by the Colonial Defence Committee," 10/1/1911, p. 14.

123. "Committee of Imperial Defence, Minutes of 108th Meeting," 1/26/1911, CAB 38/17/5, p. 5.

124. "Minutes of 100th Meeting, Committee of Imperial Defence," 24/3/1911, CAB 38/17/16, p. 5.

125. "Vice Adm. L. Winsloe to Maj. Gen. Charles Anderson," 7/4/1911, WO 32/5316.

126. "Armaments of Defended Ports: Provision of Long Range Guns," 19/11/1912, CAB 38/22/37.

127. Roger Chesneau and Eugene Kolesnik (eds.), *Conway's All the World's Fighting Ships 1860–1905* (Greenwich: Conway Maritime Press, 1979), p. 39.

128. *Brassey's Naval Annual* (1902).

129. Bernard Lowry, "The Gin Drinker's Line: Its Place in the History of Twentieth Century Fortifications," *Surveying & Built Environment*, Vol. 21, No. 2 (Dec. 2011), p. 58.

130. "Hong Kong Defence Scheme, Revised to October 1910," CAB 11/57, p. 24.

131. "Notes on the Garrison Required for the Defence of Hong Kong Under the Condition Prescribed in the Instructions for the Preparation of the Local Defence Scheme: Namely Against a Raid by a Landing Part of Three or Four Thousand Men," 6/5/1911, WO 32/5316, p. 5.

132. Ibid., pp. 3–4.

133. Created from the text of "Notes on the Garrison Required," WO 32/5316. Some structures of the line were built, see note 135.

134. "Notes on the Garrison Required," WO 32/5316, pp. 7–8.

135. Ibid., p. 10.

136. Ibid., pp. 11–2.

137. Ibid., p. 9.

138. Ibid., pp. 12–23.

139. Ibid., p. 24.

140. "Hong Kong Defence Scheme, 1911," CAB 11/58, p. 26. Rob Weir found around thirty of these blockhouses along Kowloon Hill; their exact locations are shown in the map of his article. See Rob Weir, "A Note on British Blockhouses in Hong Kong," *Surveying & Built Environment*, Vol. 22, No. 1 (2012), pp. 8–18.

141. "MO1 to GOC South China," 13/1/1912, WO 32/5316.

142. "GOC South China to WO," 14/3/1912, WO32/5316.

143. "Minutes of ADMO1," 25/4/1912, WO32/5316.

144. "DMO to GOC South China," 22/1/1913, WO32/5316, p. 1.

145. "Strength of Infantry Garrison: Note by the Secretary," 23/11/1912, CAB 38/22/38.

146. "Strength of Infantry Garrison: Memorandum by the Oversea Defence Committee," 20/11/1912, CAB 38/22/38.

147. "Committee of Imperial Defence, Minutes of the 121st Meeting," 7/1/1913, CAB/38/23/2, pp. 7–8.

148. "GOC South China to WO," 27/3/1912, WO32/5316, p. 5.

149. "DMO to CIGS," 5/6/1913, WO32/5316.

150. "FO to DMO," 22/7/1913, WO32/5316.

151. "DMO to DFW," 8/1913, WO32/5316, p. 1.

152. "GOC South China to DMO," 14/7/1913, WO 32/5316, pp. 1–13.

153. "Hong Kong Defences, GOC South China to DMO," 14/7/1913, WO 32/5316.

154. "GOC South China to WO," 9/10/1913, WO 32/5316.

155. "DMO minutes," 9/7/1914, WO 32/5316, pp. 1–2.

156. "The Allied China Squadron," *Naval Review*, Vol. 3, No. 2 (1915), pp. 312–21.

157. Rollo, *Guns and Gunners of Hong Kong*, p. 95; Harfield, p. 320.

158. Harfield, *British and Indian Armies on the China Coast*, p. 323.

159. Julian Corbett, *Naval Operations: History of the Great War Based on Official Documents* (London: Longmans, 1920), pp. 138–9.

160. "Honkon hōtai yori Shikoku Maru hōgeki no ken," 1914, Gaimushō kiroku (GK), JACAR, Ref: B11092762300.

161. Edwin Hoyt, *Kreuzerkrieg: The Gripping Story of the German East Asia Cruiser Squadron in World War I* (New York: World Publishing Company, 1968), pp. 181–213.

162. Carroll, *A Concise History of Hong Kong*, p. 89.

163. Norman Miners, "The Use and Abuse of Emergency Powers by the Hong Kong Government," *Hong Kong Law Journal*, Vol. 26, No. 1 (1996), p. 50; David French, *The British Way in Counter-Insurgency, 1945–1967* (Oxford: Oxford University Press, 2011), p. 76.

164. Phillip Bruce, *Second to None: The Story of the Hong Kong Volunteers* (Hong Kong, New York: Oxford University Press, 1991), p. 115.

165. Bruce, *Second to None*, p. 115; Tang Kaijian, Shao Guojian and Chen Jierong (eds.), *6000 Years of Hong Kong History, Prehistory to 1997* (Hong Kong: Qilun, 1998), p. 350.

166. Miners, "The Use and Abuse of Emergency Powers by the Hong Kong Government," p. 51.

167. "GOC Hong Kong to WO," 18/12/1914, CO 129/429.

168. Bruce, *Second to None*, p. 114.

169. "General Observations," *Hong Kong Government Annual Report 1914*, p. 35; "Hong Kong Funded First Fighter," *Hong Kong Military History Notes*, Issue 7, unpaginated.

170. "General Observations," *Hong Kong Government Annual Report 1914*, p. 35.

171. Tang, Shao and Chen (eds.), *6000 Years of Hong Kong History*, p. 363.

172. *The Register of the Hong Kong Memorial: Commemorating the Chinese of the Merchant Navy and Others in British Service Who Died in the Great War and Whose Graves Are Not Known* (London: Imperial War Graves Commission, 1931), pp. 2–5.

173. Ibid., p. 9. Their names may be found at the Stanley Military Cemetery.

174. Clifford Kinvig, *Churchill's Crusade: The British Invasion of Russia, 1918–1920* (London: Continuum, 2006), p. 56.

175. "Hong Kong—Storm-proof Defence and Land Fronts," 14/1/1915, WO 32/5316.

176. "Hong Kong Defences on the Land Fronts: Summary of Proposals Affecting the Defence of Kowloon," 14/1/1915, WO 32/5316.

177. "GOC China Command to WO," 3/12/1917, WO 32/5316.

178. "Observations on the Scheme for Kowloon Frontier," 21/7/1917, WO 32/5316.

179. "DFW to GOC China Command," 23/4/1918, WO 32/5316.

5   Treaty, Air Force and Landward Defence, 1920–1939

1. Quoted in Christopher Bell, *The Royal Navy, Seapower and Strategy between the Wars* (Stanford, CA: Stanford University Press, 2000), p. 61.

2. David Edgerton, *Warfare State: Britain, 1920–1970* (Cambridge, New York: Cambridge University Press, 2006), pp. 26–57, especially the chart on page 23.

3. Williamson Murray and Allan R. Millett (eds.), *Military Innovation in the Interwar Period* (Cambridge, New York: Cambridge University Press, 1996), pp. 197–203.

4. David French, *Raising Churchill's Army: The British Army and the War against Germany, 1919–1945* (Oxford, New York: Oxford University Press, 2000), pp. 12–121.

5. Paul Kennedy, *The Rise and Fall of British Naval Mastery* (London: Penguin, 2004), p. 273; Brian Farrell, *The Defence and Fall of Singapore, 1940–1942* (Stroud: Tempus, 2005), p. 31.

6. Christopher Bell, *Churchill and Sea Power* (Oxford: Oxford University Press, 2013), pp. 106–11; Andrew Field, *Royal Navy Strategy in the Far East, 1919–1939: Preparing for War against Japan* (London; Portland, OR: Frank Cass, 2004), pp. 27–9.

7. Christopher Bell, "'Our Most Exposed Outpost': Hong Kong and British Far Eastern Strategy," *Journal of Military History*, Vol. 60, No. 1 (1996), pp. 61–4.

8. "Conference on the Limitation of Armament, Washington: Treaty Between the United States of America, the British Empire, France, Italy, and Japan, Signed at Washington, February 6, 1922." http://www.ibiblio.org/pha/pre-war/1922/nav_lim.html

9. Stephen Roskill, *Naval Policy between the Wars* (New York: Walker, 1968), p. 290.

10. Denis Rollo, *The Guns and Gunners of Hong Kong* (Hong Kong: The Gunners Roll of Hong Kong, 1991), p. 98.

11. Ibid., p. 100.

12. *The Navy List*, Jan. 1920 (London: HMSO, 1920), p. 714.

13. *The Navy List*, Jul. 1939 (London: HMSO, 1939), p. 247.

14. "Copy of a letter from the Admiralty to the Secretary, CID," 1/3/1926, COS 33, CAB 53/12, p. 1.

15. Ibid., p. 1.

16. "The Defence of Ports at Home and Abroad," 9/5/1927, COS 91, CAB 53/13, p. 2.

17. "Hong Kong—Defence of," COS 44, CAB 53/12, p. 2.

18. Ibid., p. 2.

19. Song Xianlin, "Jiulongcheng dibiao zhi er: Kai Tak Bun yu Kai Tak jichang de xingjian," in Chiu Yu-lok and Chung Po Yin (eds.), *Jiulongcheng* (Hong Kong: Joint Publishing, 2001), p. 178.

20. CAB 23/58, pp. 11–2.

21. Song, "Jiulongcheng dibiao zhi er," p. 182.

22. Gordon Alderson, *History of Royal Air Force Kai Tak* (Hong Kong: Royal Air Force Kai Tak, 1972), pp. 11–2.

23. V. N. Surtees, *HMS* Emerald, *1926–1928* (London: Hiorns and Miller, 1928), p. 147. A copy of this rare book may be found in the Hong Kong Maritime Museum.

24. Alderson, *History of Royal Air Force Kai Tak*, p. 22.

25. "Honkon no bōbei zōdai ni kansuru ken," 1925, GK, JACAR, Ref: B07090356000, slide 307.

26. "Hong Kong, Coast Defences," 17/3/1928, COS 130, CAB 53/14, pp. 1, 4; "Hong Kong, Coast Defences," 5/4/1928, COS 138, CAB 53/14, p. 2.

27. "Hong Kong, Coast Defences," 26/4/1928, COS 143.

28. One of these detachments consisted of White Russian émigrés. A. D. Blue, "Piracy on the China Coast," *Journal of the Hong Kong Branch of the Royal Asiatic Society*, Vol. 5 (1965), pp. 80–1.

29. "FO to Sir M. Lampson," 23/10/1928, CO 129/507, slide 32.

30. Blue, "Piracy on the China Coast," pp. 84–5.

31. Alderson, *History of Royal Air Force Kai Tak*, p. 12.

32. Richard Hopton, *A Reluctant Hero: The Life of Captain Robert Ryder VC* (London: Pen and Sword, 2011), p. 15.

33. Martyn Sherwood, *The Voyage of the Tai-Mo-Shan* (London: Rupert Hart-Davis, 1957), p. 3.

34. *China Side*, Vol. 1, No. 1 (Dec. 1935), pp. 3–17.

35. Steven Schwankert, *Poseidon: China's Secret Salvage of Britain's Lost Submarine* (Hong Kong: Hong Kong University Press, 2014).

36. Kemp Tolley, *Yangtze Patrol: The U.S. Navy in China* (Annapolis: Naval Institute Press, 1971), p. 93.

37. "Two Wars in Hong Kong," 8/4/1940, *Life*, p. 12.

38. Augustus Muir, *The First of Foot: The History of the Royal Scots* (Edinburgh: The Royal Scots History Committee, 1961), p. 113.

39. Report of Advisory Commission for the Protection and Welfare of Children and Young People, League of Nations, 1929, p. 80.

40. "Admiralty to CO," 7/4/1924, CO129/486.

41. Norman Miners, *Hong Kong Under Imperial Rule: 1912–1941* (Hong Kong: Oxford University Press, 1987), pp. 198–9.

42. Frank Welsh, *A History of Hong Kong* (London: HarperCollins, 1997), pp. 391–2; Miners, *Hong Kong Under Imperial Rule*, p. 204.

43. Miners, *Hong Kong Under Imperial Rule*, p. 104.

44. Sit Fung-shuen and Kwong Chi Man, *Xinjie xiangyiju shi: you zujiedi dao yi guo liang zhi* (Hong Kong: Joint Publishing, 2011), particularly Chapter 5.

45. Ibid., pp. 105–6.

46. Sinclair joined the navy at the age of fourteen. He was the captain of HMS *Temeraire* in 1914 and rose to command a squadron of cruisers and battleships. He was the Commander-in-Chief of the China Station from 1925 to 1926.

47. Luard joined the army at the age of eighteen as an officer of the Durham Light Infantry. He had participated in the Boer War and became a brigadier during the First World War. He saw extensive action as a brigadier in the Middle East. In 1925, he was appointed the General Officer Commanding Hong Kong. He retired in 1929.

48. "Defence Against Overseas Attack," 17/2/1926, CO 129/498, p. 412.

49. Ibid., p. 417.

50. Wilfred Egerton was the Director of Naval Plans from 1925. He died while studying at the Royal Naval College in 1931.

51. William Dobbie was a military engineer by origin, and had participated in the Boer War and the First World War. After the war, he served in the War Office, before being appointed Inspector General of the Engineers in 1933. In 1935–1939, he was the General Officer Commanding Malaya. It was Dobbie who pointed out the vulnerability of the Malay Peninsula. From 1940 to 1942, he was the Governor of Malta.

52. Richard Peck was an infantry officer before joining the Royal Flying Corps. In 1919, he became the commander of the 84th Squadron at Iraq and was later admitted to the Army Staff College. He then served as a planning officer of the RAF before entering the Imperial Defence College in 1933. He reached the rank of Air Marshal in 1940.

53. "Defence of Hong Kong: Report of Joint Planning Sub-committee," 10/12/1927, COS 117, CAB 53/14, pp. 1–2.

54. Ibid., p. 2.

55. Ibid., p. 2.

56. Ibid., p. 3.

57. Ibid., p. 12.

58. Ibid., pp. 6–8.

59. Ibid., p. 16.

60. Ibid., pp. 15–6.

61. Ibid., p. 23.

62. Tyrwhitt joined the navy at the age of fifteen. He became the commander of a torpedo boat flotilla in 1912. During the First World War, he was commander of the Harwich Force, which was responsible for coastal defence and protection of shipping across the English Channel. He replaced Sinclair as the Commander-in-Chief of the China Station in 1926.

63. "Naval, Military and Air Force Appreciation on the Defence of Hong Kong Received from the Commander-in-Chief, China," 25/4/1928, COS 146, CAB 53/14, p. 3.

64. Ibid., pp. 3–6.

65. Ibid., pp. 7–13.

66. Ibid., p. 15.

67. Roger Bellairs was the staff officer of the Grand Fleet during the Battle of Jutland in 1916. He became the assistant of the First Sea Lord in 1919–1925, before serving as the Director of Naval Plans in 1928. In 1941, he was the British representative discussing joint strategy with the United States. See Barry Dennis Hunt, *Sailor-scholar: Admiral Sir Herbert Richmond, 1871–1946* (Waterloo, ON: Wilfrid Laurier University Press, 1982), p. 88; Haywood Hansell, Jr., *The Strategic Air War Against Germany and Japan: A Memoir* (Washington: Office of Air Force History, 1986), p. 27.

68. Liddell served as a logistics officer during the First World War. He then taught in the Staff College and was in the first batch of graduates of the Imperial Defence College in 1927. He then served in the General Staff during the 1920s and 1930s, before being given command of a division. He retired in 1942 as the Inspector of Training.

69. "Defence of Hong Kong: Report of the Joint Planning Sub-committee," 31/5/1930, COS 233JP, CAB 53/21, pp. 17–26.

70. Ibid., p. 20.

71. Ibid., p. 20.

72. Ibid., pp. 17–26.

73. Ibid., pp. 46–7.

74. "Imperial Defence Policy," 15/2/1932, COS 295, CAB 53/22, p. 2.

75. Ibid., p. 3.

76. Ibid., p. 4.

77. Ibid., p. 6.

78. "Reports by the Deputies to the Chiefs of Staff Sub-committee on the Situation in the Far East," 22/2/1932, COS 295 (D.C.), p. 4.

79. Ibid., p. 4.

80. Ibid., p. 8.

81. Ibid., pp. 12, 14.

82. "Plans for Singapore and Hong Kong," 7/4/1933, COS 304, CAB 53/23, pp. 3–5.

83. "RAF Requirements for Singapore, Hong Kong, Penang, Ceylon and Aden," 23/1/1934, COS 318, CAB 53/23, p. 3.

84. Ian Cowman, *Dominion or Decline: Anglo-American Naval Relations on the Pacific, 1937–1941* (Oxford; Washington, DC: Berg, 1996), p. 44.

85. Rollo, *Guns and Gunners of Hong Kong*, p. 105.

86. Robert Haining joined the Royal Artillery in 1901. He served in various staff and administrative posts before being appointed Director of Military Operations in 1931–1933. He was the commandant of the Imperial Defence College from 1935 to 1936.

87. Arthur Harris joined the Royal Flying Corps in 1915 and became a squadron leader by the end of the war. He then commanded various RAF formations in Iraq, India and Arabia, and was known for his bombing tactics against rebellious tribes. He served in the Air Ministry as a planning officer throughout the 1930s. During the Second World War, he was first the Vice Chief of Air Staff before serving as the Commander-in-Chief of the Bomber Command from 1942 to 1945.

88. "Hong Kong—Plan for Defence, Relief or Recapture," 30/7/1934, COS 344, CAB 53/24, p. 1.

89. Ibid., p. 1.

90. Ibid., p. 1.

91. Ibid., p. 9.

92. Ibid., pp. 11, 22.

93. "Strategic Position in the Far East with Particular Reference to Hong Kong and Air Requirements for the Far East," 29/10/1934, COS 347, CAB 53/24, pp. 5–6.

94. Reynolds Salerno, *Vital Crossroads: Mediterranean Origins of the Second World War, 1935–1940* (Ithaca, NY: Cornell University Press, 2002), p. 98.

95. "Strategic Position in the Far East with Particular Reference to Hong Kong," 16/9/1935, COS 403, CAB 53/25, pp. 3–4.

96. Ibid., pp. 8–9.

97. Ian Johnston and Ian Buxton, *The Battleship Builders: Constructing and Arming British Captial Ships* (Bransley: Seaforth Publishing, 2013), pp. 294–5.

98. Basil Liddell-Hart held an interview with John Dill, the DMO, in 1935. Dill told him that the War Office had been unwilling to send additional troops as it did not want to see an immense blow to British prestige if the colony was captured. Basil Liddell-Hart, *History of the Second World War* (London: Pan Books, 1973), p. 228.

99. "Proposals for the Acceleration of the Programme for the Defence of Ports Aboard," 4/12/1936, COS532, CAB 53/29, pp. 3–5.

100. *Hong Kong Defence Scheme, 1936*, Chapter 1, 343.01 HON (HKPRO), p. 11.

101. Ibid., Chapter 1, p. 16.

102. Ibid., Chapter 1, pp. 14–6.

103. Ibid., Chapter 2, p. 4.

104. Ibid., Chapter 4, p. 59.

105. Ibid., Chapter 4, p. 59.

106. Ibid., Chapter 4, pp. 57–9, 63.

107. "GOC Hong Kong to DMO," 30/1/1936, WO 106/5358.

108. "WO to C.W. Orde," 25/3/1936, WO 106/5358.

109. Brereton Greenhous, *"C" Force to Hong Kong: A Canadian Catastrophe, 1941–1945* (Toronto; Buffalo, NY: Dundurn Press, 1997), p. 8.

110. "Strategical Position in the Far East with Particular Reference to Hong Kong," 10/10/1935, COS 405, CAB 53/25, p. 1.

111. Thomas Phillips joined the Royal Navy in 1903 and became a lieutenant in 1909. During the First World War, he served in a destroyer. After the war, he studied at the Naval College and became the military adviser to the League of Nations from 1920 to 1922. Having briefly served as a cruiser captain in the China Station in 1934–1935, he served for the longest as a planning officer in the Admiralty throughout the 1930s. In December 1941, he died on HMS *Prince of Wales* when it was sunk by Japanese naval air force.

112. "Far East Appreciation 1937," 7/5/1937, COS 579, CAB 53/31, pp. 27, 29.

113. Ibid., p. 23.

114. Ibid., pp. 31–2.

115. Ibid., p. 57.

116. Ibid., pp. 59–60.

117. Ibid., p. 75.

118. Ibid., p. 76.

119. Ibid., p. 78.

120. Cowman, *Dominion or Decline*, p. 42.

121. "Hong Kong: Policy of Re-Fortification or Demilitarisation," 30/7/1937, COS 605, CAB 53/32, p. 2.

122. "Chiefs of Staff 217th Meeting," COS/217 Mtg, CAB 53/8, pp. 11, 13.

123. Ibid., p. 13.

124. Ibid., pp. 12–15.

125. "Defence of Hong Kong," 18/12/1937, COS 655, CAB 53/35, pp. 1–2.

126. "Defence of Hong Kong," 1/12/1937, COS 657, CAB 53/35, p. 4.

127. Ibid., p. 6.

128. Ibid., p. 7.

129. "Hong Kong—Refortification," 2/3/1938, COS 693, CAB 53/37, p. 10.

130. Ibid., p. 10.

131. Ibid., pp. 4–5.

132. Ibid., pp. 8–9.

133. Ibid., p. 9.

134. "Chiefs of Staff 234th Meeting," COS/234 Mtg, CAB 53/9, pp. 8–9.

135. Ibid., p. 11.

136. Ibid., p. 11.

137. Ibid., pp. 11–3.

138. "The Policy for the Defence of Hong Kong," 16/5/1938, COS 725, CAB 53/38, p. 5.

139. Ibid., pp. 6–8.

140. "The Policy for the Defence of Hong Kong," 26/5/1938, COS 731, CAB 53/39, pp. 6–8.

141. "The Policy for the Defence of Hong Kong," 15/7/1938, COS 740, CAB 53/39, p. 2.

142. Ibid., pp. 6–7.

143. Ibid., p. 8.

144. Carl Vincent, *No Reason Why: The Canadian Hong Kong Tragedy: An Examination* (Stittsville, ON: Canada's Wings Inc., 1981), p. 8.

145. Franco David Macri, "Abandoning the Outpost: Rejection of the Hong Kong Purchase Scheme of 1938–1939," *JRASHKB*, Vol. 50 (2010), pp. 303–16.

146. For more detail, see Bernard Lowry, "The Gin Drinker's Line: Its Place in the History of Twentieth Century Fortifications," *Surveying & Built Environment*, Vol. 21, No. 2 (Dec. 2011); Kwong Chi Man, "Reconstructing the Early History of the Gin Drinker's Line from Archival Sources," *Surveying & Built Environment*, Vol. 22 (Nov. 2012), pp. 18–35. For a map of the locations of the pillboxes, see Lawrence W. C. Lai, Stephen N. G. Davies, Ken S. T. Ching and Castor T. C. Wong, "Location of Pillboxes and Other Structures of the Gin Drinker's Line Based on Aerial Photo Evidence," *Surveying & Built Environment*, Vol. 21, No. 2 (2011), p. 69.

147. Barron first joined the army as a junior artillery officer. He served as a logistician during the First World War in Mesopotamia, and then served in the War Office as a staff officer throughout the 1920s. From 1930 to 1933 he was the fortress commander of the Southern Command, responsible for the British coastal defences facing the English Channel. He was the Inspector of Fixed Defences from 1934 to 1938.

148. "Mock Battle at Hong Kong," *The Straits Times*, 20/3/1935; "10,000 Men in Secret Battle," *The Straits Times*, 9/4/1935; "British Defences in Far East," *The Straits Times*, 18/4/1935.

149. "Report on the Defences of Hong Kong," 4/1935, WO 106/111, pp. 3–5.
150. "Report on the Defences of Hong Kong," 4/1935, WO 106/111, p. 18.
151. "Extract from DO Letter Col. Harrison, Hong Kong," 13/2/1937, WO 106/2363.
152. "Work Completed on Gin Drinker's Line," circa 1936, WO 106/2363. The following two paragraphs mainly come from Kwong, "Reconstructing the Early History of the Gin Drinker's Line from Archival Sources."
153. Please also see Kwong, "Reconstructing the Early History of the Gin Drinker's Line from Archival Sources," p. 27.
154. "Report of the Director of Public Works for the Year 1937," Annual Report 1937, 55. It is possible that they were pillboxes of the Shing Mun Redoubt, but concrete documentary evidence has yet to be found.
155. "Landward Defence," 4/1938, WO 106/2363.
156. From Lawrence Lai et al., "Decoding the Enigma of the Fall of the Shing Mun Redoubt Using Line of Sight Analysis," *Surveying & Built Environment*, Vol. 21, No. 2 (2011), p. 35.
157. Lai et al., "Location of Pillboxes and Other Structures of the Gin Drinker's Line Based on Aerial Photo Evidence," p. 69.
158. While this might be the cause of the rapid fall of the Shing Mun Redoubt during the Battle of Hong Kong in December 1941, further investigation on whether the Japanese had such knowledge before the battle and acted accordingly is needed.
159. "Kyūryū hantō okeru honbōgyo jinchi chōsa hōkoku" [The study of the main defence position on the Kowloon Peninsula], 1/1942, Shina-Dai Tōasen-Nanshi 90, Archives of the National Institute for Defense Studies of Japan (NID), slide 1473.
160. "Kyū Honkon yōsai bōgyo shisetsu no shashin" [Photos of the facilities of the old Hong Kong fortress], 1/1942, Shina Shashin 94, NID.
161. "Report on the Defences of Hong Kong," 4/1935, WO 106/111, p. 12.
162. "Minute by Director of Military Operations and Intelligence, War Office," 5/11/1938, JDC 226, AIR 2/1666, pp. 1–6.
163. "Hong Kong Coast Defences (draft)," 12/1935, AIR 2/1666, pp. 1–2.
164. Map based on WO 78/5361.
165. "Recapitulation Island Defences," WO 106/2363.
166. Rollo, *Guns and Gunners of Hong Kong*, p. 114.
167. Civil Engineering and Development Department, "Investigation of Disused Tunnels: Preliminary Report, Victoria Barrack—Disused Underground Operations Headquarters," Document #5341, Hong Kong, 10/1983, p. 5.
168. Richard Aldrich, *Intelligence and the War against Japan: Britain, America, and the Politics of Secret Service* (Cambridge: Cambridge University Press, 2000), p. 28.
169. Richard Walding, "Indicator Loops: Royal Navy Harbour Defences—Hong Kong," http://indicatorloops.com/hongkong.htm

6 The International Situation and Hong Kong Defence, 1939–1941

1.   Kent Fedorowich, "'Cocked Hats and Small, Little Garrisons': Britain, Canada and the Fall of Hong Kong, 1941," *Modern Asian Studies*, Vol. 37, No. 1 (2003), p. 123.
2.   Franco David Macri, "C Force to Hong Kong: The Price of Collective Security in China," *Journal of Military History*, Vol. 77 (2013), p. 154.

3. Chiefs of Staff Sub-committee, "Our Policy in China," 19/11/1938, COS 798, CAB 53/42, pp. 1–4.

4. John Driefort, *Myopic Grandeur: The Ambivalence of French Foreign Policy toward the Far East* (Kent, OH: Kent State University Press, 1991), p. 164. From Fedorowich, "'Cocked Hats and Small, Little Garrisons,'" p. 126.

5. Chiefs of Staff Sub-committee, "The Situation in the Far East: Report," 16/6/1939, COS 928, CAB 53/50, pp. 5–6.

6. COS 928, 16/6/1939, p. 6.

7. Fedorowich, "'Cocked Hats and Small, Little Garrisons,'" p. 128.

8. Carl Vincent, *No Reason Why: The Canadian Hong Kong Tragedy: An Examination* (Stittsville, ON: Canada's Wings Inc., 1981), p. 9.

9. Fedorowich, "'Cocked Hats and Small, Little Garrisons,'" p. 128.

10. "Hong Kong—Period Before Relief," 17/2/1940, COS (40) 238, CAB 80/8, p. 1.

11. COS (40) 238, p. 2.

12. Quoted from Ian Cowman, *Dominion or Decline: Anglo-American Naval Relations on the Pacific, 1937–1941* (Oxford; Washington, DC: Berg, 1996), p. 45.

13. Cowman, *Dominion or Decline*, pp. 44–5.

14. "Memorandum of Japanese Occupation of the Land Frontier of the New Territories, 1938–1941," 20/3/1941, CO968/132.

15. "Ekkyō ga kō seru ei-inhei no shochi ni kansuru ken," 1939, Rikugunshō dainikki (RD), NIDS, JACAR, Ref: C04121537900.

16. Chiefs of Staff Committee, "British Strategy in a Certain Eventuality," 23/5/1940, COS (40) 390, CAB 80/11.

17. Chiefs of Staff Committee, "Policy in Respect of the French Colonial Possessions," 6/1940, COS (40), CAB 80/11.

18. Chiefs of Staff Committee, "Far East: Note by the Secretary," 19/6/1940, COS (40) 477, CAB 80/13.

19. Chiefs of Staff Committee, "Immediate Measures Required in the Far East, Report by the Joint Planning Committee," 24/6/1940, COS (40) 488JP, CAB 80/13, p. 1.

20. "Policy in the Far East: Memorandum by the Chief of the Imperial General Staff," 3/7/1940, COS (40) 528, CAB 80/14, pp. 1–2.

21. Chiefs of Staff Committee, "Policy in the Far East, Aide Memoire by the Joint Planning Committee," 30/6/1940, COS (40) 506JP, CAB 80/14, pp. 1–2.

22. "Daihonei rikugunbu, daihonei kaigunbu–seikai jōsei no suii nihanpu jikyoku shori yōkōan," 7/1940, Institute of Developing Economies, Kōichi Kishi Collection, B1–144, slides 1–12. http://d-arch.ide.go.jp/kishi_collection/

23. Furūya Tetsūo, "Sensō seisaku no kakudai to mujun," *Rekishi kōron*, Vol. 4, No. 8 (1978), p. 8.

24. Chiefs of Staff Sub-committee, "The Situation in the Far East in the Event of Japanese Intervention against Us," 19/7/1940, COS (40) 555, CAB 80/15, p. 3.

25. Ibid., p. 13.

26. Ibid., p. 22.

27. Chiefs of Staff Sub-committee, "Far East Policy," 25/7/1930, COS (40) 578, CAB 80/15, p. 1.

28. Chiefs of Staff Sub-committee, "Far East—British Garrisons in China," 31/7/1940, COS (40) 591, CAB 80/15, p. 3; "Reinforcement of Garrisons Aboard," COS (40) 673, CAB 80/17, p. 2.

29. Secretary, COS Sub-committee, "The Far East," COS (40) 676, CAB 80/17, pp. 2–3.

30. "Copy of a telegram No. 2197 from H.M. Ambassador United States to Foreign Office, dated 5th October 1940," 6/10/1940, COS (40) 804, CAB 80/20, p. 2.

31. "The Local Chinese Population and the Defence of Hong Kong," 2/7/1940, COS (40) 834 (J. P.), CAB 80/20, Annex I, p. 3.

32. Ibid., p. 2.

33. "Notes by Sir Geoffry Northcote: Considerations regarding the defensibility of Hong Kong," 17/9/1940, COS (40) 834 (J. P.), Annex I, p. 4.

34. Ibid., p. 6.

35. "Defence of Hong Kong: Draft Report by the Chiefs of Staff," 15/10/1940, COS (40) 834 (J. P.), pp. 1–2.

36. Ibid., p. 2.

37. Fedorowich, "'Cocked Hats and Small, Little Garrisons'"; Macri, "C Force to Hong Kong."

38. "Appreciation by Commander-in-Chief, Far East: Note by Secretary," 8/12/1940, COS (40) 1023, CAB 80/24, p. 2.

39. Ibid., p. 3.

40. Ibid., p. 3.

41. Ibid., p. 5.

42. Commander-in-Chief, Far East, "Propaganda Policy in the Far East," 7/12/1940, COS (40) 1024, CAB 80/24, p. 1.

43. "An Attack on Hong Kong Would Be Costly," *The Straits Times*, 10/4/1941.

44. "Alert in the East," Imperial War Museum Collection, COI 122.

45. Tim Luard, *Escape from Hong Kong: Admiral Chan Chak's Christmas Day Dash, 1941* (Hong Kong: Hong Kong University Press, 2012), p. 32.

46. "Brooke-Popham to Street," 15/1/1941, Brooke-Popham 6/3/3, Liddell-Hart Archive, King's College London.

47. "Defence of Hong Kong: Copy of Telegram dated 6th January, 1941, from Commander-in-Chief, Far East to the Air Ministry," 7/1/1941, COS (41) 18, CAB 80/25, p. 1.

48. Ibid., p. 1.

49. Ibid., p. 2.

50. "Copy of a Minute dated 7 January, 1941, from the Prime Minister to Major General Ismay," 7/1/1941, COS (41) 28, CAB 80/25, p. 2.

51. "Defence of Hong Kong: Memorandum by the Chief of the Imperial General Staff," 10/1/1941, COS (41) 28, p. 1.

52. "Draft Telegram to C-in-C, Far East," COS (41) 28, p. 3; "Minutes of Meeting held on 13th January, 1941," 13/1/1941, COS (41) 16th Meeting, in CO 968/13/2.

53. "Copy of Telegram dated 18th January, 1941, from Commander-in-Chief, Far East to the Air Ministry," 18/1/1941, Annex II, COS (41) 51, CAB 80/25, p. 4.

54. Annex II, COS (41) 51, p. 5.

55. Annex I, COS (41) 51, p. 3.

56. Chief of the Imperial General Staff, "Defence of Hong Kong: Memorandum," 22/1/1941, COS (41) 51, CAB 80/25, p. 2.

57. "WO to GOC Hong Kong," 9/1/1941, CO 968/13/2; "GOC Hong Kong to WO," 10/1/1941, CO 968/12/2.

58. Yizhi, "Xianggang ruhe cai neng zhichi changqi de baowei" [How can Hong Kong withstand a prolonged siege?], *Xianshi* (Shanghai: Xianshi zazhishe, 1939), p. 26.

59. Haruo Iguchi, "Japan Foreign Policy and the Outbreak of the Asia-Pacific War: The Search for a Modus Vivendi in US-Japanese Relations after July 1941," in Frank McDonough (ed.), *The Origins of the Second World War: An International Perspective* (London: Continuum, 2011), p. 467.

60. Glen Williford, *Racing the Sunrise: Reinforcing America's Pacific Outposts, 1941–1942* (Annapolis: Naval Institute Press, 2011), p. 2.

61. Williford, *Racing the Sunrise*, pp. 36, 39, 52–3, 63–5, 77, 79.

62. Secretary, COS Sub-committee, "British, American and Dutch Technical Military Conservations: Draft Report by the Joint Planning Staff," 7/10/1940, COS (40) 807, CAB 80/20, p. 3; "Anglo-Dutch-American Technical Military Conservations," COS (40) 836, CAB 80/20, p. 2.

63. Secretary of Chiefs of Staff Sub-committee, "Allied Strategy in the Far East: Note by the Secretary," 2/11/1940, COS (40) 893, CAB 80/201, p. 2.

64. Chiefs of Staff Sub-committee, "Measures to Avert War with Japan," 6/2/1941, COS (41) 74, CAB 80/25, pp. 1–2.

65. "British-United States Staff Conversation," 2/4/1941, COS (41) 250, CAB 80/27, p. 2.

66. "British-United States Staff Conversations," 22/4/1941, COS (41) 255, CAB 80/27, p. 7.

67. Ibid., p. 8.

68. "Far East: American-Dutch-British Conference at Singapore, April, 1941," 30/4/1941, COS (41) 272, CAB 80/27, p. 1.

69. Chan Chak, "Xianggang zhan tuwei riji," 1/12/1941, in Chan On-kwok (ed.), *Chan Chak Jiangjun jinianji* (2011), p. 228.

70. "Waijiao buzhang Wang Chongwei zhi Chongqing zhi Jiang weiyuanzhang baogao Yingguo tongyi jiang Meiguo fenpei gei Yingguo zhi P-40 zhandouji yibaijia rangyu wo xiwo jiena daidian" [Minister of Foreign Affairs Wang Chongwei's Report about the British decision to send one hundred P-40 fighters given by the USA to China and their request to me to send their offer], 25/3/1941, Zhonghua minguo zhongyao shiliao chubian bianji weiyuanhui (ed.), *Zhonghua minguo zhongyao shiliao chubian— duiri kangzhan shiqi* [Selected historical sources of the Chinese Republic, Anti-Japanese War], Vol. 3, No. 2 (Taipei: Zhongyang weiyuanhui dangshi weiyuanhui, 1981), pp. 150–1.

71. "Junshi kaochatuan tuanzhang Shang Zhen tuanyuan Lin Wei baogao yu Yingguo yuandong zhongshiling Popham jiangjun tanhua neirong dian," 20/5/1941, Zhonghua minguo zhongyao shiliao chubian bianji weiyuanhui (ed.), *Zhonghua minguo zhongyao shiliao chubian—duiri kangzhan shiqi*, Vol. 2, No. 3, pp. 202–3; Hans van de Ven, *War and Nationalism in China, 1925–1945* (London: Routledge, 2003), p. 23.

72. "Assistance to China," 26/6/1941, COS (41) 401, CAB 80/29, pp. 1–2.

73. "Assistance to China," 8/8/1941, COS (41) 480, CAB 80/29, p. 1.

74. "Progressive Measures in the Far East: Note by the Secretary," Annex, 7/10/1941, COS (41) 608, CAB 80/31, p. 2.

75. "Far East: United States Attitude," Annex I, 10/5/1941, COS (41) 303, CAB 80/28, p. 1.
76. "The Far East: Note by the Secretary," 30/7/1941, COS (41) 463, CAB 80/29, p. 2.
77. "Measures to Counter Further Japanese Southward Moves," 5/8/1941, COS (41) 474, CAB 80/29, Annex, p. 7.
78. "Measures to Counter Further Japanese Southward Moves," 7/8/1941, COS (41) 479, CAB 80/29, Annex, p. 1.
79. Richard Aldrich, *Intelligence and the War against Japan: Britain, America, and the Politics of Secret Service* (Cambridge: Cambridge University Press, 2004), p. 90.
80. Williford, *Racing the Sunrise*, p. 85.
81. Herbert P. Bix, *Hirohito and the Making of Modern Japan* (New York: HarperCollins Publishers, 2000), pp. 401–38.
82. Macri, "C Force to Hong Kong," pp. 155–6.
83. Ibid., p. 154.
84. Paul Douglas Dickson, *A Thoroughly Canadian General: A Biography of General H.D.G. Crerar* (Toronto: University of Toronto Press, 2007), p. 166.
85. "Annex of COS (41) 559 dated 8th September, 1941," 8/9/1941, CO 968/13/2.
86. Untitled Document, CO 968/13/2, 9/9/1941; also see Fedorowich, "'Cocked Hats and Small, Little Garrisons,'" p. 142.
87. Untitled Document, CO 968/13/2, 11/9/1941.
88. LHCMA, Brooke-Popham Papers, 6/2/19, Brooke-Popham to Ismay, 29/10/1941; see also Fedorowich, "'Cocked Hats and Small, Little Garrisons,'" p. 135.
89. Fedorowich, "'Cocked Hats and Small, Little Garrisons,'" pp. 133, 135. Studies on the Canadian reinforcement to Hong Kong seldom mention the Australian decision to send two battalions to Timor and Ambon. These battalions were sent in October 1941 and were overrun in January 1942. The death rate of these 2,500 soldiers was even higher than that suffered by the two Canadian battalions in Hong Kong.
90. "Dominion Office to the Government of Canada," 19/9/1941, CO 968/13/2.
91. Fedorowich, "'Cocked Hats and Small, Little Garrisons,'" p. 116.
92. Carl Vincent of *No Reason Why* and Brian McKenna and Terence McKenna of *The Valor and the Horror* were champions of the "misleading" school. However, this thesis has been recently rebuked by historians. See Galen Roger Perras, "Defeat Still Cries Aloud for Explanation: Explaining C Force's Dispatch to Hong Kong," *Canadian Military Journal*, Vol. 11, No. 4 (2011), pp. 40–2.
93. Dickson, *A Thoroughly Canadian General*, p. 165.
94. Ibid., p. 166.
95. Fedorowich, "'Cocked Hats and Small, Little Garrisons,'" pp. 136–40.
96. Macri, "C Force to Hong Kong," p. 160.
97. "Extract from Minutes of COS (41) 345th Meeting held on Wednesday, 8th October, 1941," CO 968/13/2, slide 91.
98. "Government of Canada to Dominions Office," 29/9/1941, CO 968/13/2, slide 98; "WO to GOC Hong Kong," 3/10/1941, CO 968/13/2, slide 95; "WO to GOC Hong Kong," 8/10/1941, CO 968/13/2, slide 93; "GOC Hong Kong to WO," 9/10/1941, CO 968/13/2, slide 92.
99. Richard Aldrich, *Intelligence and the War against Japan*, pp. 54–7, 83–6; Robert Love (ed.), *Pearl Harbor Revisited* (Washington: Palgrave, 1994), p. 164; Michael Smith,

The Emperor's Codes: The Breaking of Japan's Secret Ciphers (New York: Arcade, 2001); Charles Beard, *President Roosevelt and the Coming of the War, 1941: A Study in Appearances and Realities* (Hamden, CT: Archon Books, 1968, 1948).

100. "Hong Kong Despatches, Appendix B, War Narrative," WO 106/2401B.
101. On 19 November, Tokyo instructed the Japanese consulates around the world that if they received "East Wind Rain" in the weather broadcast from Japan, that would mean war with the United States. "North Wind Cloud" meant war with the Soviet Union, and "West Wind Sunny" meant war with Great Britain only.
102. "Fortress War Diary," WO 106/2401A, p. 1.
103. Colin Crisswell and Mike Watson, *The Royal Hong Kong Police, 1841–1945* (Hong Kong: Macmillan, 1982), p. 166.
104. "Hong Kong Despatches, Appendix B, War Narrative," WO 106/2401B, p. 5.
105. "Fortress War Diary," WO 106/2401A, p. 1.

7   Hong Kong before the War

1.   "Report on operations (together with appendices) leading up to the surrender of Hong Kong to the Japanese Imperial Army, December 1941, with special reference to the part played by the 1st Battalion the Middlesex Regiment," WO 172/1689, p. 3.
2.   Air Raid Precaution Department, *Report on Census of the Colony of Hong Kong (exclusive of the New Territories) taken on 13th/14th and 14th/15th March, 1941* (Hong Kong: Hong Kong Government Printers, 1941).
3.   Philip Snow, *The Fall of Hong Kong: Britain, China and the Japanese Occupation* (New Haven: Yale University Press, 2003), pp. 2–22, 28–51; Xie Yongguang, *Xianggang kangri fengyunlu* (Hong Kong: Cosmos Books, 1995), pp. 2–5; Cai Rongfang, *The Hong Kong People's History of Hong Kong* (Hong Kong: Oxford University Press, 2001), pp. 173–225.
4.   Gerald Horne, *Race War: White Supremacy and the Japanese Attack on the British Empire* (New York: New York University Press, 2004).
5.   In 1937, the police had discovered the bodies of 1,353 homeless people. This shows the often difficult living conditions of the colony before the war. See David Faure (ed.), *Society: A Documentary History of Hong Kong* (Hong Kong: Hong Kong University Press, 1997), p. 181; Snow, *The Fall of Hong Kong*, pp. 17–22.
6.   Richard Aldrich, *Intelligence and the War against Japan: Britain, America, and the Politics of Secret Service* (Cambridge: Cambridge University Press, 2000), pp. 39–41; Snow, *The Fall of Hong Kong*, p. 45.
7.   George MacDonell, *One Soldier's Story 1939–1945: From the Fall of Hong Kong to the Defeat of Japan* (Toronto: Dundurn Press, 2002), pp. 57–8.
8.   Tony Banham, "Hong Kong Volunteer Defence Corps, Number 3 (Machine Gun) Company," *Journal of the Royal Asiatic Society Hong Kong Branch*, Vol. 45 (2005), pp. 113–39; Li Chaoyuan, *Rijun xi Gang ji: weikun Zhongguo de shaju Taipingyang zhan de xumu* (Ontario: Jishan shushi, 2002), p. 22.
9.   Frederic Wakeman, Jr., *Spymaster: Dai Li and the Chinese Secret Service* (Berkeley: University of California Press, 2003), p. 249.
10. Snow, *The Fall of Hong Kong*, p. 27.

11. Nonetheless, it was only a ruse with which to trick the Japanese. See Yang Tianshi, *Zhaoxun zhenshi de Jiang Jieshi: Jiang Jieshi riji jiedu* (Taiyuan: Shanxi renmin chubanshe, 2008).

12. "Governor to the Right Honourable Malcolm Macdonald," 18/1/1940, CO 129/585; Xie, *Xianggang kangri fengyunlu*, p. 171.

13. "Chūkon kyōsantō no ippan katsudō," 1942, RD, NIDS, JACAR, Ref: C01000136000; Li Guoqiang and Zhang Peixin, *Xianggang zai kangri qijian* (Hong Kong: Xianggang wenshi chubanshe, 2005), pp. 42–3; also see Xie, *Xianggang kangri fengyunlu*.

14. Yang Mingwei, "Zhou Enlai yu dongjiang zhongdui ji Xianggang kangzhan," in Chan King Tong, Yau Siu Kam and Chan Ka Leung (eds.), *The Defence of Hong Kong: Collected Essays on the Hong Kong-Kowloon Brigade of the East River Column* (Hong Kong: Hong Kong Museum of History, 2004), p. 129.

15. Liu Zhijian, "Xianggang haiyuan yu zuguo kangzhan," in Chan, Yau and Chan (eds.), *The Defence of Hong Kong: Collected Essays on the Hong Kong-Kowloon Brigade of the East River Column*, pp. 155–9.

16. W. W. Yen, *An Autobiography by W. W. Yen: East-West Kaleidoscope* (Taipei: Zhuanji wenxue, 1973), p. 242; see also Xie, *Xianggang kangri fengyunlu*, p. 55.

17. Jozef Straczek, "The Empire Is Listening: Naval Signals Intelligence in the Far East to 1942," *Journal of the Australian War Memorial*, No. 35 (2001). Website: http://www.awm.gov.au/journal/j35/straczek.asp

18. Peter Elphick, *Far Eastern File: The Intelligence War in the Far East, 1930–1945* (London: Coronet Books, 1998), p. 70.

19. Elphick, *Far Eastern File*, pp. 71–72. A listening station was later established at Little Sai Wan before the war, which was used after the war as well. However, details are sketchy. See http://www.littlesaiwan-367su.talktalk.net/history.html.

20. Aldrich, *Intelligence and the War against Japan*, pp. 25–6.

21. "Jiang weiyuanzhang zhi junshi weiyuanhui canmou zongzhang He Yingqin bingzhuan Kunming xingying zheren Yun Long gaoyi Fa yi tongyi wokou jiadao Yuenan gonghua xi jizao coufang dian" [Chiang Kai-shek to He Yingqin and Yun Long about the French decision to allow Japan to attack China from Indochina], 21/8/1938, Zhonghua minguo zhongyao shiliao chubian bianji weiyuanhui (ed.), *Zhonghua minguo zhongyao shiliao chubian—duiri kangzhan shiqi*, Vol. 2, No. 3, p. 198.

22. Robert Hanyok, "How the Japanese Did It," in *Naval History Magazine*, Vol. 23, No. 6 (Dec. 2009). Online version: http://www.usni.org/magazines/navalhistory/2009–12/how-japanese-did-it

23. Aldrich, *Intelligence and the War against Japan*, pp. 21, 23.

24. Philip Davies, *MI6 and the Machinery of Spying* (London: Frank Cass, 2004), p. 130.

25. John O'Connell, *Submarine Operational Effectiveness in the 20th Century: Part One (1939–1945)* (Bloomington: iUniverse Publishing, 2011), p. 87.

26. "Chūkon Jūkei (Chongqing) soku kōkyū tokumu kikan no gairyaku," 1942, RD, NIDS, JACAR, Ref: C01000135900; Xie, *Xianggang kangri fengyunlu*, pp. 110–2.

27. Xie, pp. 131–7.

28. Snow, *The Fall of Hong Kong*, p. 48.

29. Aldrich, *Intelligence and the War against Japan*, p. 63.

30. Sambo Hombu (ed.), *Honkon heiyo chishi* (Tokyo: Sambo Hombu, 1938), p. 125.

31. Ibid., pp. 127, 129.

32. "Honkon gunji shisetsu nikansuru chūhon i-sōryōji no setsumei no ken hashū san den," 25/5/1939, RD, NIDS, JACAR, Ref: C04121059300.

33. "Honkon bōgyo shisetsu to," 8/1939, National Diet Library Japan.

34. Aldrich, *Intelligence and the War against Japan*, p. 44.

35. Xie later surrendered again to the Nationalist government. See Brian Martin, "Shield of Collaboration: The Wang Jingwei Regime's Security Service, 1939–1945," *Intelligence and National Security*, Vol. 16, No. 4 (Winter 2001), p. 129.

36. Snow, *The Fall of Hong Kong*, p. 39.

37. "Ha shu san den," 12/10/1941, Rikugun ichihan shiryō (RIS), NIDS, JACAR, C12122326000, slide 7. Ken Kotani, "Nihongun to Intelligence: seikō to shippai no jirei karu," *NIDS Journal of Defense and Security*, Vol. 11, No. 1 (2008), pp. 55–6; Ken Kotani, *Japanese Intelligence in World War II* (Oxford, New York: Osprey, 2009), p. 49.

38. Snow, *The Fall of Hong Kong*, p. 27; Wang Zhenghua, "Kangzhan qianqi Xianggang yu Zhongguo junhuo wuzi de zhuanyun, 1937–1941," *Gang Ao yu jindai Zhongguo xueshu yantaohui lunwenji* (Taipei: Guoshiguan, 2000), pp. 393–439.

39. However, only Lin Shiliang was executed. No further investigation took place. Wakeman, *Spymaster*, pp. 325–7.

40. Cai, *The Hong Kong People's History of Hong Kong*, pp. 183–7.

41. Ma Yau-woon, *Jinghai chengjiang: Zhongguo jindai haijun shishi xinquan* (Taipei: Lianjing, 2009), pp. 474–5.

42. George Endacott, *A Biographical Sketch-book of Early Hong Kong* (Hong Kong: Hong Kong University Press, 2005), p. 38.

43. A. H. Fernyhough, *History of the Royal Army Ordnance Corps, 1920–1945* (London: Royal Army Ordnance Corps, 1966), p. 318; Kwong Chi Man and Tsoi Yiu Lun, *Gudu qianshao: Taipingyang zhanzheng zhong de Xianggang zhanyi* (Hong Kong: Cosmos, 2013), p. 83.

44. George Endacott, pp. 39–41.

45. Ibid., p. 42; Kwong Chi Man and Tsoi Yiu Lun, p. 83.

46. Endacott, *A Biographical Sketch-book of Early Hong Kong*, pp. 35–6.

47. *The Kung Sheung Daily News*, 14/10/1941.

48. Snow, *The Fall of Hong Kong*, p. 28.

49. Michael Calvert, *Prisoners of Hope* (London: Cooper, 1971), p. 41.

50. Denis Rollo, *The Guns and Gunners of Hong Kong* (Hong Kong: The Gunners Roll of Hong Kong, 1991), p. 113; *Dragon Journal* (Hong Kong: Hong Kong Ex-Servicemen's Association, 1997), pp. 14–6.

51. DGB, 8/11/1941; 11/11/1941.

52. "Prisoner of War Diary of Chief Signal Officer, China Command, Hong Kong, 1941–1945," 940 547252 PRI.

53. "C-in-C Hong Kong to Secretary of State for Colonies," 21/9/1945, CO 820/60/4; "Extract from Prologue to the Volunteers at War," Elizabeth Ride Collection, Hong Kong Heritage Project.

54. Endacott, *A Biographical Sketch-book of Early Hong Kong*, p. 45.

55. Regulations under the Emergency Regulations Ord., 1922, GA 1938 no. 775; Restrictions on alien combatants, Emergency Regulation Ord., 1922, GA 1938 no.

794; Additional Regulations, Emergency Regulation Ord., 1922, GA 1938 no. 798; Regulations regarding squatters and destitutes, Emergency Regulations Ord., 1922, GA 1938 no. 902.

56. Endacott, *A Biographical Sketch-book of Early Hong Kong*, p. 30.

57. Defence Regulations, 1939, Emergency Powers Order in Council, 1939, GA 1939 no. 703; Additional Defence Regulations, Emergency Powers (Colonial Defence), GA 1939 no. 740; Additional Defence Regulations, Emergency Powers (Colonial Defence), GA 1939 no. 747; Additional Defence Regulations, Emergency Powers (Colonial Defence), GA 1939 no. 820; Order fixing the maximum retail prices of sugar, Defence Regulations 1939, GA 1939 no. 859; Order prohibiting the export, except by license, of certain goods, Defence Regulations, 1939, GA 1939 no. 1229; George B. Endacott, p. 30.

58. Defence Regulations, 1941, GA 1940 no. 709.

59. Order prohibiting the export, except by license, of Nickel Coins, Defence Regulations, 1939, GA 1940 no. 318; Order prohibiting the importation of motor vehicles and radio receiving sets, Defence Regulations, 1939, GA 1940 no. 475.

60. Endacott, *A Biographical Sketch-book of Early Hong Kong*, pp. 31–2; Xie, *Xianggang lunxian: Rijun gong-Gang shibari zhanzheng jishi* (Hong Kong: Commercial Press, 1996), p. 10.

61. Endacott, *A Biographical Sketch-book of Early Hong Kong*, pp. 32–3.

62. Ibid., p. 49.

63. "General Statement on A.R.P. During the Period 1st January, 1939 to 31st December, 1939," *Annual Report 1939*, P (1) A.R.P., pp. 1–6.

64. *China at War*, Vol. 5 (1940), pp. 95–6. The horrendous tunnel suffocation accident during a bombing of Chongqing in 1941 had yet to happen.

65. Kwong Chi Man and Tsoi Yiu Lun, p. 92.

66. Ibid., pp. 87–89.

67. *The Kung Sheung Daily News*, 1/10/1941.

68. DGB, 3/9/1941; 4/9/1941; 5/9/1941; 1/10/1941; 3/10/1941; 14/10/1941; 16/10/1941; 17/10/1941; 18/10/1941; 21/10/1941; 1/11/1941; 2/11/1941; 5/11/1941; 8/11/1941.

69. DGB, 5/11/1941.

70. Endacott, *A Biographical Sketch-book of Early Hong Kong*, p. 52. Endacott, who relied mainly on English newspaper sources, subscribed to this myth.

71. DGB, 18/11/1941.

72. Leo Goodstadt, *Uneasy Partners: The Conflict between Public Interest and Private Profit in Hong Kong* (Hong Kong: Hong Kong University Press, 2005), pp. xv, 267.

73. "Governor to Secretary of State for the Colonies," 2/12/1941, CO 129/590.

74. Kent Fedorowich, "The Evacuation of Civilians from Hong Kong and Malaya/ Singapore, 1939–1942," in Brian Farrell and Sandy Hunter (eds.), *Sixty Years On: The Fall of Singapore Revisited* (Singapore: Eastern Universities Press, 2002), pp. 122–32.

75. Snow, *The Fall of Hong Kong*, p. 51.

8　The Fall of Hong Kong, December 1941

1. "Operations in the Far East, from 17th October 1940 to 27th December 1941," *Supplement to London Gazette*, 20/1/1948, p. 541.

2.   *Hohei dai ninihachi rentai shi* [History of the 228th infantry regiment] (Nagoya: Hohei dai ninihachi rentai shi kankōkai, 1973), p. 103.

3.   *Entries in Personal Diary Brigadier J.K. Lawson* (hereafter Lawson Diary), 1941, Library and Archives Canada, R1961–0-9, p. 1.

4.   The next day, a man died of a heart attack due to seasickness. Lawson Diary, p. 1.

5.   The officers tried to set an example by joining the physical training, but Lawson was injured in the leg as a result. Lawson got a "slight kink" at physical training on 5 November and was unable to resume until the 10th. Lawson Diary, pp. 1–2.

6.   The consequences of this incident remain elusive, but three events occurred afterwards. After *Awatea* had left Honolulu, the schedule of the *Taiyo Maru* was delayed by an extended investigation of its passengers and mails. It could not leave until 5 November, after some negotiation. Lawson wrote in his diary after the incident that the ship was the "only possible source of leakage," without any follow-up. G. Hutson, a junior engineer on board *Awatea*, recalled that "it was reported that a ship had shadowed us for several days, and it was presumed to be a Japanese warship . . ." On 15 November, when *Awatea* was just one day away from Hong Kong, it had to change course to avoid Japanese cruisers. It could be an interesting question about the relationship between this possible leakage and the sudden extension of the U.S. Customs investigation. Did *Taiyo Maru* send any intelligence report to Japan and did it have any relationship with the suspected Japanese cruisers? They are questions that await answer. "Honolulu zeikan tōyoku no Taiyo Maru jōkyaku tenimotsu kensashin nikansuru ken," Rikugunshō dainiki (RD), NIDS, JACAR, Ref: C04014873400; Lawson Diary, pp. 2–3; G. Hutson, *Awatea at War* (2010), website of New Zealand Ship and Marine Society, http://www.nzshipmarine. com/node/52.

7.   Lawson Diary, p. 3.

8.   Ibid.

9.   Ibid.

10. Lawson Diary, pp. 3–4.

11. Ronald Parker, *Deadly December: The Battle of Hong Kong, The Royal Rifles of Canada, The Winnipeg Grenadiers* (London: Lulu.com, 2008), p. 18.

12. "Telegram from C in C Far East to the War Office," 19/11/1941, CO 968/13/2, slide 72.

13. Ibid., slide 70.

14. Ibid., slide 70.

15. Ibid., slide 69.

16. Ibid., slide 67.

17. "Anti-Aircraft Allocations for December 1941," COS (41) 709, CAB 80/32.

18. "Minutes of Meeting held on Monday," 1/12/1941, CAB 79/16.

19. "Anti-Aircraft Defence of Hong Kong (Draft Report)," CO 968/13/2, slide 62.

20. "Extract from Minutes of Meeting held on Wednesday," 3/12/1941, CO 968/13/2, slides 56–58.

21. "An abbreviated narrative of events during the action at Hong Kong, December, 1941," WO 106/2401A, Appendix A, p. 1. This abbreviated narrative was the first draft of Maltby's *Supplement to the London Gazette: Operations in Hong Kong from 8th to 25th December, 1941*; however, the above quotation was omitted when it was published.

22. WO 106/2401A, Appendix A, p. 1.

23. "Letter to WO from Maj. Gen. Maltby," 21/11/1945, WO 106/2401A, p. 2.

24. Southeast to Li Muk Shue Milestone No. 7 of Castle Peak Road.

25. "Report on Operations Leading up to the Surrender of Hong Kong on the Japanese Imperial Army, December, 1941, with special reference to the part played by the 1st Battalion the Middlesex Regiment," WO 172/1689, pp. 1–2.

26. The construction of S-class destroyers started in 1917. With its tonnage of 1,075 tons, its top speed reached 36 knots. These destroyers were armed with three 4-inch rapid-firing guns, one 2-pounder machine cannon, four Lewis light machine-guns and two 21-inch torpedo tubes. HMS *Scout* and HMS *Thanet* were built in 1919 and HMS *Thracian* was built in 1923. Christopher Briggs, *Farewell Hong Kong 1941* (Carlisle: Hesperian Press, 2001), pp. 6–11.

27. Specifications of the Insect-class gunboats: 635 tons, 14 knots, two 6-inch guns, one 3-inch AA, one 2-pounder, and eight MGs; HMS *Tern*: 262 tons, 14 knots, two 3-inch rapid-firing guns and eight MGs; HMS *Robin*: 226 tons, 13 knots, one 3.7-inch howitzer, one 6-pounder gun and eight MGs.

28. These six MTBs weighed 22 tons each with a top speed of 33 knots. They were armed with two 18-inch torpedo tubes and four 0.303-inch twin machine-guns. MTBs 26 and 27 weighed 14 tons each and had a top speed of 40 knots. They were armed with two 18-inch torpedo tubes and two 0.303-inch twin machine-guns. Due to the outbreak of the Second Sino-Japanese War and the fall of Nanjing and Shanghai, the Hong Kong government held six MTBs bought by the Chinese Nationalist government in custody when the boats were being transferred to China. Two of them were bought by the Hong Kong government, which became MTBs 26 and 27; the rest later reached Wuhan.

29. Hong Kong War Diary, www.hongkongwardiary.com; Kwong Chi Man and Tsoi Yiu Lun, *Gudu qianshao: Taipingyang zhanzheng zhong de Xianggang zhanyi* (Hong Kong: Cosmos, 2013), pp. 130–1.

30. "War Narrative," WO 106/2401B, p. 3.

31. "Copy of Proceedings of the Court of Enquiry Held on 8 May 1942 in P.O.W. Camp in Argyle Street to Investigate the Circumstance Leading to the Loss of Shing Mun Redoubt," CAB 106/166, p. 15.

32. Kwong Chi Man and Tsoi Yiu Lun, p. 150.

33. Bōeishō bōei kenshusho senshishitsu, *Honkon-Chosa Sakusen* [Hong Kong-Changsha operations] (Tokyo: Asagumo, 1971), pp. 10–11.

34. Ibid., p. 25.

35. Ibid., pp. 53–4. A recently published book argues that the directives were actually drafted by the Chief of Staff of the 23rd Army, Maj. Gen. Kuribayashi Tadamichi and his colleague Lt. Col. Toda. Harayama Shigeo, *Kuribayashi Tadamichi, Imai Takeo monogatari* (Nagano: Hōzuki, 2011), pp. 142–8.

36. Bōeishō bōei kenshusho senshishitsu, *Honkon-Chosa Sakusen*, p. 36.

37. It was sometimes suggested that the Japanese were trained at the Baiyun Mountain of Guangzhou. However, no information about this has been found in Japanese documents. "Honkon kōryakusen nikansuru shoken kyu kyōkun" [Opinions and lessons on the Offensive Operation in Hong Kong], 10/1/1942, RIS, NIDS, JACAR, Ref: C13031812500.

38. "1941 nen 12 getsu ni okeru Honkon kōryaku sakusen kikoru" [Report of the Offensive Operation in Hong Kong in December 1941], RIS, NIDS, JACAR, Ref: C13031811200, pp. 18–20. See also Kwong Chi Man and Tsoi Yiu Lun, pp. 151–3.

39. Map based on the description in Bōeishō bōei kenshusho senshishitsu, *Honkon-Chosa Sakusen*, pp. 10–11.

40. "Dai ni kenshi kantai shireibu senshi nisshi" [Wartime Diary of HQ Second China Fleet], 1/12/1941–31/12/1941, Kaigun ichihan shiryō (KIS), NIDS, JACAR, Ref: C08030033500.

41. Kwong Chi Man and Tsoi Yiu Lun, p. 138.

42. "1941 nen 12 getsu ni okeru Honkon kōryaku sakusen kikoru," RIS, NIDS, JACAR, Ref: C13031811200, p. 27.

43. "1st Hong Kong Regiment HKSRA Mainland," WO 172/1688, p. 3. The war diary of the Royal Artillery provides rather different data: "ammunition was sent to gun positions on a scale of 100 rounds per gun with the same held at West Fort and 200 r.p.g. at Mau Tau Kok [*sic*] Ordnance Deport as a further reserve." "Royal Artillery Report of Operations in Hong Kong," WO 172/1687, p. 1.

44. "War Diary," WO 106/2401A, Appendix B, p. 1.

45. Ibid.

46. Ibid.

47. Kwong Chi Man and Tsoi Yiu Lun, p. 161.

48. "No.1 Company HKVDC War Diary," WO 172/1693, p. 2.

49. H. M. Montague, "Report of Proceedings from Outbreak of Hostilities with Japan at Hong Kong until His Arrival at Chungking" (hereafter "Montague's Report"), CO 968/9/4, slide 56; Bōeishō bōei kenshusho senshishitsu, *Chukoku hōmen rikugun kōkū sakusen* [Army Air Force's War in China] (Tokyo: Asagumo News, 1974), p. 255.

50. This exceptionally low level was recorded in both Japanese and British sources. The award for Takatsuki Hiraki claimed that they strafed the British aircraft at the level of little more than ten metres; Bōeishō bōei kenshusho senshishitsu, *Honkon-Chosa Sakusen*, p. 119. Maltby said the Japanese aircraft attacked "down to 60 feet" in a letter; "Letter to WO by Maj. Gen. Maltby," *Hong Kong Despatches*, WO 106/2401A, p. 6.

51. WO 106/2401A, Appendix B, p. 2. The report of the 23rd Army noted that the light bombers at the level of 4,200 metres failed to find their targets; it was the fighters at low level that destroyed the British planes. See "Honkon kōryakusen nikansuru shoken kyu kyōkun," 23rd Army, Shina-Shina shihen: nanshi-64, NID, p. 26.

52. WO 106/2401A, Appendix B, p. 2.

53. "Honkon kōryakusen nikansuru shoken kyu kyōkun," p. 10.

54. "Dai sanjuhachi shidan Honkon kōryakusen sentō shōhō" [Report of the 38th Division's Offensive Operation in Hong Kong], Shina-Shina shihen: nanshi-15, pp. 159–61.

55. Chan Chak, "Xianggang zhan tuwei riji," in Chan On-kwok (ed.), *Chan Chak Jiangjun jinianji* (2011), pp. 236–40.

56. The fall of the Shing Mun Redoubt has been comprehensively discussed by Lawrence Lai and others, based on British sources and the official Japanese history of the campaign. However, as we have pointed out the difference in the time zones used by either side, this section attempts to reconstruct events on the basis of the Japanese primary documents as well as the Shing Mun inquiry, conducted by the British in the 1950s.

For Lai's study and the comparison of his timeline with that of Tony Banham in *Not the Slightest Chance*, see Lawrence Lai et al., "Decoding the Enigma of the Fall of the Shung Mun Redoubt Using Line of Sight Analysis," *Surveying & Built Environment*, Vol. 21, No. 2 (2011), pp. 21–42.

57. *Hohei dai ninihachi rentai shi*, pp. 76–9; "Battle Progress Report of the 228th Infantry Regiment in the Hong Kong Invasion Operations in December 1941," HKMS 100–1-5, pp. 3–5.

58. According to Latham's report, Maj. Gen. Maltby described Capt. Jones as "useless" while Brig. Wallis described Capt. Jones as "weak," when Wallis was serving at the inquiry in 1942. "Notes of an Interview with Major-General Maltby, 1 October 1957," CAB 44/175, Appendix I; "Copy of Proceedings of the Court of Enquiry Held on 8 May 1942 in P.O.W. Camp in Argyle Street to Investigate the Circumstances Leading to the Loss of Shing Mun Redoubt," CAB 106/166, p. 5.

59. Where they withdrew to is not clear, but it was possibly L. 104. Please refer to the text for further details.

60. *Report on the Action of the 2nd Battalion The Royal Scots in the Fighting on the Mainland during the Hong Kong Campaign, 8th–13th December 1941*, CAB 44/175 (unpaginated).

61. There were no alternative positions for PB 400 and PB 401, as the terrain was too rough. CAB 44/175.

62. Jones mentioned in the inquiry in 1942 that he had proposed to block the dam with barbed wire but was turned down by Public Works Department, which claimed that the wire would "interfere with the water supply." No other records may be found to support his claim. CAB 106/166, p. 21.

63. "Dai sanjuhachi shidan Honkon kōryakusen sentō shōhō," Shina-Shina shihen: nanshi-15, pp. 159–61.

64. "War Diary 2nd Battalion Royal Scots," WO 172/1690, p. 5.

65. *Hohei dai ninihachi rentai shi*, p. 78.

66. Ibid., pp. 79–83.

67. Bōeishō bōei kenshusho senshishitsu, *Honkon-Chosa Sakusen*, pp. 147–8.

68. HKMS 100–1-5, p. 5; *Hohei dai ninihachi rentai shi*, pp. 79–80, 116–7.

69. CAB 106/166, p. 23.

70. Robb later broke out and withdrew to D/Rajput on Smugglers' Ridge; *Hohei dai ninihachi rentai shi*, p. 79.

71. *Hohei dai ninihachi rentai shi*, p. 79.

72. "Dai sanjuhachi shidan Honkon kōryakusen sentō shōhō," Shina-Shina shihen: nanshi-15, p. 165.

73. *Hohei dai ninihachi rentai shi*, p. 80; "Dai sanjuhachi shidan Honkon kōryakusen sentō shōhō," Shina-Shina shihen: nanshi-15, pp. 166–8.

74. Harayama, *Kuribayashi Tadamichi, Imai Takeo monogatari*, pp. 142–8.

75. CAB 106/166, p. 20; CAB 44/175.

76. CAB 44/175. In all, PBs 208, 210, 211, 212, 213 and 214 were damaged; 211 and 214 were almost destroyed. See "Kyūryū hantō okeru honbōgyo jinchi chōsa hōkoku," 1/1942, Shina-Dai Tōasen-Nanshi 90, NID.

77. WO 172/1690, p. 10.

78. Bōeishō bōei kenshusho senshishitsu, *Honkon-Chosa Sakusen*, p. 167; "Honkon kōryakusen sentō shōhō dai sanju hachi shidan hohei dai nihakusanju rentai" [Action

Report of the 230th Infantry Regiment of the 38th Division during the Hong Kong Campaign], Shina-Shina shihen: nanshi-34, NID, pp. 69–70.

79. "Events on Castle Peak Road Morning 11th Dec, 1941," WO 106/2401A, Appendix C, p. 1.

80. WO 106/2401A, Appendix C, p. 1. World Pencil Factory was located on Fuk Wah Street.

81. Bōeishō bōei kenshusho senshishitsu, *Honkon-Chosa Sakusen*, pp. 168–9.

82. CAB 44/175.

83. WO 172/1689, p. 4.

84. One of the searchlight positions was inside the present-day Tsing Yi Garden.

85. Kwong Chi Man and Tsoi Yiu Lun, pp. 199–200.

86. Chiu Lan Chu is nowadays the quarry of Anderson Road. Tai Wan Tsun is the area around the present-day Jordan Valley.

87. It was located at the entrance of Wilson Trail No. 3.

88. These Chinese non-combatants were mainly truck drivers and ship crew. They were neither regular soldiers nor volunteers. WO 106/2401A, Appendix A, p. 9.

89. WO 106/2401A, Appendix A, p. 10; Appexdix B1, p. 5.

90. "Memorandum on Dynamite Incident," WO 106/2401B.

91. "The Work of the Hong Kong Police during the Siege," CO 968/9/4, slides 2–3.

92. Philip Snow's *The Battle of Hong Kong* describes in detail the triad incident. He described Shaftain as the head of Special Branch. However, the head of Special Branch was actually H. R. S. Major. Shaftain was the head of the Criminal Investigation Department, which was responsible for the investigation of the triad societies' activities. That is the reason the report went to Shaftain. "The Work of the Hong Kong Police during the Siege," CO 968/9/4, slides 2–3.

93. Alan Birch and Martin Cole, *Captive Christmas: The Battle of Hong Kong—December 1941* (Hong Kong: Heinemann Asia, 1979), p. 60.

94. Zhou Yumin and Shao Yong, *Zhongguo banghuishi* (Wuhan: Wuhan daxue chubanshe, 2012), pp. 447–50, 498–500, 576–81, 671–5; For a description of the triads, please also see Kwong Chi Man and Tsoi Yiu Lun, *Gudu qianshao: Taipingyang zhanzheng zhong de Xianggang zhanyi*, pp. 329–31.

95. Birch and Cole, *Captive Christmas*, p. 61.

96. CO 968/9/4, slide 4. Birch and Cole, *Captive Christmas*, p. 61.

97. L. H. C. Calthrop, "Hong Kong Police War Diary—December 8th–25th, 1941," CO 129/592/4, slide 40. This line was originally deleted: the authors of this book were able to reconstruct this line letter by letter through magnifying the microfilm of the document.

98. CO 968/9/4, slide 7.

99. Birch and Cole, *Captive Christmas*, pp. 61–2.

100. He was called "Colonel" in Lavalle's account.

101. Kenneth Cambon, *Guest of Hirohito* (Vancouver: PW Press, 1990), Appendix 1, p. 138.

102. Ibid., pp. 138–40.

103. Gwen Dew, *Prisoner of the Japs* (New York: Alfred Knopf, 1943), p. 51; *Honkon-Chosa Sakusen*, p. 186.

104. "Governor to CO," 14/12/1941, CO 968/9/3, slide 127.

105. "CO to Governor," 14/12/1941, CO 968/9/3, slide 130.

106. The area is nowadays between the Fortress Hill and Quarry Bay stations. *Honkon-Chosa Sakusen*, p. 201.

107. The war diary of the 38th Division also contained detailed description of the shelling of Hong Kong Island. See "Dai sanjuhachi shidan Honkon kōryakusen sentō shōhō," Shina-Shina shihen: nanshi-15, pp. 181–96.

108. Tai Shek Ku is nowadays Shek Ku Street in Ho Man Tin.

109. This area is probably the present-day Hong Ning Road Park.

110. The E Company consisted of the replacement troops of the Winnipeg Grenadiers.

111. "War Diary East Infantry Brigade," WO 172/1686, p. 3.

112. "The Work of the Hong Kong Police during the Siege," CO 968/9/4, slide 2.

113. Three "units" (twenty 240-mm, thirty 150-mm cannon and mortar, and forty 150-mm howitzer shells) were expended for each gun.

114. WO 172/1687, p. 7.

115. Lawson Diary, pp. 4–5; "Montague's Report," CO 968/9/4, slide 58; WO 106/2401A, Appendix A, p. 13. In his book *Not the Slightest Chance: The Defence of Hong Kong, 1941* (Hong Kong: Hong Kong University Press, 2003), Tony Banham put this action on the nights of 15 and 16 December. However, HMS *Thracian*'s action was dated in the diary of Brig. Lawson, the reports of Cmdr. Montague and the original reports dated 1942 by Maj. Gen. Maltby as actually taking place on the nights of 14 and 15 December. Tom Quillam, who was on board HMS *Thracian*, mistakenly recorded the date as 15 December. Maj. Gen. Maltby also made the same mistake in his full report dated 1945. Tom Quillam, *Eye Witness Tells the* Thracian*'s Story*, 940.53 QUI, p. 4; C. M. Maltby, *Supplement to The London Gazette* (London: HMSO, 1948), p. 709.

116. WO 106/2401A, Appendix B, p. 8.

117. Ibid.

118. "Report from Kwangtung Province, December 1941/January 1942," Elizabeth Ride Collection, Hong Kong Heritage Project.

119. "G.O.C. Hong Kong to C. in C. Far East," 15/12/1941, WO 106/ 2420A; Chan Chak, "Xianggang zhan tuwei riji," p. 246.

120. E. C. Ford, "Memos of the Battle of Hong Kong and Impressions of a Prison Camp," *Letters, Memoranda, Reports Diary Extracts and Other Narratives Written by Hong Kong Residents Relating Their Experiences and Observations during the Battle for Hong Kong, the Japanese Occupation and Surrender*, HKMS100–1-6, p. 17.

121. "Montague's Report," CO 968/9/4, slide 58; "Dai ni kenshi kantai senshi nisshi sentō shōhō," 1/1/1942–31/1/1942.

122. Bōeishō bōei kenshusho senshishitsu, *Chukoku hōmen rikugun kōku sakusen*, pp. 258–9.

123. "Kanoya kōkutai hokōkitai sentō kōdō chōsho" [Action Report of the Kanoya Wing], 12/1941–2/1942, KIS, NIDS, JACAR, C08051612900.

124. "Montague's Report," CO 968/9/4, slide 58.

125. Kwong and Tsoi, *Gudu qianshao*, p. 166.

126. When they were hit by British shell fire is not certain. *Honkon-Chosa Sakusen* claimed that they were hit when returning from Tide Cove, while the record of 229th Regiment claimed that they came under fire on the way towards Tide Cove. The authors have followed the version of the latter. Bōeishō bōei kenshusho senshishitsu, *Honkon-Chosa*

Sakusen, p. 179; *Hohei dai ninikyu rentai shi* [History of the 229th infantry regiment] (Fukufukukai, 1981), p. 209. Although it was said that each regiment formed a company of capable swimmers, this event is reported only in the regimental histories of the 229th and 230th regiments.

127. Bōeishō bōei kenshusho senshishitsu, *Honkon-Chosa Sakusen*, pp. 189–90.

128. "Governor to CO," 17/12/1941, WO 106/ 2420A.

129. WO 106/2401A, Appendix B, p. 10.

130. Ibid.

131. Bōeishō bōei kenshusho senshishitsu, *Honkon-Chosa Sakusen*, pp. 202–6.

132. Ibid., pp. 223–4.

133. WO 106/2401A, Appendix B, p. 10.

134. PB 41 was at the junction of present-day Shau Kei Wan Road and Aldrich Bay Road. PB 42 is nowadays the petrol station at Tai Hong Street. *Hohei dai ninikyu rentai shi*, p. 303.

135. The beach is in present-day the area of Tai Hong Street, Tai On Street, Holy Cross Path, Hoi Ning Street and Hoi An Street.

136. "An Abbreviated Narrative of Events during the Action at Hong Kong, December, 1941," WO 106/2401A, Appendix A, p. 18.

137. Bōeishō bōei kenshusho senshishitsu, *Honkon-Chosa Sakusen*, p. 226.

138. WO106/2401A, Appendix A, p. 18.

139. "Report by O.C. 5/7 Raj (Taikoo) on Events on North Face between 0900 hours 18 Dec. 41 & 0900 hours 19 Dec. 41," WO 106/2401A, Appendix D, p. 1.

140. WO106/2401A, Appendix A, p. 19.

141. The British record of the landing time is rather confusing. The record of Rajput had mistakenly put the time of landing at 20:00, while Japanese troops were still crossing Victoria Harbour. WO 106/2401A, Appendix D, p. 1; "Dai sanjuhachi shidan Honkon kōryakusen sentō shōhō," pp. 208–10.

142. "Dai sanjuhachi shidan Honkon kōryakusen sentō shōhō," Shina-Shina shihen: nanshi-15, p. 204; "Honkon kōryakusen sentō shōhō dai sanju hachi shidan hohei dai nihaku-sanju rentai," Shina-Shina shihen: nanshi-34, NID, p. 99; Kwong Chi Man and Tsoi Yiu Lun, *Gudu qianshao*, p. 226.

143. The reservoir is now called Choi Sai Woo.

144. WO 106/2401A, Appendix D, p. 2.

145. Appendix D, 2401A; *Hohei dai ninikyu rentai shi*, pp. 296–314.

146. Appendix D, 2401A.

147. Kwong Chi Man and Tsoi Yiu Lun, *Gudu qianshao*, p. 305.

148. Chan Chak, "Xianggang zhan tuwei riji," p. 251.

149. The platoons were from the HQ Company of the Winnipeg Grenadiers.

150. Chan Chak, "Xianggang zhan tuwei riji," p. 251.

151. "Military Court for the Trial of War Criminals: The Proceedings of the Trial of Maj. Gen. Shoji Toshishige of the Imperial Japanese Army," WO 235/1015, Exhibit Z, p. 3; "Dai sanjuhachi shidan Honkon kōryakusen sentō shōhō," p. 206.

152. "Honkon kōryakusen sentō shōhō dai sanju hachi shidan hohei dai nihakusanju rentai," p. 102.

153. The British record had given Jacosta's rank as captain, but his tombstone in the Stanley War Cemetery has his rank as lieutenant. We have followed the latter here.

154. Ted Ferguson, *Desperate Siege: The Battle of Hong Kong* (Toronto: Nelson Canada, 1980), p.148.

155. *Hohei dai ninikyu rentai shi*, p. 231.

156. "Personal Account by the Hon: Major J. J. Paterson, HKVDC, On North Point Power Station," *Hong Kong Despatches*, WO 106/2401A, Appendix L; WO 172/1689, Appendix 4; WO 172/1689, Appendix 4E; *Hohei dai ninikyu rentai shi*, pp. 231–2.

157. WO 172/1689, Appendix 4.

158. "Report on the Hong Kong Chinese Regiment in the battle of Hong Kong 1941 Dec. 8–25, by Captain R. D. Scriven," CAB 106/88.

159. Royal Scots Diary, WO 172/1690, p. 26. For a survey map describing the disposition of the defenders in Wong Nai Chung Gap before the battle, see Lawrence W. C. Lai, Ken Ching, Tim Ko and Y. K. Tan, "'Pillbox 3 Did Not Open Fire!': Mapping the Arcs of Fire of Pillboxes at Jardine's Lookout and Wong Nai Chung Gap," *Surveying & Built Environment*, Vol. 21, No. 2 (2011), pp. 54–5.

160. "Honkon kōryakusen sentō shōhō dai sanju hachi shidan hohei dai nihakusanju rentai," Shina-Shina shihen: nanshi-34, NID, pp. 105–6.

161. "Honkon kōryakusen sentō shōhō dai sanju hachi shidan hohei dai nihakusanju rentai," p. 102.

162. *Hohei dai ninihachi rentai shi*, p. 88.

163. Ibid., p. 98.

164. "Dokuritsu sokushahō dai go daitai dai san chutai sentō jōhō" [Action Report of the 3rd Company of the 5th Independent Rapid-fire Gun Battalion], RIS, NIDS, JACAR, Ref: C13031807100; Lawrence Lai has suggested that PB 3 failed to engage because it was unable to train its fire on the advancing Japanese. However, the 3rd Rapid-Firing Gun Company noted that it had exchanged fire with PB 3 and silenced it. See Lai et al., "'Pillbox 3 Did Not Open Fire!'," pp. 43–57; in addition, for accurate survey maps of the battle, see the above article by Lawrence Lai.

165. A Company was then commanded by Captain K. J. Campbell; it probably regrouped after arrival at Hong Kong Island. "Account of Events in the Jardine's Lookout—Wong Nei Chong Gap Area," *Hong Kong Desptaches*, WO 106/2401A, Appendix E, p. 2.

166. "G.O.C. Hong Kong to WO at 0836," 19/12/1941, WO 106/2420A.

167. *Hohei dai ninikyu rentai shi*, pp. 231, 251–2; Tim Luard, *Escape from Hong Kong* (Hong Kong: Kong Kong University Press, 2012), pp. 44–5.

168. "Dai sanjuhachi shidan Honkon kōryakusen sentō shōhō," pp. 212–3.

169. "Dokuritsu sokushahō dai go daitai dai san chutai sentō jōhō," Ref: C13031807100.

170. Bōeishō bōei kenshusho senshishitsu, *Honkon-Chosa Sakusen*, p. 243.

171. "Honkon kōryakusen sentō shōhō dai sanju hachi shidan hohei dai nihakusanju rentai," p. 107. He died or incapicated later, as he was never in active service again throughout the war.

172. "War Narrative," WO 106/2401B, p. 36. Maltby wrote two versions of what happened next. In 1942, he wrote: "He spoke to me over the telephone and told me that the situation there was critical and that he was leaving his HQ to organize an attack on the enemy at Jardine's Lookout. I subsequently heard that he was killed instantaneously shortly after leaving his Bde HQ." In his final report in 1945, he wrote: "Brigadier J. K. Lawson reported that the HQ shelters were overrun, firing into them was actually taking

place at point blank range and that he was going outside to fight it out, after destroying telephone exchanges etc. He did so, and I regret to say he was killed, together with his Bde Major, Major Temple and personnel of HQ West Group R.A., and also C.B. Group personnel were killed too." WO 106/2401A, Appendix A, p. 24; "War Narrative," WO 106/2401B, p. 36.

173. Japanese soldiers did not discover the death of Brig. Lawson until four days later, when they completely controlled Wong Nai Chung Gap and had cleared the battlefield. According to Col. Shoji, Lawson "had died as a result of wounded fractured right leg and loss of blood. It appeared that considerable time had elapsed before his death and that necessary medical supplies had been lacking." They wrapped up the body of Lawson with the blanket of Lt. Okada, the commander of 9th Company, and buried him on site. WO 235/1015, Exhibit Z, p. 6.

174. It is nowadays the Celestial Garden at No. 5 Repulse Bay Road.

175. The owner, George Tinson, assisted the defenders with his Chinese servant; he later died during a Japanese bombardment.

176. CAB 106/88.

177. It is probably the present-day Hong Kong Tennis Centre.

178. WO 172/1690, p. 32.

179. "Account of Events at PBs 1 & 2 (Wong Nai Chung Area) by Lieut. B. C. Field, H.K.V.D.C.," WO 106/2401A, Appendix F, p. 2.

180. WO 106/2401A, Appendix B, p. 14.

181. Ibid., p. 14.

182. Nathan Greenfield, *The Damned: The Canadians at the Battle of Hong Kong and the POW Experience, 1941–45* (Toronto: HarperCollins Publishers, 2010), p. 124. There was an entry in the Fortress HQ diary for 16:55, 19 December. It reads: "A report from the R.A. at this time stated the position of the enemy at Wong Nei Chong Gap was not known. He was thought to be holding the Police Station and ridge at 225514 [south of Wong Nai Chung Reservoir] and to be working round south of the Reservoir." Since the Royal Artillery counterattack had not yet been launched, it is believed that Maj. Gen. Maltby mistook Capt. Hopkinson as personnel of the Royal Artillery. WO 106/2401A, Appendix B, p. 14.

183. "Personal Account by Lieut. I. Tamworth, Hong Kong Engineering Corps," WO 106/2401A, Appendix J, p. 1.

184. In the Fortress HQ diary, it reads "O.C. 1st H.K. Regt. H.K.S.R.A.," referring to Lt. Col. Yale. But Lt. Col. Yale was already wounded and missing. According to the war diary of the Island East Group Royal Artillery, it should be Maj. Hunt who went to Fortress HQ. WO 106/2401A, Appendix B1, p. 15; WO 172/1687, p. 14.

185. Dan Waters, "The Country Boy Who Died for Hong Kong," *JRASHKB*, Vol. 25 (1985).

186. "Examination of 9th Witness for Prosecution—G. J. White on 12th March, 1947," Military Courts for the Trial of Major General Shoji Toshishige, WO 235/1015, pp. 49–55.

187. "Montague's Report," CO 968/9/4, slide 59.

188. David Macri, "Hong Kong in the Sino-Japanese War," unpublished PhD thesis, the University of Hong Kong (2010), p. 488; CAB 106/88.

189. There were at least three versions of the casualties suffered by 230th Regiment. In his statement dated 18 November 1946, Col. Shoji claimed they had suffered 800 casualties. In the Operation Report of 38th Division, it was stated that the 230th Regiment suffered casualties of 39 officers and 629 other ranks. The Operation Report of 230th Regiment claimed the total casualties were 36 officers and 580 soldiers. WO 235/1015, Exhibit Z, p. 6; "Dai sanjuhachi shidan Honkon kōryakusen sentō shōhō," Appendix 6; "Honkon kōryakusen sentō shōhō dai sanju hachi shidan hohei dai nihakusanju rentai," Appendix 1.

190. WO 235/1015, Exhibit Z, p. 5.

191. WO 172/1690, p. 33.

192. "Dokuritsu sokushahō dai go daitai dai san chutai sentō jōhō," RIS, NDI, JACAR, Ref: C13031807100. After the battle, it was recommended that the artillerymen should be equipped also with rifles.

193. WO 106/2401A, Appendix E.

194. WO 106/2401A, Appendix B, p. 16.

195. Bōeishō bōei kenshusho senshishitsu, *Honkon-Chosa Sakusen*, pp. 259–60.

196. Benjamin Proulx, *Underground from Hong Kong* (New York: Stratford Press, 1943), p. 43.

197. Bōeishō bōei kenshusho senshishitsu, *Honkon-Chosa Sakusen*, p. 265.

198. Ibid., p. 262; "Events at Little Hong Kong: Personal Narrative by Major H. Marsh. 1 Mx.," WO 106/2401A, Appendix K.

199. Bōeishō bōei kenshusho senshishitsu, *Honkon-Chosa Sakusen*, pp. 255–6.

200. "Dai sanjuhachi shidan Honkon kōryakusen sentō shōhō," pp. 224–9.

201. WO 106/2401A, Appendix B, p. 17.

202. Ibid., p. 18.

203. Chan Chak, "Xianggang zhan tuwei riji," p. 253.

204. "Dokuritsu sanhōhei dai niju daitai honkon kōryakusen sentō shōhō," RIS, NDI, JACAR, Ref: C13031799700, slides 0976–0977.

205. "Report from Kwangtung Province, December 1941/January 1942," Elizabeth Ride Collection, Hong Kong Heritage Project.

206. WO 106/2401A, Appendix B, pp. 18–9.

207. Ibid., p. 19.

208. Ibid., p. 19.

209. Col. Doi reported that there were only two survivors who were severely wounded. HKMS 100–1-5, pp. 13–4.

210. *Hohei dai ninihachi rentai shi*, pp. 91–2, 104–6; Banham, *Not the Slightest Chance*, p. 188. Col. Doi recalled that 3rd Company had suffered 40 percent casualties. HKMS 100–1-5, p. 13.

211. "Montague's Report," CO 968/9/4, slide 60.

212. *Hohei dai ninikyu rentai shi*, pp. 253–4. The European engineers were later murdered. See "Examination of 15th Witness for Prosecution—Chan Sai-So on 20th January, 1948," Military Courts for the Trial of Lt. Gen. Ito Takeo, WO 235/1107, pp. 73–6.

213. *Hohei dai ninikyu rentai shi*, pp. 235–9, 249–59, 264–6; *Honkon-Chosa Sakusen*, pp. 269–70.

214. Grant S. Garneau, *The Royal Rifles of Canada in Hong Kong 1941–1945* (Carp, ON: The Hong Kong Veterans' Association of Canada, 1980), pp. 71–7; WO 172/1693, pp. 14–7; WO 106/2401A, Appendix B, pp. 19–22.

215. The telegram also said the Chinese hoped to operate twenty bombers against Japanese airfields from 20 December. WO 106/2401A, Appendix B, p. 21.

216. Ibid., p. 22.

217. WO 172/1686, pp. 76–7; Greenfield, *The Damned*, pp. 164–5.

218. "N.O.I.C. Hong Kong to Admiralty," 21/12/1941, WO 106/2420A.

219. Ibid.

220. "Grey 36, 1840/20," WO 106/2420A.

221. "D.M.O. P/340a," WO 106/2420A.

222. Ibid.

223. "Admiralty to Cdre. Hong Kong," 21/12/1941, WO 106/2420A.

224. "WO to G.O.C. Hong Kong," 21/12/1941, WO 106/2420A.

225. WO 106/2401A, Appendix B, p. 23.

226. Bōeishō bōei kenshusho senshishitsu, *Honkon-Chosa Sakusen*, pp. 276–7.

227. Chan Chak, "Xianggang zhan tuwei riji," pp. 253–5.

228. WO 172/1686, pp. 78–80.

229. "Personal Account by Lieut. I. Tamworth, Hong Kong Engineering Corps," WO 106/2401A, Appendix J.

230. WO 106/2401A, Appendix B, p. 23.

231. "Cdre. Hong Kong to Admiralty," 22/12/1941, WO 106/2420A.

232. WO 106/2401A, Appendix B, pp. 24, 30–1.

233. "Events at Little Hong Kong," *Hong Kong Despatches*, WO 106/2401A, Appendix K, p. 6; *Hohei dai ninihachi rentai shi*, pp. 92–3.

234. WO 106/2401A, Appendix B, p. 24.

235. "Honkon kōryakusen sentō shōhō dai sanju hachi shidan hohei dai nihakusanju rentai," p. 120.

236. "Events at Little Hong Kong," WO 106/2401A, Appendix K, p. 6.

237. WO 172/1686, p. 88.

238. Ibid., pp. 89–90.

239. It is where the Police Museum stands nowadays.

240. Hill 281 is nowadays the location of Guildford Road, Mansfield Road and Watford Road.

241. WO 106/2401A, Appendix B, pp. 27–8.

242. Mount Parrish is nowadays the location of Wah Yan College.

243. WO 106/2401A, Appendix B, p. 27.

244. Ibid., p. 28.

245. WO 172/1686, pp. 91–3.

246. WO 106/2401A, Appendix B, p. 27.

247. WO 172/1686, pp. 95–7.

248. WO 106/2401A, Appendix B, p. 29.

249. WO 172/1686, p. 103.

250. *Hohei dai ninikyu rentai shi*, pp. 239–40, 259–61. This searchlight probably belonged to PB 28.

251. "Statement by Sgt. H.F. Hopkins, HKVDC," WO 106/2401B, Appendix Q, p. 83.

252. "Recommendations for Honours and Awards," WO 106/2401B, Appendix Q, pp. 80–4.

253. WO 106/2401A, Appendix B, p. 29.

254. *Hohei dai ninikyu rentai shi*, pp. 241–3; WO 172/1689, Appendix 2b, pp. 5–7; WO 172/1686, pp. 106–7.

255. Wallis claimed in his war diary that on the evening of 24 December, "I learned to my astonishment some European nurses were at St. Stephens College. I sent an ambulance with water and succeeded in evacuation [*sic*] 3, the others had been killed during the fighting, to the Fort." There were no survivors of the evacuation mentioned. Most of the nurses were trapped inside the main building until capitulation. St. Stephen's College was used as a military hospital; wounded soldiers from Red Hill, Repulse Bay and Middle Spur were housed inside the main building. When Wallis planned the in-depth defence of Stanley Peninsula, St. Stephen's College was somehow cut into two by the second line, with the main building at its front. It seems possible that Brig. Wallis chose not to withdraw the wounded into either Stanley Prison or Stanley Fort, as these two places were either out of water or lacked enough space. The military hospital continued to function as fighting in Stanley Village continued. WO 172/1686, p. 100.

256. Bōeishō bōei kenshusho senshishitsu, *Honkon-Chosa Sakusen*, pp. 307–8.

257. WO 106/2401A, Appendix B, p. 31.

258. WO 172/1690, pp. 38–9.

259. WO 106/2401A, Appendix B, p. 31.

260. Ibid., p. 31.

261. "Letter to the Secretary of State for the Colonies from Sir Mark Young," CO 968/98/6, slide 52.

262. "Governor, Straits Settlements to Colonial Office," 25/12/1941, WO 106/2420A.

263. By then, Wallis did not have enough time to destroy the Stanley and Bluff Head batteries; they were taken over unscathed by the Japanese.

264. *Hohei dai ninihachi rentai shi*, p. 103; *Hohei dai ninikyu rentai shi*, p. 286.

265. Chan On-kwok (ed.), "Chan Chak jiangjun zhuanlue," *Chan Chak Jiangjun jinianji* (2011), p. 98.

266. "Sir A. Clark Kerr to FO," 15/12/1941, CO 129/590.

267. Chan On-kwok (ed.), "Xianggang kangzhan tuwei zongbaogao," *Chan Chak Jiangjun jinianji* (2011), p. 279.

268. Ibid., p. 279.

269. Ibid., p. 282.

270. Ibid., pp. 95, 101–2.

271. Ibid., pp. 283–4.

272. L. H. C. Calthrop, "Hong Kong Police War Diary: December 8th–26th December," CO 129/592/4, p. 52.

273. Chan On-kwok (ed.), "Xianggang kangzhan tuwei zongbaogao," p. 284.

274. Luard, *Escape from Hong Kong*, pp. 58–9.

275. Chan On-kwok (ed.), "Xianggang kangzhan tuwei zongbaogao," pp. 259, 285.

276. Luard, *Escape from Hong Kong*, p. 77.

277. Luard, *Escape from Hong Kong*, p. 52.

278. "Montague's Report," CO 968/9/4, slide 61; Luard, *Escape from Hong Kong*, pp. 79, 89–94. When Chan Chak and his men were breaking out, they met "Two-Gun" Cohen, the bodyguard of Dr. Sun Yat-sen. Cohen had been left behind after escorting the Soong sisters to Kai Tak airfield. MacDougall asked Cohen to join them, but he insisted on

staying in Hong Kong. Cohen was arrested and interned in Stanley Internment Camp until 1943.

279. Luard, *Escape from Hong Kong*, pp. 80–5.

280. "Montague's Report," CO 968/9/4, slide 63; Tim Luard, pp. 103–11.

281. Luard, *Escape from Hong Kong*, pp. 112–5; Chan On-kwok (ed.), "Xianggang kangzhan tuwei zongbaogao," p. 260.

282. "Dai sanjuhachi shidan Honkon kōryakusen sentō shōhō," p. 113.

283. "Dai ni kenshi kantai senshi nisshi sentō shōhō," 1/1/1942–31/1/1942, Ref: C08030033500.

284. "Montague's Report," CO 968/9/4, slide 64.

285. Chan On-kwok (ed.), "Xianggang kangzhan tuwei zongbaogao," pp. 262–3.

286. WO 106/2401A, Appendix P.

287. "Prisoner of War Diary of Chief Signal Officer, China Command, Hong Kong, 1941–1945," 940 547252 PRI.

288. "Dai sanjuhachi shidan Honkon kōryakusen sentō shōhō," Appendix; Kwong and Tsoi, *Gudu Qianshao*, pp. 350–1.

289. "Honkon kōryakusen nikansuru shoken kyu kyōkun," 10/1/1942, RIS, NIDS, JACAR, Ref: C13031812400.

290. *Chukoku hōmen rikugun kōkū sakusen* (Tokyo: Asagumo News, 1974), p. 262.

9 Hong Kong under the Japanese Occupation, 1942–1945

1. "J. D. Clague to G. B. Endacott," 21/5/1971, HKMS 100–1-1. Also quoted in Kwong Chi Man, "The Failure of Japanese Land-Sea Cooperation: Hong Kong and the South China Coast as an Example, 1942–1945," *Journal of Military History*, forthcoming.

2. "Jōkyō hōkoku," 2/4/1942, RD, NIDS, JACAR, Ref: C01000250100.

3. Ibid.

4. "Senshi getsuhō nikansuru ken," 4/1942, RD, NIDS, JACAR, Ref: C01000412800.

5. "Hensei kanketsu no ken," 20/2/1942, RD, NIDS, JACAR, Ref: C01000272200.

6. "Dai ni kenshi kantai senshi nisshi sentō shōhō," 1/1/1942–31/1/1942, Kaigun ichihan shiryō (KIS), NIDS, JACAR, Ref: C08030033600.

7. "Jōkyō hōkoku," Ref: C01000250100.

8. "Dai ni kenshi kantai senshi nisshi sentō shōhō," Ref: C08030033600.

9. Tony Banham, *The Sinking of the* Lisbon Maru: *Britain's Forgotten Wartime Tragedy* (Hong Kong: Hong Kong University Press, 2006); Tony Banham, *We Shall Suffer There: Hong Kong's Defenders Imprisoned, 1942–45* (Hong Kong: Hong Kong University Press, 2009); Geoffrey Charles Emerson, *Hong Kong Internment, 1942–1945: Life in the Japanese Civilian Camp at Stanley* (Hong Kong: Hong Kong University Press, 2011).

10. "Dai ni kenshi kantai senshi nisshi sentō shōhō," 1/3/1942–31/3/1942, KIS, NIDS, JACAR, Ref: C08030033700.

11. "Dai ni kenshi kantai senshi nisshi sentō shōhō," 1/11/1942–30/11/1942, KIS, NIDS, JACAR, Ref: C08030033800.

12. Ibid.

13. Ibid.

14. "Combat Chronology of the United States Army Air Forces in World War II," October 1942, http://www.usaaf.net/chron/42/oct42.htm

15. "Dai ni kenshi kantai senshi nisshi sentō shōhō," Ref: C08030033800.

16. "Combat Chronology."

17. Mark Parillo, *The Japanese Merchant Marine in World War II* (Annapolis: Naval Institute Press, 1993), p. 7.

18. "Dai ni kenshi kantai senshi nisshi sentō shōhō," 1/1/1944–31/1/1944, KIS, NIDS, JACAR, Ref: C08030032400, slides 0683–0684.

19. "Dai ni kenshi kantai senshi nisshi sentō shōhō," 1/11/1944–30/11/1944, KIS, NIDS, JACAR, Ref: C08030033200.

20. Choi Cho-hong, "Hong Kong in the Context of the Pacific War," unpublished MPhil thesis (1998).

21. "Dai san hen, dai ichi shō, dai roku setsu, engan hōmen tai bei senbi no shidō" [Part III, Chapter 1, Section 6: Coastal Defence Against U.S.], Shina hōmen sakusen kiroku Shina hakengun no tōsui [Operation record of the Supreme Command of the China Expeditionary Army], RIS, NIDS, JACAR, Ref: C11110627200.

22. Samuel Morison, *History of United States Naval Operations in World War II*, Vol. 14 (Urbana: University of Illinois Press, 2001–2002), p. 170.

23. "Tokumukan Shin-i senshi nisshi sent ō shōhō" [Wartime diary of special warship "Shin-i"], 1/4/1944–31/3/1945, KIS, NIDS, JACAR, Ref: C08030588000.

24. Austin Coates, *Whampoa: Ships on the Shore* (Hong Kong: SCMP, 1980), p. 230.

25. Morison, *History of United States Naval Operations in World War II*, p. 171.

26. Zen Nippon Kaiin kumiai [All Japan Seamen's Union], "Sembotsu shita sen to kaiin no shoryō kan" [Database of merchantmen sunk and merchant seamen killed], http://www.jsu.or.jp/siryo/sukaiinnk/tairyou.html

27. "Dai san hen, dai ichi shō, dai roku setsu, engan hōmen tai bei senbi no shidō," Ref: C11110627200.

28. Ibid.

29. "Dai san hen, dai ni shō, dai yon setsu, Nanshi hōmen sakusen shidō no henkō" [Part III, Chapter 2, Section 4: Change of war plan for South China], Shina hōmen sakusen kiroku Shina hakengun no tōsui [Operation record of the Supreme Command of the China Expeditionary Army], RIS, NIDS, JACAR, Ref: C11110627700.

30. "Dai nijusan gun sakusen yōkō," RIS, NIDS, JACAR, Ref: C13031950000, slide 2033; "Shina engan bōgyo kyubi shusen chokuzen no jōkyō," RIS, NIDS, JACAR, Ref: C13031949500, slide 1946.

31. "Chukoku butai sakuinbo," 8/1945, RIS, NIDS, JACAR, Ref: C13031990300.

32. Lawrence W. C. Lai, Ken S. T Ching and Y. K. Tan, "Survey Findings on Japanese World War II Military Installations in Hong Kong," *Surveying & Built Environment*, Vol. 21, No. 2 (Dec. 2011), pp. 78–94.

33. For detailed discussion about BAAG, see Charles Cruickshank, *SOE in the Far East* (Oxford: Oxford University Press, 1983); Edwin Ride, *BAAG: Hong Kong Resistance, 1942–1945* (Hong Kong: Oxford University Press, 1981); Chan Sui-jeung, "The British Army Aid Group," in Chan King Tong, Yau Siu Kam and Chan Ka Leung (eds.), *The Defence of Hong Kong: Collected Essays on the Hong Kong-Kowloon Brigade of the East River Column* (Hong Kong: Hong Kong Museum of History, 2004), p. 129.

34. "Japanese Trial against Newnham, Haddock, Ford, Gray, Hardy and Routledge," 28/3/1947.

35. Gordon Alderson, *History of Royal Air Force Kai Tak* (Hong Kong: Royal Air Force Kai Tak, 1972), pp. 51–3.
36. Marshall Getz, *Subhas Chandra Bose: A Biography* (Jefferson, NC: McFarland, 2002), pp. 97–8.
37. Chan Sui-jeung, "The British Army Aid Group," pp. 124–32.
38. Yang Mingwei, "Zhou Enlai yu dongjiang zhongdui ji Xianggang kangzhan," in Chan, Yau and Chan (eds.), *The Defence of Hong Kong*, pp. 133–9, 141.
39. Chan Sui-jeung, *East River Column: Hong Kong Guerrillas in the Second World War and After* (Hong Kong: Hong Kong University Press, 2009), pp. 44–9.
40. "Gangjiu duli dadui shi" bianxiezu, *Gangjiu duli dadui shi* (Guangzhou: Guangdong renmin chubanshe, 1989), p. 27.
41. Chan, *East River Column*, pp. 42–9, 63–4.
42. Huang Yunpeng, "Gangjiu dadui zai Xianggang kangri zhanzheng de diwei he zuoyong," in Chan, Yau and Chan (eds.), *The Defence of Hong Kong*, p. 165.
43. "Dai ni kenshi kantai senshi nisshi sentō shōhō," 1/9/1944–30/9/1944, KIS, NIDS, JACAR, Ref: C08030033100.
44. He Fa and Liang Shaoda, "Riben touxiang hou de Xinjie ziweidui," in Chan, Yau and Chan (eds.), *The Defence of Hong Kong*, p. 258.

10 The Defence of Hong Kong during the Early Stages of the Cold War, 1945–1960

1. Scott Lucas et al., "A Very British Crusade: The Information Research Department and the Beginning of the Cold War," in Richard Aldrich (ed.), *British Intelligence, Strategy, and the Cold War, 1945–51* (London, New York: Routledge, 1992), p. 85.
2. Peter Smith, *Task Force 57: The British Pacific Fleet* (London: Crecy Books, 1994), pp. 188–9.
3. "Defence of Hong Kong," 3/5/1949, CAB 129/34. Also see Karl Hack, "South East Asia and British Strategy, 1944–1951," in Aldrich (ed.), *British Intelligence, Strategy, and the Cold War*, p. 316.
4. "Statement Relating to Defence: Memorandum by the Minister of Defence," 7/2/1947, CAB129/17, p. 5.
5. Hack, "South East Asia and British Strategy, 1944–1951," p. 316.
6. "Situation in Malaya and Hong Kong," 5/3/1949, CAB 129/33, p. 1.
7. CAB 129/33, pp. 2–3.
8. "Conclusions of a Meeting of the Cabinet," 26/5/1949, CAB 128/15, p. 51.
9. "Conclusions of a Meeting of the Cabinet," 8/3/1949, CAB 128/15, pp. 98–9.
10. "Conclusions of a Meeting of the Cabinet," 8/3/1949, CAB 128/15, p. 98.
11. "Defence of Hong Kong," 3/5/1949, CAB 129/34, pp. 3–4.
12. Christine Loh, *Underground Front: The Chinese Communist Party in Hong Kong* (Hong Kong: Hong Kong University Press, 2010), pp. 79–80.
13. "Defence of Hong Kong," 3/5/1949, CAB 129/34, p. 7.
14. "Conclusions of a Meeting of the Cabinet," 26/5/1949, CAB 128/15, p. 52.
15. "Defence of Hong Kong," 3/5/1949, CAB 129/34, p. 1.
16. Ibid., p. 7.

17. "Threat to Hong Kong," 3/5/1949, CAB 129/34, pp. 3–5; "Defence of Hong Kong," 3/5/1949, CAB 129/34, pp. 7–8.

18. Peter Melson, *White Ensign—Red Dragon: the History of the Royal Navy in Hong Kong, 1841–1997* (Hong Kong: Edinburgh Financial Publishing [Asia], 1997), p. 81.

19. "Hong Kong: Report by the Chiefs of Staff," 3/5/1949, CAB 129/34, pp. 1–2; "Defence of Hong Kong: Memorandum by the Minister of Defence," 24/5/1949, CAB 129/35, p. 2.

20. "Defence of Hong Kong: Memorandum by the Minister of Defence," 24/5/1949, CAB 129/35, p. 2.

21. Ibid.

22. "Conclusions of a Meeting of the Cabinet," 26/5/1949, CAB 128/15, p. 53.

23. Mark Chi-kwan, *Hong Kong and the Cold War: Anglo-American Relations 1949–1957* (Oxford: Clarendon, 2004), p. 15.

24. "Visit to Hong Kong, 6th June–9th June, 1949," 17/6/1949, CAB 129/35, p. 1.

25. Ibid., pp. 1–2.

26. Ibid., p. 6.

27. Ibid., pp. 3–4.

28. Ibid., pp. 5–6.

29. "Conclusions of a Meeting of the Cabinet," 23/6/1949, CAB 128/15, p. 80.

30. "Hong Kong, Memorandum by the Secretary of State for Foreign Affairs and the Secretary of State for the Colonies," 19/8/1949, CAB 129/36, p. 3.

31. "Conclusions of a Meeting of the Cabinet," 24/8/1949, CAB 128/16, p. 161.

32. "Recognition of the Chinese Communist Government: Memorandum by the Secretary of State for Foreign Affairs," 12/12/1949, CAB 129/37, pp. 3, 5.

33. Hack, "South East Asia and British Strategy, 1944–1951," p. 317.

34. Loh, *Underground Front*, p. 80.

35. "U.S. Policy on Hong Kong," 11/6/1960, NSC 6007/1, in Paul Kesaris, *Documents of the National Security Council, 1947–1977*, Supplementary 4, Reel 3, p. 6.

36. Jin Yaoru, *Zhonggong Xianggang zhengce miwen shilu: Jin Yaoru wushinian xiangjiang yiwang* (Hong Kong: Tianyuan shuwu, 1998), pp. 1–8.

37. Mark, *Hong Kong and the Cold War*, pp. 40–1.

38. Ibid., p. 48.

39. "Implication of a Possible Chinese Communist Attack on Foreign Colonies in South China," JCS 1330/51, in Paul Kesaris, *Records of the Joint Chiefs of Staff. Part II, 1946–53: The Far East*, Reel 1 (Washington, DC: University Publications of America, 1979), pp. 358–9.

40. "Memorandum for the Secretary of Defence," 15/7/1949, NSC 55, in Paul Kesaris, *Documents of the National Security Council, 1947–1977*, Reel 1 (Frederick, MD: University Publications of America, 1980), pp. 1–2.

41. M. E. B. Groves, "The Royal Artillery and Hong Kong 1842–1976," *Journal of the Royal Artillery*, Vol. 103, No. 2 (Sep. 1976), p. 128.

42. Michael Share, *Where Empires Collided: Russian and Soviet Relations with Hong Kong, Taiwan, and Macao* (Hong Kong: The Chinese University Press, 2007), p. 5.

43. "Conclusions of a Meeting of the Cabinet," 17/7/1949, CAB 128/18, p. 146.

44. Quotation from Mark, *Hong Kong and the Cold War*, p. 50.

45. Ibid., p. 53.

46. "Pacific Defence: Memorandum by the Minister of State," 9/2/1951, CAB 129/44, p. 4.

47. "Additional Measures by the United Nations against China: Memorandum by the Secretary of State for Foreign Affairs," 3/4/1951, CAB 129/45, p. 4.

48. Mark, *Hong Kong and the Cold War*, p. 54.

49. "British Overseas Obligations: Memorandum by the Secretary of State for Foreign Affairs," 18/6/1952, CAB 129/53, p. 7.

50. "Economic Policy: Note by the Secretary of the Cabinet," 23/5/1952, CAB 129/52, p. 2.

51. "U.S. Policy on Hong Kong," 17/7/1957, NSC 5717, in Paul Kesaris, *Documents of the National Security Council, 1947–1977*, Supplementary 5, Reel 2, p. 4.

52. Mark, *Hong Kong and the Cold War*, pp. 56–7.

53. "A Report to the National Security Council," 6/4/1953, NSC 148, in Paul Kesaris, *Documents of the National Security Council, 1947–1977*, Supplementary 3, Reel 3, pp. 1–3.

54. "A Report to the National Security Council," 6/4/1953, NSC 148, pp. 14–7.

55. Ibid., p. 6.

56. "U.S. Policy on Hong Kong," 17/7/1957, NSC 5717, pp. 8–9.

57. *The China Mail*, 30/11/1961.

58. "U.S. Policy on Hong Kong," 11/6/1960, NSC 6007/1, p. 10.

59. "U.S. Policy on Hong Kong," 17/7/1957, NSC 5717, pp. 6–8.

60. Reginald Hunt, Geoffrey Russell and Keith Scott, *Mandarin Blue: RAF Chinese Linguists—1951–1962—in the Cold War* (Oxford: Hurusco Books, 2008); The 367 Association Website, http://www.littlesaiwan-367su.talktalk.net/history.html

61. Richard Baum has suggested that the institute might also have been sponsored by the CIA, but no evidence was put forward. See Richard Baum, *China Watcher: Confessions of a Peking Tom* (Seattle: University of Washington Press, 2010), pp. 234–5.

62. László Ladány, *The Communist Party of China and Marxism, 1921–1985: A Self Portrait* (Stanford, CA: Hoover Institution Press, Stanford University, 1988), pp. v, ix.

63. "U.S. Policy on Hong Kong," 17/7/1957, NSC 5717, p. 7.

64. "U.S. Policy on Hong Kong," 11/6/1960, NSC 6007/1, p. 15.

65. Quotation from Mark, *Hong Kong and the Cold War*, p. 56.

66. Quotation from ibid., p. 60.

67. "Conclusions of a Meeting of the Cabinet," 7/4/1954, CAB 128/27, pp. 6–7.

68. "Conclusions of a Meeting of the Cabinet," 15/4/1954, CAB 128/27, p. 3.

69. "United Kingdom Defence Policy: Memorandum by the Chiefs of Staff," 23/7/1954, CAB 129/69, p. 5.

70. Mark, *Hong Kong and the Cold War*, p. 60.

71. Quoted from ibid., p. 65.

72. "The Far East: Note by the Secretary of State for Foreign Affairs," 17/2/1955, CAB 129/73.

73. "The Defence of Hong Kong: Memorandum by the Minister of Defence," CAB 129/78, p. 1; Melson, *White Ensign—Red Dragon*, p. 87.

74. CAB 129/78, pp. 2–3.

75. "JDB Shaw to High Commissioners in Ottawa, Canberra, and Wellington," 19/8/1957, DEFE 11/300; Also quoted in Mark, *Hong Kong and the Cold War*, p. 69.
76. "U.S. Policy on Hong Kong," 17/7/1957, NSC 5717, pp. 1–15.
77. "Statement on Defence, 1957," 26/3/1957, CAB 129/86, p. 8; "Statement on Defence, 1957," 28/3/1957, CAB 129/86, p. 8.
78. "Statement of Defence, Note by the Minister of Defence," 6/2/1958, CAB 129/91, pp. 9–10.
79. "Naval Reorganisation: Note by the First Lord of the Admiralty," 11/2/1958, CAB 129/91, p. 6.
80. Alan Harfield, *British and Indian Armies on the China Coast, 1785–1965* (London: A and J Partnership, 1990), p. 469.
81. Gordon Alderson, *History of Royal Air Force Kai Tak* (Hong Kong: Royal Air Force Kai Tak, 1972), p. 86.
82. "Anglo American Relations," 10/4/1958, CAB 129/92, p. 3.
83. "Anglo American Relations, Annex," 10/4/1958, CAB 129/92, pp. 10–2.
84. Quote from "UK Pondered China Nuclear Attack," BBC News. The BBC article quoted a letter from Alec Douglas-Home to the Prime Minister (22/2/1961, PREM 11/3277). http://news.bbc.co.uk/2/hi/uk_politics/5130524.stm
85. "Future Policy Study," 24/2/1960, CAB 129/100, p. 36.
86. Ibid.
87. "Special Report on Hong Kong (NSC 5717)," 28/12/1959, in Paul Kesaris, *Documents of the National Security Council, 1947–1977*, Supplementary 4, Reel 2.
88. "U.S. Policy on Hong Kong," 11/6/1960, NSC 6007/1, pp. 1–2.
89. *Hong Kong Annual Report 1951* (Hong Kong: Hong Kong Government Press, 1951), pp. 36–7.
90. *Hong Kong; Report for the Year 1968* (Hong Kong: Hong Kong Government Press, 1969), p. 36.
91. *Dragon Journal* (1997), pp. 29, 33, 145, 146.
92. Harfield, *British and Indian Armies on the China Coast*, p. 473.
93. "Statement on the Defence Estimates, 1969: Memorandum by the Secretary of State for Defence," 27/1/1969, CAB 129/140, p. 24.
94. Royal Corps of Transport, *Hong Kong: Year Book 1967* (Hong Kong: Royal Corps of Transport, 1968). The English caption reads: "Now, doubtless you chaps are saying to yourself, what could one platoon do if three hundred Chinese divisions attacked from, say, that direction?"; The equally sarcastic Chinese caption reads: "Chaps, if three hundred Chinese Communist divisions attacked from this direction, what strategy can we use to defeat them?"
95. Ibid., pp. 24–5.
96. *The Straits Times*, 2/11/1958.
97. Interview Record of Phillip Thompson, 30/8/2013.
98. Interview Record of Yau Wai Kee and Kong Kim Hung, 3/9/2013.
99. Alderson, *History of Royal Air Force Kai Tak*, p. 81.
100. John Fleming, *Hong Kong: The Pearl River Incident: The Untold Story of H.M.M.L. 1323* (Lancaster: Scotforth Books, 2002).
101. Alderson, *History of Royal Air Force Kai Tak*, p. 81.

102. Melson, *White Ensign—Red Dragon*, p. 86.

103. Interview of Capt. Chan Yik Chung, 12/12/2011; Philip Bruce, *Second to None: The Story of the Hong Kong Volunteers* (Hong Kong, New York: Oxford University Press, 1991), pp. 288–9.

104. "Manpower Statement of the Auxiliary Defence Services Hong Kong: Male Membership by Races as at 31 March, 1959," HKRS 369/11/2.

105. Interview of Capt. Chan Yik Chung, 12/12/2011.

106. Mark Chi-kwan, "Vietnam War Tourists: US Naval Visits to Hong Kong and British-American-Chinese Relations, 1965–1968," *Cold War History*, Vol. 10, No. 1 (Feb. 2010), p. 28.

107. Stanley S. K. Kwan with Nicole Kwan, *The Dragon and the Crown: Hong Kong Memoirs* (Hong Kong: Hong Kong University Press, 2009), p. 97; Bryce Harland, *Collision Course: America and East Asia in the Past and the Future* (Singapore: Institute of Southeast Asian Studies, 1996), pp. 145–6.

108. Alderson, *History of Royal Air Force Kai Tak*, p. 92.

109. "The Future of Hong Kong," 2/8/1957, DEFE 11/300.

110. *Report on the Riots in Kowloon and Tsuen Wan* (Hong Kong: Hong Kong Government, 1956), pp. 5–7, 9.

111. Ibid., pp. 22–7.

112. Ibid., pp. 15–7.

113. Ibid., pp. 31–2.

114. Mark, *Hong Kong and the Cold War*, p. 70.

115. *Report on the Riots in Kowloon and Tsuen Wan*, pp. 33–6.

116. Georgina Sinclair, "'Hong Kong Headaches': Policing the 1967 Disturbances," in Robert Bickers and Ray Yep (eds.), *May Days in Hong Kong: Riot and Emergency in 1967* (Hong Kong: Hong Kong University Press, 2009), pp. 91–2.

117. Gary Cheung Ka-wai, *Hong Kong's Watershed: The 1967 Riots* (Hong Kong: Hong Kong University Press, 2009), p. 17.

118. Ibid., pp. 30–1.

119. Ibid., pp. 43–5.

120. Ibid., pp. 45–7.

121. Ibid., p. 52.

122. Ibid., p. 66.

123. "Confidential Annex," 11/7/1967, CAB 128/46, p. 1.

124. Ibid., p. 2.

125. Thanks are due to Mr. Chan Sui-jeung for the information.

126. Bruce, *Second to None*, p. 300; Interview of Capt. Chan Yik Chung, 12/12/2011.

127. Melson, *White Ensign—Red Dragon*, p. 90.

128. "Reinforcement of Hong Kong: Joint Theatre Plan (East) No. 30: Operation Galaxy," 14/10/1971, DEFE 5/19/13, pp. 1–4.

129. "Replacement of Local Labour in Hong Kong: Joint Theatre Plan (East) No. 68: Operation Halibut," 22/11/1971, CAB 5/191/25, pp. 1–4.

130. Alderson, *History of Royal Air Force Kai Tak*, p. 97.

Appendices

1. Malcolm Murfett et al., *Between Two Oceans: A Military History of Singapore from First Settlement to Final British Withdrawal* (Singapore: Marshall Cavendish Academic, 2004).

2. Kathleen Harland, *The Royal Navy in Hong Kong, 1841–1980* (Hong Kong: Royal Navy, 1981); Peter Melson, *White Ensign—Red Dragon: The History of the Royal Navy in Hong Kong, 1841–1997* (Hong Kong: Edinburgh Financial Publishing [Asia], 1997).

3. Gerald Graham, *The China Station: War and Diplomacy 1830–1860* (Oxford: Clarendon Press, 1978).

4. Donald Oxley, *Victoria Barracks, 1842–1979* (Hong Kong: British Forces Hong Kong, 1979); Alan Harfield, *British and Indian Armies on the China Coast, 1785–1965* (London: A and J Partnership, 1990).

5. Gordon Alderson, *History of Royal Air Force Kai Tak* (Hong Kong: Royal Air Force Kai Tak, 1972).

6. Phillip Bruce, *Second to None: The Story of the Hong Kong Volunteers* (Hong Kong, New York: Oxford University Press, 1991).

7. Denis Rollo, *The Guns and Gunners of Hong Kong* (Hong Kong: The Gunners Roll of Hong Kong, 1991).

8. Tim Carew, *Fall of Hong Kong* (London: Anthony Blond, 1960); George Endacott, *Hong Kong Eclipse* (Hong Kong: Oxford University Press, 1978).

9. Carl Vincent, *No Reason Why: The Canadian Hong Kong Tragedy: An Examination* (Stittsville, ON: Canada's Wings, 1981).

10. Brereton Greenhous, *"C" Force to Hong Kong: A Canadian Catastrophe, 1941–1945* (Toronto; Buffalo, NY: Dundurn Press, 1997).

11. Galen Roger Perras, "Defeat Still Cries Aloud for Explanation: Explaining C Force's Dispatch to Hong Kong," *Canadian Military Journal*, Vol. 11, No. 4 (2011), pp. 37–47; Kent Fedorowich, "'Cocked Hats and Small, Little Garrisons': Britain, Canada and the Fall of Hong Kong, 1941," *Modern Asian Studies*, Vol. 37, No. 1 (2003), pp. 111–57; Christopher Bell, "'Our Most Exposed Outpost': Hong Kong and British Far Eastern Strategy," *Journal of Military History*, Vol. 60, No. 1 (1996), pp. 61–88.

12. Franco David Macri, "C Force to Hong Kong: The Price of Collective Security in China," *Journal of Military History*, Vol. 77 (2013), pp. 141–71.

13. Tony Banham, *Not the Slightest Chance: The Defence of Hong Kong, 1941* (Hong Kong: Hong Kong University Press, 2003); Oliver Lindsay, *The Battle for Hong Kong 1941–1945: Hostage to Fortune* (Hong Kong: Hong Kong University Press, 2005); Nathan Greenfield, *The Damned: The Canadians at the Battle of Hong Kong and the POW Experience, 1941–45* (Toronto: HarperCollins Publishers, 2010).

14. Philip Snow, *The Fall of Hong Kong: Britain, China and the Japanese Occupation* (New Haven, CT: Yale University Press, 2003).

15. Xie Yongguang, *Xianggang kangri fengyunlu* (Hong Kong: Cosmosbooks, 1995); Xie Yongguang, *Xianggang lunxian: Rijun gong-Gang shibari zhanzheng jishi* (Hong Kong: Commercial Press, 1996).

16. Edwin Ride, *BAAG: Hong Kong Resistance, 1942–1945* (Hong Kong: Oxford University Press, 1981); Chan Sui-jeung, *East River Column: Hong Kong Guerrillas in the Second World War and After* (Hong Kong: Hong Kong University Press, 2012).

17. Gillian Bickley, *Hong Kong Invaded! A '97 Nightmare* (Hong Kong: Hong Kong University Press, 2001).

18. Patrick Hase, *The Six-Day War of 1899: Hong Kong in the Age of Imperialism* (Hong Kong: Hong Kong University Press, 2008).

19. Lee Kam Keung et al., *Modern Chinese Naval History: New Perspectives* (Hong Kong: Hong Kong Museum of Coastal Defence, 2004); Ma Yau-Woon, *Jinghai chengjiang: Zhongguo jindai haijun shishi xinquan* (Taipei: Lianjing, 2009).

20. Such as Franco David Macri, "Abandoning the Outpost: Rejection of the Hong Kong Purchase Scheme of 1938–1939," *Journal of Royal Asiatic Society Hong Kong Branch* , Vol. 50 (2010), pp. 303–16; Stephen N. G. Davies, Lawrence W. C. Lai and Y. K. Tan, "World War II Small Coastal Casemates, Pillboxes, and Open Machine Gun Positions on Hong Kong Island in Photos," *JRASHKB*, Vol. 49 (2009), pp. 57–67; Lawrence W. C. Lai, "Recollections of the Battle of Hong Kong and the Life of a POW by Arthur Ernesto Gomes, 5th Company (Machine Gun), HKVDC," *JRASHKB*, Vol. 48 (2008), pp. 26–50; Lawrence W. C. Lai, Daniel C. W. Ho, P. Yung, "Survey of the Pottinger Battery," *JRASHKB*, Vol. 47 (2007), pp. 90–114; Tony Banham, "Hong Kong Volunteer Defence Corps, Number 3 (Machine Gun) Company," *JRASHKB*, Vol. 45 (2005), pp. 117–42.

21. Mark Chi-kwan, *Hong Kong and the Cold War: Anglo-American Relations 1949–1957* (Oxford: Clarendon, 2004).

22. Lawrence W. C. Lai, "The Gin Drinker's Line: Reconstruction of a British Colonial Defence Line in Hong Kong Using Aerial Photo Information," *Property Management*, Vol. 27, No. 1 (2009), pp. 16–41; Lawrence W. C. Lai, Stephen N. G. Davis, Ken S. T. Ching and Castor T. C. Wong, "Decoding the Enigma of the Fall of the Shing Mun Redoubt Using Line of Sight Analysis," *Surveying & Built Environment*, Vol. 21, No. 2 (Dec. 2011), pp. 21–42; Lawrence W. C. Lai, Stephen N. G. Davis, Ken S. T. Ching and Castor T. C. Wong, "Location of Pillboxes and Other Structures of the Gin Drinker's Line Based on Aerial Photo Evidence," *Surveying & Built Environment*, Vol. 21, No. 2 (Dec. 2011), pp. 69–70.

23. Donald Mackenzie Schurman, *Imperial Defence, 1868–1887* (London; Portland, OR: Frank Cass, 2000); Greg Kennedy and Keith Neilson, *Far Flung Lines: Essays on Imperial Defence in Honour of Donald Mackenzie Shurman* (London: Frank Cass, 1997); Greg Kennedy, *Imperial Defence: The Old World Order, 1856–1956* (London: Routledge, 2008).

24. David Edgerton, *Warfare State: Britain, 1920–1970* (Cambridge, New York: Cambridge University Press, 2006); George Paden, *Arms, Economics and British Strategy: From Dreadnoughts to Hydrogen Bombs* (Cambridge: Cambridge University Press, 2007).

25. Richard Aldrich, *Intelligence and the War against Japan: Britain, America, and the Politics of Secret Service* (Cambridge: Cambridge University Press, 2004).

References

PRIMARY SOURCES

Archival Sources and Compilation of Archives

National Archives, UK

AIR 2: Air Ministry and Ministry of Defence: Registered Files

CAB 7: Colonial Defence Committee, and Committee of Imperial Defence, Colonial Defence Committee, later Overseas Defence Committee: Minutes, Reports and Correspondence

CAB 11: Colonial Defence Committee, and Committee of Imperial Defence, Colonial Defence Committee, later Overseas Defence Committee: Defence Schemes

CAB 23: War Cabinet and Cabinet: Minutes

CAB 24: War Cabinet and Cabinet: Memoranda

CAB 38: Committee of Imperial Defence: Minutes and Memoranda

CAB 44: Committee of Imperial Defence, Historical Branch and Cabinet Office, Historical Section

CAB 53: Committee of Imperial Defence: Chiefs of Staff Committee: Minutes and Memoranda

CAB 54: Committee of Imperial Defence: Deputy Chiefs of Staff Committee: Minutes and Memoranda

CAB 57: Committee of Imperial Defence: Standing Inter-departmental Committee on National Service in a Future War and Sub-committee on Man-Power: Minutes and Memoranda

CAB 58 Cabinet: Committee of Civil Research, later Economic Advisory Council and Sub-committees: Minutes and Memoranda

CAB 66: War Cabinet and Cabinet: Memoranda

CAB 80: War Cabinet and Cabinet: Chiefs of Staff Committee: Memoranda

CAB 94: War Cabinet: Overseas Defence Committee: Minutes and Papers

CAB 128: Cabinet: Minutes

CAB 129: Cabinet Minutes and Papers

CO 129: War and Colonial Department and Colonial Office: Hong Kong, Original Correspondence

CO 820: Colonial Office: Military Original Correspondence

CO 968: Colonial Office and Commonwealth Office: Defence Department and successors: Original Correspondence

DEFE 5: Ministry of Defence: Chiefs of Staff Committee: Memoranda

DEFE 11: Records of the Defence Chiefs of Staff

DEFE 25: Ministry of Defence: Chief of Defence Staff: Registered Files

DEFE 70: Ministry of Defence (Army): Registered Files and Branch Folders

PREM 11: Prime Minister's Office: Correspondence and Papers, 1951–1964

WO 100: War Office: Campaign Medal and Award Rolls (General Series)

WO 106: War Office: Directorate of Military Operations and Military Intelligence, and predecessors: Correspondence and Papers

WO 172: War Office: British and Allied Land Forces, South East Asia: War Diaries, Second World War

WO 235: Judge Advocate General's Office: War Crimes Case Files, Second World War

Japan Center for Asian Historical Records (JACAR)

Gaimushō kiroku (GK, Ministry of Foreign Affairs Papers)

Kaigun ichihan shiryō (KIS, General Records of the Imperial Japanese Navy)

Kaigunshō kōbun bikō (KKB, General Reference Documents, Imperial Japanese Navy)

Rikugun ichihan shiryō (RIS, General Records of the Imperial Japanese Army)

Rikugunshō dainikki (RD, Daily Records of the Imperial Japanese Army)

Archives of the National Institute for Defense Studies of Japan (NID)

"Honkon kōryakusen nikansuru shoken kyu kyōkun" [Experiences of and lessons from the Hong Kong operation], 23rd Army, Shina-Shina shihen: nanshi-64.

"Honkon kōryakusen sentō shōhō dai sanju hachi shidan hohei dai nihakusanju rentai" [War diary of the 228th Infantry Regiment of the 38th Division during the operations against Hong Kong], Shina-Shina shihen: nanshi-34.

"Kyū Honkon yōsai bōgyo shisetsu no shashin" [Photos of the facilities of the old Hong Kong Fortress], 1/1942, Shina Shashin 94.

"Kyūryū hantō okeru honbōgyo jinchi chōsa hōkoku" [The study of the main defence position on the Kowloon Peninsula], 1/1942, Shina-Dai Tōasen-Nanshi 90.

Australian War Memorial

The Imperial Defence College Register, 1927–1967 (London, Imperial Defence College, 1968)

Liddell Hart Centre for Military Archives, King's College, University of London

BROOKEPOPHAM: 6: Papers relating to service as Commander in Chief, Far East, 1940–1953

Documents of the National Security Council, the United States of America

JCS 1330/51, Paul Kesaris, *Records of the Joint Chiefs of Staff. Part II, 1946–1953: The Far East*, Reel 1. Washington, DC: University Publications of America, 1979.

NSC 55, Paul Kesaris, *Documents of the National Security Council, 1947–1977*, Reel 1. Frederick, MD: University Publications of America, 1980.

NSC 148, Paul Kesaris, *Documents of the National Security Council, 1947–1977,* Supplementary 3, Reel 3.

NSC 5717, Paul Kesaris, *Documents of the National Security Council, 1947–1977,* Supplementary 5, Reel 2.

NSC 6007/1, Paul Kesaris, *Documents of the National Security Council, 1947–1977,* Supplementary 4, Reel 3.

Public Records Office, Hong Kong

"Battle Progress Report of the 228th Infantry Regiment in the Hong Kong Invasion Operations in December 1941," HKMS 100–1-5.

CO 129: War and Colonial Department and Colonial Office: Hong Kong, Original Correspondence

CO 968: Colonial Office and Commonwealth Office: Defence Department and Successors: Original Correspondence

"The Diary of Lt. James Sutcliffe, RAOC, During Japanese Hostilities in Hong Kong, from 7th December to 14th August 1945," 940.547252 D2A 1945.

Hong Kong Defence Scheme, 343.01 HON

"Hong Kong Volunteers Defence Corps Scrap Book," HKRS 219–1-32.

"Prisoner of War Diary of Chief Signal Officer, China Command, Hong Kong, 1941–1945," 940 547252 PRI.

Report on the Riots in Kowloon and Tsuen Wan. Hong Kong: Hong Kong Government, 1956. 《九龍及荃灣暴動報告書，一九五六年十月十日至十二日》。香港：政府印務局，1956。

"War Diary No. 3 Company HKVDC," HKPRO, HKRS 255–1-48–2.

Hong Kong Heritage Project

Elizabeth Ride Collection

Others

"Alert in the East," Imperial War Museum Collection, COI 122.

Entries in Personal Diary Brigadier J. K. Lawson, 1941. Library and Archives Canada, R1961–0-9

Irish University Press Area Studies Series, British Parliamentary Papers. China, Vols. 24–28. Shannon: Irish University Press, 1971.

Zhonghua minguo zhongyao shiliao chubian bianji weiyuanhui (ed.). *Zhonghua minguo zhongyao shiliao chubian—duiri kangzhan shiqi* [Selected historical sources of the Chinese Republic, Anti-Japanese war]. Taipei: Zhongyang weiyuanhui dangshi weiyuanhui. 中華民國重要史料初編編輯委員會。《中華民國重要史料初編——對日抗戰時期》。中國國民黨中央委員會黨史委員會，1981。

Newspapers and Periodicals

Brassey's Naval Annual, 1887. Portsmouth: J. Griffin & Co., 1887.

Brassey's Naval Annual, 1902. Portsmouth: J. Griffin & Co., 1902.

The China Mail

China Side, Vol. 1, No. 1, December 1935 (publication of HMS *Medway*, the submarine
     tender of the China Station during the 1930s)

Dragon Journal (Hong Kong Military Service Corps/Hong Kong Ex-Servicemen's
     Association), 1970–1997.

Gongshang ribao《工商日報》(1941)

Hong Kong Government Annual Reports

Hong Kong Government Gazette

Hong Kong Government Sessional Papers

Hong Kong Military History Notes

The Kung Sheung Daily News

London Gazette

The Navy List: Corrected to the 18th December, 1919. London: HMSO, 1920.

The Navy List: Corrected to the 18h June, 1939. London: HMSO, 1939.

The Navy List: Corrected to the 20th June, 1948. London: John Murray, 1848.

The Naval Review, 1915–1932.

The Royal Engineers Journal

Singapore Free Press and Mercantile Advertiser

South China Morning Post

The Star

The Straits Times

Supplement to London Gazette

Ta kung pao《大公報》(1941)

The Times

UK Parliament Hansard

SECONDARY SOURCES

Air Raid Precaution Department. *Report on Census of the Colony of Hong Kong (exclusive of
     the New Territories) taken on 13th/14th and 14th/15th March, 1941.* Hong Kong: Hong
     Kong Government Printers, 1941.

Alden, Dauril, J. S. Cummins and Michael Cooper. *Charles R. Boxer: An Uncommon Life:
     Soldier, Historian, Teacher, Collector, Traveller.* [Lisbon:] Fundação Oriente, 2001.

Alderson, Gordon. *History of Royal Air Force Kai Tak.* Hong Kong: Royal Air Force Kai Tak,
     1972.

Aldrich, Richard (ed.). *British Intelligence, Strategy, and the Cold War, 1945–51.* London, New
     York: Routledge, 1992.

———. *Intelligence and the War against Japan: Britain, America, and the Politics of Secret
     Service.* Cambridge: Cambridge University Press, 2000.

Andrew, Christopher and Jeremy Noakes (eds.). *Intelligence and International Relations,
     1900–1945.* Exeter: University of Exeter Press, 1987.

Ashton, Nigel. "Harold Macmillan and the 'Golden Days' of Anglo-American Relations
     Revisited, 1967–1963." *Diplomatic History*, Vol. 29, No. 4 (2005).

Banham, Tony. "Hong Kong Volunteer Defence Corps, Number 3 (Machine Gun) Company." *Journal of the Royal Asiatic Society Hong Kong Branch*, Vol. 45 (2005), pp. 113–39.

———. Hong Kong War Diary, www.hongkongwardiary.com

———. *Not the Slightest Chance: The Defence of Hong Kong, 1941*. Hong Kong: Hong Kong University Press, 2003.

———. *The Sinking of the* Lisbon Maru: *Britain's Forgotten Wartime Tragedy*. Hong Kong: Hong Kong University Press, 2006.

———. *We Shall Suffer There: Hong Kong's Defenders Imprisoned, 1942–45*. Hong Kong: Hong Kong University Press, 2009.

Baum, Richard. *China Watcher: Confessions of a Peking Tom*. Seattle: University of Washington Press, 2010.

Beard, Charles. *President Roosevelt and the Coming of the War, 1941: A Study in Appearances and Realities*. Hamden, CT: Archon Books, 1968 [1948].

Beeler, John. "Steam, Strategy and Shurman: Imperial Defence in the Post Crimean Era, 1856–1905." In Greg Kennedy and Keith Neilson (eds.), *Far Flung Lines: Essays on Imperial Defence in Honour of Donald Mackenzie Shurman*. London: Frank Cass, 1997.

Bell, Christopher. *Churchill and Sea Power*. Oxford: Oxford University Press, 2013.

———. "'Our Most Exposed Outpost': Hong Kong and British Far Eastern Strategy." *Journal of Military History*, Vol. 60, No. 1 (1996).

———. *The Royal Navy, Seapower and Strategy between the Wars*. Stanford: Stanford University Press, 2000.

Bickers, Robert and Ray Yep (eds.). *May Days in Hong Kong: Riot and Emergency in 1967*. Hong Kong: Hong Kong University Press, 2009.

Bickley, Gillian. *Hong Kong Invaded! A '97 Nightmare*. Hong Kong: Hong Kong University Press, 2001.

Biddle, Tami Davis. *Rhetoric and Reality in Air Warfare: The Evolution of British and American Ideas about Strategic Bombing, 1914–1945*. Princeton, Oxford: Princeton University Press, 2002.

Birch, Alan and Martin Cole. *Captive Christmas: The Battle of Hong Kong—December 1941*. Hong Kong: Heinemann Asia, 1979.

Bix, Herbert. *Hirohito and the Making of Modern Japan*. New York: HarperCollins Publishers, 2000.

Blue, A. D. "Piracy on the China Coast." *Journal of the Hong Kong Branch of the Royal Asiatic Society*, Vol. 5 (1965), pp. 69–85.

Bōeishō bōei kenshusho senshishitsu (Military History Research Section, National Institute for Defence Studies). *Chukoku hōmen kaigun sakusen*. Vol. 2. Tokyo: Asagumo shimbun, 1975. 防衛省防衛研修所戰史室。《中國方面海軍作戰》（2）。東京：朝雲新聞社，1975。

———. *Chukoku hōmen kōku sakusen* [Air battle on the China front]. Tokyo: Asagumo shimbun, 1974.《中國方面航空作戰》。東京：朝雲新聞社，1974。

———. *Honkon-chosa sakusen* (Hong Kong-Changsha Operation). Tokyo: Asagumo shimbun, 1971.《香港長沙作戰》。東京：朝雲新聞社，1971。

Bond, Brian and Kyoichi Tachikawa (eds.). *British and Japanese Military Leadership in the Far Eastern War, 1941–1945*. London, New York: Frank Cass, 2004.

Briggs, Christopher. *Farewell Hong Kong 1941*. Victoria Park, WA: Hesperian Press, 2001.

Bruce, Phillip. *Second to None: The Story of the Hong Kong Volunteers*. Hong Kong, New York: Oxford University Press, 1991.

Cai Rongfang. *The Hong Kong People's History of Hong Kong*. Hong Kong: Oxford University Press, 2001. 蔡榮芳。《香港人之香港史，1841–1945》。香港：牛津大學出版社，2001。

Calvert, Michael. *Prisoners of Hope*. London: Cooper, 1971.

Cambon, Kenneth. *Guest of Hirohito*. Vancouver: PW Press, 1990.

Carew, Tim. *Fall of Hong Kong*. London: Anthony Blond, 1960.

Carroll, John. *A Concise History of Hong Kong*. Lanham, MD: Rowman & Littlefield, 2007.

Chan Chak. "Xianggang zhan tuwei riji," 1/12/1941. In Chan On-kwok (ed.), *Chan Chak Jiangjun jinianji*, 2011.

Chan King Tong, Yau Siu Kam, Chan Ka Leung (eds.). *The Defence of Hong Kong: Collected Essays on the Hong Kong-Kowloon Brigade of the East River Column*. Hong Kong: Hong Kong Museum of History, 2004. 陳敬堂、邱小金、陳家亮編。《香港抗戰：東江縱隊港九獨立大隊論文集》。香港：香港歷史博物館，2004。

Chan, Lau Kit-ching. *China, Britain and Hong Kong 1895–1945*. Hong Kong: The Chinese University Press, 1990.

Chan, Ming K. and John Young. *Precarious Balance: Hong Kong between China and Britain, 1842–1992*. Hong Kong: Hong Kong University Press, 1994.

Chan On-kwok (ed.). *Chan Chak Jiangjun jinianji*, 2011. 陳安國編。《陳策將軍紀念集》，2011。

Chan Sui-jeung. "The British Army Aid Group." In Chan King Tong, Yau Siu Kam and Chan Ka Leung (eds.), *The Defence of Hong Kong: Collected Essays on the Hong Kong-Kowloon Brigade of the East River Column*. Hong Kong: Hong Kong Museum of History, 2004.

———. *East River Column: Hong Kong Guerrillas in the Second World War and After*. Hong Kong: Hong Kong University Press, 2009.

Chesneau, Roger and Eugene Kolesnik (eds.). *Conway's All the World's Fighting Ships 1860–1905*. Greenwich: Conway Maritime Press, 1979.

Cheung, Gary Ka-wai. *Hong Kong's Watershed: The 1967 Riots*. Hong Kong: Hong Kong University Press, 2009.

Chiu Yu-lok and Chung Po Yin (eds.). *Jiulongcheng*. Hong Kong: Joint Publishing, 2001. 趙雨樂、鍾寶賢編。《香港地區史研究之一：九龍城》。香港：三聯，2001。

Choi Chohong. "Hong Kong in the Context of the Pacific War." Unpublished MPhil thesis (1998), Hong Kong University.

Chow Kai Wing. "Shijiu shiji Zhongguo waijiaoguan lun Xianggang zai haifang shang de zhongyaoxing." *Jindai Zhongguo haifang guoji yantaohui* (Hong Kong: The Chinese University of Hong Kong, 1998). 周佳榮。〈十九世紀中國外交官論香港在海防上的重要性〉，《近代中國海防國際研討會》。香港：香港中文大學，1998。

Civil Engineering and Development Department, Hong Kong. "Investigation of Disused Tunnels: Preliminary Report, Victoria Barrack—Disused Underground Operations Headquarters." Document #5341 (1983).

Coates, Austin. *Whampoa: Ships on the Shore*. Hong Kong: SCMP, 1980.

Colomb, John Charles Ready. *The Defence of Great and Greater Britain: Sketches of Its Naval, Military and Political Aspects (1880)*. London: Eilbron, 2005.

"Combat Chronology of the United States Army Air Forces in World War II," October 1942. http://www.usaaf.net/chron/42/oct42.htm

"Conference on the Limitation of Armament, Washington: Treaty between the United States of America, the British Empire, France, Italy, and Japan, Signed at Washington, February 6, 1922." http://www.ibiblio.org/pha/pre-war/1922/nav_lim. html

Corbett, Julian. *Naval Operations: History of the Great War Based on Official Documents*. London: Longmans, 1920.

Cowman, Ian. *Dominion or Decline: Anglo-American Naval Relations on the Pacific, 1937–1941*. Oxford; Washington, DC: Berg, 1996.

Crisswell, Colin and Mike Watson. *The Royal Hong Kong Police, 1841–1945*. Hong Kong: Macmillan, 1982.

Cruickshank, Charles. *SOE in the Far East*. Oxford: Oxford University Press, 1983.

"Daihonei rikugunbu, daihonei kaigunbu–seikai jōsei no suii nihanpu jikyoku shori yōkōan," 7/1940, Institute of Developing Economies, Kōichi Kishi Collection, B1–144, slides 1–12. http://d-arch.ide.go.jp/kishi_collection/（大本営陸軍部・大本営海軍部「世界情勢ノ推移ニ伴フ時局処理要綱」）。昭和十五年7月 （7/1940），來自アジア経済研究所。「岸幸一コレクション—南方関係軍政・海軍資料を中心に」。B1–144。

Davies, Philip. *MI6 and the Machinery of Spying*. London: Frank Cass, 2004.

Davies, Stephen N. G., Ken S. T. Ching and Castor T. C. Wong. "Location of Pillboxes and Other Structures of the Gin Drinker's Line Based on Aerial Photo Evidence." *Surveying & Built Environment*, Vol. 21, No. 2 (2011).

Davies, Stephen N. G., Lawrence W. C. Lai and Y. K. Tan. "World War II Small Coastal Casemates, Pillboxes, and Open Machine Gun Positions on Hong Kong Island in Photos." *JRASHKB*, Vol. 49 (2009).

Davison, Robert. *The Challenges of Command: The Royal Navy's Executive Branch Officers, 1880–1919*. London: Ashgate, 2011.

Dew, Gwen. *Prisoner of the Japs*. New York: Alfred Knopf, 1943.

Dickson, Paul Douglas. *A Thoroughly Canadian General: A Biography of General H.D.G. Crerar*. Toronto: University of Toronto Press, 2007.

Driefort, John. *Myopic Grandeur: The Ambivalence of French Foreign Policy toward the Far East, 1919–1945*. Kent, OH: Kent State University Press, 1991.

Dyal, Donald H. *Historical Dictionary of the Spanish American War*. Westport, CT: Greenwood Press, 1996.

Edgerton, David. "Liberal Militarism and the British State." *New Left Review*, No. 185 (1991). Online version: http://www.newleftreview.org/?view=1624

———. *Warfare State: Britain, 1920–1970*. Cambridge, New York: Cambridge University Press, 2006.

Elphick, Peter. *Far Eastern File: The Intelligence War in the Far East, 1930–1945*. London: Coronet Books, 1998.

Emerson, Geoffrey Charles. *Hong Kong Internment, 1942–1945: Life in the Japanese Civilian Camp at Stanley*. Hong Kong: Hong Kong University Press, 2011.

Endacott, George. *A Biographical Sketch-book of Early Hong Kong*. Hong Kong: Hong Kong University Press, 2005.

———. *Hong Kong Eclipse*. Hong Kong: Oxford University Press, 1978.

Farndale, Martin. *The Far East Theatre, 1941–1946*. London: Brassey's, 2000.

Farrell, Brian. *The Basis and Making of British Grand Strategy, 1940–1943: Was There a Plan?* Lewiston, NY: E. Mellen Press, 1998.

———. *The Defence and Fall of Singapore, 1940–1942*. Stroud: Tempus, 2005.

Farrell, Brian and Sandy Hunter (eds.). *Sixty Years On: The Fall of Singapore Revisited*. Singapore: Eastern Universities Press, 2002.

Faure, David (ed.). *Society: A Documentary History of Hong Kong*. Hong Kong: Hong Kong University Press, 1997.

Fedorowich, Kent. "'Cocked Hats and Small, Little Garrisons': Britain, Canada and the Fall of Hong Kong, 1941." *Modern Asian Studies*, Vol. 37, No. 1 (2003).

———. "The Evacuation of Civilians from Hong Kong and Malaya/Singapore, 1939–1942." In Brian Farrell and Sandy Hunter (eds.), *Sixty Years On: The Fall of Singapore Revisited*. Singapore: Eastern Universities Press, 2002.

Ferguson, Ted. *Desperate Siege: The Battle of Hong Kong*. Toronto: Nelson Canada, 1980.

Fernyhough, A. H. *History of the Royal Army Ordnance Corps, 1920–1945*. London: Royal Army Ordnance Corps, 1966.

Field, Andrew. *Royal Navy Strategy in the Far East, 1919–1939: Preparing for War against Japan*. London; Portland, OR: Frank Cass, 2004.

Fleming, John. *Hong Kong: The Pearl River Incident: The Untold Story of H.M.M.L. 1323*. Lancaster: Scotforth Books, 2002.

French, David. "The British Army and the Empire, 1856–1956." In Greg Kennedy (ed.), *Imperial Defence: The Old World Order, 1856–1956*. Abingdon: Routledge, 2008.

———. *The British Way in Counter-Insurgency, 1945–1967*. Oxford: Oxford University Press, 2011.

———. *Raising Churchill's Army: The British Army and the War against Germany, 1919–1945*. Oxford, New York: Oxford University Press, 2000.

Furūya Tetsūo. "Sensō seisaku no kakudai to mujun," *Rekishi kōron*, Vol. 4, No. 8 (1978). 古屋哲夫。（戦争政策の拡大と矛盾），《歷史公論》，4卷8号，1978年8月。

"Gangjiu duli dadui shi" bianxiezu. *Gangjiu duli dadui shi*. Guangzhou: Guangdong renmin chubanshe, 1989. 《港九獨立大隊史》編寫組。《港九獨立大隊史》。廣州：廣東人民出版社，1989。

Garneau, Grant S. *The Royal Rifles of Canada in Hong Kong, 1941–1945*. Carp, ON: Baird O'Keefe for The Hong Kong Veterans' Association of Canada, 1980.

Getz, Marshall. *Subhas Chandra Bose: A Biography*. Jefferson: McFarland, 2002.

Goodstadt, Leo. *Uneasy Partners: The Conflict between Public Interest and Private Profit in Hong Kong*. Hong Kong: Hong Kong University Press, 2005.

Government of India. *Frontier and Overseas Expeditions from India*, Vol. 4. Government of India, 1911.

Graham, Gerald. *The China Station: War and Diplomacy 1830–1860*. Oxford: Clarendon Press, 1978.

Gray, Edwyn. *Nineteenth-century Torpedoes and Their Inventors*. Annapolis, MD: Naval Institute Press, 2004.

Greenfield, Nathan. *The Damned: The Canadians at the Battle of Hong Kong and the POW Experience, 1941–45*. Toronto: HarperCollins Publishers, 2010.

Greenhous, Brereton. *"C" Force to Hong Kong: A Canadian Catastrophe, 1941–1945*. Toronto; Buffalo, NY: Dundurn Press, 1997.

Grimes, Shawn. *Strategy and War Planning in the British Royal Navy, 1887–1918*. Woodbridge: Boydell, 2012.

Groves, M. E. B. "The Royal Artillery and Hong Kong 1842–1976." *Journal of the Royal Artillery*, Vol. 103, No. 2 (Sep. 1976), pp. 119–28.

Groves, Robert. "Militia, Market and Lineage: Chinese Resistance to the Occupation of Hong Kong's New Territories in 1899." *Journal of the Hong Kong Branch of the Royal Asiatic Society*, Vol. 9 (1969).

Hack, Karl. "South East Asia and British Strategy, 1944–1951." In Richard Aldrich (ed.), *British Intelligence, Strategy, and the Cold War, 1945–51*. London, New York: Routledge, 1992.

Halpern, Paul. *A Naval History of World War I*. London: Routledge, 1994.

Hamilton, Sheilah. *Watching Over Hong Kong: Private Policing 1841–1941*. Hong Kong: Hong Kong University Press, 2008.

Hansell, Haywood, Jr. *The Strategic Air War against Germany and Japan: A Memoir*. Washington: Office of Air Force History, 1986.

Hanyok, Robert. "How the Japanese Did It." *Naval History Magazine*, Vol. 23, No. 6 (2009). Online version: http://www.usni.org/magazines/navalhistory/2009–12/how-japanese-did-it

Harayama Shigeo. *Kuribayashi Tadamichi, Imai Takeo monogatari*. Nagano: Hōzuki, 2011. 原山茂夫。《栗林忠道・今井武夫物語》。長野：ほおずき書籍株式会社，2011。

Harfield, Alan. *British and Indian Armies on the China Coast, 1785–1965*. London: A and J Partnership, 1990.

Harland, Bryce. *Collision Course: America and East Asia in the Past and the Future*. Singapore: Institute of Southeast Asian Studies, 1996.

Harland, Kathleen. *The Royal Navy in Hong Kong, 1841–1980*. Hong Kong: Royal Navy, 1981.

Hase, Patrick. *The Six-Day War of 1899: Hong Kong in the Age of Imperialism*. Hong Kong: Hong Kong University Press, 2008.

He Fa and Liang Shaoda. "Riben touxiang hou de Xinjie ziweidui." In Chan King Tong, Yau Siu Kam and Chan Ka Leung (eds.), *The Defence of Hong Kong: Collected Essays on the Hong Kong-Kowloon Brigade of the East River Column*. Hong Kong: Hong Kong Museum of History, 2004.

Hevia, James. *The Imperial Security State: British Colonial Knowledge and Empire-Building in Asia*. Cambridge: Cambridge University Press, 2012.

Hide, Richard. "Escape from Hong Kong—Admiral Chan Chak's Final Hours—The Definitive Account." www.hongkongescape.org/

HMS "Enterprise": Story of the First Commission April 7th, 1926, to December 19th, 1928. London: Gale and Polden, 1928.

Hoe, Susanna and Derek Roebuck. *The Taking of Hong Kong: Charles and Clara Elliot in China Waters*. Hong Kong: Hong Kong University Press, 2009.

Hohei dai ninihachi rentai shi [History of the 228th infantry regiment]. Nagoya: Hohei dai ninihachi rentai shi kankōkai, 1973.

"Honkon bōgyo shisetsu to," 8/1939, National Diet Library Japan. 《香港防御施設圖》。日本國立國會圖書館藏。

Hopton, Richard. *A Reluctant Hero: The Life of Captain Robert Ryder VC*. London: Pen and Sword, 2011.

Horne, Gerald. *Race War: White Supremacy and the Japanese Attack on the British Empire*. New York: New York University Press, 2004.

Hoyt, Edwin. *Kreuzerkrieg: The Gripping Story of the German East Asia Cruiser Squadron in World War I*. New York: World Publishing Company, 1968.

Huang Yunpeng. "Gangjiu dadui zai Xianggang kangri zhanzheng de diwei he zuoyong." In Chan King Tong, Yau Siu Kam and Chan Ka Leung (eds.), *The Defence of Hong Kong: Collected Essays on the Hong Kong-Kowloon Brigade of the East River Column*. Hong Kong: Hong Kong Museum of History, 2004.

Hunt, Barry Dennis. *Sailor-Scholar: Admiral Sir Herbert Richmond, 1871–1946*. Waterloo, ON: Wilfrid Laurier University Press, 1982.

Hunt, Reginald, Geoffrey Russell and Keith Scott. *Mandarin Blue: RAF Chinese Linguists—1951 to 1962—in the Cold War*. Oxford: Hurusco Books, 2008.

Hutson, G. *Awatea at War* (2010). Website of New Zealand Ship and Marine Society, http://www.nzshipmarine.com/node/52

Iguchi, Haruo. "Japan Foreign Policy and the Outbreak of the Asia-Pacific War: The Search for a Modus Vivendi in US-Japanese Relations after July 1941." In Frank McDonough (ed.), *The Origins of the Second World War: An International Perspective*. London: Continuum, 2011.

Jane's Fighting Ships of World War I. London: Studio Editions, 1990.

Jarman, R. L. *Hong Kong Annual Administration Reports, 1841–1941*. Farnham Common: Archive Editions, 1996.

Jin Yaoru. *Zhonggong Xianggang zhengce miwen shilu: Jin Yaoru wushinian xiangjiang yiwang*. Hong Kong: Tianyuan shuwu, 1998. 金堯如。《中共香港政策秘聞實錄：金堯如五十年香江憶往》。香港：田園，1998。

Johnson, Robert. *Far China Station: The U.S. Navy in Asian Waters, 1800–1898*. Annapolis, MD: Naval Institute Press, 1979.

Johnston, Ian and Ian Buxton. *The Battleship Builders: Constructing and Arming British Captial Ships*. Bransley: Seaforth Publishing, 2013.

Kennedy, Greg. *Imperial Defence: The Old World Order, 1856–1956*. London: Routledge, 2008.

Kennedy, Greg and Keith Neilson. *Far Flung Lines: Essays on Imperial Defence in Honour of Donald Mackenzie Shurman*. London: Frank Cass, 1997.

Kennedy, Paul. *The Rise and Fall of British Naval Mastery*. London: Penguin, 2004.

Kinvig, Clifford. *Churchill's Crusade: The British Invasion of Russia, 1918–1920*. London: Continuum, 2006.

Kotani, Ken. *Japanese Intelligence in World War II*. Oxford, New York: Osprey, 2009.

————. "Nihongun to Intelligence: seikō to shippai no jirei kara." *NIDS Journal of Defense and Security*, Vol. 11, No. 1 (2008). 小谷 賢。（日本軍とインテリジェンス-成功と失敗の事例から）。《防衛研究所紀要》第11卷，第1號，2008年11月。

Kwan, Stanley S. K. with Nicole Kwan. *The Dragon and the Crown: Hong Kong Memoirs*. Hong Kong: Hong Kong University Press, 2009.

Kwong Chi Man. "Reconstructing the Early History of the Gin Drinker's Line from Archival Sources." *Surveying and Built Environment*, Vol. 22 (Nov. 2012).

Kwong Chi Man and Tsoi Yiu Lun. *Gudu qianshao: Taipingyang zhanzheng zhong de Xianggang zhanyi*. Hong Kong: Cosmos, 2013.

Ladány, László. *The Communist Party of China and Marxism, 1921–1985: A Self Portrait*. Stanford, CA: Hoover Institution Press, Stanford University, 1988.

Lai, W. C. Lawrence. "The Gin Drinker's Line: Reconstruction of a British Colonial Defence Line in Hong Kong Using Aerial Photo Information." *Property Management*, Vol. 27, No. 1 (2009).

————. "Recollections of the Battle of Hong Kong and the Life of a POW by Arthur Ernesto Gomes, 5th Company (Machine Gun), HKVDC." *JRASHKB*, Vol. 48 (2008).

Lai, W. C. Lawrence et al. "Decoding the Enigma of the Fall of the Shing Mun Redoubt Using Line of Sight Analyses." *Surveying & Built Environment*, Vol. 21, No. 2 (2011).

Lai, W. C. Lawrence, Daniel Ho et al. "A Survey of the Pottinger Battery, Devil's Peak, Hong Kong." *JRASHKB*, Vol. 47 (2008).

Lai, W. C. Lawrence, Stephen N. G. Davies, Ken S. T. Ching and Castor T. C. Wong. "Location of Pillboxes and Other Structures of the Gin Drinker's Line Based on Aerial Photo Evidence." *Surveying & Built Environment*, Vol. 21, No. 2 (2011).

Lai, W. C. Lawrence, Ken Ching, Tim Ko and Y. K. Tan. "'Pillbox 3 Did Not Open Fire!': Mapping the Arcs of Fire of Pillboxes at Jardine's Lookout and Wong Nai Chung Gap." *Surveying & Built Environment*, Vol. 21, No. 2 (2011).

Lai, W. C. Lawrence, Ken S. T. Ching and Y. K. Tan. "Survey Findings on Japanese World War II Military Installations in Hong Kong." *Surveying & Built Environment*, Vol. 21, No. 2 (Dec 2011).

Lee Kam Keung et al. *Modern Chinese Naval History: New Perspectives*. Hong Kong: Hong Kong Museum of Coastal Defence, 2004. 李金強等編。《我武維揚：近代中國海軍史新論》。香港：政府物流服務署，2004。

Li Chaoyuan. *Rijun xi Gang ji: weikun Zhongguo de shaju Taipingyang zhan de xumu*. Ontario: Jishan shushi, 2002. 李超源。《日軍襲港記》。安大略省：繼善書室，2002。

Li Guoqiang and Zhang Peixin. *Xianggang zai kangri qijian*. Hong Kong: Xianggang wenshi chubanshe, 2005. 李國強、張佩新編。《香港在抗日期間》。香港：香港文史出版社有限公司，2005。

Liddell-Hart, Basil. *History of the Second World War*. London: Pan Books, 1973.

"Life in Hong Kong's ARP Tunnels." Gwulo: Old Hong Kong. http://gwulo.com/life-in-hong-kongs-ARP-tunnels?page=1

Lim, Patricia. *Forgotten Souls: A Social History of the Hong Kong Cemetery*. Hong Kong: Hong Kong University Press, 2011.

Lindsay, Oliver. *The Battle for Hong Kong 1941–1945: Hostage to Fortune*. Hong Kong: Hong Kong University Press, 2005.

Liu Cunkuan (ed.). *Zujie Xinjie*. Hong Kong: Sanlian shudian (Hong Kong), 1995.

Liu Zhijian. "Xianggang haiyuan yu zuguo kangzhan." In Chan King Tong, Yau Siu Kam and Chan Ka Leung (eds.), *The Defence of Hong Kong: Collected Essays on the Hong Kong-Kowloon Brigade of the East River Column*. Hong Kong: Hong Kong Museum of History, 2004.

Loh, Christine. *Underground Front: The Chinese Communist Party in Hong Kong*. Hong Kong: Hong Kong University Press, 2010.

Love, Robert (ed.). *Pearl Harbor Revisited*. Washington: Palgrave, 1994.

Lovell, Julia. *The Opium War: Drugs, Dreams and the Making of China*. London: Picador, 2012.

Lowry, Bernard. "The Gin Drinker's Line: Its Place in the History of Twentieth Century Fortifications." *Surveying & Built Environment*, Vol. 21, No. 2 (2011).

Luard, Tim. *Escape from Hong Kong*. Hong Kong: Kong Kong University Press, 2012.

Lucas, Scott et al. "A Very British Crusade: The Information Research Department and the Beginning of the Cold War." In Richard Aldrich (ed.), *British Intelligence, Strategy, and the Cold War, 1945–51*. London, New York: Routledge, 1992.

Ma Yau-Woon. *Jinghai chengjiang: Zhongguo jindai haijun shishi xinquan*. Taipei: Lianjing, 2009. 馬幼垣編。《靖海澄疆：中國近代海軍史事新詮》。臺北：聯經出版事業股份有限公司，2009。

MacDonell, George. *One Soldier's Story 1939–1945: From the Fall of Hong Kong to the Defeat of Japan*. Toronto: Dundurn Press, 2002.

Macri, David. "Hong Kong in the Sino-Japanese War." Unpublished PhD thesis (2010), the University of Hong Kong.

Macri, Franco David. "C Force to Hong Kong: The Price of Collective Security in China." *Journal of Military History*, Vol. 77 (2013), pp. 141–71.

Maltby, C. M. *Supplement to The London Gazette*. London: HMSO, 1948.

Mao Haijian. *Tianchao de bengkui: yapian zhanzheng zai yanjiu*. Beijing: Sanlian shudian, 1995. 茅海建。《天朝的崩潰：鴉片戰爭再研究》。北京：三聯書店，1995。

Marder, Arthur. *Old Friends, New Enemies: The Royal Navy and the Imperial Japanese Navy*. Oxford: Clarendon Press, 1981–1990.

Mark, Chi-kwan. *Hong Kong and the Cold War: Anglo-American Relations 1949–1957*. Oxford: Clarendon, 2004.

———. "Vietnam War Tourists: US Naval Visits to Hong Kong and British-American-Chinese Relations, 1965–1968." *Cold War History*, Vol. 10, No. 1 (Feb. 2010).

Martin, Brian. "Shield of Collaboration: The Wang Jingwei Regime's Security Service, 1939–1945." *Intelligence and National Security*, Vol. 16, No. 4 (2001).

Matzke, Rebecca Berens. *Deterrence through Strength: British Naval Power and Foreign Policy under Pax Britannica*. Lincoln: University of Nebraska Press, 2011.

Melson, Peter. *White Ensign—Red Dragon: The History of the Royal Navy in Hong Kong, 1841–1997*. Hong Kong: Edinburgh Financial Publishing (Asia), 1997.

Miners, Norman. *Hong Kong Under Imperial Rule: 1912–1941*. Hong Kong: Oxford University Press, 1987.

———. "The Use and Abuse of Emergency Powers by the Hong Kong Government." *Hong Kong Law Journal*, Vol. 26, No. 1 (1996).

Mitchell, William and Leonard Sawyer. *The Empire Ships*. London, New York, Hamburg, Hong Kong: Lloyd's of London Press, 1990.

Mitsuru, Hagiwara. "The Japanese Air Campaigns in China, 1937–1945." In Mark Peattie, Edward Drea and Hans van de Ven (eds.), *The Battle for China: Essays on the Military History of the Sino-Japanese War of 1937–1945*. Stanford, CA: Stanford University Press, 2011.

Morison, Samuel. *History of United States Naval Operations in World War II*, Vol. 14. Urbana: University of Illinois Press, 2001–2002.

Munn, Christopher. *Anglo-China: Chinese People and British Rule in Hong Kong, 1841–1880*. Hong Kong: Hong Kong University Press, 2009.

Murfett, Malcolm and Brian Farrell et al. *Between Two Oceans: A Military History of Singapore from First Settlement to Final British Withdrawal*. Singapore: Marshall Cavendish Academic, 2004.

Murray, Williamson and Allan R. Millett (eds.). *Military Innovation in the Interwar Period*. Cambridge, New York: Cambridge University Press, 1996.

Ng Chi-wah. "*Backdoor* and Coastal Defence of Hong Kong." In Lee Kam Keung et al. (eds.), *Modern Chinese Naval History: New Perspectives*. Hong Kong: Hong Kong Museum of Coastal Defence, 2004.

Ngo, Tak-Wing. *Hong Kong's History: State and Society under Colonial Rule*. London: Routledge, 1999.

Norton-Kyshe, James. *The History of the Laws and Courts of Hong Kong from the Earliest Period to 1898*. Hong Kong: Vetch and Lee, 1971.

O'Connell, John. *Submarine Operational Effectiveness in the 20th Century: Part One (1939–1945)*. Bloomington: iUniverse Publishing, 2011.

Oxley, Donald (ed.). *Victoria Barracks, 1842–1979*. Hong Kong: British Forces Hong Kong, 1979.

Paden, George. *Arms, Economics and British Strategy: From Dreadnoughts to Hydrogen Bombs*. Cambridge: Cambridge University Press, 2007.

Papastratigakis, Nicholas. *Russian Imperialism and Naval Power: Military Strategy and the Build-up to the Russian-Japanese War*. London, New York: I.B. Tauris, 2011.

Parillo, Mark. *The Japanese Merchant Marine in World War II*. Annapolis, MD: Naval Institute Press, 1993.

Parker, Ronald. *Deadly December: The Battle of Hong Kong, The Royal Rifles of Canada The Winnipeg Grenadiers*. London: Lulu.com, 2008.

Peattie, Mark, Edward Drea and Hans van de Ven (eds.). *The Battle for China: Essays on the Military History of the Sino-Japanese War of 1937–1945*. Stanford, CA: Stanford University Press, 2011.

Perras, Galen Roger. "Defeat Still Cries Aloud for Explanation: Explaining C Force's Dispatch to Hong Kong." *Canadian Military Journal*, Vol. 11, No. 4 (2011).

Perry, Matthew. *Narrative of the Expedition to the China Seas and Japan, 1852–1854*. Mineola, NY: Dover Publications, 2000.

"Pillbox Construction—Suffolk Anti-invasion Defences." http://pillboxes-suffolk.webeden. co.uk/pillbox-construction/4556138817

"Price Index 1750 to 1998." UK Parliament, http://www.parliament.uk/documents/commons/lib/research/rp99/rp99–020.pdf

Proulx, Benjamin. *Underground from Hong Kong.* New York: Stratford Press, 1943.

Qiu Yi et al. *Weicheng kuzhan: baowei Xianggang shiba tian.* Hong Kong: Chunghwa, 2013. 邱逸等。《圍城苦戰》。香港：中華書局，2013。

The Register of the Hong Kong Memorial: Commemorating the Chinese of the Merchant Navy and Others in British Service Who Died in the Great War and Whose Graves Are Not Known. London: Imperial War Graves Commission, 1931.

Renfrew, Barry. *Forgotten Regiments: Regular and Volunteer Units of the British Far East: With a History of South Pacific Formations.* Amersham, Bucks, UK: Terrier Press, 2009.

Rennie, David Field. *British Arms in North China and Japan: Peking 1860; Kagoshima 1862.* London: John Murray, 1864.

Ride, Edwin. *BAAG: Hong Kong Resistance, 1942–1945.* Hong Kong: Oxford University Press, 1981.

Rollo, Denis. *The Guns and Gunners of Hong Kong.* Hong Kong: The Gunners Roll of Hong Kong, 1991.

Roskill, Stephen. *Naval Policy between the Wars.* New York: Walker, 1968.

Ross, Steven. *American War Plans, 1890–1939.* London; Portland, OR: Frank Cass, 2002.

Salerno, Reynolds. *Vital Crossroads: Mediterranean Origins of the Second World War, 1935–1940.* Ithaca, NY: Cornell University Press, 2002.

Sambo Hombu (ed.). *Honkon heiyo chishi.* Tokyo: Sambo Hombu, 1938. 參謀本部編。《香港兵要地誌》。東京：參謀本部，1938。

Schurman, Donald Mackenzie. *Imperial Defence, 1868–1887.* London; Portland, OR: Frank Cass, 2000.

Schwankert, Steven. *Poseidon: China's Secret Salvage of Britain's Lost Submarine.* Hong Kong: Hong Kong University Press, 2014.

Sellick, Douglas. *Pirate Outrages: True Stories of Terror on the China Seas.* Fremantle, WA: Fremantle Press, 2010.

Share, Michael. *Where Empires Collided: Russian and Soviet Relations with Hong Kong, Taiwan, and Macao.* Hong Kong: The Chinese University Press, 2007.

Sherwood, Martyn. *The Voyage of the Tai-Mo-Shan.* London: Rupert Hart-Davis, 1957.

Sinclair, Georgina. "'Hong Kong Headaches': Policing the 1967 Disturbances." In Robert Bickers and Ray Yep (eds.), *May Days in Hong Kong: Riot and Emergency in 1967.* Hong Kong: Hong Kong University Press, 2009.

Sit Fung-shuen and Kwong Chi Man. *Xinjie xiangyiju shi: you zujiedi dao yi guo liang zhi.* Hong Kong: Joint Publishing, 2011. 薛鳳旋、鄺智文。《新界鄉議局史：由租借地到一國兩制》。香港：三聯書店（香港）有限公司，2011。

Smith, Michael. *The Emperor's Codes: The Breaking of Japan's Secret Ciphers.* New York: Arcade, 2001.

Smith, Peter. *Task Force 57: The British Pacific Fleet.* London: Crecy Books, 1994.

Snow, Philip. *The Fall of Hong Kong: Britain, China and the Japanese Occupation.* New Haven: Yale University Press, 2003.

Song Xianlin. "Jiulongcheng dibiao zhi er: Kai Tak Bun yu Kai Tak jichang de xingjian." In Chiu Yu-lok and Chung Po Yin (eds.), *Jiulongcheng.* Hong Kong: Joint Publishing, 2001.

Spiers, Edward. *The Army and Society, 1815–1914.* London: Longman, 1980.

Straczek, Jozef. "The Empire Is Listening: Naval Signals Intelligence in the Far East to 1942." *Journal of the Australian War Memorial,* No. 35 (2001). Website: http://www.awm.gov.au/journal/j35/straczek.asp

Surtees, V. N. *HMS* Emerald, *1926–1928.* London: Hiorns and Miller, 1928.

Swann, Sebastian. *Japan's Imperial Dilemma in China: The Tientsin Incident, 1939–1940.* London: Routledge, 2012.

Tang Kaijian, Shao Guojian and Chen Jierong (eds.). *6000 Years of Hong Kong History, Prehistory to 1997.* Hong Kong: Qilun, 1998.

367 Association Website. http://www.littlesaiwan-367su.talktalk.net/history.html

Tolley, Kemp. *Yangtze Patrol: The U.S. Navy in China.* Annapolis, MD: Naval Institute Press, 1971.

Tsang, Steve. *A Modern History of Hong Kong.* Hong Kong: Hong Kong University Press, 2004.

Tucker, Spencer. *The Encyclopaedia of Spanish-American and Philippine-American Wars: A Political, Social, and Military History,* Vol. 1. Santa Barbara: ABC-CLIO, 2009.

Vaid, Kanwal. *The Overseas Indian Community in Hong Kong.* Hong Kong: Centre of Asian Studies, the University of Hong Kong, 1972.

Van de Ven, Hans. *War and Nationalism in China, 1925–1945.* London: Routledge, 2003.

Vincent, Carl. *No Reason Why: The Canadian Hong Kong Tragedy: An Examination.* Stittsville, ON: Canada's Wings, 1981.

Wakeman, Frederic, Jr. "Drury's Occupation of Macau and China's Responses to Early Modern Imperialism." *East Asian Studies,* No. 28 (2004), pp. 27–34.

———. *Spymaster: Dai Li and the Chinese Secret Service.* Berkeley: University of California Press, 2003.

Walding, Richard. "Indicator Loops: Royal Navy Harbour Defences—Hong Kong." http://indicatorloops.com/hongkong.htm

Wang Zhenghua. "Kangzhan qianqi Xianggang yu Zhongguo junhuo wuzi de zhuan-yun, 1937–1941." In *Gang Ao yu jindai Zhongguo xueshu yantaohui lunwenji* (Taipei: Guoshiguan, 2000), pp. 393–439. 王正華。〈抗戰前期香港與中國軍火物資的轉運〉（民國26至30年）。載港澳與近代中國學術研討會論文集編輯委員會編，《港澳與近代中國學術研討會論文集》。新店：國史館，2000。

Ward, Iain. *Sui Geng: The Hong Kong Marine Police 1841–1950.* Hong Kong: Hong Kong University Press, 1991.

Waters, Dan. "The Country Boy Who Died for Hong Kong." *JRASHKB,* Vol. 25 (1985).

Weir, Rob. "A Note on British Blockhouses in Hong Kong." *Surveying & Built Environment,* Vol. 22, No. 1 (2012), pp. 8–18.

Welsh, Frank. *A History of Hong Kong.* London: HarperCollins, 1997.

Wesley-Smith, Peter. *Unequal Treaty 1898–1997: China, Great Britain and Hong Kong's New Territories.* Hong Kong: Oxford University Press, 1980.

Williford, Glen. *Racing the Sunrise: Reinforcing America's Pacific Outposts, 1941–1942.* Annapolis: Naval Institute Press, 2011.

Winfield, Rif and David Lyon. *The Sail and Steam Navy List: All the Ships of the Royal Navy 1815–1889.* Chatham: Chatham Publishing, 2004.

Wong Kam C. *Policing in Hong Kong*. Farnham, Surrey; Burlington, VT: Ashgate, 2012.

Wright-Nooth, George. *Prisoner of the Turnip Heads: The Fall of Hong Kong and Imprisonment by the Japanese*. London: Cassell, 1999.

Xie Yongguang. *Xianggang kangri fengyunlu*. Hong Kong: Cosmos Books, 1995. 謝永光。《香港抗日風雲錄》。香港：天地圖書，1995。

———. *Xianggang lunxian: Rijun gong-Gang shibari zhanzheng jishi*. Hong Kong: Commercial Press, 1996.《香港淪陷：日軍攻港十八日戰爭紀實》。香港：商務，1996。

———. *Xianggang zhanhou fengyunlu*. Hong Kong: Mingpao, 1996.《香港戰後風雲錄》。香港：明報，1996。

Yang Bafan and Yang Xing'an. *Yang Quyun jia zhuan*. Hong Kong: Xintian chuban, 2010.

Yang Mingwei. "Zhou Enlai yu dongjiang zhongdui ji Xianggang kangzhan." In Chan King Tong, Yau Siu Kam and Chan Ka Leung (eds.). *The Defence of Hong Kong: Collected Essays on the Hong Kong-Kowloon Brigade of the East River Column*. Hong Kong: Hong Kong Museum of History, 2004.

Yang Tianshi. *Zhaoxun zhenshi de Jiang Jieshi: Jiang Jieshi riji jiedu*. Taiyuan: Shanxi renmin chubanshe, 2008. 楊天石。《找尋真實的蔣介石：蔣介石日記解讀（二）》。太原：山西人民出版社，2008。

Yen, W. W. *An Autobiography by W. W. Yen: East-West Kaleidoscope*. Taipei: Zhuanji wenxue, 1973. 顏惠慶著、姚崧齡譯。《顏惠慶自傳》。臺北：傳記文學出版社，1973。

Yizhi (pen name). "Xianggang ruhe cai neng zhichi changqi de baowei" [How can Hong Kong withstand a prolonged siege?]. *Xianshi*. Shanghai: Xianshi zazhishe, 1939.

Yu Shengwu and Liu Cunkuan. *Shijiu shiji de Xianggang* [Hong Kong in the nineteenth century]. Hong Kong: Qilun, 1993. 余繩武、劉存寬編。《十九世紀的香港》。香港：麒麟，1993。

Zen Nippon Kaiin kumiai [All Japan Seamen's Union]. "Sembotsu shita sen to kaiin no shoryō kan" [Database of merchantmen sunk and merchant seamen killed]. http://www.jsu.or.jp/siryo/sukaiinnk/tairyou.html

Zhou Yumin and Shao Yong. *Zhongguo banghuishi*. Wuhan: Wuhan daxue chubanshe, 2012.

Index

2nd China Fleet (Imperial Japanese Navy), 170–1, 189, 192, 226–7

6th Rajputana Rifles (British Army), 119–20, 144

7th Rajput Regiment (British Army), 145, 165–6, 171, 177–8, 180, 182, 186, 193–5, 197–8, 201–2, 205–6, 211, 215–7, 231, 306

14th Punjab Regiment (British Army), 165–7, 173, 180–1, 186, 197, 201–3, 205–6, 208, 210–1, 215, 219

14th U.S. Army Air Force (14th USAAF), 227, 228

38th Division (Imperial Japanese Army), 161, 168–9, 171–4, 179, 181, 185, 187, 190, 192, 213, 216, 222, 225–6

40th Fortress Company (Royal Engineers), 38

51st Infantry Brigade (British Army), 251

228th Infantry Regiment (228 Rgt., Imperial Japanese Army), 168, 171, 173–7, 181, 184, 192, 194–6, 198–200, 203–4, 207–8, 211, 215–6, 219–20

229th Infantry Regiment (229 Rgt., Imperial Japanese Army), 168, 172–3, 175, 180–2, 192–7, 199–200, 203–11, 214–20

230th Infantry Regiment (230 Rgt., Imperial Japanese Army), 168, 172–5, 177–8, 181, 192, 194–204, 206, 210–1, 214–8, 220, 222

Alexander, Albert, 239–40

Alexander-Sinclair, Edwyn (Royal Navy), 82–3, 275

Amethyst, HMS, 238

Anderson, Charles (British Army), 33, 59–65, 67, 69, 89, 273

Angels of Wan Chai, 80

Anglo-Satsuma War, 17, 261

Asiatic Squadron (U.S. Navy)
Fleet, 35, 80, 132
East Indian Squadron, 17

Australia, 19–20, 47, 57, 73, 100, 123, 130, 132, 136–8, 146, 151, 158, 159, 235, 242–3, 247

Automedon, SS, 126

Back Door, The (novel), 48–9, 68, 270

Banham, Tony, 226, 270, 306, 308

Barker, George (British Army), 47–8, 273

Barron, Frederick (British Army), 3, 92, 107–8, 111, 293

Bartholomew, Arthur (British Army), 94–5, 107, 110, 273

Battle-box (Hong Kong), 112–4

Bias Bay, 13, 78–9, 84, 106, 229, 234

Black, Wilsone (British Army), 48–9, 273

Bokhara Battery, 111–2, 200

Boxer, Charles (British Army), 120, 185, 190

Boxer Protocol, 34

Boxer Rebellion, xiii, 34, 38, 53, 261, 272, 285

Breech Loader, xxi, xxiii, 19, 39, 41, 68

Brennan torpedo, 42–3, 54–7, 68, 261

British Army Aid Group (BAAG), 226–7, 230–4

British Pacific Fleet, 237

Broadwood, Robert (British Army), 55, 57, 59, 273

Brooke-Popham, Robert, Sir (Royal Air Force), 2, 117–8, 126–31, 133–5, 138–9, 141–2, 147, 161, 163, 242, 263

Burma Road, 121–3, 161

C Force (Canadian Army), 139–40, 162–4, 223; *see also* Chapter 8

Calvert, Michael (British Army), 154, 232

Cambridge, Duke of, 25, 31

Cameron, William (British Army), 46–9, 273

Canton-Hong Kong Strike, of 1926, xii, 72

Carnarvon, Earl of, 26–31, 40

Chan Chak, xvi, 3, 133–4, 148, 182–3, 188, 190, 191, 195, 206, 213, 220–2

Chatfield, Lord (Royal Navy), 101, 104

Chiang Kai-shek, 100, 117–8, 122, 133, 137–8, 145, 148, 151, 159, 161, 231

Chief of Imperial General Staff (CIGS), 35, 74, 92, 101, 104, 121, 129, 133–4, 136, 164, 212

Chief of Naval Staff, 71, 101, 104, 285

Chiefs of Staff Committee (COS), 73, 77–80, 83, 90, 92–3, 96, 101–2, 104–6, 111, 113, 117–8, 121, 125–30, 132–8, 141–2, 154, 164, 183, 196–7, 207–8, 211, 215, 237–9, 242–3, 246–7, 264

China Air Task Force (CATF, U.S. Army Air Force), 227

China Station, 4, 8, 12–3, 17–8, 23, 30–1, 34–7, 49, 57, 66, 75–6, 79–80, 82, 84, 86, 97, 118, 125, 146, 150, 167, 235, 237, 254, 261, 269

downgrading to Far Eastern Squadron, 235

Eastern Fleet, 271–2

organization, 271–2

size of, 13, 17, 35–6, 75, 76

Chindits, 232

Chinese Communist Party (CCP), 144–7, 221, 225, 229, 237–45, 247, 249, 250, 263

Chinese Nationalist government, 101, 106, 133, 145, 148, 150, 151, 157, 168, 172, 182, 206, 220, 222, 229, 232, 237, 244, 246, 255–6

activities in Hong Kong, 145, 148, 182–4, 244, 255

cooperation in Hong Kong defence, 133, 157, 172, 182, 222

sale of NT sovereignty, 106

Churchill, Winston, 71–3, 123, 126, 129, 138–9, 141–2, 161–2, 185, 212, 245–6

Chusan Islands, 9–10, 15

Colomb, John, 4, 17, 20, 26–7, 34

Colonial Defence Committee (CDC), 35, 46–7, 49, 54–8, 52–3, 264

Colonial Office, 25, 37, 42, 48, 50, 80, 82, 106, 124, 137, 158–9, 219, 240–1, 247, 264

Committee of Imperial Defence (CID), 35, 52–5, 57–8, 64, 74–5, 77–8, 79, 82, 90–2, 101–2, 104, 118, 264

Contagious Disease Ordinance (Act), 12, 37

Convention of Chuenpee, 9–10

Cosmopolitan Dock, 34, 64

Crerar, Henry (Canadian Army), 136, 139

Crimean War, 13–4, 19, 22, 261

D'Aguilar, George (British Army), 9–10, 272

Defence of Great and Greater Britain, The (book), 17, 20

Dill, John (British Army), 95, 129, 133, 292

Directorate of Military Operations (DMO, British Army), 35, 63–5, 95, 291

Directorate of Naval Intelligence (Royal Navy), 35

discipline (of the British garrison), 18–9, 25, 31, 37, 80, 252

Donovan, Edward (British Army), 18–9, 37, 80, 252

Dupuy de Lôme (French Navy), 40

East Asia Squadron (Imperial German Navy), 33

East Brigade, 193, 202–3, 208–11, 214, 217–8

East River Column, 146, 221, 227, 230–3

Eden, Anthony, 134, 138–9, 141, 246

Eisenhower, Dwight, 245–6, 248

Elliot, Charles, 9–10

Far Eastern Combined Bureau (FECB), 114, 140, 146–7, 150

Festing, Francis (British Army), 239, 273

First Opium War, xi–xiii, 9–10, 16, 261, 272

food, 10, 17, 80, 96, 124, 155–7, 184, 212, 217, 220, 240, 245

Foreign Office, Foreign Secretary, 35, 57, 64, 78–9, 101–2, 106, 118, 125, 134, 139, 241, 245, 248

France, 13–16, 19, 31–3, 35, 36, 38, 40, 46, 48–49, 53, 55–6, 66, 71–2, 74, 90, 118, 120–3, 131, 150, 158, 168, 235, 262
    cooperation to defend Hong Kong, 66, 90, 118
    Crimean War, 13
    fall of, in 1940, 120–6
    Second Opium War, 14–5
    Sino-French War, 35, 38

French, John (British Army), 55–7

Fumimaro Konoe, 122, 136

Germany, 33, 54, 56, 65, 72, 89, 96, 99, 118, 121–2, 132, 136, 159, 164, 262

Gibraltar, 20, 32, 90, 127

Gin Drinker's Line, xvi, 1–3, 85–6, 88–95, 97, 101–11, 114–5, 118, 120, 129, 140, 149, 151, 163–5, 169–71, 173–4, 178–9, 184, 223, 229, 239, 262–3, 271
    design of, 107–11
    early idea and planning, 85–6, 88–94
    fall of, in 1941, 174–9
    Japanese use of, 229

Gneisenau, SMS (Imperial German Navy), 66

Gordon, Charles (British Army), 30–1

Gough Battery, 44–6, 60, 64, 108

Government Cipher School; Government Communication Headquarters (GCHQ), 146, 244

Governor of Hong Kong, 1, 12–5, 23–6, 30, 37, 50, 54–5, 66, 77, 82, 115, 124–5, 143–4, 146, 155–6, 158, 162, 185, 211–3, 217–9, 237, 239–41, 245–6, 256, 264
    Blake, Henry, 50
    Bowring, John, 12–5
    Clementi, Cecil, 77, 82, 125
    Grantham, Alexander, 239–41, 245–6, 256
    Hennessy, John Pope, 1, 12, 23–6, 30, 37, 115, 264
    Lugard, Federick, 54–5
    May, Henry Francis, 50, 66
    Northcote, Geoffrey, 124–5, 143, 155–6, 264
    Young, Mark, 143–4, 146, 158, 162, 185, 211–3, 217–9, 237, 264

Grant, James Hope (British Army), 18–9, 24–5, 273

Grasett, Edward (British Army), 106, 118–21, 125, 128, 130, 136–8, 142, 273

Grey, Edward, 57

Guangzhou (Canton), xi–xii, 4, 9, 14, 15, 38, 50, 63, 86–7, 101–2, 104, 106, 117, 120, 144–5, 147, 151, 155, 159, 168, 172, 228–9, 232, 263

Guangzhouwan, 33

Harris, Arthur (Royal Air Force), 71, 91, 96, 99–100, 291

Hennessy, Patrick (Canadian Army), 162, 206, 215

Hermes, HMS, 75–6, 78, 82, 258

Ho Chi Min, 147

Ho Tung, 144, 159

Hong Kong (Chinese) Regiment (HKR), 154–5, 197, 201, 222

Hong Kong Military Service Corps (HKMSC), 250–1, 253

Hong Kong Royal Naval Volunteer Reserve (RNVR), 201, 216
Hong Kong Singapore Royal Artillery (HKSRA), 13, 67, 166, 171–2, 180
Hong Kong Submarine Mining Company, 38, 43
Hong Kong Volunteer Company, 231
Hong Kong Volunteer Defence Force (later Corps, HKVDC), Royal Hong Kong Regiment (The Volunteers, RHKR), 15, 18, 62, 67, 85, 94–5, 128, 141, 145, 155, 165–6, 172, 180, 186–8, 195–8, 205–6, 208–9, 211, 214–5, 217–8, 230–1, 253, 254, 258, 266, 269
Hongkong and Shanghai Bank, 146–7, 157
Horsley (RAF fighter), 78

Imperial Defence College, 118, 128, 139, 290–1
indicator loop, 114

Japan, 1–3, 8, 13–4, 17, 33–4, 36–7, 44–5, 49, 53, 55–8, 60, 63–4, 66, 71–8, 81, 83–92, 94–106, 110, 112, 114–5, 117–56, 159, 161–234, 235, 237, 242–3, 261–3, 266, 269–71
    Anglo-Japanese Alliance, 53, 55, 57–8, 73, 75, 83, 102, 148, 261–2
    invasion of Hong Kong, 171–224
    occupation period, 225–34
    preparation against Hong Kong, 149–51, 167–71
    seen as potential enemy, 53–8
Jervois, William (British Army), 20–2
Jinmen, 242, 246
Joint Planning Sub-committee (JPC), 73, 83–9, 91–2, 96–8, 101, 107, 121–3

Kai Tak, RAF Kai Tak, xii, 77–8, 87, 115, 120, 141, 163–4, 166, 171–2, 174, 187, 198, 220, 227, 228, 231, 234, 248, 252, 265, 269, 314
    attack on, in 1941, 172
    Kai Tak under Japanese control, 227–8
Kellett Island, 10, 21

Kelly, Francis (British Army), 64–8, 273
Keyes, Roger (Royal Navy), 51, 71, 285
Kidd, G. R. (British Army), 165, 202, 208
King, Mackenzie, 137, 139
King's Shropshire Light Infantry (KSLI, British Army), 38
KMT, see Chinese Nationalist government
Kowloon Docks, 23–4, 27–8, 30, 41, 43–4, 228
Kowloon Ridge, 5–6, 53, 57, 59–63, 68–9, 84, 87, 89, 94, 165, 180, 262–5

La Gloire, 19
Lambton, Hedworth (Royal Navy), 54–5, 58, 274–5
land, military and naval, 7, 10–1, 17–8, 24, 36–9, 49, 68, 77, 81–2, 250, 254
Lawson, John (Canadian Army), 140, 162–3, 166, 186–7, 195–8, 200–1, 204, 206, 215, 303, 310–1
Li Zongren, 95
Lin Zexu, 9
Luard, Charles (British Army), 82–3, 273
Lyemun, 6, 7, 11, 21–2, 42–6, 49, 53–4, 56, 60, 62, 68, 108, 152–3, 166, 185–6, 189, 190–1, 193–5, 201
Lyemun Redoubt, 42–3, 49, 56, 60, 62, 68, 108, 194

Macmillan, Harold, 248
Mainland Brigade, 95, 165, 167, 180–1
Malta, 20, 32, 43, 90, 290
Maltby, Christopher (British Army), 139–41, 162–5, 167, 171, 174, 177–80, 182, 185–9, 198, 200–1, 203, 205–6, 208, 211–23, 265, 272–3
Middlesex Regiment, 67, 143, 154, 166, 180, 186, 191, 195–7, 202, 205–6, 211, 214, 216–9, 305–6, 308, 310–11
military contribution, 17–8, 35–6, 81–2, 250, 264–6
Milne Committee, 21–7, 31
Mimi Lau, 157–8
Ministry of Defence, 248, 249, 259
Mirs Bay, 35, 52, 60, 78, 94, 222

Montgomery-Massingberd, Archibald
      (British Army), 92
Mount Davis Fortress, 45–6, 56, 58, 60, 62,
      64, 68, 108, 111–3, 166, 186–90
Murray Barracks, 10, 157, 172, 219
Murray Battery, 10, 11, 22, 41–2

National Security Council (NSC, U.S.),
      243, 248–9
New Jersey, USS (U.S. Navy ship), 254
New Territories, the, xii, 1, 5–7, 32–3, 35,
      43, 49–52, 57, 60–1, 68, 82–4, 86,
      91, 94, 102, 106–8, 111, 141, 164–5,
      168–9, 173, 223, 225, 229, 232, 239,
      241, 252, 258, 262, 270
   battle of, in 1899, 49–52
   terrain of, 5–7
Noble, Percy (Royal Navy), 118, 150, 275
Norton, Edward (British Army), 143,
      156–7
nuclear weapon, 235–6, 248–9, 259

Oriskany, USS (U.S. Navy ship), 254
Osborn, John (Canadian Army), 203–4
Overseas Defence Committee (ODC), 63
Owen Committee, 44–6, 54

Pakshawan Battery, 43–5, 49, 62, 64, 66,
      111, 113, 186, 188–9, 195
Paracel and Spratly islands, 117
People's Liberation Army (PLA), 237–9,
      243, 246, 248, 253
Phillips, Thomas (Royal Navy), 96, 99, 119,
      292
piracy, 13–4, 16, 78–9, 226
Port Arthur (Lüshun), 4, 33–4, 45, 53
Poseidon, HMS, 80
Postbridge, 201, 204–5
Pottinger Battery, 44, 60, 108
Prince of Wales, HMS, 133, 272, 292
prostitution, *see* venereal disease

Qing dynasty, xi–xii, 4, 6, 9–10, 14–6, 38,
      43, 46, 49–50

Qingdao (Tsingtao), 33, 54, 71
Qishan, 9
Qiying, 10

Radford, Arthur (U.S. Navy), 245
reservoir, 6, 29, 59–60, 63, 92, 108, 174–6,
      178–9, 185–7, 191, 194–5, 201–2,
      208–9, 215, 223, 309, 311
riots, in 1956 and 1967, 1, 236, 253, 254,
      255–9, 260, 263
Rizal, José, 35
Rose, H. B. (HKVDC), 206, 208, 215
Royal Air Force (RAF), 71–2, 77–8, 86–7,
      92, 96, 102–3, 105, 113, 119, 128, 141,
      147, 171–2, 187, 217, 231, 244, 248,
      250, 252, 253–4, 259, 269, 271, 290
Royal Army Ordnance Corps (RAOC),
      152, 154, 199–200, 203, 211
Royal Army Service Corps (RASC), 154,
      211
Royal Artillery, 13, 35, 42–4, 93, 145, 166,
      189, 201–2, 231, 269, 291
Royal Corps of Signals, 146, 154, 219, 222,
      244
Royal Hong Kong Auxiliary Air Force, 254
Royal Naval Dockyard, 34, 38–9, 56, 67,
      180, 187, 192, 207, 213, 219, 253–4,
      265
   capability, 34, 38–9
   decommissioning of, 253
Royal Naval Volunteer Reserve (RNVR),
      201, 216
Royal Navy, 4, 9, 12–3, 15–6, 18–20, 24,
      29–32, 38–9, 43–4, 46–9, 52–4, 56,
      58, 68, 72–5, 80, 87–8, 91–2, 96, 99,
      101, 105, 114, 117, 119, 123, 132, 136,
      139, 146–9, 152, 154, 167, 170, 180,
      187, 223, 226, 243, 248, 251–3, 261–2,
      269, 271–2, 277, 281–3, 288, 292; *see
      also* China Station, War Memorandum
      [Eastern], Royal Naval Dockyard
   submarine of, 39, 55, 57–8, 75–6, 79–80,
      87–8, 90–1, 94, 97, 102–3, 127, 142,
      147–8

Royal Rifles (Canadian Army), 140, 166,
    186–7, 194–5, 205–7, 209–11, 214–8
Royal Scots Regiment (British Army),
    120, 165, 171, 174, 176, 178–81, 193,
    197–9, 201–5, 207–8, 211, 216, 219,
    231
Russia (incl. Soviet Union), 13–6, 21–2,
    26–7, 30–4, 36, 46–9, 53–4, 56, 67,
    71, 75, 83, 98–100, 102, 118, 121, 131,
    136, 138–9, 142, 147–8, 162, 184, 235,
    238, 242–3, 299
    plan against Hong Kong, 47

Sai Wan, 62, 64, 112, 166, 189–90, 193,
    195, 197
    anti-air battery, 189–90, 193, 195, 197
    massacre, 195
Sargent, John (British Army), 49, 273
Scharnhorst, SMS (Imperial German Navy),
    66
Seamen's Strike of 1922, 144
Second Opium War, xi–xiii, 14–6, 19, 25,
    261, 272
Secret Intelligence Service (SIS), 147
Sembawang Naval Base, 34
Shang Zhen (Chinese Nationalist govern-
    ment), 133
Shing Mun Redoubt, 108–9, 149–50,
    165–6, 174, 176, 178, 181, 294, 305–6
    design of, 108–9
    fall of, 174–8
signal intelligence, 114, 146, 157, 244
Simmons, John, 21, 26, 27
Singapore, 1, 3–4, 13, 16–7, 20–2, 25–6, 31,
    34, 51, 67, 73, 75, 77–80, 82, 86, 90–2,
    94, 97–8, 100, 105, 113–4, 118, 121–3,
    127–8, 132–5, 140, 142, 145–7,
    158–9, 166–7, 171, 228, 235, 247–8,
    259, 262–3, 269, 271–2
Southeast Asia Treaty Organization
    (SEATO), 245–6
Soviet Union, *see* Russia
Special Constables, 155, 157, 224

Stanley, 5, 10, 111–3, 149, 166, 193, 200,
    203, 205, 211, 214–8
    battle of, in 1941, 214–8
    massacre at, in 1941, 218
Starling Inlet, 7, 84–5, 94, 97, 104, 229
Steele-Perkins, Arthur (Royal Air Force),
    156–8
Stewart, Herbert (British Army), 202, 219
Swiftsure, HMS, 58

Taikoo Dockyard, 34, 42, 62, 151–3, 186–7,
    191–6, 201, 228, 265
Taiping Rebellion, 30
Taiwan, 35, 72–3, 77, 84, 86–8, 97, 102,
    104, 114, 117, 132, 227–8, 241–2,
    246–7
Tamar, HMS, 66, 146, 167, 180, 200
Task Force 38 (TF38, U.S. Navy), 228
Tōjō Hideki, 136
Tongmenghui, 35, 148
Treasury, 27, 72, 71–2, 89, 90, 262
    Ten Years Rule, 72, 89, 90, 262
Treaty of Nanjing (Nanking), xi, 10
Treaty of Peking, 15, 17
Treaty of Tianjin, 15
Triumph, HMS, 58, 66
Truman, Harry, 242
Tyrwhitt, Reginald (Royal Navy), 86, 167,
    275, 290

Union Research Institute, 244–5
United States, 2, 12–3, 15–7, 21, 33–5, 50,
    56, 63, 71–2, 74, 78, 80, 90, 98–101,
    118, 121–7, 130–42, 145, 151–4,
    162–3, 225–8, 236–8, 241–9, 250,
    256–7, 259, 261, 263, 271
    actions over Hong Kong during the
        Pacific War, 227–9
    cooperation with Britain before Japanese
        invasion, 101, 121–34
    post-WWII cooperation with Britain,
        242–50
    use of Hong Kong, 244–5

use of Hong Kong during Spanish
    American War, 12, 35, 50

venereal disease (VD), 12, 37, 80–1, 266
Ventris, Francis (British Army), 68, 273
Victoria Barracks, 161, 269
Vildebeest (RAF torpedo bomber), 78, 172

Wallis, Cedric, 165, 174–5, 177–80, 182,
    186–7, 195, 197, 200, 205–6, 208–11,
    214–9
War Memorandum (Eastern), 73–4, 77, 84,
    91, 96, 100, 132
War Office, 10, 20, 24–9, 35, 37, 42–4, 47,
    57, 60, 63–4, 67–8, 94–5, 109–11,
    118, 134, 154, 163, 198, 212–4, 272
War Plan Orange, 131–2
Warrior, HMS, 19
Washington Treaty, 74–5, 77–8, 83, 86,
    93–4, 107

Weihaiwei, 4, 33–4, 49, 261, 272
West Brigade, 198–200, 202, 206, 208,
    210–1, 215–9
Whampoa Docks, 151–3
White, S. E. H. E. (British Army), 165,
    174–8, 201
Whitfield Barracks, 38–9, 254
Winnipeg Grenadiers (Canadian Army),
    140, 166, 177, 179–80, 186, 195,
    197–203, 205–8, 211, 214–5, 217
Winsloe, Alfred (Royal Navy), 58, 274
Wong Nai Chung Gap, 5, 48, 53, 62, 112,
    163, 186–9, 191, 195, 197–201, 204,
    210, 211, 214, 216, 223, 224, 310–1
battle of, in 1941, 197–204

Zhenjiang, 10
Zhou Enlai, 232, 241, 244, 257

9 789888 208715